Second City Television

Second City Television
A History and Episode Guide

JEFF ROBBINS

foreword by Sheldon Patinkin

McFarland & Company, Inc., Publishers
Jefferson, North Carolina, and London

LIBRARY OF CONGRESS CATALOGUING-IN-PUBLICATION DATA

Robbins, Jeff, 1971–
    Second City Television : a history and episode guide / Jeff Robbins ; foreword by Sheldon Patinkin.
        p.   cm.
    Includes bibliographical references and index.

    ISBN-13: 978-0-7864-3191-5
    softcover : 50# alkaline paper ∞

    1. Second city television (Television program)   I. Title.
PN1992.77.S39R63   2008
791.45'72 — dc22   2007021187

British Library cataloguing data are available

©2008 Jeff Robbins. All rights reserved

No part of this book may be reproduced or transmitted in any form or by any means, electronic or mechanical, including photocopying or recording, or by any information storage and retrieval system, without permission in writing from the publisher.

On the cover: (screen image) The cast of *Second City Television* (NBC/Photofest); (background) Shutterstock

Manufactured in the United States of America

McFarland & Company, Inc., Publishers
  Box 611, Jefferson, North Carolina 28640
    www.mcfarlandpub.com

*To my parents, for allowing a ten-year-old kid
to stay up late to watch* SCTV;

*to my wife, for allowing a thirtysomething-year-old kid
to stay up even later to watch every episode of* SCTV
again for "book research";

*to my son Danny, for providing me
with more laughter than anything since* SCTV;

*and to my daughter Julia,
the best "second" since "Second City."*

Contents

Foreword by Sheldon Patinkin 1
Preface 5

Part One. The Half-Hour Shows (1976–1981) 11
    The First Season 12
    The Second Season 44
    The Third Season 71

Part Two. The Ninety-Minute Shows (1981–1983) 103

Part Three. The Forty-Five-Minute Shows (1983–1984) 227

Appendix A. The Compilations 253
Appendix B. SCTV on DVD 257
Bibliography 259
Index 263

Foreword
by Sheldon Patinkin

I'm amazed at Jeff Robbins's comprehensive knowledge of the *SCTV* oeuvre. He's clearly a comedy nerd of the first order and, I hope, proud of it.

The first season, the first 26 half-hour episodes, are all of *SCTV* that I worked on, mostly in the editing room. I've always been a better editor than writer of comedy material — not that comedy writers like their material edited. Looking through this extraordinarily comprehensive book, I found many pieces I'd forgotten about. I was even glad to be reminded of some of them.

The first couple of shows were written as whole shows. Each was a full day's programming at SCTV, this really cheap and inept TV station coming to you from Melonville. Each of the first two also had a backstage story, the first one centering around the crackup of star Johnny LaRue, the second around security guard Gus Gusstofferson and the shooting of Captain Combat's puppeteer. We were hoping to be more like *Monty Python* than like *SNL*.

Global, the small Canadian network we were doing the show for, started complaining almost immediately about expense and asking if we couldn't shoot all the scenes together that happen on the same set, no matter which show they were intended for. Soon we were thinking about scenes rather than shows: "Words to Live By" (parodies of the sermon that many TV stations closed the night with), "Sunrise Semesters" (parodies of the kind of show some TV stations started the day with), a bunch of parody commercials (the first piece in the first show was a parody commercial, "Lasermatic," with the worst prop ever), Johnny LaRue restaurant reviews (like the one at the Italian restaurant just as Al Pacino killed Sterling Hayden and that other guy in *The Godfather*), Earl and Floyd newscasts (take your pick), fake promos for nonexistent movies and TV shows we'd never broadcast ("The Man Who Would Be King of the Popes" with Joe as Peter

O'Toole, John as Richard Burton, Dave as Richard Harris, and Catherine as Katharine Hepburn — every bit as good an impersonation as Marty Short's), movie parodies ("Grapes of Mud" was one of my favorites, though who can forget "Lust for Paint"?), commercials (one of my all-time favorite pieces of the entire 26 was Catherine O'Hara's one-take, two-minute commercial for "Milk of Amnesia"; she drank it at the top of the shot and had amnesia by the end of it), and any other kind of scene that seemed funny to enough of us. It was my job to oversee making 27-minute shows out of the pieces. (When we sold the shows to syndication in the U.S., they had to be around two minutes shorter, which often meant reediting whole shows.)

Editing the shows was a three-step process:

1. I sat alone in a tiny, windowless room within the *SCTV* offices in a building next to Second City on Lombard Street in Toronto. (I know that sounds like Dickens, but it didn't feel that way.) In that room I had a stopwatch, VCR transfers numbered second by second of everything shot that wasn't already in a show, and primitive equipment run with a joystick on which I'd make dummy shows. Since we had, at all times, three cameras shooting from different angles, all of them recording every take, each show was like editing a 27-minute movie, with a 25-minute version of it for American consumption. I had no experience at doing this. It was many all-nighters, but God knows it was never boring.

2. I'd then bring the information, most importantly the starting numbers of each shot to be used, to the editing room at Global where editor Ted Rogers, production assistant Roseanne Ironstone, and I spent many all-nighters making the final edit, including hours at a time of "down time" when the equipment broke down. It was not a wealthy TV station.

3. Then the edited tape went to a studio where graphics, music, sound effects, and voice-overs were added. Oh yes, and so was that damn laugh track (called sweetening). We couldn't shoot in front of an audience because we weren't on a set — we were on set after set. There wouldn't have been room for an audience anyway. We tried a real audience once (I think it was either show three or show four) by showing the completed show to a bunch of people and recording their laughs. We still had to sweeten it.

A couple of words about my two onscreen appearances. The first was the ending of a Chekhov parody that we referred to as "Waiting for Chekhov." Most of the cast sat around in Russian period costumes talking about how bored they were while waiting for Chekhov. When he finally appeared, it was Dave as the *Star Trek* Chekhov beamed down. He then had Scottie beam himself and everyone else up, leaving an empty set. Then I ran out as the director, confused about where everyone went and how we were going to finish the piece. It was clear in the editing room that the piece ended best with everyone getting beamed up. (I thought it was clear on the set.) Besides, I'm a lousy actor. So I cut me out. I don't think anyone even noticed.

In my other onscreen appearance, which is in show 13, it wasn't I who was cast in the role of Jesus in our parody of *Ben-Hur*. It was my really stupid looking blue and white checked pants that were cast, and I was wearing them. (I think I'd bought them in L.A. when I was working there once and trying to appear cool. Blue and white checked pants were cool in L.A. in the late '60s.) I had no problem about playing the role since I knew that only the pants and my hands were going to be on camera. And even I could act mixing and serving martinis, which is what I did in my two appearances as Jesus. I was nervous, but I don't think you can tell watching it.

Ben-Hur was the most expensive and longest piece we'd written till then. It cost the entire budget for the show, but it wasn't long enough to be the whole show. I had to fill it in with leftover stuff from other shoots. (It's been stated elsewhere that the piece wasn't working till John started doing Ben Hur as Curly from the Three Stooges, but no one acknowledges that it also helped when Eugene and Dave started doing the Roman guards or whatever they were as Abbott and Costello.)

My phone number was in another piece because I was stupid and put it in as the number to call for ordering a recording of Babe Ruth's greatest hits (which were, of course, the sound of a bat hitting a ball over and over again). It never occurred to me that anyone would really call. I got calls whenever the ad aired in Toronto, always from giggling teenagers. Not wanting to deal with the temptation to take advantage of their youth, I stopped answering the phone the nights it was on.

We salvaged an early and really bad movie parody of boring Hollywood biographical films of the '30s and '40s, and in particular of Greer Garson and Walter Pidgeon in *Madame Curie*, which nobody much had even heard of by the '70s. We shot it, we hated it, but we couldn't afford to drop it. I don't remember whose idea it was, probably either Joe's or Harold's, to use it as the movie on a show to be called "Monster Chiller Horror Theatre" with Joe as newscaster Floyd Robertson doing a terrible impersonation of Bela Lugosi's Dracula as Count Floyd, the ghoulish host of the show. The Count kept on pretending that this boring movie that wasn't even meant to be scary was "*Scaaary*." We thought it was a pretty funny way to deal with a total dud. Unfortunately it was still a total dud, but it did at least introduce "Monster Chiller Horror Theatre" and Count Floyd. (There were many viewers who didn't understand that it was the character Floyd Robertson playing Count Floyd as another of his jobs at SCTV. There were even people who didn't realize that both Floyds were played by the same actor — that's how good Joe was, and is, at seeming to be the next character he's playing. Catherine's always been particularly good at that too.)

What's most important to me isn't how good *SCTV* was, which it was, and how talented they all were, and they were, and I'm not just talking about the first 26. What's most important to me is how much we all learned from doing it, and how what we learned has stood us all in good stead ever since. I am, by the way, happy to know that somebody thought enough people would buy this book to make it worth the investment. That's really cool.

Sheldon Patinkin is Chair, Theater Department, Columbia College, Chicago, and artistic consultant to the Second City and to Steppenwolf Theatre.

Preface

Television has always been a copycat business. Even in the 1970s — before there was FOX, the WB, UPN, the CW, My Network TV, and hundreds of cable channels to choose from. Before there was iTunes, podcasts, Innertube, NBC Rewind, YouTube, on demand, pay-per-view ... in short, even when there was less demand for content and less content to copy, television was a copycat business. The logic has always been that if something worked once, it can work again.

So it was that when a meeting was called among a talented group of performers and writers in the spring of 1976, the impetus behind the gathering wasn't to create what Canada's newsmagazine *Macleans* would later call "one of the most successful pieces of television art ever made"; rather, the goals were to get rich and to get famous — something that was quickly happening to the stars, writers, and producers of a new late-night NBC television program called *Saturday Night*.

The assemblage was held in Toronto on Lombard Street at the Old Firehall, a reconverted fire station, which, not coincidentally, happened to be the Canadian home of the Second City, the famed improvisational comedy theatre company that was originally founded in Chicago in 1959 and had expanded to Toronto in 1973. Second City revues, then as now, featured a first half of scripted comedy scenes, followed by a second half of improvisations based on ideas submitted by the audience. Early alumni of the Second City included Alan Arkin, Joan Rivers, Robert Klein, Fred Willard, and Peter Boyle.

The group gathered on that day — especially Second City stage performers Joe Flaherty, Eugene Levy, Harold Ramis, and Dave Thomas — had more reason than most to want to duplicate the success of *Saturday Night*'s Not Ready for Prime Time Players. Three of the emerging stars of NBC's new sketch show, Dan Aykroyd, John Belushi, and Gilda Radner, had honed their comedic skills at the Second City. Driven by envy, pride, and the knowledge that *Saturday Night* producer Lorne Michaels hadn't drafted anywhere near all of Second City's best talent, the decision to mount another television show was made.

The concept of *Second City Television*—a satire of television programming presented in the format of a broadcast day from a low-budget TV station — arose fairly quickly during the meeting, and has most often been specifically credited to Second City stage director Del Close and eventual *SCTV* associate producer Sheldon Patinkin. The concept was a brilliant one and stuck for 135 shows — 52 half-hours for Canada's Global TV, 26 half-hours for the Canadian Broadcasting Corporation, 39 90-minute shows for NBC, and 18 45-minute shows for Cinemax. But the cast, who doubled as writers, and who at various times included (in addition to Flaherty, Levy, Ramis, and Thomas) Second City stage veterans John Candy, Catherine O'Hara, Andrea Martin, Martin Short, Robin Duke, Tony Rosato, and former disc jockey Rick Moranis, was too ambitious to forever stay within the confines of that concept.

Only the first few *SCTV* episodes actually presented a "broadcast day" from the sign-on program "Sunrise Semester" to the sign-off sermonette "Words to Live By." Sketches soon became longer and more complex. The cast introduced countless characters and then evolved them far more dramatically than the characters their former Second City colleagues were performing on *Saturday Night Live*: Levy's Bobby Bittman went from hack comedian to hack dramatic actor in a remake of *On the Waterfront*. Candy's Johnny LaRue went from sleazy showbiz mogul to sleazy political candidate. Flaherty's unctuous host Sammy Maudlin went from presiding over a parody of Sammy Davis, Jr.'s talk show *Sammy & Company* to presiding over a parody of Alan Thicke's talk show *Thicke of the Night*.

SCTV's actors and writers decided early on that it wasn't always enough to parody one television show or film at a time or even one genre of TV show or film at a time: Their style of "multi-layered" parodies became perhaps the show's signature ingredient. The show-length "Fantasy Island" sketch in *SCTV*'s second season (show 44), which combined elements of the frothy ABC primetime hit, the Bob Hope–Bing Crosby series of "road" movies, and the film classics *Casablanca* and *The Wizard of Oz*, is the most successful example of this groundbreaking comedic style.

Another early innovation was to introduce viewers of *SCTV* not just to the station's programming, but also to the station's backstage machinations. These behind-the-scenes segments evolved exponentially when NBC picked up the program in 1981, scheduled it after *The Tonight Show* on Friday nights, and expanded its length from 30 to 90 minutes. Some of *SCTV*'s most celebrated installments feature these ambitious storylines (usually referred to as "wraparounds" for how they "wrapped around" stand-alone sketches) that were produced during the NBC years, such as the Emmy Award–winning Moral Majority (show 84) and Sweeps Week (show 115) episodes, the Russian Show (show 88), and the extended *Godfather* parody (show 93).

It was during the NBC years, 1981–1983, that *SCTV* reached arguably its creative and critical apex. Although the show had had a convoluted production and distribution history — moving from Global TV to the CBC to NBC — and often seemed to be on the brink of extinction, it landed on American network TV at the right time: What passed for comedy on the three major networks at the beginning of the eighties was largely terrible, and, most significantly for *SCTV*, its main competitors, *Saturday Night Live* and especially *Fridays*, were reviled for presenting mostly juvenile drug-based humor. Television critics universally hailed *SCTV* as one of the best things on the air.

Unfortunately, *SCTV*'s critical success never fully transformed into massive commercial success, and after two years on NBC, it became clear that *SCTV* was not going to rival *Saturday Night Live* for longevity. *SCTV* was expensive to produce (especially considering the very late hour at which it aired), its ratings were stagnant, Rick Moranis and Dave Thomas had left to produce the Bob and Doug McKenzie film *Strange Brew*, Catherine O'Hara had also defected, and it was inevitable that *SCTV*'s biggest star, John Candy, would also depart to focus on feature films.

After negotiations with NBC — which are humorously recalled by Flaherty and Levy on one of *SCTV*'s DVD releases — fell apart, *SCTV* became the first original programming on the fledgling cable network Cinemax, which aired the show's final season of 18 episodes from November of 1983 to July of 1984. Despite declarations from the cast and producers that being on cable television would rejuvenate *SCTV* by freeing it from broadcast network restrictions, the final season — dubbed *SCTV Channel* — was sub-par. The four-person cast was too small (some of the cast rejected plans to expand the group by bringing in interested outsiders such as Jim Carrey, Jim Belushi, and Billy Crystal), and the writers were burned out. It didn't help that since Cinemax had only two million subscribers, leaving most *SCTV* fans simply unable to watch. *SCTV* faded away, this time for good, after Cinemax aired its final episode — *SCTV*'s 135th — on July 17, 1984.

But *SCTV* continued to thrive after production ceased: A year after its run on Cinemax ended, newly repackaged syndicated reruns appeared. Since many markets aired these reruns in more accessible time periods than *SCTV* had previously been afforded, the show was given another chance to expand its audience. Perhaps more significantly, the show's legacy and influence continued to grow enormously in the comedy world; one could argue that although without *Saturday Night Live* there would have been no *Fridays*, without *SCTV*, there might have been no *Ben Stiller Show*, *Kids in the Hall*, *The State*, *Upright Citizens Brigade*, or *Mr. Show*. (*Entertainment Weekly* dubbed *The Ben Stiller Show* "*SCTV* with Better Hair.") Conan O'Brien has been one of the more vocal and visible devotees of *SCTV*, even hosting a cast reunion at the 1999 Aspen U.S. Comedy Arts Festival, which appears on Volume One of the *SCTV* DVDs. A listen to DVD commentaries of influential programs such as *Freaks & Geeks*, *Undeclared*, and even *The Simpsons* reveals creators' debts to *SCTV*.

More significant in relation to the book you are holding is the impact *SCTV* had on me, which began when I was just nine years old. But my earliest remembrances of the show are not of laughter, but of sheer terror. It was show 12's "Movie of the Week" sketch — *not* a Count Floyd piece; every *SCTV* fan knows there's nothing scary about Count Floyd or the movies he presents — that I found horrifying. The sketch featured John Candy as a taxidermist who takes his girlfriend home to meet his parents. But his parents, like the numerous animals adorning their walls, are also dead and stuffed. The piece ends with Candy's petrified girlfriend frantically phoning for a police officer, who arrives quickly but is of little help as he too is dead and stuffed.

Somehow this initially disturbing exposure to *SCTV* did not deter me from tuning in again; upon further viewing I realized that the program was a comedy show unlike any I had ever seen. Quickly *SCTV* began to play a huge role in my adolescence, particularly when the program moved from first-run syndication to NBC on May 15, 1981. The night of the network premiere was especially exciting, and I distinctly recall watching the first NBC installment in my bedroom — on my tiny black-and-white set — while my parents and older sister slept. Although I could have watched *SCTV* on a bigger (and color) TV, there was something appealing about watching *my* show on *my* TV. And since no one else in my fourth-grade class knew of the program, I felt strongly that *SCTV* was *my* show.

Which brings me to *my* book: Despite the show's unparalleled comedic legacy, despite its loyal fan base of TV critics and viewers, despite producing such stars as John Candy, Eugene Levy, Catherine O'Hara, and Martin Short, despite its special star on Canada's Walk of Fame, despite being named a "Masterwork" by the Audio-Visual Preservation Trust of Canada, and despite its recent resurgence on "TV on DVD" shelves, precious little of substance has been written about *SCTV*. Dave Thomas has collected a very enjoyable book of cast remembrances, while Sheldon Patinkin's book *The Second City: Backstage at the World's Greatest Comedy Theater*, included a single chapter devoted to *SCTV*.

But nearly nothing has been written on what makes *SCTV* such a standout: the shows themselves. Which is a shame, since not only does *SCTV* deserve such treatment, but, given the density of its material and its often-obscure targets for parody, it almost demands it. The purpose of this book is therefore to provide followers and newcomers alike with an ultimate *SCTV* reference guide, which traces not only the appearances, evolution, and development of its many legendary characters, but also reveals the sources of *SCTV*'s parodies, most of which aren't as obvious or well-known (especially decades after production) as show 15's *Leave It to Beaver* satire or show 113's lampoon of *Cagney & Lacey* ("Koffler & Meltzer"). In short, this book is a history of the *Second City Television* programming that originated from the fictional town of Melonville. (For a backstage history of *SCTV* that originated from the very real towns of Toronto and Edmonton, I recommend that you track down Dave Thomas's *SCTV: Behind the Scenes.*)

To complete this task, I visited and revisited innumerable times my extensive *SCTV* tape library, which I have been compiling since 1981 (when my parents bought their first VCR) and which grew in the late nineties through Internet tape-trading. For adding to the archives, I need to thank Dwight Hodge, Michael Delaney, and others whose names have sadly been deleted along with erased e-mail correspondence. I compared and contrasted different versions of sketches and shows culled from Canadian syndication, American syndication, NBC, Cinemax, and various best-of incarnations. In the latter stages of compiling this book, Shout! Factory began to release *SCTV* DVDs, which in many cases (largely due to the difficulty of obtaining music clearances) presented even additional variations of material. I also rented or purchased and studied countless films — many not easy to find and many of which I admit I was initially unfamiliar with — in order to detail how they were then parodied by *SCTV*. (Special thanks here to my good friend Jeremy Fredriksen for tracking down a copy of the out-of-print film disaster — *not* disaster film — *The Oscar.*) Lastly, I revisited my library of reviews and other writings on *SCTV* that I've compiled since the early eighties. These reference sources and others are noted at the back of this volume.

In summation, this book is not just for those who were paying attention when *SCTV* was originally in production. It is also for those who are just now catching up with *SCTV* on DVD. Although the show ended its run on July 17, 1984, *SCTV* will always be for me and for many others — as the show's opening credits proudly proclaim — "on the air!"

For each episode detailed on the following pages, the list of sketches is a chronological account of major pieces on that show. Bumpers, opening credits, and commercial breaks are not listed. Also, if a sketch played as a whole but was interrupted by a real commercial break, the piece is listed as one sketch and not as a "two-parter." Conversely, if a sketch was interrupted for a commercial parody or other *SCTV*-produced piece, the interrupted sketch is noted as having two (or more) parts.

PART ONE

The Half-Hour Shows (1976–1981)

The first 78 episodes — three seasons — of *SCTV* were produced in a half-hour format. Seasons one and two were completed for Canada's Global TV Network and season three was created for the Canadian Broadcasting Corporation. (With the shift to the CBC came a title change, from *Second City Television* to *SCTV Television Network*, beginning with show 53.) All three seasons were later syndicated in the United States.

The first season — which premiered in the fall of 1976 in Canada and was syndicated in the U.S. the following year — featured the cast of John Candy, Joe Flaherty, Eugene Levy, Andrea Martin, Catherine O'Hara, Harold Ramis, and Dave Thomas. Apart from being produced cheaply — the first seven shows cost a total of $35,000 — one of the most distinctive characteristics of the first 26 episodes is the brevity of the sketches, particularly when compared with later seasons. Even when the cast created long pieces — show 13's *Ben-Hur* parody, for example — they were cut into several short segments.

The first season is also notable for the number of recurring characters that were introduced, including news anchors Floyd Robertson and Earl Camembert, mogul Johnny LaRue, talk show host Sammy Maudlin, funnyman Bobby Bittman, and "Monster Chiller Horror Theatre" mainstays Count Floyd, Dr. Tongue, and Bruno (a.k.a. Woody Tobias, Jr.). The quality of *SCTV*'s first year was aided immeasurably by the early introduction of these strong recurring characters.

As the show neared its second season, Harold Ramis left to write feature films. While not the group's best performer, Ramis was the show's head writer, an associate producer, and its strongest creative voice. Fortunately, Ramis was heavily involved in writing *SCTV*'s second season before his departure. The second season sees the cast gaining the confidence to write longer, more ambitious, and more sustained pieces, such as the "SCTV Solid Gold Telethon" (show 30) and the show's first attempt at parodying television election coverage (show 32). The finest examples of these complex sketches are two of *SCTV*'s crowning achievements, the *Fantasy Island* parody (show 44) and Bobby Bittman's remake of *On the Waterfront* (show 45), both of which came in the show's second year. But *SCTV*'s sophomore season was also the show's most inconsistent, as the material veered between brilliant and surprisingly amateurish. The poor stretch of shows late in the season is arguably *SCTV*'s lowest creative point.

After a year-and-a-half hiatus and the loss of key cast members John Candy and Catherine O'Hara, *SCTV* returned for a third season, this time for the CBC. Thanks to a bigger budget, the addition of several new writers (most notably Paul Flaherty, Dick Blasucci, and Mike Short), and new cast member Rick Moranis, *SCTV* rebounded with its best season yet and arguably its finest ever. Moranis and Dave Thomas formed a quick partnership and produced much of the show's strongest material that season, including "Play It Again, Bob" (show 59), as well as no fewer than 25 "Great White North" segments featuring new creations Bob and Doug McKenzie. Moranis and Thomas were not alone; Flaherty, Levy, and Martin also contributed material of remarkable quality. Two other cast members who joined for the third season, Robin Duke and Tony Rosato, were overshadowed by Moranis and would later go on to join *Saturday Night Live*, while Flaherty, Levy, Martin, Moranis, and Thomas would reunite with Candy and O'Hara to create an ambitious 90-minute version of the program for NBC entitled *SCTV Network 90*.

THE FIRST SEASON

Show 1 *(Second City Television)*

1. Lasermatic Commercial
2. Sunrise Semester with Moe Green: Essentials of Bookkeeping
3. Unnecessary Surgeon / Ted Gordon: Malpractice Lawyer promo
4. The Johnny LaRue Show
5. SCTV AM News Today: Big News / Little News
6. Evelyn Woods Speed Talking School commercial
7. Backstage
8. Stop Those Depressing Ads PSA
9. Masterpiece Theatre: The Girls of Vienna
10. SCTV PM News: Johnny LaRue
11. Words to Live By: Joni Newton Buffy

What to watch for: The Johnny LaRue Show.
This first episode features the introduction of three important characters (Johnny LaRue, Floyd Robertson, and Earl Camembert), but it is Candy's introduction of LaRue — here as an out-of-shape exercise show host who finds it prudent to respond to viewer confusion concerning his sexuality ("I'm not gay")— that stands out.

As with most other premiere installments of successful TV shows, the first episode of *Second City Television* only hints at the show's potential. What is immediately striking is how established the *SCTV* format is at this primitive stage; this debut introduces elements — entertainment programs, newscasts, promos, original characters, celebrity impersonations, even backstage storylines — that would sustain *SCTV* through network changes, cast defections, and the next 134 episodes.

Early on, the show stays close to its initial concept (although usually credited to Del Close or Sheldon Patinkin, others cite executive producer Bernie Sahlins, Flaherty, or Ramis) of presenting a *complete day's* worth of programming — from the early morning "Sunrise Semester" show to the sign-off program "Words to Live By"— of a small television station. Soon the programming day would become more of a programming sampler and later, as more intricate backstage storylines were introduced, "on-air" programming would become something of an afterthought.

Speaking of backstage storylines, this first show features a rather crude plot involving the personal problems (alcoholism, impotence) and professional setbacks (cancellation, bankruptcy) of Candy's Johnny LaRue. (The material lacks polish largely due to heavy editing; the first cut of the 30-minute episode came in at one hour.) The majority of the plot is presented within a program entitled simply "Backstage," but the storyline eventually bleeds over into later sketches, cutting short a dull "Masterpiece Theatre" sketch and becoming the focus of the "SCTV PM News."

Floyd Robertson (Flaherty) and Earl Camembert (Levy), the co-anchors of the "SCTV News," are introduced here in a sketch perfected on the Second City stage. More than anything, the piece serves as a set-up for the characters: Robertson is a serious journalist who reports on major stories such as fighting in the Middle East and important scientific discoveries, while Camembert is a bumbling hack who presents trivial items such as a report about a harmless fire in a local health food store. Camembert also notably lacks professionalism, as demonstrated by his attempt to one-up Robertson with an outrageously false story about a rabies-infected herd of caribou or, when that fails, to leak potentially embarrassing personal information about his co-anchor. Robertson in turn makes no secret of his lack of respect for Camembert.

While Camembert, Robertson, and LaRue's characters are already fairly well developed, Harold Ramis's Moe Green is not — here he appears both as a bookkeeper on "Sunrise Semester" and as Johnny LaRue's accountant; it would not be until show 24 that Green would be introduced as SCTV's station manager. Similarly, note Joe Flaherty's appearance in "Backstage" as a network president. When Flaherty tells Johnny LaRue, "I'm canceling your show," he is using a line that he will repeat many times in the future under the guise of his later creation, SCTV president Guy Caballero.

Even though he didn't yet exist, the thrifty Caballero would be proud of at least one aspect of the first few *SCTV* shows: They were made cheaply (approximately $5,000 each) and they look it: Sets are virtually nonexistent, and those few sets are forced to do double duty — note, for example, how Johnny LaRue's dressing room in "Backstage" looks remarkably like the sitting room used in "Masterpiece Theatre." Props are also amateurish — Dave Thomas says he "felt sick" when presented with the prop for this show's "Lasermatic" camera commercial parody. *SCTV* also didn't seem to be able to afford makeup: In a funny spot, Flaherty does a fine Gregory Peck impression, but his outward appearance is that of Joe Flaherty. The production values for *SCTV* would mercifully improve (particularly starting with the third season); the budgetary increases would be a key element of *SCTV*'s overall improvement during most of those later years.

Despite budgetary limitations, there are moments of brilliance in this first episode. Besides "LaRue" and the news, the first show contains the first classic *SCTV* promo, here for the programs "Unnecessary Surgeon" and "Ted Gordon: Malpractice Lawyer." (Note Thomas's Ted Gordon character would return a full 90 shows later with the piece "Ted Gordon: Overbooked Attorney.") Writing short promos ensured that a comedic idea could be explored without having to present a longer "show" sketch. As evidenced in this first show, these fake promos would result in some of *SCTV*'s funniest and quickest sketches as well as one of the program's best-known running gags: Seemingly every SCTV show promoted airs "Thursday at Nine." That joke was not yet perfected, as "Unnecessary Surgeon" is scheduled "Thursday at *Eight*."

Show 2 *(Second City Television)*

1. Swami Banananda: Flexibility of Legs
2. Captain Combat
3. Fat Chance for the Sub Sahara PSA
4. English for Beginners
5. SCTV AM News Today: News Service Writers' Strike
6. Stan Musial's Greatest Hits commercial
7. SCTV AM News: Gus Gusstofferson interview
8. England for Sale commercial
9. Gus Gusstofferson: Security Guard
10. SCTV Movie of the Week: Wara! Wara! Wara!
11. SCTV PM News: Earl teaches Floyd to shuffle papers

What to watch for: SCTV AM News Today.
One of the shortest of the early "SCTV News" pieces, its brevity blamed on a strike that shut down the major news services. Despite having nothing to report on, Floyd (Flaherty) still manages to look more professional than Earl (Levy), simply by tossing the story to an indignant Earl ("I'm not a fiction writer!"). Just two shows in, the Floyd and Earl pieces were already becoming highlights.

SCTV takes a step backward with this weak episode. Several segments, while unsuccessful, are noteworthy for their place in the show's continuing evolution. Chief among these is *SCTV*'s first "Movie of the Week" sketch. Soon *SCTV* would be celebrated for producing intricately detailed film parodies far superior to this spoof of the 1970 film *Tora! Tora! Tora!* entitled "Wara! Wara! Wara!" The original film told the story of the attack on Pearl Harbor from both American and Japanese points of view; this version tells the story of the Italian surrender from both American and Italian viewpoints. The sketch is humorless and confusing in how it inexplicably uses characters from earlier and completely unrelated segments.

Two characters appearing in "Wara! Wara! Wara!" are Captain Combat (Thomas) and security guard Gus Gusstofferson (Levy), who also figure prominently in a wraparound story involving the murder of a puppeteer. The *Captain Kangaroo* spoof on which the puppeteer is killed is *SCTV*'s first attempt at parodying children's shows; in addition to substituting Captain Combat for Captain Kangaroo, the sketch features Mr. Green Fatigues (Ramis) instead of Mr. Green Jeans and Mr. Gunny Rabbit in place of Mr. Bunny Rabbit. Children's shows that feature warfare lingo and tips on cleaning firearms is a promising concept, but the sketch fails in its execution. (For a sketch that mixes kids and guns, show 90's "Mrs. Falbo's Tiny Town," with Thomas as G. Gordon Liddy, is much more successful.) The Gusstofferson-led investigation into the puppeteer's death is particularly dull. Oddly enough, the character of Gusstofferson would completely disappear for years before resurfacing on a regular basis on the NBC shows. Captain Combat would make just one more appearance before being eliminated for good.

The only other notable sketch here is the "English for Beginners" piece. This segment, originally done on the Second City stage, introduces a foreigner named Pirini Scleroso (Martin) who insists on repeating everything in unintelligible gibberish. The sketch is passable, but it doesn't leave one wanting more of Scleroso; despite this, Martin would repeatedly bring back this one-joke character, with her only worthwhile sketch being show 53's *My Fair Lady* parody. (Strangely, "English for Beginners" would be completely re-shot for inclusion into show 79.)

Show 3 *(Second City Television)*

1. Harold Ramis: Racial and Ethnic Humor

2. Sunrise Semester with Dr. Ernest Bruter: Gypsy Mythology
3. The Leutonian Hour
4. Plainclothes Mountie promo
5. Out-Patient
6. Hints for Homemakers: Amish Food
7. North American Stethoscopy Institute commercial
8. Theatre North America: We're Gonna Be All Right, You Creep, Leaving Home and All, Eh?
9. Golden Hits of the 11th Century commercial
10. Words to Live By: Dr. Ernest Bruter

What to watch for: Plainclothes Mountie.
Harold Ramis stars in this episode's quickest and funniest sketches. In one, he is a proud spokesperson for a questionable institute that specializes in nothing more than the study of the stethoscope. Even better is a promo for "Plainclothes Mountie" that features Ramis as an "undercover" member of the Royal Canadian Mounted Police. His attempts to work covertly, as when he tries to get information from a stoned Thomas and O'Hara, are severely limited by the fact that he is on horseback. These two pieces prove that although Ramis was not as versatile an actor as his fellow cast members, as head writer he excelled at creating good material that he was comfortable performing.

This episode features an unusual reliance on ethnic stereotypes; much of the show's humor comes at the expense of Gypsies, who are depicted either as thieves ("Hints for Homemakers"), beggars ("Theatre North America"), or people with bizarre religious views ("Sunrise Semester" and "Words to Live By"). The group is also seen as despised and inferior, specifically on the nonsensical program "The Leutonian Hour" (*SCTV*'s first of many references to the fictional country Leutonia). An opening disclaimer from Harold Ramis intends to reprimand the program for its ethnic humor but instead piles on more racial jokes. (Note that Ramis, addressing viewers on behalf of the "management of SCTV," is speaking as himself, and not as a fictional character. Repeats of the episode would identify him on-screen as "SCTV Station Manager Maurice Green.")

The appropriateness of some of this show's material is certainly debatable; however, a good portion of what is offensive is also quite funny. Best is Levy's nerdish Dr. Bruter who, in "Words to Live By," echoes the supposed Gypsy belief that the Ten Commandments do not exist: "Where is it written that thou shalt not steal nor thou shalt not covet thy neighbor's wife," Bruter drones. "I would love to covet my neighbor's wife. She's a gorgeous woman."

Also helping to make the ethnic material more palatable is the fact that *SCTV* devotes plenty of time to mocking its own country of origin in a play supposedly written to help Canadians find their identity. The piece, entitled "We're Gonna Be All Right, You Creep, Leaving Home and All, Eh?" was first done on The Second City stage; a 1974 stage recording of the sketch is available on a CD packaged with the 2000 book *The Second City*. Note also that the *SCTV* version of the sketch marks Dave Thomas's first appearance as his ever-evolving Chinese character Lin Ye Tang.

This episode also features a juvenile but humorous piece entitled "Out-Patient," which involves three men (Candy, Levy, Flaherty) getting vasectomies. The piece was judged too crude by American syndicators and was deleted in favor of a "Dining with LaRue" sketch that was in turn not seen in Canada. The "LaRue" piece, which was obviously filmed much later than the other material in this episode, features Johnny LaRue at a Greek restaurant; because of the piece's Greek setting and characters (including the United States's introduction to Flaherty's Alki Stereopolis character), the sketch fits the ethnic theme of the episode better than "Out-Patient." But since "Out-Patient" has long since been restored for U.S. syndication, the "LaRue" sketch is as of this writing out of circulation.

Show 4 *(Second City Television)*

1. The Sammy Maudlin Show: Premiere
2. Sunrise Semester with Alki Stereopolis: Classical Greek
3. Spray On Socks commercial
4. The $211,000 Triangle
5. Cooking with LaRue
6. Backstage: Lorna Minelli
7. Masterpiece Theatre: Crosswords part 1
8. The Exorcist of Oz promo
9. Masterpiece Theatre: Crosswords part 2
10. Shakespeare's Greatest Jokes commercial
11. Words to Live By: Father Michael Meyer

What to watch for: The Sammy Maudlin Show.
What would become arguably SCTV*'s finest recurring sketch gets a remarkably assured premiere. Despite the rudimentary set (four chairs and a small coffee table offset by some distracting lighting), nearly all of the classic elements of the "Maudlin" sketches are here, the most obvious being the sickening adulation exchanged between talk show host Sammy Maudlin (Flaherty), sidekick William B. Williams (Candy), and his guests, funnyman Bobby Bittman (Levy) and Lorna Minnelli (Martin).*

*Joe Flaherty sums up the origins of Sammy Maudlin best: "Sammy Davis, Jr. had a show on the air [*Sammy and Company*] that was a frenzy of self-congratulations and mutual admiration and I just wanted to do something on it so badly ... I didn't want to do Sammy Davis, Jr. per se. I just wanted to do something suggesting that type of show business guy." Both Flaherty and Levy have their characters down cold at this early stage, in no small part because they had already played Maudlin and Bittman on the stage prior to filming this sketch.*

The most unusual element in this premiere piece is the fact that someone — guest Trish Nutley (O'Hara) — actually has the chutzpah to reprimand the panel for their sycophancy. Never again would anyone challenge Maudlin, nor would Nutley ever again appear in the "Maudlin" sketches, as O'Hara would in the next season discard Nutley in favor of her Lola Heatherton character.

This is *SCTV*'s first classic episode, with a strong series of sketches highlighted not only by the original "Maudlin," but also by the first memorable commercial parody ("Spray-On Socks"), and the first game show parody, "The $211,000 Triangle." A spoof of *The $25,000 Pyramid*, "Triangle" includes the episode's second appearance of Bobby Bittman; this time he is a woefully inept celebrity contestant who can't begin to answer any of the program's tough questions. Bittman is not the only character to make multiple appearances in this program; Martin's Lorna Minnelli is also featured in a brief episode of "Backstage" as well as in a promo for "The Exorcist of Oz" in which she valiantly attempts to croon "Over the Rainbow" even while fighting off demonic possession.

Besides strong sketches featuring Flaherty's Alki Stereopolis ("Sunrise Semester") and Candy's Johnny LaRue ("Cooking with LaRue"), the other most notable sketch in this episode has to be the "Masterpiece Theatre" segment featuring unlikely guest stars Sir Ralph Richardson and Sir John Gielgud. Seeing these two acting legends on *SCTV* at any time in the show's history would be jarring enough, but it's particularly odd to see them appear while the program was still in its infancy.

The two thespians, in Toronto performing in a Harold Pinter play, agreed to be on the show only if they could approve the final script. Several ideas were tried and rejected — including the fine "Shakespeare's Greatest Jokes" commercial included in this episode — and it was only after Gielgud and Richardson gave the cast an assignment to create something that referenced their hobbies was something written that they agreed to perform. But after all the bother, the sketch, as Dave Thomas succinctly put it, "stunk." However, the segment is such a fascinating oddity that it does not detract from the rest of this stellar episode.

Show 5 *(Second City Television)*

1. Baa, Baa, Black and White Sheep promo
2. Sunrise Semester with Dr. Cheryl Kinsey: The Inability to Fake Orgasms
3. It's An Unusual World, Isn't It? promo
4. Witness to Yesterday
5. SCTV AM News Today: Earl's Report from San Francisco
6. The Amanda II commercial
7. "So You're Dead ... Now What?" PSA
8. Match Unto My Feet
9. AC/DC promo
10. Words to Live By: Father John Duffy

What to watch for: Sunrise Semester.
Another piece transferred from the Second City stage, this sketch is the definitive Dr. Cheryl Kinsey segment. Kinsey, a horribly repressed "sexologist" who has the dis-

tinction of fidgeting and twitching at the slightest hint of sexual discussion, would prove to be one of Andrea Martin's best characters. Here Kinsey is given plenty of opportunities to convulse, as the piece — a lecture to women on how to fake orgasms — is one of the most sexually frank SCTV would ever produce. Kinsey's advice is dubious — she claims that men will interpret emotionless utterances of "I've got the music in me" and "Make me a woman, big boy" as orgasmic squeals — and Martin spasms and quivers through every word.

In addition to Martin's Dr. Kinsey, this strong episode also sees the premiere of Eugene Levy's elderly Sid Dithers. Here Dithers is the patriarch of a Jewish family commemorating Passover in the sketch "Match Unto My Feet," a parody of the long-running religious program *Lamp Unto My Feet*. Levy, who named the character Morris for this first outing, summarized how Dithers's diminutive stature came to be: "The scene took four or five hours to do. When I watched the playbacks, I found myself more and more reclined in my seat, so by the end of the scene, I seemed to be lower than when I started. The look was kind of funny."

This episode is also notable for the appearance of Second City stage actress Brenda Donohue in no less than three sketches. Donohue's biggest role comes in a parody of the Canadian TV program *Witness to Yesterday*, which featured a host "interviewing" a historical figure. In *SCTV*'s version, John Candy plays real-life host Patrick Watson who interviews an actress playing Joan of Arc (Donohue). The problem is that Donohue is only prepared to answer questions as Cleopatra.

Harold Ramis continues to search for an identity for his Moe Green character — here Green is identified as a "licensed chiropractor" informing viewers of several warning signs that they may be dead. Contrary to Green, the personas of anchors Earl Camembert and Floyd Robertson were set early and Levy and Flaherty would just continue to improve in the roles. Here Earl's journalistic integrity takes another hit as his decision to drive rather than fly to San Francisco to file a report on earthquakes results in an embarrassing story about car trouble that prevented him from even reaching California.

Show 6 *(Second City Television)*

1. Labrador Slugger commercial
2. SCTV AM News Today: Earl is tired
3. Heavenly Bodies
4. Mr. Science
5. The House of Beauty commercial
6. SCTV News Today: Black & Feminist Perspectives
7. Corna-Bix commercial
8. Masterpiece Theatre: New season promo
9. Hooker Handbook commercial
10. The Memoirs of Anton Chekhov

11. Plainclothes Mountie promo (repeat from show 3)
12. SCTV News: Floyd can't stop laughing

What to watch for: Mr. Science.
"Mr. Science" finds Johnny LaRue as the terrifically unfit host of a children's science program modeled on the educational show Mr. Wizard. *As the show starts, LaRue is "sleeping one off" when he is awoken by his junior assistant Donald (child actor Donald Cowper, making his first of several* SCTV *appearances); since LaRue is in no shape for any legitimate scientific experiments, he instead teaches Donald about making coffee, smoking cigarettes, and watching TV (they watch the first episode of* Second City Television*).*

A strong show with no less than three "SCTV News" sketches. One of the news segments — "Black Perspective" — ranks as one of *SCTV*'s most controversial pieces: Unlike *Saturday Night Live*, *SCTV* saw no need to diversify its cast with non–White performers (this can be at least partially explained by looking at the show's origins — non–Whites were a rarity on the Second City stage as late as the 1970s), a situation that did not prevent the actors from performing as non–White characters, the most glaring examples being the Asian ones (Lin Ye Tang and Tim Ishimuni) attempted by Dave Thomas.

Here Thomas's decision to portray someone of a different race — he dons crude blackface to offer the "Black Perspective" on the news — is initially more shocking yet ultimately *less* offensive than his Asian personas. While Thomas's makeup is clearly reprehensible, it is quickly condemned by Flaherty's Floyd Robertson as "the most racist thing I've ever seen in my life" and a "tasteless display of White arrogance." Thomas's explanation — the regular "Black Perspective" reporter called in sick — can be interpreted as not only a commentary on the embarrassing lack of minorities working in television news but as a commentary on the embarrassing lack of minorities working on *SCTV* itself. Sadly, *SCTV* never corrected its failure to diversify its cast or writing staff.

The rest of the episode is less controversial: Joe Flaherty's interest in the works of Anton Chekhov and Dave Thomas's interest in *Star Trek* results in the inspired idea of *Star Trek*'s Chekov (Thomas) being transported into the performance of a play based on Anton Chekhov's memoirs. (Note that while Thomas soon favored an impression of "Bones" McCoy, he impersonated the *Star Trek* character of Chekov first.)

Other fine moments include the revelation of the vast salary disparity between Floyd Robertson and Earl Camembert — Earl makes $200 a week while Floyd pulls in a startling $7,000 a week. And Flaherty and Candy are a riot as famed hockey players Darryl Sittler and Guy Lafleur trying to get through the taping of a cereal commercial.

Show 7 *(Second City Television)*

1. Homelier You commercial
2. An SCTV Before-School Special: Beauty and the Beets
3. SCTV AM News Today
4. Lasermatic commercial (repeat from show 1)
5. Firing Squad with William F. Buckley
6. Famous Philosophers' School commercial
7. Alice the Wonder Dog
8. Dialing for Dollars: Changing Partners part 1
9. Evelyn Woods Speed Talking School commercial (repeat from show 1)
10. Dialing for Dollars: Changing Partners part 2
11. 15 Minutes promo
12. Dialing for Dollars part 3

What to watch for: *15 Minutes.*
This brief sketch promoting a 60 Minutes–*type magazine show with Floyd Robertson and Earl Camembert is one of the characters' finest first season pieces, no small achievement considering the quantity and quality of news segments done in the first 26 shows.*

The disparity between Floyd and Earl continues to grow as the two reveal their reports for "15 Minutes": Somehow Floyd was sent to cover a combination gourmet restaurant/bordello in New Orleans, while Earl was assigned to spend ten days inside a "scummy prison" for a look at solitary confinement. The prison story tease leads to one of SCTV's most shocking exchanges as Floyd callously asks Earl about the prison rape he suffered while covering the story. Robertson's total lack of concern for his partner is one of the most telling moments in all of the Floyd and Earl sketches.

A fairly strong episode noted for two particularly bizarre sketches: "Beauty and the Beets" is a so-called "cautionary tale" for children that depicts a beautiful young princess (O'Hara) being graphically tortured for refusing to eat her beets. Apparently the tale is meant to caution young children whose parents just happen to have a torture chamber in their basement. "Alice the Wonder Dog" is equally strange — the real dog in the sketch does absolutely nothing to earn the title of "Wonder Dog," but her complete lack of activity is nevertheless praised mightily by her owner (Levy).

Here Harold Ramis's Moe Green character finally settles into something of a stable role as the host of "Dialing for Dollars." Green is adamantly unwilling to part with the show's jackpot of $2,400, going so far as to hang up on viewers before they get a chance to name the movie and win the cash. The movie shown is a funny softcore porn film starring Trish Nutley (O'Hara) as a nymphomaniac who pays for things — even regular mail delivery — with sex.

O'Hara was often called upon to be "sexy" on *SCTV*; the perception of her as more desirable than Andrea Martin was never more bluntly portrayed than in this episode's "Homelier You" commercial. In the spot, O'Hara plays a target of a co-worker's sexual advances; to fend off the colleague, O'Hara uses a de-beautifying product to turn herself into Martin, whose appearance immediately repulses the co-worker. The amenable Martin should have quickly rejected this insulting sketch.

Show 8 *(Second City Television)*

1. Harold Ramis: Parental Advisory
2. Extreme Close-Up promo
3. Dining with LaRue: Italian Restaurant
4. 50 Practical Jokes You Can Do for Free commercial
5. The Wacky World of Poverty
6. Al Pro commercial
7. Eye On Science
8. A Fistful of Ugly preview
9. Shock Theatre
10. Margot Fontaine at the Russian Circus promo

What to watch for: Shock Theatre.
This sketch, about a father (Flaherty) who attempts to get his son (Donald Cowper) to sleep by telling the boy scary stories, is arguably the most unsettling of any sketch in SCTV's canon. The final shot of the son having been literally scared to death is particularly unforgettable, thanks to a remarkable make-up job (especially considering the show's low budget) and an equally remarkable job by Cowper at convincingly playing dead.

The sketch features even more gruesomeness: An earlier story, acted out by the cast, ends rather horrifically with a mother (Martin) killing her daughter (O'Hara) with a kitchen knife. As the story ends, quick edits intercut the mother hacking away at her daughter with shots of the kitchen window becoming increasingly covered in blood. (And apparently real blood at that—the show's end credits thank the Blood Bank of Toronto.) Though we never see the knife entering O'Hara's body, that doesn't dilute the sketch's grisliness.

Actually, the shocking moments in "Shock Theatre" are quite funny in the context of the sketch: Yes, a mother butchering her daughter is disturbing, but the fact that she does so because the daughter has so many pimples she is unrecognizable to the mother makes the scene humorous. Likewise the ghastly shot of the boy scared to death is ultimately hysterical because the story that killed him was not frightening in the least.

Despite the success of this piece (and of show 12's creepy "Taxidermist" sketch), SCTV's experiments with mixing comedy and horror would ultimately be few in number. Either the show decided that "Shock Theatre" simply couldn't be improved upon, or the Blood Bank of Toronto refused future requests for more blood.

A remarkable show with several classic bits: Besides "Shock Theatre," the game show parody "The Wacky World of Poverty" is the best piece here; a parody of both *The Gong Show* and *Let's Make a Deal*, this sketch satirizes those two shows for ridiculing poor people in exchange for giving them the chance to win cash and prizes. *SCTV* takes these shows a step further by filling an audience with miserably destitute people and requiring them to perform potentially deadly stunts for the chance to win a few measly dollars.

Nearly as funny is a "Dining with LaRue" sketch that parodies the famous scene in *The Godfather* in which Al Pacino takes care of family business in an Italian restaurant. Candy's Johnny LaRue is the only customer who stays in the restaurant when some gangsters arrive; he and the waiter (Ramis) are the only witnesses when Flaherty returns from the washroom and loudly shoots Thomas and Levy at point-blank range. In his book, Thomas remembers being quite uneasy with this scene, particularly since *SCTV* had no budget for a firearms supervisor.

Despite the fact that *SCTV* was steadily improving, there was still confusion about who was in charge of the fictional television station. Here Harold Ramis is credited as being the SCTV station manager; his alter ego Moe Green would eventually take over in show 24. Meanwhile Moe Green is credited as being an "author, playwright, and critic" in a promo for a show called "Extreme Close-Up." If Green is indeed so esteemed, why is he slumming as the host of the cheapo "Dialing for Dollars"?

Show 9 (Second City Television)

1. Good-Bye America: The State of Motion Pictures
2. Sunrise Semester with Dr. Cheryll Height: Self-Defense for Women
3. Bath Talk promo
4. SCTV AM News Today: Earl "punches it up"
5. Philosophy Street
6. S & M Airlines commercial
7. Total Woman with Cassy Mackerel
8. SCTV Movie of the Week: A Fistful of Ugly
9. Longjeans G-11 commercial
10. Feedback

What to watch for: Philosophy Street.
A wickedly funny parody of the venerable Sesame Street, *this sketch attempts to teach kids about different types of materialism, and also how to tell the difference between realism, idealism, and existentialism. Best of all is a series of exchanges between hoodlum Dave Thomas and brain Eugene Levy — Levy purports to teach the uninterested Thomas about value judgments and factual judgments, but instead Thomas teaches him about bad judgment and armed robbery. A much smarter mixture of children and violence than show 2's "Captain Combat."*

This episode earns its place in *SCTV* history by featuring, during the Moe Green (Ramis) phone-in show "Feedback," the first appearance of SCTV president Guy Caballero. Granted, only Caballero's voice is heard in this initial sketch, but Flaherty seems to already have a grasp of the character, particularly the vicious and cruel manner with which he deals with his employees. Not only does Caballero call Green's show "terrible," "lousy," and "the worst thing I've ever seen on television," but he also fires Green on the spot and forces him out of the studio. A funny introduction to what would prove to be a classic, if ultimately overused, character.

Despite some fine commercial parodies on this episode — one for the sadistic S&M Airlines and another for an ordinary watch that touts itself as a "vegetable dicer and slicer" and a "mini gym"— this episode falters on its longer pieces. The centerpiece sketch, a "family" version of a Sergio Leone spaghetti western, is particularly tedious, as violent confrontations between "the Sheriff with no name" (Ramis) and others (including Johnny LaRue as "the Mexican") are hinted at and then avoided.

Other notable sketches include the first of two parodies of Geraldo Rivera's *Good Night America*; the piece, lampooning several notable film critics, features Andrea Martin as "Pauline Kale" [sic]. Over 100 episodes later, Mary Charlotte Wilcox would impersonate the same critic for the second and last time on *SCTV*. Also, the "Sunrise Semester" sketch features Andrea Martin's Dr. Cheryl Kinsey character, although here she is mysteriously renamed Dr. Cheryll Height.

Show 10 *(Second City Television)*

1. SCTV News: Earl in New Deli
2. Sunrise Semester with Dr. Hammond Greer: Political Sciences 101
3. Robco Up-Your-Nose Pollution Filter commercial
4. SCTV News: Action Line / FDA report
5. Dining with LaRue: Tang Gardens
6. Silver Bullet Suppositories commercial
7. Northern Ireland Perspective '77 with Lou Jaffe
8. National Drugstore Association PSA
9. SCTV Foreign Film of the Week: Thérèse et Joe
10. SCTV News: Earl's commentary on terrorists

What to watch for: *Thérèse et Joe.*
While not as sophisticated as SCTV's movie parodies would soon become, this brief satire of French New Wave films is still enjoyable. "Thérèse et Joe" recognizes three of the masters of the French New Wave movement—Jean-Luc Godard, Alain Resnais, and François Truffaut; the sketch is credited to "Jean-Luc Resnais," while the title is clearly a play on Truffaut's most famous film, Jules et Jim.

To detractors, French New Wave films were nonsensical, which is the most glaring characteristic of "Thérèse et Joe." In the title roles, Andrea and Joe are obviously lovers, but their actions—kissing passionately, eating, discussing politics in an abrupt and superficial manner, and simply behaving silly (he impersonates Jerry Lewis, she rides him like a horse)—hardly constitute the plot of a traditional film. Most illogical of all is the film's end, when Joe suddenly jumps out the window, prompting Thérèse to remark, "I understand now." Certainly Thérèse is alone in her understanding of Joe's fatal action, but that is precisely the point.

A weak episode most noteworthy for featuring the first recognizable appearance of Dave Thomas's classic announcer character Harvey K-Tel, who is heard (and not seen) in an otherwise uninspired commercial for personal pollution filters. (Oddly enough, Eugene Levy's announcer counterpart, Lou Jaffe, also debuts in this episode, in a substandard sketch involving therapy groups in Northern Ireland.)

Thomas fares better in two other sketches: He is quite funny in a "Sunrise Semester" sketch working himself up into a lather over claims that scientists are stealing his electricity, his mail, and even the top third of cereal from his cereal boxes. Oddly enough, Thomas thought that he got himself "locked into the seriousness" of the character and was "embarrassed" when the sketch aired. On the contrary, the fact that Thomas is convincingly angry about the absurd notion of a scientist conspiracy only makes the sketch more effective. (Thomas would later use belligerent anger to even better effect with his finest creation — Bill Needle, *SCTV*'s self-described "critic-at-large.")

Thomas, as Lin Ye Tang, is the funniest thing in a sloppy "Dining with LaRue" segment; while both he and Candy are playing drunk, Thomas alone appears to realize the weakness of the material and seems more interested in breaking up Candy. Thomas doesn't succeed, but his presence makes the sketch at least passable.

Show 11 *(Second City Television)*
1. Bell Telephone commercial: Three Fishermen
2. Sunrise Semester with Mort Finkel: Do-It-Yourself Dentistry
3. SCTV News: Earl's Helsinki Report
4. Dining with LaRue: The Scorched Earth
5. Broads Behind Bars
6. An Evening with Col. Sanders promo

What to watch for: Sunrise Semester.
One of the best of all the "Sunrise Semester" sketches and one of Harold Ramis's funniest performances. Here Ramis lectures on the topic of do-it-yourself dentistry, which he claims can save its practitioners thousands of dollars. But the savings come at the steep price of having to drill your own cavities, which Ramis does while screaming in intensely excruciating pain. Ramis cries out so convincingly that the scene is almost uncomfortable to watch.

Note that in the sketch, Ramis remarks that because do-it-yourself dentists aren't licensed to administer Novocain, he recommends as a substitute shots of rum, which he proceeds to quickly ingest. Ramis claims that the crew supplied actual rum for the scene and he finished the shoot drunk. The finished sketch backs up Ramis's story, as he gives the crew a couple of knowing looks as he downs the shots.

An episode notable for its lengthier sketches; the show has half as many pieces as most of the episodes in the first season.

The most ambitious sketch here is "Broads Behind Bars," a parody of fifties women-in-prison films like *Caged* (1950) and *Women's Prison* (1955). (The stars of *Women's Prison* include Audrey Totter and Jan Sterling; "Broads Behind Bars" stars Audrey Tawdry and Jan Silver.) The black-and-white piece, while featuring fine comic performances from Andrea Martin as the leader of the inmates and John Candy as a female prison guard, is the low point of the episode. The reason the piece doesn't work better is because women's prison movies are camp to begin with; what *SCTV* has done here is parody a genre that parodies itself. "Broads Behind Bars" is no funnier or sillier than the movies it purports to mock.

Elsewhere, John Candy's Johnny LaRue stars in yet another "Dining with LaRue" segment; although the sketch is beginning to wear out its welcome, placing the distinctly unhealthy LaRue at a health food restaurant is a funny premise, and the piece is successful. Even better is another "SCTV News" segment, as Earl wastes time showing slides from his trip to Helsinki. Notably, Earl also shows a slide of a drunken Robertson, which is the first hint of Robertson's drinking problem that will become a recurring element in future "SCTV News" sketches.

Finally, Dave Thomas pulls off a tour de force performance in a sketch with an unlikely premise: A one-man show with Kentucky Fried Chicken's Colonel Sanders. Somehow Thomas's Sanders manages to interweave chicken and major historical figures of the 20th century: Upon finding out in 1934 that Adolf Hitler hated chicken, Sanders claims to have said, "'Mark my words. There's a man who will start a Holocaust!"

Show 12 *(Second City Television)*
1. Nuclear-Sized Baggys commercial
2. Farm Report
3. Welcome Back President Kotter
4. The Glass Menagerie promo
5. Alistair Cook's Armenia
6. SCTV Mystery Movie of the Week: The Taxidermist
7. 20 Depressing Hits by Connie Franklin commercial
8. SCTV News: Earl coughs

What to watch for: The Taxidermist.
Before Count Floyd ever appeared to falsely declare certain sketches as "scary," SCTV *did have a couple of pieces that, if not exactly "scary," were at least creepy. One of the most notable examples is this unnerving sketch featuring John Candy as a taxidermist and Catherine O'Hara as Candy's girlfriend who is invited to Candy's home to meet his parents, only to find that Candy has killed and stuffed them like game.*

The sketch is certainly not without laughs—when Ramis falls off the couch, Candy callously remarks that Dad is "always the clown"—but what sets the piece apart from the other material in SCTV*'s history is that it is, like show 8's "Shock Theatre," legitimately unsettling. Ramis and Martin do look grotesque, and O'Hara does a fine job of playing the damsel in distress. But the sketch belongs to Candy, who does a brilliant job of shifting from the friendly boyfriend to a hostile killer. A true original of the* SCTV *canon. Count Floyd would approve.*

A solid episode marred only by a muddled sketch about the birthplace of carpeting as well as a forgettable debut of Flaherty's Big Jim McBob character. It would be another season before Big Jim McBob would pair up with Candy's Billy Sol Hurok to become two of *SCTV*'s most memorable characters (noted most for their enthusiasm for seeing people "blowed up real good"). The premiere of McBob's "Farm Report" program is quite different from those later installments — Flaherty simply reads a list of commodity prices and interviews a representative from the Department of Agriculture (Thomas). No Billy Sol Hurok, no talk of movies, and certainly nothing getting "blowed up." And not many laughs.

Much better is a parody of the then-current sitcom *Welcome Back Kotter*, a rare example of *SCTV* doing a straightforward parody of a mass-appeal program. (John Candy once told David Letterman that satirizing popular shows was difficult because shows were often "parodies of themselves," citing a shelved *Laverne & Shirley* parody as an example.) This sketch finds Mr. Kotter (Eugene Levy's Gabe Kaplan) as President of the United States, presiding not over the Sweathogs, but a similarly disrespectful and troublemaking staff, including Harold Ramis as the Attorney General who breaks up the meeting to go "find some chicks." Catherine O'Hara also makes an appearance impersonating Marcia Strassman in her thankless role as Kotter's wife.

Finally, Andrea Martin is gloomy singer Connie Franklin peddling her album "20 Depressing Hits," a record that features lyrics like "I'm losing my hearing / I've lost sight in one eye / I'm sorry I can't hear you / Did you really say goodbye." One of *SCTV*'s strongest in a long line of record album commercials.

Show 13 *(Second City Television)*

1. Moe Green: Introduction
2. Ben-Hur: Part 1
3. Moe Green: "Was that ever moving"
4. Ben-Hur: Part 1 continued
5. Moe Green: Intermission
6. AMCO Dolls commercial
7. Masquerade Funeral promo
8. Moe Green: Pit Stop
9. Ben-Hur: Part 2
10. Top Secret commercial
11. Tobacco Paste commercial
12. Ben-Hur: Part 2 continued
13. Moe Green: Stephen Boyd
14. Ben-Hur: Conclusion
15. Moe Green: Dialing for Dollars

What to watch for: *Ben-Hur*.
A landmark sketch in style and concept more than in execution and substance, "Ben-Hur," as SCTV's first extended film parody, lays a foundation upon which the show would improve.

Many accounts of SCTV *have documented the gestation of this ambitious piece: The fact that the "Ben-Hur" sets, though miserably primitive, nevertheless destroyed the episode's budget to the point that the entire episode had to be built around the sketch; the fact that the sketch seemed, in the words of Harold Ramis, "terrible" and "flat as could be" in rehearsal; the fact that John Candy, playing the title role, began delivering his lines as Curly from The Three Stooges and the idea was hatched that Candy should just play Ben-Hur as Curly. Ramis credits this acting choice for turning the sketch into a "classic."*

It's too easy to say that a change, however major, in how Candy read his lines was enough to turn a "terrible" piece into a "classic" sketch; it wasn't, and "Ben-Hur" would have ultimately been better had Joe Flaherty played the lead doing his Charlton Heston impression (which he had yet to introduce on SCTV). But the decision does show that SCTV was not afraid to attack even the most revered film with extreme silliness—a formula that was to serve the show well even as its parodies got smarter and more complex. (The mud slinging in show 23's "Grapes of Mud" or the woodchuck CPR in show 106's "Garth and Gord and Fiona and Alice.") Indeed, it was when SCTV's film parodies were too literal—"New York Rhapsody" (show 92) or "Oliver Grimley" (show 129), for example—that the program lost its way.

It helps when viewing SCTV's "Ben-Hur" to visualize the sketch as a filmed version of a stage performance; this mind game makes the piece's extreme budgetary limitations easier to accept. Interestingly enough, long before William Wyler directed the definitive film version of General Lew Wallace's novel, Ben-Hur *was done as a highly successful theatrical production. How the stage version presented the film's most technically challenging sequence—the famous chariot race—actually mirrors how* SCTV *presented the same scene: Both used video backdrops to help give the illusion of motion (although the stage version did use live horses running on treadmills; horses were apparently beyond the limitations of* SCTV*'s budget).*

One of the most memorable aspects of the sketch is the appearance of a man in plaid pants who pours a martini to a parched and enslaved Ben-Hur. The scene is a parody of the sequence in the original film in which a longhaired man appears out of nowhere to offer water to Heston's Ben-Hur. The face of neither savior is seen; in the film, it is obvious that the figure is Jesus, but it is not obvious nor does it matter that the figure in SCTV's version is associate producer and writer Sheldon Patinkin. Thomas claims the casting amounted to an inside joke because Patinkin played a "god-like role in the editing room." But the reasons for casting Patinkin are ultimately irrelevant; the sight of Ben-Hur receiving a cocktail from a man in garish pants is simply unforgettable.

With the cast perhaps demonstrating a lack of confidence that it could sustain such a lengthy piece, SCTV presents the "Ben-Hur" sketch with an incredible amount of interruptions for Moe Green asides, commercial parodies, and promos (i.e., SCTV's usual fare). While the other sketches improve the overall show, their existence makes "Ben-Hur" choppy and badly paced. SCTV would correct this problem when the piece was rerun in two long segments on show 95. Finally, SCTV would later poke fun at itself for how it originally presented the sketch: On a 1988 Best of SCTV *special, an investigatory panel presents an even* more *frequently interrupted version of "Ben-Hur" as evidence that SCTV exceeds industry standards for commercial time.*

Show 14 *(Second City Television)*

1. Those Funny Guys promo
2. SCTV Sports Central part 1
3. Hefty part 1
4. SCTV News promo
5. Shoplifting PSA
6. 50 Psalms commercial
7. The Hefty Neil Story part 2
8. Emergency Orderly and Court Clerk promo
9. SCTV Sports Central part 2

What to watch for: Emergency Orderly and Court Clerk.
This promo harkens back to show 1's "Unnecessary Surgeon"/"Malpractice Lawyer" spot, but improves upon that earlier piece. Spotlighting two highly unglamorous occupations, SCTV nevertheless tries to sell these shows as action-packed blockbusters. For example, "Emergency Orderly" is not just a show about a guy (Levy) who cleans bedpans; it's sold as showcasing "experiences that ordinary men never see." Levy is particularly funny as he disgustingly pushes an elderly woman (O'Hara) onto the floor to change her soiled sheets.

For the second straight episode, a lengthy piece acts as a wraparound element around a series of much shorter sketches. However, the longer piece here—a parody of *Rocky* starring John Candy as boxer Hefty Neil—can't improve on the *Ben-Hur* spoof of show 13. Not that the wraparound is without merit: John Candy turns in a fine performance in the title role, moving effortlessly from slapstick (eating raw meat instead of training with it) to seriousness (speaking up for all of the "bums and losers in this lousy stinking world"). Also notable is the appearance of *SCTV*'s first filmed (as opposed to videotaped) sequences.

The highlight of the wraparound comes at the finale, which features SCTV's much-hyped live coverage of Hefty Neil's heavyweight title bout. Unfortunately, the fight is over after one punch, leaving studio analysts Keith Hampshire (Thomas), Phyllis Gumbel (O'Hara), and ringside announcer Lou Jaffe (Levy) scrambling to fill airtime. Overall, *Hefty*, like the fight itself, is *not* one for the ages.

Much better are most of the short pieces that surround *The Hefty Neil Story*, particularly a "SCTV News" promo (foreshadowing a later, similar piece in show 115) that features Earl previewing some deliciously sensationalistic news stories. Flaherty shines in a PSA as a demented assistant excited about the prospect of torturing a female shoplifter (O'Hara). And all of the male cast members generate laughs in a promo that lampoons the stereotypical characters often found in sitcoms ("Those Funny Guys").

Show 15 *(Second City Television)*

1. Library Police promo
2. Exorcising with Reagan Blair

3. SCTV AM News Today: Earl Jr.
4. Chickadee Chickette Chicken Style Loaf commercial
5. Leave It to Beaver 25th Anniversary Party
6. Quick Wash Dish Laundry commercial
7. Kids Can Play on the Wagon PSA
8. Blind Fists of the Furious Dragon preview
9. Dr. Tongue and His Animal Friends
10. Family Detective commercial
11. Dialing for Dollars: Moe calls "Mrs. Green"

What to watch for: Leave It to Beaver.
An ingenious sketch that presents a disturbingly dark vision of the Cleaver household had the popular sitcom remained on the air for 25 years. According to SCTV, June Cleaver (O'Hara) would have run off with neighbor Fred Rutherford, Ward (Flaherty) would be a hopeless drunk, Wally (Levy) would be divorced four times and flat broke, and the Beaver (Candy) would be depressed, unemployed, and on welfare. Eddie Haskell (Thomas), while still a jerk, would also change, as he confides here to Wally: "I'm gay and I'm proud of it." (Note that not only are the Cleavers dysfunctional, they're also brazenly intolerant: Upon hearing Eddie's confession, Wally says, "Gee, Eddie, maybe you'd better stop coming around here anymore.")

The plot of the sketch involves the Beaver's dislike of Eddie, a problem to which Beaver's friend Whitey (Ramis) offers this solution: "Why don't you kill him?" As Candy innocently replies "Gee, Whitey, I don't know," it becomes apparent that SCTV is using one of America's most beloved fictitious families to comment on how things have gone wrong since the fifties: That in the 1970s, plotting to murder someone could be discussed as casually as plotting to go the movies might have been chatted about twenty years earlier.

After killing Haskell, Beaver — as the character always did when he was caught doing something wrong — gets his punishment from his strict but loving father; but this time, it's not straight to bed without supper, it's a phone call to the police. Ward hopes that "maybe 35 years in the slammer will teach the Beaver something." Unfortunately, SCTV never followed up this sketch with a "Beaver in jail" piece. Instead, we are left with this, arguably SCTV's most realized parody of classic television.

Besides the "Beaver" sketch, this show has other memorable moments: Notable among them is John Candy's first appearance as Dr. Tongue. But this is not the Dr. Tongue that *SCTV* fans know from such classics as "3-D House of Stewardesses" (show 84); this Dr. Tongue is the host of a children's program about animals. The character had first appeared in a similar context on the Second City stage; five shows later he would evolve again into the star of most of the films featured on "Monster Chiller Horror Theatre."

Dave Thomas's versatile Lin Ye Tang is featured in one of the character's most tolerable sketches, a preview for a "shtick-fu" film called "Blind Fists of the Furious Dragon." In the movie, Tang is a master of a new martial arts style that calls for tricking opponents with slapstick gags straight out of Three Stooges films; seeing him fool an adversary (Levy) into falling off a bridge just by utilizing the old "follow my hand" routine is particularly inspired.

This show is also unique for the many appearances of Donald Cowper; the child actor appears in no less than four sketches, most memorably as Earl Camembert's son in another solid "SCTV News" segment. Cowper is also quite good in a PSA about juvenile alcoholism. This last sketch is noteworthy for one of the most blatant examples of *SCTV*'s small budget: A kitchen set in the PSA is exactly the same kitchen set used earlier in the "Leave It to Beaver" sketch.

Show 16 *(Second City Television)*
1. Absolutely and Positively Nothing commercial
2. Winning Chess with Boris Morris
3. SCTV AM News Today: Earl's clothes / Roda Barret
4. 20 Depressing Hits by Connie Franklin commercial (repeat from show 12)
5. "So You're Dead ... Now What?" PSA (repeat from show 5)
6. Good-Bye America with Heraldo Rivera: Johnny LaRue's Penthouse Party part 1
7. Sex commercial
8. Good-Bye America with Heraldo Rivera: Johnny LaRue's Penthouse Party part 2

What to watch for: Good-Bye America.
This sketch is key in the evolution of John Candy's Johnny LaRue character. Until this point, LaRue was something of an oxymoron: He was purported to be a big mogul, yet whenever he appeared on-camera, it was in cheap programs such as "Cooking with LaRue" or "Mr. Science." This second installment of "Good-Bye America" brings LaRue much more into focus.

Here LaRue is presented in all of his glory: At his beck and call are dozens of hangers-on (including many beautiful women known as "Gerbils," which are LaRue's answer to Hugh Hefner's "Bunnies"), all of whom he can "squash like bugs" should the mood strike him. And when he's not entertaining in his lavish 95th floor penthouse apartment, LaRue maintains a multi-million dollar empire that he can control from the comfort of his own bed. This portrayal of LaRue as powerful, wealthy, selfish, and cruel is the image of Johnny LaRue that will persist throughout the character's remaining appearances, particularly in the NBC episodes when he often butts heads with the equally powerful and conceited Guy Caballero.

Although this piece was created to showcase Candy's main character, it is Eugene Levy, as party guest Bobby Bittman, who gets the segment's biggest laughs. Here Bittman begins an evolution of his own, as the funnyman's unprovoked rage at fellow partygoers provides the first indication of the comedian's troubled soul. As was happening already, Bittman would prove to be even more interesting than LaRue throughout the remainder of SCTV*'s run.*

Beside the LaRue sketch, there is little of interest on this episode. Even "SCTV News" is sub-par, as much of the segment is given over to a pedestrian piece featuring Catherine O'Hara as gossip columnist Rona Barrett. Worst yet is a tedious sketch featuring Harold Ramis and Andrea Martin as immature chess players.

The most successful piece here is a parody of then-current Stove Top Stuffing commercials; in *SCTV*'s version, Mrs. Maurice Green (Martin) is shocked to learn that her husband would prefer sex (not stuffing) to mashed potatoes.

Show 17 *(Second City Television)*

1. Diving for Dollars
2. Sunrise Semester with Edith Prickly: Elevator Conversation part 1
3. Serfs commercial
4. Sci-Fi Theatre with Bradley Omar: Galaxy 66
5. To Tell the Truth promo
6. Mrs. Prickley's Jelly commercial
7. The Swish Buckler promo
8. Pyramid Power commercial
9. Beside the Point
10. Bald & Brassy commercial
11. Words to Live By: Dr. Bradley Omar

What to watch for: Beside the Point.
This parody of public affairs programs features a perfect execution of a very simple idea: A host, a panel of newspaper editors, and a guest gather to discuss an issue of current public interest. The problem is that no one can stay focused on the topic at hand—they all go off on tangents that are "beside the point." Flaherty, playing a one-eyed leader of an Israeli right-wing party, gets increasingly incensed at digressions that include the host (Ramis) going on about his car problems and a panelist (Levy) who asks him how the loss of one eye has impacted his golf game. However, when given a relevant question, Flaherty himself goes on and on with a completely irrelevant airport anecdote.

Just as show 9 will live in *SCTV* history as the first show to feature Guy Caballero, this episode is best remembered as the first to introduce Andrea Martin's Edith Prickley character, although Prickley's role as SCTV's station manager would not be defined until episode 36. In this initial episode, the character appears in both a "Sunrise Semester" sketch and in a commercial for homemade jellies. The fact that Martin had most of Prickley's characteristics — her love of leopard-spotted clothing, her obnoxious laugh — already down is due to the fact that she created the part on the Second City stage. But it wasn't until Harold Ramis left the show and Edith Prickley became Guy Caballero's right-hand woman that the character was given proper direction. That Prickley appears in not one but two sketches in her first show is prescient of the fact that Martin would appear as Prickley far too many times in the years ahead.

Though Martin inarguably has a handle on Prickley, neither of her sketches are actually very funny. Nor is an overlong parody of the 1960s show *Route 66* done as a sci-fi show called "Galaxy 66." In his book, Dave Thomas admits that the sketch was based on a "stupid idea," but he also uses "Galaxy 66" to grouse about the inadequate makeup people that *SCTV* had in its early days. He has a point — the makeup in the sketch is amateurish, but so are the costumes, special effects, and, most importantly, the script. Thomas's frustrations even find their way into the sketch, as a mutant (Candy) mocks the protagonists (Thomas and Flaherty) for their "nice heads." Candy's taunts are the most memorable aspect of the piece.

Two brief sketches are sophomoric but work: In a mint commercial, Candy and Levy play two drunk drivers ("I think you hit that old lady") who are overly concerned about bad breath, while all of the male cast members shine in a promo for a show about effeminate buccaneers called "The Swish Buckler." *Saturday Night Live* would later copy "The Swish Buckler" for a similar sketch called "The Raging Queen."

Show 18 *(Second City Television)*

1. Recriminalize Marijuana PSA
2. The Texas Chainsaw Massacres preview
3. Dante's Inferno
4. Fillips Milk of Amnesia commercial
5. SCTV AM News Today: Earl's Women Newscaster Editorial
6. Meatball Heroes promo
7. Monster Chiller Horror Theatre: Madame Blitzman part 1
8. Venerable Electric commercial
9. Tornado Warning
10. Monster Chiller Horror Theatre: Madame Blitzman part 2

What to watch for: Dante's Inferno.
A game show parody with a twist: The contestants on "Dante's Inferno" desperately don't want to be on the show, in no small part because one out of three participants is guaranteed to be thrown into a large flaming pit. This sketch, named for the description of Hell found in Dante Alighieri's The Divine Comedy, *tests contestants on sins they have committed in the past as well as sins they may be willing to commit in the future. Besides boasting one of the most striking sets created thus far for SCTV, the segment works expertly. Assisting admirably are Eugene Levy and Dave Thomas, who agreed to don ridiculous demon costumes for the piece; for their trouble, they get to rend Harold Ramis's flesh with giant pitchforks.*

"Monster Chiller Horror Theatre," featuring "Floyd Robertson as Count Floyd," makes an unimpressive debut in this episode. While much of Count Floyd's shtick is already present here — his vampire call, his apologies for the recent rash of non-scary films, his promises that on next week's show "we'll have a real good one for you" — the *Madame Curie* parody that comprises the bulk of the sketch is a bore. Entitled "Madame Blitzman," the piece revolves around the relationship between a student (Martin) and her mentor and husband (Levy). There's nothing scary about the movie, a fact that sets Floyd off on a rant of excuses ("We send away for these films and they send them in packages. They send two or three scary films and the rest are all clinkers."); unfortunately, there's nothing humorous or interesting about the movie either, nor is there any indication the "Monster Chiller Horror Theatre" sketches would soon become one of *SCTV*'s most successful recurring pieces.

Elsewhere, this show contains a high number of quality sketches, the best being Catherine's commercial for a stress-relieving product called "Milk of Amnesia" that "helps you forget why you took it." Associate Producer Sheldon Patinkin would later single out the sketch as "one of the best pieces of sustained comic acting I've ever seen." Just as good is Earl Camembert's outrageously sexist commentary on women news anchors: He's against them because of their "high and squeaky" voices and also because he's "too busy looking at their chests" to hear what they have to say. Levy excelled at finding new ways to make Camembert look ridiculous; this is one of his finest efforts.

Show 19 *(Second City Television)*

1. Dr. Benson: The Credit Psychiatrist commercial
2. Wake Up with Alki Steriopoulous
3. Fluffy Puff commercial
4. SCTV AM News Today: Problems with Earl's film
5. Labels PSA
6. Fat Masterson Private Eye promo
7. $129,000 Question
8. The Point Shave and Haircut System commercial
9. Elvira Mad Again Part II
10. Dom Perignon commercial
11. Words to Live By: Father Chick Murphy

What to watch for: *$129,000 Question.*
Another in a long line of excellent game show parodies. Hosted by Harold Ramis's Moe Green, this sketch takes Green's reluctance to award prize money on "Dialing for Dollars" one step further: Faced with a fireman contestant (Flaherty) who is coming frighteningly close to winning the jackpot, Green purposefully unnerves him by reminding him of the gruesome death of his best friend and then by doubting his wife's fidelity. Ramis is unspeakably sleazy and underhanded—wrongly thinking that Flaherty was trying to cheat, he snidely adds, "Don't pick up your wife's filthy habits." Eventually Flaherty cracks and Green saves his miserly station the $129,000 prize.

A solid episode containing several strong bits, including two commercial parodies wisely revived for use on the NBC episodes. In one, Dave Thomas does an inspired variation on his already well-established Harvey K-Tel pitchman; here he is a psychiatrist who peddles his services like a used car salesman peddles Volvos. He even offers easy payment plans and displays recent patients like new vehicles fresh on the lot. Putting his real-life experience as an advertising copywriter to great use, Thomas was an expert at parodying hard-sell commercials. This is one of his best.

Rivaling that spot is a commercial for an all-in-one haircut and shaving system called "The Point." The contraption looks like a pencil sharpener, and it leaves its users looking like — what else — freshly sharpened pencils, with haircuts that foreshadow Martin Short's Ed Grimley character.

Starring in a longer but equally successful piece is Flaherty's smooth-talking Greek Alki Steriopoulous, who is featured here in a sketch that is designed to make female viewers feel as if they are waking up next to Alki, presumably after a night of passion. What makes the piece so darkly funny is that Flaherty for the first time introduces us to the cruelty of this playboy — when Alki's partner (represented by the camera shot) refuses to fetch him some jam, Alki reacts by throwing a cup of hot coffee on her.

Two sketches dealing with the death of characters played by Dave Thomas meet with mixed results: In one, Thomas plays a police commissioner who has a heart attack while announcing his retirement. The film of this dramatic event is introduced several times by Earl Camembert on "SCTV News," but for technical reasons the film is never properly shown. The result foreshadows a similar, even funnier sketch in show 55. Unfortunately, a piece parodying the finale of the Swedish film *Elvira Madigan* doesn't work: In this version, Thomas's Sixten tries desperately to kill himself at the request of O'Hara's Elvira, only to discover too late that she was playing an ill-conceived joke.

Show 20 *(Second City Television)*

1. Attention Span PSA
2. Sunrise Semester with April Squall: Meteorology 101
3. Mick Mason: Police Photographer promo
4. It Was That Way with Keith Hampshire
5. Join the Shelley People promo
6. Pocket Belt, Pocket Hat, and Spare Sock Caddy commercial
7. I Cry Each Day I Die
8. Monster Chiller Horror Theatre: Dr. Tongue's Evil House of Wax
9. SCTV Boogie

What to watch for: Dr. Tongue's Evil House of Wax.
Just two shows after a weak debut, SCTV quickly comes up with a better way to utilize Count Floyd's "Monster Chiller Horror Theatre," resulting in this marvelous sketch. Here for the first time John Candy's Dr. Tongue is joined by his grotesquely hunchbacked assistant Bruno (Levy), and the two delight in thrusting themselves and other objects at the screen to obtain an effect something like 3-D. This sketch also contains Count Floyd's first sales pitch to the kids at home to get their "special 3-D glasses"; as always, the price of the glasses (here it's $18) seems to be whatever exorbitant figure happens to pop into Floyd's head. The trio of Count Floyd, Dr. Tongue, and Bruno would later be responsible for funnier sketches (show 84's "House of Stewardesses") and certainly more complex sketches (show 117's "Midnight Cowboy II"), but this is a solid premiere.

An odd episode in that the first two-thirds of the show is mediocre, while the final third of the show is early *SCTV* at its best. After the premiere of his Bruno character, Levy introduces dance show host Rockin' Mel Slirrup. Unlike many of Levy's characters that he brought to *SCTV* fully formed (a process aided in many cases by prior stage experimentation), it would take some time for Levy to define Slirrup.

In the later "Mel's Rock Pile" sketches, Slirrup is a quintessential nerd; here Levy plays him as more of a detached stoner moving lifelessly among the "groovy kids" on the dance floor. With a goofy smile pasted on his face and a tendency to refer to everything as "boss" ("boss school," "boss grade," "boss outfit"), it seems Slirrup is interacting with hallucinations and not the awkward teenagers that the rest of the cast are portraying. (Note that O'Hara's character is named "Robin Duke," a Second City stage performer and later *SCTV* cast member.) Levy would eventually bring back an improved version of Slirrup, but it would take him another 26 shows to do so. It would be another 16 shows after that before he would thoroughly grasp the character on the "Mel's Rock Pile" sketches. But "SCTV Boogie" remains a fine beginning for Levy's Slirrup.

Apart from a promo for "Mick Mason: Police Photographer" ("He came from the cushy world of commercial photography looking for something different"), the rest of this show is forgettable. Particularly weak is a "Sunrise Semester" piece featuring Andrea Martin as an unbearably perky meteorologist; the character is every bit as aggravating as the vapid local TV weather broadcasters she's trying to parody. Martin also features prominently in an interesting failure of a sketch that consists of nothing but a series of false endings strung together. The sketch, titled "I Cry Each Day I Die," is well edited but offers nothing else of interest.

Show 21 *(Second City Television)*

1. Counterattack commercial
2. Paul's Workshop with Paul Fistinyerface
3. Barretta's Bird promo
4. SCTV AM News Today: Earl's Dog Fetish / Rhoda Barret in Hollywood
5. James Whitmore Tonight promo
6. The Sammy Maudlin Show: Bobby Bittman / Sir Kenneth Clark part 1
7. Serfs commercial (repeat from show 17)
8. The Sammy Maudlin Show: Bobby Bittman / Sir Kenneth Clark part 2
9. Shoplifting PSA (repeat from show 14)
10. Dialing for Dollars: Moe phones Sandy Moss

What to watch for: The Sammy Maudlin Show.
The initial "Sammy Maudlin Show" (show 4) was such a success that why Flaherty waited 17 shows for its return is a mystery. Perhaps he felt the premise of the sketch — the sickening oiliness exuded by Sammy and his phony show-biz

guests—was a one-joke affair not worth repeating. Luckily, Flaherty would bring Maudlin back many more times, beginning with this outrageous piece.

Here we discover that not only are Sammy, William B. (Candy), and perennial guest Bobby Bittman (Levy) sycophantic, but they are also spectacularly cruel. Bittman is particularly horrific as he shows supposedly hilarious outtakes that consist of one of his co-stars being electrocuted and another being cruelly and undeservedly fired. In turn, Sammy finds the outtakes so knee-slappingly hysterical that it's difficult to determine who between Bobby and Sammy is the most gleefully distasteful. With this piece, SCTV discovers that the "Maudlin Show" wasn't a solitary piece but would instead become arguably SCTV's most brilliant recurring sketch.

A program made up of a mixed bag of sketches with an unusually high number of connections to pieces in other episodes. Following a debut stint as one of the dancers on the previous episode's "SCTV Boogie," John Candy makes his second appearance as the ridiculously named Paul Fistinyerface. This time Fistinyerface is the host of a home improvement show, which foreshadows a sketch in show 113 in which Candy plays another ridiculously named (Karl Bildenhausen) host of a similar show. This weak sketch also features Dave Thomas doing an early version of a slimy and feeble character sometimes referred to, in a none-too-subtle jab at the types that populate a certain show business agency, as "William Morris."

Andrea Martin is featured as former and future Indian Prime Minister Indira Gandhi in an unfunny piece that spotlights Gandhi's new nightclub act. The idea of Gandhi as a song-and-dance woman would later be used to much better effect in the classic "Indira" promo (show 80).

Also, in an illuminating example of just how undefined a character Moe Green (Ramis) was, here on "Dialing for Dollars," Green calls his girlfriend just six shows after calling his wife. Either Green got a quickie divorce or he is dim enough to call a woman whom he is cheating with on television. Either way the piece is funny, as is Dave Thomas's sequel to his "Evening with Colonel Sanders" sketch (show 11); this time he is character actor Hal Holbrook playing character actor James Whitmore. And Earl Camembert's dog fetish highlights yet another excellent "SCTV News."

Show 22 *(Second City Television)*

1. Head and Chest commercial
2. Passport to Adventure: Africa
3. Klägg promo
4. The World of Mystery with Orson Welles: Sandwich on the Orient Express
5. Sleepfast commercial
6. Homelier You commercial (repeat from show 7)
7. World at War
8. Stay White commercial
9. Lowell Thompson Remembers: 1937

What to watch for: ***Klägg.***
At this point, it seems redundant for SCTV *to feature another sketch about a strangely unique defender of the law. In the last two episodes alone,* SCTV *presented promos for "Barretta's Bird" and "Mick Mason: Police Photographer." But the sight of Harold Ramis as a Swedish detective who captures criminals by using his enormous wooden shoes ("Stop or I shoe!") nevertheless works. (Note that a "Klägg" scene in which Flaherty is chased down would be almost exactly duplicated in show 57's "Danny Eubanks" promo.)*

This show presents a surprising amount of distinctly unique pieces — while no classic, it illustrates that even late in the season, *SCTV* was not content to simply trot out the many recurring characters the show had already originated.

Most successful of the experimental pieces is a parody of the 1974 World War II mini-series *World at War*. This wonderfully edited and very clever sketch combines old war footage, archival baseball material, and mock interviews to present the case that Hitler tried to demoralize Americans by wiping out Major League Baseball. This piece marks *SCTV*'s first lengthy attempt to mine humor out of stock footage, a comedic strategy that would reach its apex in show 77's *Cisco Kid* parody as well as in the final episode. Here the cast takes a backseat to the sketch's premise, although Eugene Levy in particular is memorable as a former manager who wanted Hitler to kill all of the members of his team's biggest rival. (Note that Dave Thomas would adopt the same narrative style used here for 1984's Candy-Levy documentary *The Last Polka*.)

Not quite as successful but interestingly bizarre is a parody of *Murder on the Orient Express* featuring a homicidal sandwich. This piece is one of the best contributions by writer Brian Doyle-Murray; but it wouldn't work without the cast ably playing such silly material so seriously. Joe Flaherty is particularly good as the man who foolishly brings the murderous sandwich on board; Flaherty never breaks character even while muttering a line such as "I think you'll find the sandwich's gun permit is in order." Flaherty is also solid as forgetful historian Lowell Thompson in the sketch that closes the show.

Much worse is the introduction of Dave and Catherine's annoying Bob and Betty Wilson characters, who host a travel show called "Passport to Adventure." The joke here is that the two aren't adventurous at all, as their trip to Africa basically consists of them remaining inside their Holiday Inn because of "bacteria." Meandering along with nary a laugh, the sketch feels like lazy improvisation. Fortunately, it would be another 25 shows before these characters would return in what would thankfully be their final appearance.

Show 23 *(Second City Television)*

1. Muley's Roundhouse: The Three Dummies
2. Library Police promo (repeat from show 15)
3. SCTV AM News Today: Terrorist Picnic

4. Spray On Socks commercial (repeat from show 4)
5. SCTV Movie of the Week: The Grapes of Mud part 1
6. Mrs. Prickley's Jelly commercial (repeat from show 17)
7. Disco Farming
8. SCTV Movie of the Week: The Grapes of Mud part 2

What to watch for: The Grapes of Mud.
A significant SCTV first: The show's first sustained classic film parody. While the lengthy Ben-Hur send-up in show 13 asserted that SCTV could present ambitious parodies of revered films, the fact that the sketch was broken up into many small segments underlined a lack of confidence SCTV had in presenting such material. But just ten shows later, SCTV had the courage to broadcast this stronger parody of The Grapes of Wrath *(almost) without interruption.*

"The Grapes of Mud" isn't any more highbrow than Curly Howard starring as Ben-Hur: On the contrary, the sketch (starring Flaherty as "Henry Fondue") is quite silly; in this version of John Steinbeck's story, mud storms force the Joads to leave their land in California in search of drier ground in Oklahoma. Several times during the sketch, the storms manifest themselves as mud thrown at the cast from off-camera. Unlike later movie parodies, familiarity with the original film is not necessary. Mud in the face is pretty much mud in the face.

Along with "Ben-Hur," "The Grapes of Mud" is one of the most ambitiously staged pieces of SCTV's first year. Necessary concessions were certainly made to conform to the show's minuscule budget: The piece is shot indoors instead of the outdoor setting the material calls for, the sets and props are minimal at best, and obvious lighting and staging tricks abound (note that when Levy's preacher is picked up by the Joads, he shuffles closer to the stationary truck to give the illusion that the truck is in motion). But overall the piece looks surprisingly cinematic in scope. Here SCTV figures out how to do movie parodies on the cheap; the results would be even better once they had the budget necessary to realize their ever-increasingly ambitious ideas.

Despite the presence of three repeat sketches, this show is a highlight of the first season, and not just because of "The Grapes of Mud." There are also satisfying shorter pieces here, highlighted by one of Dave Thomas's darkest bits: A "SCTV News" segment with the bored host of *Truth or Consequences* throwing sulfuric acid into the eyes of a horrified contestant. The same sketch also includes video of a terrorist picnic, presented by Earl as a soft news item despite the fact that the occasion resulted in twelve people dying "horrible deaths."

The only misfire of the episode is a toothless Three Stooges parody so similar to the real thing that it comes across as a homage rather than as a spoof. Apparently *SCTV* had more respect for Larry, Moe, and Curly than for John Steinbeck, John Ford, and Henry Fonda.

Show 24 *(Second City Television)*

1. Maurice Green: SCTV's license renewal
2. A.M. Little America

3. Dan Money promo
4. SCTV AM News Today: Organized Crime
5. Civil Opportunities PSA
6. AC/DC promo (repeat from show 5)
7. Officer Friendly
8. The Undersea World of Marcel Cousteau promo
9. Masterpiece Theatre: All the Long-Leggedy Beasties
10. Dream Interpretation

What to watch for: All the Long-Leggedy Beasties.
Undoubtedly the finest of the many "Masterpiece Theatre" sketches SCTV *would present, this piece strikes just the right balance between being superficially highbrow (and thus the sort of fare offered up by* Masterpiece Theatre*) while simultaneously being quite silly in its details. A parody of the 1974 British film* All Creatures Great and Small, SCTV*'s version features Thomas as a quietly psychotic Scottish veterinarian who delights in putting animals to sleep before they're faced with any debilitating health problems. His unconventional philosophy is matched only by his unconventional methods: He uses a machine gun to put down a dog and a rabbit (fortunately off-camera). (Note that Pittsburgh native Joe Flaherty — as Alistair Cooke — credits the piece to L.C. Greenwood, who was in fact a defensive end for the Pittsburgh Steelers.)*

"All the Long-Leggedy Beasties" was written by Thomas and Flaherty, Thomas crediting this specific collaboration as being crucial in cementing a solid working partnership between him and Joe. This partnership would prove to be critical to SCTV*'s future, particularly in the third season, when the two found themselves as the only original cast members involved with the show on a full-time basis.*

Two significant occurrences distinguish this strong episode: Harold Ramis's Moe Green character is finally introduced as SCTV's station manager (though his reign would be extremely short-lived), and Eugene Levy's sleazy Dr. Raoul Wilson makes his premiere appearance.

Levy's Wilson is arguably *SCTV*'s most underused recurring character. Although not fully apparent in this episode's "Dream Interpretation" sketch (except for a quick gag of him looking up Andrea Martin's dress), Wilson would evolve into the most outrageously chauvinistic and sexist persona ever created for *SCTV*. By his last appearance (show 67's "Men on Women"), perhaps even Levy found the character too repulsive, as he toned him down to create the more acceptable Rawl Withers persona.

Elsewhere, two otherwise unrelated sketches are oddly linked together by a similar joke involving bribery. In the first, Joe Flaherty stars as "Dan Money," a cop with deep pockets who doesn't hesitate to bribe people to get information. What makes the sketch work is the fact that Money's reputation so obviously precedes him, forcing him to open his wallet even when simply asking someone for the time. "Dan Money" is immediately followed by a rare "SCTV News" misfire that features Earl Camembert bribing a head of organized crime for information.

Finally, Catherine O'Hara shines as *Wonder Woman*'s Lynda Karter [sic] in a *Today Show* knock-off called "A.M. Little America." Wearing her superhero's silly but sexy costume, O'Hara's Karter drones on about wanting to perform Shakespeare or Chekhov, while Dave Thomas (credited as Tom Brokraw; Tom Brokaw was the host of *Today* at this time) unrespectfully leers at her body and laughs about her unattainable acting goals. One of O'Hara's funniest and sexiest first-season roles.

Show 25 *(Second City Television)*

1. Tiny Tops commercial
2. Morning Facial with Princess Carlotta part 1
3. Check Please promo
4. Morning Facial with Princess Carlotta part 2
5. The Man Who Would Be King of the Popes preview
6. Mr. Coffee Table Book commercial
7. The Uncle Earl Show
8. Harry Filth preview
9. Insights
10. Get Tough commercial
11. Grumbles commercial
12. Enough About Me

What to watch for: Harry Filth.
A parody of Clint Eastwood's Dirty Harry *films, this piece is* SCTV *at its slapstick best. John Candy is a hotheaded cop who doesn't think twice about killing bystanders while tracking down criminals ("I'd hit a hundred innocent bystanders if it got punks like that off the street!"). The brief piece evolves into Filth acquiring a big gun for a big job; he finally settles on a ridiculously large firearm that he can barely fit through a set of double doors. Not just funny, but a keen comment on the relentless violence of the* Dirty Harry *films (and their countless imitators).*

A frustrating episode in that it features several brilliant sketches but several forgettable ones as well. Besides "Harry Filth," the most notable piece here is a lengthy preview for "The Man Who Would Be King of the Popes." In his book, Dave Thomas discusses this sketch at length as the first time that the cast "stacked" impressions: Joe's Peter O'Toole, Dave's Richard Harris, Catherine's Katharine Hepburn, and John's Richard Burton (the latter Flaherty claimed was actually a combination of Burton and Jackie Gleason). Thomas claimed that this piece (and later ones such as show 33's "How the Middle East Was Won") worked because the cast were always trying to out-do each other's impressions.

Most *SCTV* fans know that Flaherty's Floyd Robertson (as Count Floyd) hosted the kids' show "Monster Chiller Horror Theatre." Often overlooked is the fact that Robertson's co-anchor, Earl Camembert, also tried his hand at children's television in an obvious rip-off of *Mister Rogers' Neighborhood* called

"The Uncle Earl Show." Unlike the several "MCHT" sketches that made it to air, only one "Uncle Earl Show" aired on *SCTV*—the final one. Here Earl employs pathetic ventriloquism to have stuffed animal characters inform the boys and girls watching that the network executives who made the decision to cancel "The Uncle Earl Show" are "morons" and "stupid jerks." Another fine sketch for Eugene's Earl Camembert.

Other solid sketches include a promo for a situation comedy starring *Star Trek*'s Bones McCoy (Thomas) and Dr. Spock (Ramis). The sitcom, set in a "diner in the future where the food gets whipped up at warp speed," overhauls the two sci-fi characters as a futuristic Flo and Mel from the sitcom *Alice*. Thomas's belligerent McCoy is especially funny; thankfully Thomas would bring this impression back in later episodes.

There are a surprising number of weak pieces in this episode: Particularly unfunny is "Morning Facial with Princess Carlotta," a program starring Martin (looking and sounding exactly like Edith Prickley) as a woman of means. Equally weak is Catherine's "Enough About Me" sketch in which she plays a talk show host who chatters on endlessly about herself. The character is written to be humorously annoying; unfortunately, she's just annoying.

Show 26 *(Second City Television)*

1. Dialing for Dollars: Introduction
2. Lust for Paint: Part 1
3. Lust for Paint: Part 2
4. Celebrity Tattletales promo
5. Dialing for Dollars: Moe has phone disconnected
6. Lust for Paint: Part 2 continued
7. The Babe Ruth Story promo
8. 50 Practical Jokes You Can Do for Free commercial (repeat from show 8)
9. Lust for Paint: Part 3
10. Mick Mason: Police Photographer promo (repeat from show 20)
11. Lust for Paint: Conclusion
12. Pluffy Puff commercial (repeat from show 19)
13. Dialing for Dollars: Caballero cancels program

What to watch for: The Babe Ruth Story.
Despite the impressive achievement of "Lust for Paint," the funniest piece in this show is a promo for "The Babe Ruth Story," which parodies the legend of Babe Ruth promising to hit a home run for a sick child. The scene was enacted for the 1948 movie of the same name, but in SCTV's version, the child (Donald Cowper in his final SCTV appearance) isn't satisfied with just one home run. After a series of impossible requests culminating with the Babe (Candy) being asked to stand on his head while eating 50 hot dogs, the Babe physically attacks the sick child he came to cheer up.

For the final show of its first season, *SCTV* duplicates the format from show 13: A lengthy movie parody presented by Ramis's Moe Green, with several interruptions for unrelated and brief sketches. This time out, "Dialing for Dollars" plays a large role, as the program is cancelled after the show's telephone is disconnected because of overdue bills. The oft-repeated "Dialing for Dollars" program would indeed not appear in *SCTV*'s second season, returning in the third year with the inspired selection of Walter Cronkite (Thomas) as host.

"Lust for Paint," an ambitious parody of the 1952 film *Moulin Rouge* with a title borrowed from 1956's Vincent Van Gogh biopic "Lust for Life," is one of the most notable triumphs of the season, encompassing several different sets, period costumes, significant roles for every cast member, and a script that shifts easily from being quite literate to quite sophomoric. (Note that the beating up of dummies, soon to become a *SCTV* staple, was begun here.)

Moulin Rouge told the story of the diminutive late 19th century painter Toulouse-Lautrec and featured José Ferrer in a dual role as Lautrec and as the painter's unsupportive father. In the Ferrer roles, Joe Flaherty is outstanding, while Andrea Martin is also good as Marie (a role originated by Colette Marchand), a cruel woman who Lautrec inconceivably loves. Her jabs at Lautrec's height and Lautrec's enraged reactions to her insults — which featured prominently in the original film — are impressively exaggerated here.

Lautrec's penchant for sketching on the Moulin Rouge's tablecloths proves unlikely but successful fodder for *SCTV*'s parody. In the original, Lautrec was a favorite customer of the famed nightclub; here the club's employees chastise him for ruining their tablecloths. In the original, Lautrec naturally paints on canvases while in his home studio, whereas Flaherty's Lautrec paints only on tablecloths, even while at home. And at the end of the original, as the painter lies on his deathbed, his father informs him that the famous Louvre Art Museum has accepted a collection of his paintings; in *SCTV*'s inspired conclusion, Lautrec's father tells Lautrec that his "tablecloths are in the Louvre. They're in the cafeteria. They want to know if you've done any napkins."

The conclusion of *Moulin Rouge*, in which Lautrec is visited by visions of friends from his life, is parodied here in the finest part of the sketch; anyone not familiar with the original would surely believe that when O'Hara (as a Moulin Rouge dancer) tells Lautrec, "We heard you were dying. We just had to come by," she was reciting a line written for *SCTV*, but a similar character in the original speaks nearly the exact same line. Also, *SCTV*'s version fudges matters a little — Lautrec is visited not just by friends who featured prominently in his life, but also by Candy's Babe Ruth, who featured prominently in an earlier sketch. A fine finale to a successful first season.

Despite an upcoming and unexpected departure of one of the show's principal players, *SCTV* was primed for a winning — if surprisingly uneven — second season.

Although show 26 signaled the end of *SCTV*'s first season, a compilation show was added for air in the United States. The episode included one original sketch: A strong "Sunrise Semester" piece on beekeeping featuring Dave Thomas's Lin Ye Tang. The sketch was not added for later syndication packages and is out of circulation as of this writing.

THE SECOND SEASON

Show 27 *(Second City Television)*

1. Moe Green: SCTV's second season
2. Ernest Kirsch & Guy Caballero part 1
3. Lola Heatherton in Concert promo
4. Love Craft promo
5. Water Spray from Pocketpic commercial
6. SCTV News: Chit Chat
7. Words to Live By: Ernest Kirsch
8. The Incredible Bulk
9. Moxwell House commercial
10. Feedback
11. Ernest Kirsch & Guy Caballero part 2

What to watch for: Lola Heatherton in Concert.
Catherine O'Hara begins her second SCTV *season with the unveiling of her signature character: volatile singer, actress, and sexpot Lola Heatherton. Although O'Hara has often skirted the issue, Heatherton is most assuredly modeled on Joey Heatherton, who at this time was fresh off her starring role in* The Happy Hooker Goes to Washington.

In this initial spot, Catherine has already perfected Lola, even including what will eventually become her catchphrase: "I want to bear your children!" Though Heatherton would soon become a character as celebrated as Bobby Bittman or Johnny LaRue, here Lola is nearly upstaged by her dancers: Joe, Eugene, and Dave, foreshadowing the later shtick of the Juul Haalmayer Dancers.

SCTV opens its second season while undergoing a significant if not immediately noticeable change: After being recruited to write the film *Caddyshack*, Harold Ramis is no longer a member of *SCTV*'s cast, appearing only in two second season shows. Despite his disappearance on-camera, Ramis did have a hand in writing much of the year's material. Note that as the season wears on and *SCTV* apparently runs out of Ramis scripts, the shows get particularly weak.

But as Ramis and his signature persona Moe Green leave, a much more significant character finally arrives in the flesh — SCTV president Guy Caballero.

Heard only via telephone in the first season, Flaherty's creation is immediately arresting, particularly his trademark of transporting himself via wheelchair — not because of any handicap, but simply for "respect." As Caballero would evolve, becoming more charismatic and less cruelly hostile, Flaherty would get sharper and funnier in the role.

The only character physically interacting with Caballero here is SCTV staff writer Ernest Kirsch, a Dave Thomas creation that would only appear in two episodes. While the notion that the SCTV network would have only one writer churning out scripts for all of its programs is a humorous one, Thomas decided that as far as Kirsch was concerned, "no one was interested in continuing it, especially me." Nevertheless, Thomas is quite funny in the role, especially when a lack of scripts forces him to resurrect last season's sign-off program "Words to Live By" at 12 noon.

Apart from the Kirsch/Caballero/Green storyline, the episode is surprisingly uneven. A highlight is a lengthy promo for a *Love Boat* parody called "Love Craft" starring Flaherty's Greek womanizer Alki Stereopolis as the captain. Conversely, a send-up of *The Incredible Hulk* is simply awful; while storming around in an ill-fitting green bodysuit, Candy tries his best to hide the fact that the endless sketch plays like something the unsubtle *Carol Burnett Show* would have rejected as being too broad. There would be more missteps to come during *SCTV*'s new season.

Show 28 *(Second City Television)*

1. Monster Chiller Horror Theatre: The House of Cats
2. SCTV Sports Central: Bob Hope Desert Classic preview
3. Delay commercial
4. Betty Bain: Professional Juror
5. Masterpiece Theatre: Naughty Chambermaids
6. Bob Hope Desert Classic

What to watch for: *Masterpiece Theatre*.
Although the "Bob Hope Desert Classic" is usually cited as Dave Thomas's first SCTV appearance as Bob Hope, in actuality Thomas first appeared as the legendary comedian during this "Masterpiece Theatre" sketch, in which Thomas's Hope interrupts Flaherty's Alistar Cook [sic] to plug his golf special.

Hope was well known at the time as the only entertainer given carte blanche to interrupt Tonight Show *tapings, a freedom Hope took advantage of frequently. (After this appearance, Thomas would twice more mock Hope's propensity to interrupt TV shows: in show 63's "Sammy Maudlin Show" and on a 2001 episode of Martin Short's* Primetime Glick, *in which a wrinkled Hope interrupts Glick's interview with Eugene Levy.)*

Of course Johnny Carson always appeared delighted to see Hope; here Flaherty's Cook is furious that his "classy production" is being interrupted by "cheap show-biz plugs." He then surprisingly pulls out a switchblade ("C'mon, let's go, Hope"), which finally sends Hope coolly striding off the set. As played by Thomas, Hope was eternally unflappable.

Without a doubt, had Dave Thomas and Rick Moranis not created Bob and Doug McKenzie, Thomas would have left *SCTV* best known as the cast member who did the brilliantly wicked impression of Bob Hope. Thanks to a suggestion from make-up artist Beverly Schechtman, whom Thomas lovingly credits with helping him work out his impression, Thomas had Hope perfected from the start.

The lingering question is whether Thomas's impression is flattering — the viewpoint Thomas maintains — or whether it's malicious. A look at any of Thomas's limited appearances as Hope seem to suggest the latter: For example, in the "Bob Hope Desert Classic" Thomas mocks the obvious edits found in Hope's TV specials whereby a medium-shot of Hope delivering a punchline cuts quickly to a close-up of Hope basking in canned laughter and applause.

Unfortunately, despite the brilliance of Thomas's impression, the "Bob Hope Desert Classic" is a chaotic sketch. Intended as a combination of two of Hope's passions, golf and entertaining troops, the piece begins promisingly but degenerates as a golf tournament unravels into a land conflict between Palestinians and Israelis with Hope caught in the middle ducking golf balls being hit between the two sides. The piece is not a total loss, though: Moses ("Chuck Heston, ladies and gentlemen") appears to part a pipeline interfering with Golda Meir's game, while Thomas uncharacteristically breaks up at Flaherty's Richard Nixon, who appears to promote his upcoming engagements with Bobby Vinton and Doc Severinsen.

Having found the right ingredients for "Monster Chiller Horror Theatre," Flaherty, Candy, and Levy present another 3-D "semi-classic" with "The House of Cats." Candy is particularly enjoyable as he single-handedly (without special effects) tries to convey that timid household cats are capable of brutal attacks. (Note that the ever-fluctuating price of 3-D glasses has gone up — they will now set you back $27.) And in a unique sketch, Andrea Martin is quite good as a woman who makes a profession out of sitting on juries. "Betty Bain: Professional Juror" is the sort of joke that *SCTV* would normally tell much more efficiently in a promo ("I love you, darling, but I'm afraid I love the jury system more"), but the piece does work as a longer segment.

Show 29 *(Second City Television)*
1. Moe Green: Leutonian Liberation Front
2. Donna
3. Master Sergeant Chef promo
4. SCTV News: Moe Green Kidnapping
5. Cup 'n Soup commercial
6. Petty Claims Court
7. Linkin Murcurry Salvador Dali Edition / K-Tel Stash Wax commercial
8. SCTV Movie of the Week promo: Nice Kids from Hell
9. SCTV News Bulletin: Moe Green in captivity

What to watch for: SCTV News Bulletin.
A rare chance to see newscasters Floyd Robertson and Earl Camembert actually getting along, this piece provides a satisfying conclusion to the episode's running storyline involving Moe Green's abduction by the fictitious Leutonian Liberation Front. Here Floyd and Earl callously giggle and snicker at an audiotape of a prepared message that a terrified Green has been forced to read. Funnier still is their solidarity in supporting SCTV's decision to not pay the paltry $2,000 ransom requested by the Leutonians. Above all, it's a welcome change just to see Robertson and Camembert on the same side, united in their shared indifference toward Moe Green.

The very clever storyline of Green's kidnapping was done as a way to write Harold Ramis off *SCTV*— this show would mark Ramis's final appearance on the program until he guested on show 107. But the saga of Moe Green would not end here — his name would be mentioned several times in upcoming shows, most notably in show 67, when a member of the Leutonian Liberation Front would call Guy Caballero to beg him to take Green off their hands.

Although this episode is essential viewing due to Harold Ramis's final appearance as a regular cast member, the show is far from *SCTV* at its best and begins the post–Ramis *SCTV* era on very shaky ground.

The worst of the sketches, an endless parody of Dinah Shore's syndicated talk show, is notable for featuring Andrea Martin's first on-screen appearance as Barbra Streisand. Martin's impression is outstanding; however, she is so skilled at capturing Streisand's narcissism that the impression quickly becomes as grating as Streisand herself.

Other pieces aren't as time-consuming but are equally pointless. A sketch taking place at a petty claims court is one of the sloppiest pieces *SCTV* would ever present, as three lowlifes played by Martin, Thomas, and Candy simply ramble incoherently for two minutes.

Even sketches that should be slam dunks miss the mark: A promo for "Master Sergeant Chef," featuring Thomas as a Green Beret turned head chef at the Waldorf Astoria, has a funny premise but is far too leisurely paced to be effective. The piece needs the quicker editing style utilized in earlier promos such as "Emergency Orderly" (show 14).

The overall success of the pieces devoted to Moe Green would lead *SCTV* to further experiment with linking sketches and themed episodes in the shows ahead. The relative success of these experiments would eventually lead to more complicated wraparounds, culminating in the ninety-minute programs of *SCTV*'s NBC run.

Show 30 *(Second City Television)*

1. SCTV Solid Gold Telethon: Maudlin, Bittman, LaRue
2. Beef & Booze commercial
3. SCTV Solid Gold Telethon: Heatherton, Captain Combat, Lawrence and Gorme

4. Max Lax commercial
5. SCTV Solid Gold Telethon: Pirini Scleroso
6. SCTV Solid Gold Telethon: Lorna Minelli

What to watch for: SCTV Solid Gold Telethon.
An often-overlooked classic in SCTV's oeuvre, this episode is just as significant in SCTV's evolution as the celebrated "Ben-Hur" sketch from show 13. Not only does the "SCTV Solid Gold Telethon" mark the first of many times that this commercial station would ask for additional public funding, but this episode is also the first time that SCTV devotes (nearly) an entire show to a single sketch starring characters created for the program. It surely took a leap of confidence on the part of the cast to think that Sammy Maudlin, Bobby Bittman, Johnny LaRue, and others could sustain a twenty-minute piece, but the experiment paid off handsomely.

With Maudlin, Bittman, and LaRue as hosts, it's not surprising that the telethon—a more obvious send-up of Jerry Lewis's annual MDA drives than later "pledge week" sketches featuring Guy Caballero—is awash in phoniness and showbiz sycophancy. In fact, the three hosts love and respect each other so much that they—particularly Bittman—repeatedly take the audience to task for not showing them the love that they show for each other: Not happy with the feedback to a particularly heartfelt musical number, Bittman points to the audience and furiously asks Maudlin, "Where did you find these people, Poland?"

Candy nearly steals the piece with one of his best performances as Johnny LaRue. Obviously committed to the telethon, LaRue pledges to keep drinking until their goals are met; once he is completely plastered, he then vows to donate his weight in gold only to back down after learning the true value of his pledge (around $750,000).

Though Flaherty, Levy, and Candy own the show, the other cast members do get some airtime, particularly Dave Thomas and Catherine O'Hara, who do a bitterly cruel song as Steve Lawrence and Eydie Gorme. The song, a cheerfully delivered jazzy ode to hatred ("You make me puke" / "Your creation was satanic"), directly contradicts Steve and Eydie's image as a blissfully happy husband and wife team. Thomas also scores with the unlikely return of Captain Combat: In a nod to the infamous 1965 incident in which Soupy Sales asked children to send him their parents' money, Combat encourages kids to deliver their parents' gold items to the studio.

The telethon ends with the station meeting its goal of 2,000 pounds of gold. Against all odds, SCTV's telethons tended to be successful; in fact, the only time that SCTV staged a telethon in which the station did *not* meet its monetary goal was in the final episode, which resulted in the end of SCTV. Proof that Caballero really did need viewer contributions to stay afloat.

Show 31 *(Second City Television)*

1. Restless Doctors
2. SCTV News Bulletin: Ernest Kirsch on strike
3. Master Ralph Roister Doister
4. Palmoval commercial
5. SCTV News: Earl and Floyd write own items

6. LaRue By Night part 1
7. Harlett Romances commercial
8. LaRue By Night part 2
9. Kirsch signs contract

What to watch for: Restless Doctors.
This soap opera parody, named after the dramas The Young and the Restless *and* The Doctors, *works on two levels: Most obviously, it satirizes the simplistic dialogue and overwrought acting common to the genre, as Eugene Levy overplays a—what else—restless doctor. ("Nothing changes," Levy laments. "People get sick, they come to us, we operate, they get better, they go home, they die.") Also present in this piece is a skewering of soap opera actors, particularly in respect to how they compare with the* SCTV *cast; whereas* SCTV's *actors were well trained in the art of improvisation, these performers are completely speechless when, due to a writers' strike, they find themselves without lines to read. A fine start to the episode.*

Years before the strike episode that saw SCTV turn to CBC programming (show 106), *SCTV* ran this less ambitious and less successful installment, which details the on-air ramifications when staff writer Ernest Kirsch (Thomas, playing the character for the final time) goes on a work stoppage. Instead of importing another station's programs, this episode finds SCTV exploring several programming options that are available even when scripts are not—reruns (a sitcom that shares the name of an English comedy written in the sixteenth century), news, and unscripted shows ("LaRue By Night," a precursor to the later "Street Beef").

Apart from *Restless Doctors*, the news segment works the best, as Floyd and Earl's differing personalities lead them to take a wildly different approach when forced to write their own news items—Floyd's items are melodramatic ("Dateline, New York City. This is a tough town, but a damn good one."), while Earl's pieces are spiced up with words he found in a thesaurus but doesn't understand.

Otherwise, "Master Ralph Roister Doister" comes across as a *Monty Python* reject, while "LaRue By Night," a sketch in which nothing happens, is as interesting as a sketch in which nothing happens. A funny parody of ads for the Harlequin line of trashy romance novels thankfully provides a few moments of respite in the middle of the weakest Johnny LaRue sketch to date.

Note that this is the first *SCTV* episode to include appearances from both Edith Prickley and Guy Caballero, though they don't feature in the same sketch: Flaherty continues to play Caballero as an insufferable bully; here he uses physical threats to force Ernest Kirsch to sign a terrible contract. Martin's Prickley, meanwhile, is still a character looking for a forum. Upon finding it, Prickley's airtime would significantly increase.

Show 32 *(Second City Television)*

1. Paid Political Announcement: Johnny LaRue for city council
2. The Silly Bastard promo
3. Election Central part 1: The Great Debate
4. One is Enough promo
5. Moxwell House commercial (repeat from show 27)
6. Election Central part 2
7. Matchbook Advertising commercial
8. Election Central part 3: Earl at LaRue headquarters

What to watch for: The Great Debate.
Eugene Levy's news anchor Earl Camembert, one of SCTV's best characters, hits a new low in professionalism in this political debate sketch. Camembert unashamedly moderates a city council debate while simultaneously acting as the campaign manager of one of the candidates (Candy's Johnny LaRue). This lapse of judgment leads to an obviously biased debate, as Camembert tells a female candidate (O'Hara) that women should stay out of politics and "start baking more cookies." (Earl's rampant sexism was first seen in show 18's commentary on women newscasters.) Earl also sports LaRue campaign buttons throughout the proceedings.

With this episode, *SCTV* continues to expand beyond television and films for its subject matter. While show 28's "Bob Hope Desert Classic" rather clumsily made light of Middle Eastern conflict, this episode finds *SCTV* making much more pointed attacks at a subject nearer to home — North American politics. Note this example from the debate sketch as Thomas's candidate unveils his political platform: "What we need basically is something to unite the people. A war," Thomas cheerfully suggests. "We need hatred to bring the people back together again." History is full of examples of politicians employing this strategy to get elected or stay elected.

Just as show 31's subject matter was revisited by *SCTV* in their NBC days, so too was this show's theme of Melonville municipal elections. But whereas show 31 was greatly improved upon in show 106, this episode holds its own against the more complex NBC version (show 108).

Much of the reason behind this show's success was the inspired decision to have Candy's Johnny LaRue attempt a run for city council. Why LaRue would decide to enter politics isn't important; his sadistic and hard-drinking persona makes him a terrible candidate while providing many highlights of this episode. Best is the paid political announcement in which, to prove his love for people, he brings on a family — not his family, of course — and then promptly fires them all after one of the children is disobedient. Also interesting is the continuation of the backstory that LaRue has mafia connections (first planted in the previous episode) and that he is a homosexual (first planted in the first episode); he denies being gay again here, but the fact that the spot is paid for by the Sicilian Homophile Society lends credence to both notions. Exploring either aspect of LaRue's life in more detail might have been interesting fodder for future episodes, but apart from a couple of quick assertions of his heterosexuality, neither idea is ever brought up again.

Helping to bolster the strength of this episode are some quality sketches outside of the election material. Dave Thomas is a convincing moron in a parody of the 1978 TV movie *The Bastard*. Thomas is upstaged, however, by John Candy's impression of Tom Bosley playing the part of Benjamin Franklin. Candy plays Bosley (who did actually play Franklin in the original TV movie) as confused over whether he is playing Franklin or his *Happy Days* role of Howard Cunningham, telling others of "his son Richie" and of the hardware store he owns in America.

In an odd bit of prophesizing, Catherine O'Hara stars as an obvious Suzanne Somers clone in a promo for a show called "One Is Enough," the joke being that after Somers's infamous contract negotiations got her fired from *Three's Company*, she would star in an even more vacuous solo sitcom. The joke makes sense until the realization sets in that this sketch aired years before Somers actually left *Three's Company*.

Show 33 *(Second City Television)*

1. Guy Caballero: Welcome, Arabs
2. Farm Film Report: The Red Hat
3. Cup 'n Soup commercial (repeat from show 29)
4. The Millionaire
5. Falcons and Oysters
6. Speaking of Talk with Lou Jaffe
7. Grease commercial
8. How the Middle East Was Won preview

What to watch for: The Millionaire.

The strongest show-specific parody since show 15's "Leave It to Beaver" sketch, "The Millionaire" takes the 1950s show and gives it a twist: What if John Beresford Tipton, the millionaire known for giving away a million dollars each week to a total stranger, ran out of money?

Broke but still having a generous heart, Tipton (Flaherty) decides that rather than quit his altruistic ways, he will merely curtail them, giving his male servant (Candy) a check for the underwhelming amount of $50 to deliver to a bitterly unhappy couple (Thomas and O'Hara, who deliver a scene of intricately choreographed quarreling).

Disgusted and humiliated, Candy returns to expose the previously unseen Tipton, who loses his last link to sanity when he loses his anonymity. Tipton is soon back in the high life, though; in the conclusion, a wealthy Arab (Levy) enters to present Tipton with a million dollar check, thereby bringing the original series full circle and initiating a spin-off, "The Millionaire of Mecca."

After the more experimental nature of the previous shows, *SCTV* returns here with one of their finest collections of stand-alone sketches, in the process introducing two elements — "Farm Film Report" and messages from SCTV president Guy Caballero — that will be regular pieces for years to come.

"Blowed up real good." That expression, usually attributed to farmers turned film critics Billy Sol Hurok (Candy) and Big Jim McBob (Flaherty) and one of *SCTV*'s most successful catchphrases, was first uttered in this episode. Beginning as an uninspired parody of farm programs back on show 12, the re-emergence of Flaherty's Big Jim McBob character is *SCTV* getting something out of what initially seemed like nothing. Thanks to the new partnership with Candy and the pair's atypical obsession with seeing things "blowed up," the "Farm Film Report" sketches would become one of *SCTV*'s signature pieces, not only turning Hurok and McBob into solid repeatable characters, but also providing an uncomplicated forum for the *SCTV* cast to showcase their impressions. From here until Candy's final show as a *SCTV* regular, these sketches were as dependable as the show got.

Besides saving Big Jim McBob from the one-off pile, Flaherty also continued to tweak station president Guy Caballero, here seen delivering his first of many direct messages to the home viewer. Besides being made up to seem older than in his previous appearances, Flaherty successfully tones down the character, replacing much of his bluster with oily charm as he tries to recruit "free-spending Arabs" to "invest heavily in the SCTV network." Flaherty would overuse Caballero in the years to come, a crime that would be much more offensive if the character wasn't usually so hilariously sleazy.

This episode has more celebrated pieces: The first and only pairing of hyperactive announcers Harvey K-Tel (Thomas) and Lou Jaffe (Levy) has the two comparing larynxes and discovering a deep admiration for each other's abilities to read commercial copy. A funny commercial featuring Johnny LaRue seems to exist not only to further refute rumors of his homosexuality but also to show LaRue's (and maybe Candy's?) increasing sensitivity about his weight. Finally, "How the Middle East Was Won" is an even better sequel to show 25's "The Man Who Would Be King of the Popes," with Flaherty, Candy, and Thomas bringing back their impressions of Peter O'Tool [sic], Richard Berton [sic], and Richard Hariss [sic]. Having the three "blowed up good" as a nod to "Farm Film Report" is an especially inspired touch and a fine climax to one of the best shows of the second season.

Show 34 *(Second City Television)*

1. The Mirthmakers with Orsan Welles part 1
2. Max Lax commercial (repeat from show 30)
3. The Mirthmakers with Orsan Welles part 2
4. SCTV News: Earl's happy endings
5. Modular Shoe Kit commercial
6. Chinese Fairy Tales with Lin Ye Tang

7. Triple Feature Movie
8. Pit Stop commercial
9. Triple Feature Movie conclusions

What to watch for: SCTV News.
Miraculously not fired after the Johnny LaRue campaign fiasco (show 32), Earl Camembert (Levy) follows that unethical decision with one that is simply boneheaded: He begins lightening up his news stories by tagging them with ridiculously inappropriate happy endings. Nothing positive about a tornado destroying a family's home? At least it gets the homeowners' names in the paper, offers Camembert. And the news isn't all bad when cutbacks close an old age home and force residents out on the streets: Those elderly people now have a goal in life, argues Camembert: "Namely, survival." Earl's optimistic outlook has the opposite effect on his partner Floyd Robertson (Flaherty), who for the first time physically attacks Camembert on-air. One of the best news segments of the second season.

This episode, while not offering a linking storyline of any kind, nevertheless does feature several sketches that are connected to each other through a common "happy ending" theme. This weak device indicates that *SCTV* was trying too hard, after the successes of shows 30 and 32, to inject more shows with an overall subject matter.

Apart from the outstanding "SCTV News" sketch, the themed humor doesn't work here, most notably in the overly cute "Triple Feature Movie" piece, which presents three extremely similar scenes from three extremely similar movies followed by their extremely similar happy endings. Thomas's "Chinese Fairy Tales" sketch fares better, thanks to Lin Ye Tang's annoyance at having to infuse what he considers to be fake happiness into his stories; he doesn't understand why a children's story can't conclude with "The prince had killed his foster parents and sister with a blunt ax and they died a miserable death. The end."

Oddly enough, the most promising sketch falls the flattest: An examination of funnyman Bobby Bittman done by the decidedly unfunny Orsan [sic] Welles (Candy) is occasionally humorous, but ultimately unmemorable. In "The Mirthmakers," Bittman comes off as outrageously superficial and self-congratulatory, but those traits of the character's personality had already been exposed in earlier, stronger sketches. What's missing here is any new information about Bittman, such as that found in Levy's overlooked Cinemax special, *The Enigma of Bobby Bittman*, or in show 114's "People and Things" sketch. The former fully exposed Bittman's maliciousness, while the latter gave a surprisingly sad look at the meaninglessness of Bittman's existence. Unfortunately, "The Mirthmakers" is simply meaningless.

Show 35 *(Second City Television)*

1. Me and You and Yoga and Me
2. Water Spray from Pocketpic commercial (repeat from show 27)

3. High Q
4. LaRue Towers commercial
5. Marriage Counsellor
6. Botch & Lamb commercial
7. Jacques Cousteau's Undersea World

What to watch for: High Q.
This piece, arguably SCTV's finest game show sketch, stands out prominently in the middle of this otherwise subpar episode. Consisting of two teams of high school students playing to win college scholarships, "High Q" also marks the first appearance of Eugene Levy's flustered game show host Alex Trebel, who would later suffer even more aggravation as the host of "Half Wits" (first seen in show 112). Levy is a marvel here, slowly unraveling while getting more and more annoyed at the grotesque ignorance of his contestants.

Apart from Levy, the star of the sketch is Catherine O'Hara, whose contestant Margaret Meehan insists on repeatedly buzzing in long before Trebel finishes reading the questions. The interplay between O'Hara and Levy is priceless; O'Hara's Meehan would be the sole contestant brought back for the sketch's sequel (show 89) and she is the main reason that Trebel finally loses his composure and challenges audience members to a brawl ("Still in your sexual prime? Come on up here!").

Funny people have a knack for not only being funny, but knowing what isn't funny. Suffice it to say a lot of funny people worked on *SCTV*, and while these funny people usually worked to produce funny material, undoubtedly some unfunny pieces got through. Undoubtedly these funny people knew what pieces weren't funny, because when these unfunny pieces aired, the laugh track would be turned up so high that the unfunny lines being said are nearly inaudible.

Two sketches on this episode prove this point: On "Me and You and Yoga and Me" and the Botch & Lomb commercial parody, the laugh track is deafening, a situation made more obvious by the fact that there is not a scintilla of humor in either of these pieces. But *SCTV* gets credit for doing their best to sell these stinkers as comedic gems. Two other pieces, an insufferable marriage counselor sketch and a Jacques Cousteau parody in which Cousteau (Flaherty) explores an outdoor well, are equally bad, or maybe they're slightly better but seem less funny than they are because the laugh track is toned down to normal levels for them. At least that seems to be the logic at work here.

Actually, there is one very smart piece besides "High Q"—a commercial for Johnny LaRue's affordable housing project called LaRue Towers. This is LaRue at his best; he pretends to care for those less fortunate than him, but he so bullies a family living in one of his dilapidated apartments that they cower in his presence. When he hears of problems—a faulty stove, a broken window—his answer is clear: "If you don't like it, then get out!" A second bright spot in an overall dim episode.

Show 36 *(Second City Television)*

1. Shoot at the Stars
2. SCTV News: Earl's editorial on his neighbor
3. Guy Caballero: Edith Prickley
4. Jaws 23
5. Sunrise Semester with Paul Fistinyourface: Town Pride
6. Sore Losers promo
7. Words to Live By: Edith Prickley

What to watch for: Shoot at the Stars.

"Shoot at the Stars," a game show in which winning contestants get the chance to shoot and kill celebrities John Ritter (Thomas), Charo (Martin), and Robert Goulet (Flaherty) is one of the most morally bankrupt pieces ever presented on SCTV. But it's also wickedly hilarious, largely thanks to the unrelenting cheeriness with which the show and its host Geoff Edwards (Levy) encourage murder; the program proudly promotes itself as the only show in which a contestant "holds the power of life and death over a real Hollywood celebrity."

While the "Farm Film Report" sketches encouraged the blowing up of celebrities, the violence in those pieces were cartoon-like; the hosts were also blown up every segment, but returned unharmed in the next. "Shoot at the Stars" pulls no such punches: The sketch ends with the three stars most definitely dead. While SCTV routinely savaged the entertainment industry, there is no better example of the show's contempt for shallow "show biz" performers than "Shoot at the Stars."

After several unspectacular appearances, Andrea Martin's Edith Prickley character finally finds her niche in this episode, as Guy Caballero introduces her as SCTV's new station manager. Defining Prickley's role seems to help Martin define Prickley, and she is solid in the role for the first time. Brash, bold, and assertive, Prickley even has the guts to push around the brutish Caballero, who up to this point had delighted in making mincemeat out of weaker personalities like Moe Green and Ernest Kirsch. The chemistry between Flaherty and Martin as SCTV's combative yet mutually respectful management team helped to make Caballero and Prickley *SCTV*'s most important (if not most popular) on-screen partnership: It is no coincidence that Prickley and Caballero are the final characters seen on *SCTV*'s final episode.

Although this episode doesn't quite fulfill Prickley's promise to present shows with "boobs," "bums," and "good looking hunky guys," much of its material is first-rate. A *Jaws* parody in which townspeople lament the disappearance of sharks because they are good for tourism is delightfully bizarre. Also solid is a hard-hitting Earl Camembert editorial about his inconsiderate neighbor ("Lady, get your act together!").

The sole misfire on this show is the only second season appearance of former favorite "Sunrise Semester," this time featuring John Candy's fortunately short-lived character Paul Fistinyourface. Since the "Sunrise Semester" program supposedly signals the start of a programming day, its placement here in the middle of the show is odd if understandable given the superiority of the material slotted earlier in the episode. Despite the weakness of this piece, *SCTV* would return to the "Sunrise Semester" concept with a vengeance in the next season, presenting no fewer than eleven such sketches.

Show 37 *(Second City Television)*

1. SCTV 30th Anniversary Show: Introduction
2. SCTV 30th Anniversary Show: HUAC Hearings
3. Palmoval commercial (repeat from show 31)
4. SCTV 30th Anniversary Show: Westerns
5. Delay commercial (repeat from show 28)
6. SCTV 30th Anniversary Show: What's My Shoe Size?

What to watch for: What's My Shoe Size?

A parody of the long-running quiz show What's My Line?, *"What's My Shoe Size?" features a four-person panel (including a standout performance by Flaherty as guest panelist Kirk Douglas) asking questions of a contestant in the hopes of guessing not the person's occupation but— you guessed it— his or her shoe size.*

This sketch, in which Candy's contestant succeeds in stumping the entire panel because of his gargantuan size 16s (Douglas: "Must be some kind of freak!"), is preceded by an introduction from Dr. Cheryl Kinsey (Martin) and Lola Heatherton (O'Hara). The two women— Lola immeasurably more comfortable talking about sex than the sexologist Kinsey— disagree about the presence of sexual tension in the show; Kinsey finds the show a relic from more innocent times, whereas Lola enthusiastically contends that panelist Arlene Franklin "wanted to get into [fellow panelist] Bennett Cerb's pants!"

Later airings of this sketch would suffer from the excising of this introduction, as one of the delights of the piece is realizing that Franklin (Martin) and the uptight, verbose Cerb (Thomas) display absolutely no hint of sexual chemistry whatsoever.

After several less ambitious episodes, *SCTV* successfully returns to the theme shows common earlier in the season. But whereas the material in this show is nearly as strong as the "Solid Gold Telethon" (show 30) or "Election Central" (show 32) episodes, there is an odd artificiality in presenting a 30th anniversary of SCTV: No matter how many grainy 1950s clips are presented, the idea of SCTV as a long-running television station (begun in 1948?!) contradicts the concept of SCTV as a presentation of programming from a new underground network, an idea detailed in the opening titles of season two ("There were six people who loved to watch television. But they didn't like what they saw. So they decided to do something about it").

Nevertheless, there are some memorable pieces here, particularly a re-invention of Senator Joseph McCarthy's HUAC Hearings of the early fifties as an investigation into Communism at SCTV. Like film director Elia Kazan, then–SCTV Station Manager Merle Camembert (Earl Camembert's father), buckles quickly and identifies several communists working at SCTV, including his own mother. This clip also provides a possible explanation as to how the inept Earl Camembert is able to keep his job at SCTV; perhaps his father still held some power at the station that he used to keep his son employed despite Earl's persistent incompetence.

While the episode ends too abruptly, it's worth noting two incidents under the closing credits: Heatherton hits on Camembert, proving that she'll sleep with anyone, and, more curiously, Floyd Robertson swipes a liquor bottle from Johnny LaRue. This throwaway physical business is the subtlest indicator of Robertson's alcoholism, a problem that will be explored in later episodes.

Show 38 *(Second City Television)*

1. Mr. Science with Johnny LaRue
2. Matchbook Advertising commercial (repeat from show 32)
3. SCTV News: SCTV is haunted
4. Fireside Chat with Mayor Tommy Shanks
5. 4th Degree
6. Monster Chiller Horror Theatre: Whispers of the Wolf
7. Words to Live By: Mulciber Arimaspians

What to watch for: Whispers of the Wolf.
Arguably the finest of all "Monster Chiller Horror Theatre" sketches and surely the strongest that doesn't rely on either the "miracle" of 3-D or the team of Dr. Tongue (Candy) and Bruno (Levy). Here the cast, obviously gaining confidence, takes on the lofty target of acclaimed Swedish filmmaker Ingmar Bergman with a sketch that derives its name from two of Bergman's films, the classic Cries and Whispers *and the lesser-known* Hour of the Wolf.

At first glance, the piece would seem to be a direct parody of Hour of the Wolf, *Bergman's only foray into "horror" films. But the sketch is more a send-up of Bergman's directorial style, with pretentious shots, uniquely framed close-ups, and a crushingly leaden pace. Catherine and Andrea (as Bergman regulars Liv Ullmann and Harriet Andersson) are effectively cold, distant, and wooden, while the dialogue tweaks Bergman's tendency to be overwhelmingly depressing ("Petra is dying. Life makes him vomit."). "Whispers of the Wolf" is not just a smart piece; by taking on one of the masters of world cinema, SCTV's comedic range continued its impressive expansion.*

(Note that while Flaherty has the character of Count Floyd perfected, SCTV does not yet have the staging of the "Monster Chiller Horror Theatre" pieces quite right. When the segment was rerun in show 81, it was given new titles, music, and sound effects.)

An odd episode that features three clumsy pieces dealing with evil supernatural forces at SCTV. In the worst of the three, Damian, the Antichrist child from the *Omen* films, visits Johnny LaRue's "Mr. Science" program. Damian, poorly played by an uncredited child actor, forces LaRue to drink acid before he telepathically hurls knives and other sharp objects into LaRue's body. Despite (or because of) LaRue's penchant for sleaziness, he is still a well-liked character; seeing him impaled is not a welcome sight. Moreover, the tone of the sketch is uncomfortably vague; *SCTV* doesn't seem to know whether this material is meant to be funny or scary. Unfortunately, it's neither.

The most successful pieces on the episode are those not dealing with the occult; most notable is John Candy's very first "Fireside Chat" as taciturn Melonville Mayor Tommy Shanks. Shanks would give many of these brief chats in the future, most of which wouldn't go beyond a simple remark about the weather. This first installment shows Shanks more verbose than his later greetings would be, covering not only the temperature but also the types of logs he uses in his fires. Diametrically opposed to the overly relaxed Shanks is the overly intense Chuck Clark (Flaherty), who hosts a program called "4th Degree." Clark ruthlessly interrogates and beats Governor Jerry Brown (Thomas) as if he were a cop looking for a confession. "4th Degree" would spawn an equally enjoyable sequel, "Flashing Eyes" (show 62).

Show 39 *(Second City Television)*

1. Donohue in the Morning promo
2. Sid Dithers Private Eye
3. UFO Sharkey promo
4. Enough About Me 2
5. Fish Police promo
6. Biller Hi-Lite commercial
7. Bad Acting in Hollywood

What to watch for: Fish Police.
A wonderfully silly promo for a program about fish that "disregard the laws" and the cops who work tirelessly to keep them in line. Basically a string of one-liners (the best being Catherine's "My watch. Stop that fish!" and Dave's "You'll fry for this"), this sketch proves that while SCTV's horizons were expanding, the show could still produce moments of unbridled stupidity.

A strong episode slowed down only by the inexplicable return of Catherine O'Hara's infuriating "Enough About Me" sketch for the second (and thankfully last) time.

Eugene Levy's diminutive Sid Dithers makes his second appearance (and his first since show 5, when he was named Morris) in a humorous sketch that casts him as a private investigator who succeeds in uncovering a prostitution ring and returning a teenaged girl (O'Hara) back to her loving father (Flaherty). The piece has but one joke — Dithers is too old, too slow, and too deaf to be a private eye — but it's brief and Levy is funny in the role.

Much more complex is the "Bad Acting in Hollywood" piece, which is basically a rip-off of the "Bad" ("Bad Ballet," "Bad Conceptual Art," "Bad Playhouse") series of *Saturday Night Live* sketches hosted by Dan Aykroyd's Leonard Pinth-Garnell. *SCTV*'s version is hosted by Candy as *Happy Days* patriarch Tom

Boslee [sic] and features a wretched courtroom scene from a 1940s movie entitled "Johnny Dark Always Rings Twice." Why this sketch ultimately fails to live up to its *SNL* counterparts is that *SCTV* for once underestimates the intelligence of its audience — in the *SNL* sketches, Aykroyd doesn't interrupt the proceedings to point out, for example, that the "Bad Ballet" is *really* bad. *SCTV*, conversely, finds it necessary to have Boslee continually point out how ridiculous the scene is, which only serves to kill the jokes before they come. But nevertheless, the piece does contain some good (bad?) work, particularly the ending, when the scene suddenly morphs from a murder trial into an embarrassingly patriotic call to arms when Levy's defense attorney announces that Pearl Harbor has been attacked.

Though both the Sid Dithers sketch and "Bad Acting in Hollywood" would later be rerun on NBC, the best pieces on this episode are the shorter sketches. In addition to "Fish Police," Candy unleashes a maniacal Don Rickles (here named "Rinkles") impression in a parody of Rickles's then-recently cancelled sitcom *CPO Sharkey*. Candy has the comic's insult humor down cold, mocking a Mexican (Flaherty) for smoking peyote and blaming a fire on an African-American who supposedly decided "to cook me some ribs."

Show 40 *(Second City Television)*

1. Only for Women
2. Hats of the West
3. Consumer Concern promo
4. Long Distance commercial
5. SCTV Special Presentation: Melonville Snooker Championships
6. Alfred Hitchcock Presents part 1
7. The Devil's Towering 10-G Upside Down Inferno commercial
8. Alfred Hitchcock Presents part 2: Murder is Bad for Your Health

What to watch for: Only for Women.
Whereas the previous episode was bogged down for an interview sketch featuring Andrea Martin and Catherine O'Hara, a similar sketch is this episode's highlight. A wonderfully funny discussion on the aftermath of divorce, this piece is notable not only for its humor, but also for its casting: The more typically understated Martin takes the sketch's strong, confident role, whereas the usually sexier Catherine plays a shy, mousy part.

At least that's how the sketch, with Martin punishing O'Hara for being "such a suck" for whining about her departed husband, begins. But soon Martin joins Catherine in tears as she realizes the very independence she champions has left her bitterly lonely and depressed. The initially feminist sketch ends up as a parody of feminism, with both women crying for the long-lost company of men or, barring that, at least a better look at the perverts who expose themselves on the subway. A solid statement by Martin and O'Hara that they could create material just as strong — even stronger — as the men in the cast.

Leaving the thematic shows of past episodes behind, this show presents a wildly eclectic series of sketches. The most ambitious of them is a parody of the TV series *Alfred Hitchcock Presents*, featuring John Candy doing an uncanny impression of the "Master of Suspense." Perhaps feeling a bit stifled as the stodgy filmmaker, Candy finishes the sketch by having Hitchcock perform a rant during which he reenacts parts of his films *Psycho* and *The Birds*. (Borrowing a trick most famously used in show 13's *Ben-Hur* parody, Candy segues into Curly Howard for part of the monologue.)

The film shown within the "Hitchcock Presents" sketch is a well-staged piece entitled "Murder is Bad for Your Health" featuring Joe Flaherty as a husband attempting (and miserably failing) to murder his wealthy wife, played by Andrea Martin. The piece, set in "merry old England" (Hitchcock's words), is a loose parody of the 1940 English film *Angel Street*, which was subsequently remade in America in 1944 as *Gaslight*. Appropriately enough, Americanized versions of these same characters would appear in a parody of *Gaslight* in show 60.

Two far simpler pieces also stand out here: Best is the western "Hats of the West," with Thomas as the Sundance Kid and Flaherty as a hat salesman who tries to sell him a different hat because his current one "doesn't accentuate the highlights" in his hair. The sketch is also notable for featuring Peter Aykroyd (Dan's brother, soon to become a featured player on *SNL*) and future *SCTV* cast member Tony Rosato in his first significant speaking role (sharp-eyed viewers will have noticed Rosato's appearance as an extra in several sketches by this point).

Show 41 *(Second City Television)*

1. Undercover Policewoman promo
2. SCTV News: Earl is high
3. Daylea Yogurt commercial
4. Masterpiece Theatre with Alistair Cook: Season Preview
5. Mike's Mercenaries commercial
6. SCTV Movie of the Week: Fighting Air Dogs Over the Pacific

What to watch for: SCTV News.

Beginning a stellar run of "SCTV News" segments over the next several episodes, this sketch finds Levy's Earl Camembert going on air unapologetically stoned. SCTV tempers the inappropriateness of Camembert's behavior by explaining that his condition is the result of a government-sanctioned experiment, but the apparent legalization of Camembert's activities doesn't make eating junk food or playing with a Slinky any more appropriate for a live newscast.

In stark contrast to SNL, SCTV largely refrained from drug humor, which on SNL repeats now seems dated at best and irresponsible at worst. This lack of drug material can be attributed to the fact that drugs were not a large part of SCTV's backstage culture. But when done in connection to an established character or impression (here and show 74's David Brinkley commentary), drug humor did account for a small number of SCTV highlights.

Another solid if unspectacular collection of sketches. Thomas continues to wear out his Lin Ye Tang character, this time in a pointless World War II film parody entitled "Fighting Air Dogs Over the Pacific." Not only is the sketch — basically a well crafted but overlong series of shots between Japanese and American fighter pilots — devoid of humor, the piece also further underlines the sloppy racial arbitrariness of Thomas's Asian caricature: Tang, previously defined as Chinese, is unchanged here, except for the fact that he is now suddenly Japanese.

Thomas fares better in a three-part "Masterpiece Theatre" preview: First up, Thomas and Flaherty star in a re-creation of "history's foremost duel of dialect"— the famed Lincoln-Douglas debates. In *SCTV*'s version, the two men are outrageously immature, implying that each others' grandmothers are whores and exchanging cries of "Stinkin' Lincoln" and "Dirty Douglas." Thomas is also an accused "Indian lover" who changes his tune when Eugene's Native American proves to not be an endangered species in "Mohicans Galore," a spoof of *The Last of the Mohicans*. Finally, in the most inspired segment, *SCTV* restages the British play *The Admirable Crichton*, which is about a family shipwrecked on a deserted island, as a spoof of *Gilligan's Island*, which of course was also about a group of people shipwrecked on a deserted island. Even though Flaherty's Alistair Cook dismisses "Cretin's Island" as a "low-brow rip-off of a cheap television series," it is an early example of *SCTV*'s multi-layered parodies (combining a much-maligned TV show with a highbrow British play, no less), a style soon to reach an early apex with show 44's "Fantasy Island."

Catherine O'Hara deserves mention for her performance as a bedridden cop in a promo for a show called "Undercover Policewoman," a parody of the 1970s Angie Dickinson drama *Police Woman*. (Note Catherine's character is named "Paprika," a cheap joke on the fact that Dickinson's character was nicknamed "Pepper.") Catherine rolling her bed down a flight of stairs to pin a crook (Tony Rosato) is one of the supreme examples of physical comedy in *SCTV*'s oeuvre.

Show 42 *(Second City Television)*

1. The Amazing Kretin
2. The Heys of our Lives
3. SCTV News: Earl at Melonville State Penitentiary
4. Phil's Nails commercial
5. William Castle Presents Agatha Christie's Death Takes No Holiday

What to watch for: *Phil's Nails*.
Phil (no last name given), a manic pitchman played by Eugene Levy, is the flip side of Thomas's Harvey K-Tel or Levy's Lou Jaffe. Whereas K-Tel and Jaffe are polished

professionals, Phil is outrageously nervous on-camera, a fact most evidenced by the constant movement of his arms. But the wild arm gestures at least draw attention away from his ratty hair, unkempt beard, bad clothes, horrible line readings, and bad jokes. Phil would have a hard enough time giving away free money, and unfortunately for him, he's trying to sell nails at a store that is "right next to a pile of old tires."

Two standout performances by Eugene Levy and one of the most ambitious (and lengthy) sketches to date highlight this episode. Besides "Phil's Nails," Levy also shines in a darkly comic "SCTV News" segment in which Earl Camembert actually has his throat slit (not fatally, of course) by a vindictive group of prisoners. What's interesting here is not only the darkness of the piece — as *SCTV* gets laughs out of a brutal act of violence perpetrated on one of the show's dimmest but most endearing characters — but also the reaction of co-anchor Floyd Robertson (Flaherty). At first shocked, Robertson then laughs at Camembert's injury, a callous response that takes the level of contempt that Floyd has for Earl to a new low. If there is any victory at all here for Earl, it is that the prisoners injured Earl because of his influential editorials and reports that supposedly assisted in their capture and incarceration — rare evidence that Camembert is a journalist of some clout.

In sharp contrast to "Phil's Nails" and "The Heys of Our Lives" — a silly soap opera parody in which nearly every line spoken includes the word "hey" ("Hey, are we going on that hay ride tonight?") — stands the lengthy "Death Takes No Holiday" piece. One of *SCTV*'s most elaborately costumed and staged pieces yet, this parody of *Murder on the Orient Express* features John Candy as Agatha Christie's favorite detective Hercule Poirot and Andrea Martin as Christie herself, who has the power to control the actions of others simply by what she writes in her book.

The piece, though long, is a success, particularly the inspired ending featuring Dave Thomas as producer William Castle, who appears to poll the audience on their preferred ending. In one of *SCTV*'s earliest attacks on meddling producers, Christie and Poirot argue against Castle's audience poll gimmick, and when Castle won't listen to reason, they simple strangle him. (The real William Castle, who never met a gimmick he didn't like, did include such an audience poll in his 1961 film *Mr. Sardonicus*; however, the device was a ruse: Only one ending was ever shot, so no matter how the audience voted, they saw the same conclusion.)

Show 43 *(Second City Television)*

1. Cooking with Edith Prickley part 1
2. Tex and Edna Boil's Organ Emporium commercial: Rhythm Ace
3. Cooking with Edith Prickley part 2
4. Masterpiece Theatre Library promo

5. Mind Games commercial
6. SCTV News: Earl's impacted wisdom tooth
7. Stop Smoking PSA with Lola Heatherton
8. Masterpiece wigs commercial
9. SCTV Mail Bag
10. Rock Concert

What to watch for: Rock Concert.
One of the best developments of SCTV's second season was the pairing of John Candy's Billy Sol Hurok and Joe Flaherty's Big Jim McBob and their newfound obsession with people getting blowed up good. But after the premiere sketch in show 33, it seemed John and Joe didn't know what to do with these characters, as they placed them in various supporting roles with mostly tepid results. That uncertainty ended with this sketch, which lays the groundwork for the "Farm Film Celebrity Blow-Up" sketches of the NBC years.

Here, in a parody of the TV show of the same name, Billy Sol and Big Jim simply introduce various musical acts, including Freddy Fender (Levy), Randy Newman (Thomas), Patti Smith (Martin), Helen Reddy (O'Hara), and the Village People (Flaherty, Levy, Candy, and Thomas), and then, after each performer has sung a few lyrics, they blow them up. All of the impressions, particularly Martin's Patti Smith, are excellent, but that's not really the point of the piece: Later "Farm Film" sketches would rely more on the celebrity impressions for laughs, but this sketch is simply about blowing people up; the fact that the bizarre idea is given an appropriately bizarre execution is why the piece succeeds.

A wildly uneven episode containing several weak sketches foreshadowing the poor episodes to come.

Besides "Rock Concert," the most notable aspect of this show is the debut of Edith Prickley's sister, Edna Boil (also played by Martin) and her husband, Tex (Thomas), who sell organs. Their premiere spot, in which the call-and-response of "Right, Tex?" and "That's right, Edna" is already in place, is solid. In his book, Thomas didn't hide his preference for writing and performing with O'Hara over Martin; ironically, this partnership with Martin would prove to be more fruitful for the show than any he would ever have with O'Hara.

The Tex and Edna Boil spot interrupts a cooking program hosted by Edith Prickley, which marks Martin's first appearance as the character since she was named SCTV's station manager. A station executive hosting such a low-budget program recalls Prickley's predecessor, Moe Green, lording over the rinky-dink "Dialing for Dollars." Martin is terrific in the piece, particularly when she very enthusiastically stuffs a turkey while singing "Macho Man" (a tune reprised in the "Rock Concert" sketch) to the sound of one of Tex and Edna's Rhythm Ace machines.

Besides another fine "SCTV News" segment, the rest of the program is weak. Most interesting among the tepid segments is Dave Thomas's debut of a belligerent character named Bob Clark who hosts a viewer mail program;

Thomas would vastly improve on this character type next season with his creation of SCTV's "critic at large," Bill Needle.

Show 44 *(Second City Television)*
1. Fantasy Island part 1: Guests arrive on island
2. Fantasy Island part 2: Hope and Crosby in harem
3. Ronco No Sweat Sauna commercial
4. Fantasy Island part 3: Rick's Café Americain

What to watch for: Fantasy Island (what else?).
It is surprising that a parody of a cheesy ABC drama could result in one of SCTV's best sketches and arguably the finest example of the show's famed "multi-layered" parodies, but that's what this spoof of Fantasy Island *is. A comic masterpiece, "Fantasy Island" combines a lampoon of the Ricardo Montalban / Herve Villechaize program with parodies of* Casablanca, The Wizard of Oz, *a Bob Hope / Bing Crosby road picture, and Montalban's then-popular Chrysler Cordoba ads and works them flawlessly into a single brilliant piece.*

The opening is where the sketch most resembles the ABC program, as Levy's Mr. Roarke and Candy's Pattoo, Mr. Roarke's pint-sized assistant, welcome the visitors to Fantasy Island. Through special effects, Levy and the miniature Candy are able to share the frame, and their interplay is convincing enough to buy the video manipulation as reality. In later scenes, an obvious dummy would stand in for Candy, partly to ease production but also to provide cheap laughs while absorbing Levy's physical abuse.

The guests include Martin as a bored concert violinist looking for mystery and intrigue, O'Hara as a klutzy princess who wants to become glamorous, and Thomas and Flaherty as rock musicians who want to become comedians. Although Thomas and Flaherty have the best roles of the guests (not surprising since he and Flaherty wrote the sketch), it is Candy who steals the scene when the extremely horny Pattoo ("Oh, Boss, I love chicks!") takes Andrea's payment—an original Stradivarius violin—and makes violent love to it.

The focus of the sketch then shifts from a Fantasy Island *parody to a satire of the Bing Crosby / Bob Hope "road" pictures, as Joe and Dave have been transformed from rockers to the famous comedy team who are here posing as undercover bra salesmen. Thomas's Hope, the only time on SCTV that he would be portrayed as a young man, is of particular interest—his delivery is razor-sharp and void of the smug narcissism that Thomas used in show 28's "Bob Hope Desert Classic" sketch.*

Hope and Crosby soon find themselves hiding out in Rick's Café Americain, which signals the introduction of the Casablanca *parody. Here Andrea's bored violinist emerges as Ingrid Bergman to John Candy's Humphrey Bogart (Martin self-deprecatingly would later say her Ilsa looked more like Mother Teresa than Ingrid Bergman). All of the characters converge in this setting, as the sketch gets sillier (particularly as Thomas's Hope falls under a curse that makes him think he's a dog) but no less entertaining. Even Eugene and John have their funniest exchange here as Roarke angrily calls Pattoo "a cheap little device for exposition" while ripping a huge patch of hair out of Pattoo's head. Sadly left out is O'Hara, whose princess has become Ginger Rogers; O'Hara has a brief dance number with a Fred Astarie look-alike, but no good lines.*

Catherine has better luck as Glinda, the Good Witch of the North, who appears to help Thomas and Flaherty escape their fantasy; her appearance signals a shift to a Wizard of Oz parody. Suddenly Rick's becomes Dorothy's twister-engulfed Kansas home, spinning violently as images of Pattoo, Mr. Roarke ("this would have been a smoother ride in a Cordoba!") and, in another Oz nod, the Wicked Witch of the West appear outside the café's windows. In Oz, Dorothy wakes to find herself back in Oz; here Dave and Joe's musicians wake to find themselves back with their band, echoing Oz's sentiments that there is indeed no place like home.

A dense, masterful sketch that further broadened the scope of what SCTV could and would do, while laying much of the groundwork for the path the show would take when it expanded to ninety minutes.

Show 45 *(Second City Television)*

1. The Sammy Maudlin Show part 1: Edith Prickley
2. Dr. Chet Vet the Dead Pet Remover commercial
3. LaRue Toys commercial
4. The Sammy Maudlin Show part 2: Bobby Bittman & Lola Heatherton
5. Evelynn Wolf School of Speed Eating commercial
6. The Sammy Maudlin Show part 3: Lin Ye Tang

What to watch for: *The Sammy Maudlin Show.*
Impressively, SCTV matches the brilliance of "Fantasy Island" with this edition of "Maudlin," featuring Bobby Bittman (Levy), Lola Heatherton (O'Hara), and Lin Ye Tang (Thomas) promoting their new film, "On the Waterfront Again," a massively ill-conceived and wretchedly executed remake of On the Waterfront. *Bittman, making his directorial debut, matches the inexcusable casting of himself as Terry Molloy with the wrongheaded selections of Heatherton as Edie Doyle, and Tang as Terry's brother, Charley.*

Thanks to Bittman's screening of two clips from the finished film, we see just enough of the remake to appreciate its wonderful despicableness. In particular, Bittman and Heatherton take overacting to a new extreme; note Bittman's reaction upon finding his brother's lifeless body—he stumbles forward like a drunk, vigorously rubs his temples as if he is starring in a commercial for a headache remedy, and covers and uncovers his eyes like a child playing peekaboo. But it is his overwrought reading of the vengeful line "I'll take it out on their skulls!" where Bittman truly becomes grotesque.

The other clip viewed—a re-creation of the classic scene between Charley and Terry in which Terry laments the sad direction of his life—is equally bad: Terry's despondence comes across as hollow when his fingers are weighted down with several gaudy rings that Bittman inexplicably wears throughout the film. But as enjoyable as these clips are, they pale in comparison to the "Maudlin" panel discussion portions of the sketch, during which Maudlin and sidekick William B. Williams tearfully fawn all over the film's stars, citing their "dynamite acting" that has left them "so moved" and "speechless." Even here, though, Levy's egotistical Bittman steals the sketch, as he becomes increasingly annoyed with the attention paid to Heatherton and the laughter afforded Lin Ye Tang's rotten jokes ("Good actors are like a big ball of steamed rice. They stick together!").

Sammy Maudlin and Bobby Bittman were two of the finest characters created for SCTV; this sketch not only features them at their best but is SCTV at its best. (Note: This is the first "Maudlin" sketch— but not the last— to give Candy's William B. Williams a significant role. The sketch was also the first— again not the last— "Maudlin" not to be joined "already in progress.")

Because the "Maudlin" sketch is shorter than the previous episode's "Fantasy Island" piece, this show also features three fine commercial parodies. Thomas's manic dead pet remover spot is the most unforgettable, but also notable is the Evelynn Wolf School of Speed Eating commercial, which also features a course in "speed drinking" (depicted as drinking ten shots before immediately passing out) as created by Johnny LaRue.

Show 46 *(Second City Television)*

1. The Butch Grant Show promo
2. Oil of Oil commercial
3. Those Two Zany Ambulance Drivers promo
4. Women Say the Darndest Things promo
5. Ronco Weiner Skinner commercial
6. Tex and Edna Boil's Organ Emporium commercial: Budgie transportation
7. SCTV News: Earl attacks crew inefficiency
8. Captain O'Shaunnessy Table Top Smoke Alarm commercial
9. SCTV Disco

What to watch for: SCTV News.
Towering over the episode's other material is this "SCTV News" segment in which Earl Camembert reprimands the crew for failing to provide what he considers to be satisfactory work conditions. As welcome as it is to see Camembert worked into a tizzy, the highlight of the sketch comes when the crew storms the set prepared to inflict injury on the dim-witted newsman. Not wanting to get beat up himself and obviously relishing the prospect of Camembert getting pummeled, Floyd Robertson is quick to thank the crew for their fine work.

As surprising at it is to see *SCTV* follow the classic "Fantasy Island" with the equally remarkable "On the Waterfront Again," it is equally stunning to witness the near total collapse of quality in this installment. Perhaps everyone involved exhausted themselves with the previous two ambitious episodes, as the show is reduced to running on fumes for the remainder of the season.

Part of the reason for the show's decline at this time could have been cast morale. As detailed in Dave Thomas's book, there was a "penniless aura" that surrounded the show, and the cast was growing tired of the producers' habit of paying them late. That situation could explain some of the lazy material featured here, including several cringe-inducing commercial parodies, the worst offender being one for a product known as a "Weiner Skinner." Another spot for a product called Oil of Oil is notable for being copied years later (show 127) in a funnier parody featuring Martin's stellar Sophia Loren impression.

Besides "SCTV News," there is some semblance of humor in this show: "Those Two Zany Ambulance Drivers" is stupid but funny, while Thomas's "Women Say the Darndest Things" is a daring send-up of sexism. And this show does feature another step in the evolution of Eugene Levy's Rockin' Mel Slirrup character; though the sketch in which the character is featured, "SCTV Disco," is awful, Levy does have the character's look, voice, and (almost) his trademark dance fine-tuned. Just as *SCTV* itself, Rockin' Mel Slirrup would emerge much improved in the next season.

Show 47 *(Second City Television)*
1. Passport to Adventure: Pain-Free Home Entertaining
2. Tax Advice promo
3. SCTV News Bulletin: Mayor Tommy Shanks
4. Taps Friendly No-Name Supermarket commercial
5. The Dr. Braino Hour
6. Pipeline

What to watch for: Tax Advice.
Dave Thomas premieres his fine impression of Liberace in this promo in which the showman promises to explain how to claim a million dollars for wardrobe and thousands of dollars for jewelry, Caesar salads, and booze.

SCTV continues its sharp late second season decline with arguably the single worst *SCTV* installment ever.

Besides the "Tax Advice" promo, the only bearable piece is the "SCTV News Bulletin" featuring an address from Candy's Mayor Tommy Shanks. Though most of the time spent by Floyd and Earl trying to analyze Shanks's meaningless remarks is wasted, *SCTV* does provide another clue to Floyd's burgeoning alcoholism when he disgustedly remarks that instead of covering "these stupid fireside chats, I could be home having a drink."

Compared with the remainder of the program, the aforementioned sketches are genius. Worst is a program called "The Dr. Braino Hour," which features John Candy and Joe Flaherty as stoners who "get off" while listening to The Grateful Dead and Quicksilver Messenger Service. An astonishingly amateurish piece devoid of humor, written and performed from the false assumption that simply acting stoned is funny, "The Dr. Braino Hour" is a contender for the single worst *SCTV* sketch ever.

Not much better is "Pipeline," a ridiculously lengthy documentary examining the day in the life of a plumber, played by Eugene Levy. While Levy's performance is fine, the jokes—customers are stunned when they receive Levy's bill, for instance—are remarkably lazy. Elsewhere, Dave Thomas and Catherine O'Hara unwisely bring back Bob and Betty Wilson, the insufferable hosts of "Passport to Adventure." (And why would a travelogue show cover the topic of home entertaining?)

Clearly, by the end of the second season, the cast and writers needed a break. Unbeknownst to the cast, they were soon to get one that would last well over a year.

Show 48 *(Second City Television)*
1. The Young Weasels promo
2. Fireside Chat with Mayor Tommy Shanks: State of the Economy
3. Simple Touch Whitener commercial
4. Tex and Edna Boil's Organ Emporium commercial: Budgie Bait
5. Family Crisis
6. Graft recipes commercial
7. SCTV News: Consumer Action Line

What to watch for: Graft Recipes.
A clever parody of Kraft's famous commercials that showed only a woman's hands as she prepared recipes using Kraft products. Here Eugene Levy's hands struggle to construct a revolting sandwich as quickly as his own voice-over speeds through the unique blend of ingredients, including uncooked duck fat, sliced beets, smelts, and of course, "Graft" cheese. The sketch is infantile, but the finished sandwich is humorously disgusting.

Another weak show notable for the exclusion of the lengthy Johnny LaRue game show sketch "Family Crisis" from all syndication repeats. Why the segment was pulled and replaced with "Wara! Wara! Wara!" from show 2 is unknown.

"Family Crisis" couldn't have been pulled for quality reasons; if that were the criteria for expurgation, most of this episode would never see the light of day again. The most frustrating aspect of this show is its reliance on already exhausted bits; Dave and Andrea's Tex and Edna Boil make their third appearance in six shows, going from funny to aggravating in the process. And although John Candy's brief "Fireside Chats" as Mayor Tommy Shanks remain amusing, running two carbon copy sketches in two successive episodes reveals an alarming lack of inspiration.

Elsewhere, Dave Thomas and Joe Flaherty are featured as two men raised by weasels; these "Young Weasels" predictably find success as television executives, an unflattering portrayal of TV power brokers that would eventually be replicated (somewhat more successfully) by Rick Moranis and Dave Thomas's "pig" characters, who notably stood in for *SCTV* producers Andrew Alexander and Len Stuart in show 97.

Even the normally reliable "SCTV News" bombs in this episode, as a long segment is made even more interminable by the unwelcome appearance of Andrea's Pirini Scleroso character as a "foreign correspondent." Worse is an overlong installment of "Consumer Action Line" that consists of Earl Camembert calling a drapery store and being placed on hold. By the time Earl embarrassingly discovers that the "sniveling greedy robber baron" on the other end of the line is an important sponsor, the sketch has long overstayed its welcome. Not unlike the entire episode.

Show 49 *(Second City Television)*

1. Take the Money and Run promo
2. Natalie Ringneck: Raised by Geese
3. Ronco No Sweat Sauna commercial (repeat from show 44)
4. Big Giant Restaurant commercial
5. Relaxing with Raoul
6. National Council for Antique and Restricted Automatic Weapons PSA
7. Biller Hi-Lite commercial (repeat from show 39)
8. Dining with LaRue: French restaurant

What to watch for: Relaxing with Raoul.
This sketch almost—almost—makes this otherwise putrid episode worth watching. Toned down in his premiere appearance (show 24), this is Eugene Levy's outrageously perverted Raoul Wilson character at his depraved best. First seen holding an enormously phallic cigar and salivating over a copy of Swank, *Wilson is soon introducing us to what promises to be a relaxing mind game. But instead he gets himself sexually aroused thinking about taking a girl to an "empty warehouse" and tying her up. Levy is a marvel here in one of the most morally questionable sketches the show would produce; the piece is so extreme that it prematurely takes the character of Wilson about as far as he could go. Levy would only appear twice more as Wilson.*

Show 47's humorless "Dr. Braino Hour" is arguably the worst *SCTV* sketch; the only argument is likely to come from anyone familiar with this episode's "Natalie Ringneck" segment. A pitiful piece starring Andrea Martin as a nursery school teacher who was raised by geese (another lazy idea, since the previous episode featured a sketch about two humans raised by weasels), the sketch is an embarrassment filled with cringe-inducing moments (Martin "honks" while she talks and eats grubs out of a bucket). Excruciating.

In comparison to "Natalie Ringneck," the remainder of the episode is barely more tolerable. The "Dining with LaRue" sketch is particularly frustrating; as much as we want to laugh when we see Candy's Johnny LaRue, there is simply nothing funny happening here. *SCTV*, normally so brazenly original, tries to pass off this lengthy sketch by suggesting that French food is expensive and that French waiters can be snooty. If those ideas weren't unoriginal enough, the sketch also imports a couple of the better jokes from previous "Dining with LaRue" pieces. A mess.

Finally, it's doubtful that anyone watching the episode or even anyone who worked on the show can explain the point behind the Big Giant restaurant commercial. Is it that giants are bigger than ordinary people? Or that giants have big booming voices? Or that giants make a lot of noise when they walk? Whatever the intent was, it's probably best forgotten — just like most of this episode.

Show 50 *(Second City Television)*
1. The Two Goofs Grocery Store commercial
2. Don Strom: Mental Illness PSA
3. Insights with Hugh Betcha
4. Meet the Pawnbroker promo
5. SCTV News: Earl eats
6. Polordak ESP1 commercial
7. William F. Buckley & Meatloaf: Latin PSA
8. An SCTV Big Cultural Event: The Flaming Turkey.

What to watch for: Mental Illness PSA.
Eugene Levy gives an impressively demented performance in this brief spot that purports to present seven warning signs that "you're going completely schnutz." The concept is similar to show 5's "seven warning signs that you might be dead," but here crazed actor Don Strom offers only three signs before falling prey to one of them — short mental blackouts or lapses of consciousness — himself.

With this episode, *SCTV* breaks out of its slump — sort of. While this show doesn't match the highs of the season, it escapes the lows of recent installments. This show is also significant in that it features John Candy and Catherine O'Hara making their last appearances in original *SCTV* material for over two years. The pair would sit out the next season, which itself wouldn't begin for well over a year after the close of this one.

Candy and O'Hara feature together here in a game show parody called "Meet the Pawnbroker," in which an elderly woman, having been forced to sell her 35-year-old wedding ring for a measly $100, must fight through a tough street gang in order to keep the money. The pawnbroker is none other than Johnny LaRue, making a strong appearance after last episode's "Dining with LaRue" disaster.

While not on screen together, both also star in the episode's longest sketch, a remarkably silly ballet called "The Flaming Turkey." Although a second rip-off of Dan Aykroyd's Leonard-Pinth Garnell series of sketches on *Saturday Night Live* (one of which was indeed "Bad Ballet"), the sketch — which tells the story of the death of a turkey — is still entertaining. As the turkey, Andrea Martin steals the sketch with an elongated death scene, while O'Hara is convincing doing the "dance of the peasant girl going nuts because she lost her turkey."

Perhaps most welcome is another fine "SCTV News" segment, in which Earl Camembert (Levy) decides to eat his dinner while reading the news, his reasoning being that many viewers are probably doing the same during the broadcast. (This idea is reminiscent of a *Tonight Show* episode in which Johnny Carson was wheeled in relaxing comfortably in a bed.) While certainly distracting in and of itself, Camembert can't resist the temptation to comment on his meal (even comparing a story on Angolan politics to his cold peas), which finally forces Floyd to throw the meal on the floor, much to Camembert's disgust. A classic Floyd and Earl piece, of which there would be many more to come in the next season.

Show 51 *(Second City Television)*
1. Lola Heatherton in Concert promo (repeat from show 27)
2. Donna (repeat from show 29)
3. UFO Sharkey promo (repeat from show 39)
4. What's My Shoe Size? (repeat from show 37)
5. Phil's Nails commercial (repeat from show 42)
6. Bob Hope Desert Classic (repeat from show 28)

The first of two shows consisting of repeat sketches, including the inexplicable recycling of the Dinah Shore parody with Andrea Martin's Barbra Streisand, and the overrated "Bob Hope Desert Classic."

Show 52 *(Second City Television)*
1. Speaking of Talk with Lou Jaffe (repeat from show 33)
2. Long Distance commercial (repeat from show 40)
3. Family Crisis (repeat from show 48)
4. Tex and Edna Boil's Organ Emporium commercial: Rhythm Ace (repeat from show 43)
5. The Millionaire (repeat from show 33)
6. Rock Concert (repeat from show 43)

The second of two episodes with repeat material, though this one betters the first in terms of quality. [Note that material from shows 51 and 52 were combined into a single best-of for the U.S. market.]

THE THIRD SEASON

Show 53 *(SCTV Television Network)*
1. Edith Prickley: Lee A. Iococca's Rock Concert
2. Rhoda promo
3. My Fair Lady promo
4. SCTV News teaser
5. Great White North: New boots
6. SCTV News: Earl mispronounces words
7. My Life One More Time promo
8. Lee A. Iococca's Rock Concert

What to watch for: Lee A. Iococca's Rock Concert.
A vicious parody of Chrysler head Lee A. Iacocca and his demands for a government bailout of his destitute company (a bailout that was eventually granted), this sketch — which also doubles as a parody of The Midnight Special *and* Don Kirschner's Rock Concert — *is a highlight of the season. Thomas writes in his book*

that he felt the assistance granted Chrysler was a "travesty," a travesty that Thomas exaggerates here as his Iococca asks for no less than $1.5 billion in federal assistance to save his "Rock Concert" from cancellation.

The piece also allows the cast to deliver some inspired musical impressions, the most memorable being Andrea Martin and Joe Flaherty as Barbra Steisand and yodeler Slim Whitman performing "You Don't Bring Me Flowers." New cast member Rick Moranis unveils an uncanny impression of comedian George Carlin, ruthlessly mocking the comedian's observational style of humor ("Why are there no sideways escalators? Weird."). Most bizarre is Eugene Levy's interpretation of Gino Vanelli, whose rendition of "Stop" is overshadowed by the fact that the singer slowly turns into an ape throughout his performance — a sophomoric but very funny comment on Vanelli's (and Levy's) hairiness.

At the end of the second season, it appeared that *SCTV*'s best days were behind it. The loss of head writer Harold Ramis eventually took its toll and the show floundered with weak material late in its sophomore year. Add to the loss of Ramis the departures of John Candy and Catherine O'Hara and *SCTV* appeared to be in creative trouble as its third season began.

But despite these personnel losses, *SCTV* not only survived but thrived: Thanks to new director John Blanchard and a new financial arrangement between producers Andrew Alexander and Len Stuart and businessman Dr. Charles Allard, the cast was able to produce their most visually appealing shows to date. More importantly, they produced their smartest and funniest ones as well. New writers Paul Flaherty, Dick Blasucci, and Mike Short certainly had a great deal to do with the quality of the scripts, but the most obvious reason *SCTV* improved in its third season was Dave Thomas's recruitment of Rick Moranis.

Although the other new performers, Robin Duke and Tony Rosato, had their moments, they were greatly overshadowed by Moranis. On his first episode alone, the former disc jockey unleashes not only his George Carlin impression, but also his eerily convincing Woody Allen impersonation in a promo that mocks Allen's self-absorption by pairing him with a female counterpart (Andrea Martin) that looks and speaks just like him. Moranis would employ this same idea with even better results in his first "Dick Cavett Show" sketch (show 60).

Elsewhere, Andrea Martin stars in a *My Fair Lady* parody that signals the finest use of her Pirini Sclereso character. The verbally challenged Sclereso as the verbally challenged Eliza Doolittle makes such perfect sense that it's a surprise the idea wasn't tried earlier. Martin is also funny in an Edith Prickley opening that connects the show to its past — "I took over from that shmoe Moe Green" — while also foreshadowing a year in which the station management characters Prickley and Guy Caballero (Flaherty) would be used more frequently than before. Two characters that would continue to be a significant part of the show in this third season are "SCTV News" co-anchors Floyd Robertson and Earl Camembert; the characters return here with a solid segment.

And then there is this episode's historic introduction of Bob and Doug McKenzie. It's easy to belittle the McKenzie brothers as being below the bar intellectually from the material normally produced by *SCTV* (Thomas notes in his book that "other characters we did were much smarter and more worthy of recognition"), but not only were the "Great White North" segments almost always humorous, they provided a welcome balance from some of *SCTV*'s headier material. In the long run, Bob and Doug should be applauded simply for bringing more attention to the often-overlooked *SCTV*.

[Note that for the first and last time, the third season's end credits do not credit the cast alphabetically, but instead list them in a hierarchical order, with newly appointed head writers Joe Flaherty and Dave Thomas first and new cast members Tony Rosato and Robin Duke last, with Eugene Levy, Rick Moranis, and Andrea Martin in the middle. Also note that the participation from Levy and Martin for the third season was officially "part-time" but that is belied by how often the two are featured in seemingly every episode.]

Show 54 *(SCTV Television Network)*

1. Guy Caballero: Thursday Night
2. Thursday Night
3. Great White North: Doug has his earmuffs on
4. Dat's da Name of dat Tune promo
5. Bittman Does Dallas promo
6. K-Tel's Fast Talking Playhouse: Who's Afraid of Virginia Woolf?
7. Guy Friday promo
8. Half Legs commercial
9. Point/Counterpoint: Alcohol

What to watch for: Thursday Night.

Comparisons between SCTV *and* Saturday Night Live *are inevitable; Dave Thomas even devoted an entire chapter to the subject in his book, in which it becomes apparent that many people who worked on* SCTV *were envious of the success of* SNL, *especially since they believed that* SCTV *was the better show.*

Surprisingly not mentioned in Thomas's book, the best revenge SCTV *ever got on* SNL *was this brutal parody, which finds much to mock in the NBC late-night institution:* SNL's *often-pointless behind-the-scenes sketches are sent up here with a meaningless backstage vignette about script organization;* SNL *creator Lorne Michaels's on-camera appearances are replaced by a cameo from producer Guy Caballero;* SNL's *drug humor is skewered by future* SNL *cast member Tony Rosato, who causes the audience to squeal with delight simply by saying "I'm really hungry, because I'm really stoned";* SNL's *bee characters are replaced by pig characters; Frequent host Steve Martin's catchphrase "Excuuuuuse me" becomes guest host Earl Camembert's "I beggggg your pardon."*

Best of all is the opening credit crawl for "Thursday Night," featuring an endless list of cast members (17!), a satire of SNL's *then-current ever-expanding company of stars and featured players. The final touch is the mention of Lorne Michaels's friend and ubiquitous* SNL *guest Paul Simon as the show's musical performer. Since "Thursday Night" aired before the monumentally bad 1980–1981 season of Saturday* Night *that saw producer Jean Doumanian fired after twelve shows, the* SCTV *parody was surprisingly prophetic, particularly the sketch's reliance on foul language, which foreshadowed the infamous incident when* SNL *cast member Charles Rocket said "fuck" live on the air.*

The best-known sketch of this fine second show features an inspired new venue for Thomas's manic pitchman Harvey K-Tel; he appears as the host and co-star of a brazenly abbreviated version of *Who's Afraid of Virginia Woolf?* ("Pretty classic stuff, huh? And best of all it didn't take up a lot of your time!") Besides another "Great White North," Thomas's new partnership with Rick Moranis results in the first of many pairings of newsmen Walter Cronkite (Thomas) and David Brinkley (Moranis). Here the two drunkenly discuss alcoholism, or more specifically, the question of "what the hell is wrong with alcohol?" Not satisfied with painting Brinkley as a lush, Moranis would soon portray him as a stoner as well (show 74).

Also included are two classic promos, one featuring the sole speaking appearance of Rick Moranis's Guy Friday character. Although such a stereotypical gay character is as potentially offensive as Dave Thomas's Lin Ye Tang, after eight seasons of *Will & Grace*, it's difficult to be as indignant at the sight of Guy Friday and his friend (Thomas) breathlessly perusing a gay publication ("Let's get one!"). Equally noteworthy is the season's first appearance of Levy's Bobby Bittman, featured in a promo for a hackneyed country and western special featuring the Dallas Cowboy Cheerleaders. In what is billed as his "singing debut," Levy gives oily performances of several Texas-themed numbers, while still finding time for a teary tribute to the Alamo. Best is Bittman's Southern-flavored variation on his famous catchphrase, which for the special becomes "How are ya, *y'all?*"

Show 55 *(SCTV Television Network)*

1. Words to Live By: Rabbi Karlov and Angus Crock
2. Elvis 'n' Costello promo
3. SCTV News teaser
4. Great White North: Problem of the French from point of view of back bacon and beer
5. Melba's Disco Jeans commercial
6. SCTV News: Film delay
7. Crazy Crafts with Molly Earl: Craft review
8. Guy Caballero: SCTV Live Theatre
9. SCTV Live Theatre: Death of a Salesman

What to watch for: SCTV Live Theatre.
This piece, promoted by Guy Caballero as "highly unique and unusual," is a variation on previous multiple impression sketches like "How the Middle East Was Won"

(show 33) and "The Man Who Would Be King of the Popes" (show 25). The difference here is that the script allows the cast members the freedom to do even broader impressions since none of the celebrities being portrayed seem to have any interest in presenting a recognizable interpretation of Death of A Salesman.

So we have Eugene Levy as Fantasy Island star Ricardo Montalban as Willy Loman, determining that "I should be getting back to the island," and Andrea Martin as Wizard of Oz star turned coffee spokesperson Margaret Hamilton as Linda Loman, concluding that all problems can be solved by switching to a different coffee. As the Loman boys, Dave Thomas and Rick Moranis are Star Trek's DeForest Kelley and comedian George Carlin; Kelley can't help referring to his fellow actors as "Jim" and "Spock," while Carlin (Moranis's second appearance as the comedian in three shows) can't stop working on his bits ("Why is there no green wine?"). As Willy's deceased brother Ben, Tony Rosato unveils an uncannily accurate John Belushi impression, encapsulating both Belushi's Joliet Jake Blues persona and his "but noooooo" catch phrase. No one outside of Willy can see Ben until Belushi manically informs the cast "a seed popped out of my joint and set the scenery on fire!" The ensuing blaze brings "SCTV Live Theatre" to a quick close.

Joining the cast of *SCTV* couldn't have been easy for either Robin Duke or Tony Rosato. Not only were they attempting to fill the void left by John Candy and Catherine O'Hara, they were also quickly eclipsed by fellow newcomer Rick Moranis. But in this episode Robin Duke gets her first major break as Molly Earl, the elderly host of an arts and crafts program. The character — who walks with a distinctive waddle while proudly showing off tacky creations such as a lamp made from a melted record and an empty bottle of gin — and the sketch both work well, giving Duke her first recurring role.

Not willing to be outshone by Duke, Andrea Martin brings back her Melba the Disco Queen character with infinitely more success than she had the first time (show 46's "SCTV Disco"). Melba stars in a commercial for blue jeans that do the dancing for you when you zip them up.

Moranis and Dave Thomas continue their impressively fertile partnership with the debuts of Rabbi Karlov (Moranis) and Scotsman Angus Crock (Thomas) in the return of "Words To Live By." (Note "Words to Live By" used to close the show in the first season; here it opens the show.) In the sketch, Karlov argues for the use of anti–Gentile slurs as a good defense against anti–Semitic remarks. The sketch would be edgier if the insults used weren't so silly (Crock: "Hey, Jew, is that your real nose?" Karlov: "Hey, hoodlum, Why don't you go and buy a living room set from a catalog?").

Not to be outdone, Flaherty and Levy continue their string of outstanding "SCTV News" sketches; here Earl tosses to some news footage that is never aired. Instead Camembert just sits and fidgets uncomfortably for well over a minute — a masterful job of silent comic acting by Levy.

Show 56 *(SCTV Television Network)*
1. The Young and the Wrestling promo
2. Money Talks with Brian Johns: William E. Douglas
3. Great White North: Kids being able to use calculators in school
4. Make Me Barf promo
5. Dialing for Dollars: Cronkite calls Kennedy
6. SCTV Money Movie: My Factory, My Self part 1
7. Dialing for Dollars: Cronkite calls angry viewer
8. SCTV Money Movie: My Factory, My Self part 2
9. Dialing for Dollars: Cronkite makes prank calls

What to watch for: My Factory, My Self.
An often-overlooked piece, "My Factory, My Self" is one of the most ambitious and successful achievements of SCTV's third season, marking another example of the show's multi-layered parodies. As a precursor to her feminist character Libby Wolfson, Andrea Martin plays a woman who forms a union at the nuclear-powered textile plant where she works.

*Reflecting the many films and actresses mocked in the piece, Martin is credited as Sally Jane-Clayburgh Streep, an amalgamation of Sally Field (*Norma Rae*), Jane Fonda (*Coming Home, The China Syndrome*), Jill Clayburgh (*An Unmarried Woman*), and Meryl Streep (*Kramer vs. Kramer*). What's fascinating about the piece is how seamlessly the sketch brings together elements of all these different movies: Commencing as a parody of* Norma Rae, *Martin comes home to discover her blubbering husband (Flaherty) is leaving her for another woman, which is a scene directly out of* An Unmarried Woman. *Rushing off to do her volunteer work at the veterans' hospital, Martin has a quick physical encounter with a disabled vet (Thomas)—shades of* Coming Home. *Back home, a still-tearful Flaherty struggles to get their son to eat his dinner, a different take on a famous scene from* Kramer vs. Kramer. *Then it's back to the plant for more* Norma Rae *material, then a nod to* The China Syndrome *courtesy of a nuclear explosion at the plant, then finally a stellar ending ("Can you work with* these *hanging over your shoulder?") that, depending on your point of view, either celebrates or mocks feminists in power. A complicated, extremely funny sketch that is the first worthy successor to show 44's landmark "Fantasy Island" piece.*

Besides "My Factory, My Self," another highlight of this episode is the inspired choice of Thomas's Walter Cronkite as the new host of "Dialing for Dollars." These new installments of the sketch are an improvement over the Moe Green segments from the first season; Thomas delights in showing Cronkite in a different light, whether it's cursing out callers ("Why don't you just go fuck yourself?"—bleeped but obvious) or making juvenile crank calls ("Is Jose there?").

Elsewhere, the premiere installment of "Money Talks," hosted by Levy's nerdy Brian Johns, is another noteworthy piece: Interviewing a wealthy industrialist (Rick Moranis) at his home, Johns shuns Moranis's thoughtful insight, caring only about how rich he is and how much his things cost ("How much would a pool like this cost? Are your neighbors rich?").

Show 57 *(SCTV Television Network)*
1. Sunrise Semester with Marcello Sebastiano: Communicating in Italian
2. Monster Chiller Horror Theatre teaser
3. Bubie's Chicken Medication commercial
4. Great White North: Snow chains
5. Edna's Back commercial
6. Danny Eubanks: Seminarian / Rookie Cop promo
7. Monster Chiller Horror Theatre: Death Motel

What to watch for: Danny Eubanks.
A throwback in style to some of the first season promos, this sketch features Thomas as Eubanks, a man who promised his dad he would become a priest, until "his dad got bumped off and Danny swore to avenge his death." Note the scene between Thomas and Flaherty and its extraordinary similarity to a scene between Ramis and Flaherty from show 22's "Klägg" promo.

The first forgettable episode of the third season. Kudos to Tony Rosato for bringing back the long-dormant "Sunrise Semester" series, but his lecture on Italian body language (his first appearance as future cooking show host Marcello Sebastiano) goes nowhere. (Andrea Martin would steal the idea with better results in show 114.) Two brief commercial parodies aren't any better; particularly poor is a spot for chicken soup medication.

More disappointing is the first "Monster Chiller Horror Theatre" piece of the new season; the sketch is the first solo venture for Eugene Levy's hunchback Bruno and the first season three sketch to truly suffer from the absence of John Candy, whose Dr. Tongue is gravelly missed.

Although the film starring Bruno ("Death Motel") is devoid of laughs, an interview segment between the actor who plays Bruno (Woody Tobias, Jr., also Levy) and Count Floyd works. Not only is the substance of the interview very funny — Floyd offends him several times, particularly when commenting on his dead father's "little stumpy feet" — the idea of Tobias, Jr., an actor whose movie dialogue is normally limited to grunts, calmly and fluently discussing his career is humorous.

Show 58 *(SCTV Television Network)*
1. Sunrise Semester with Norman Gorman: Conversational New Yorkese
2. Tex and Edna Boil's Organ Emporium commercial: Trip to Brazil
3. Great White North: Back bacon and snow chains
4. Donohue promo
5. 60/20
6. Guy Caballero: SCTV Satellite Raising Fund
7. Be a Foster Boss PSA
8. The Lone Ranger Show

What to watch for: 60/20.
A spoof of newsmagazine shows 60 Minutes *and* 20/20 *hosted by Levy's Earl*

Camembert, this sketch particularly takes off with the appearance of Rick Moranis as newsman Mike Wallace. The respected Wallace puts the inept Camembert on the defensive, turning what began as an examination of media effects into a 60 Minutes–style exposé of the SCTV anchor's background, complete with close-ups of a sweating Earl as Wallace charges him with nepotism. (Note here Camembert is said to have gotten his job because his father was SCTV's Chairman of the Board; in show 37, Earl's father was said to have been a former station manager.) Besides being very funny, the sketch also makes a serious point about the responsibility TV viewers have to question ratings-hungry journalists.

Although this episode isn't quite up to the quality of the first four shows of the season — misfires include another appearance by Martin's Pirini Sclereso and a weak debut for Joe Flaherty's New Yorker Norman Gorman — the episode is overall much stronger than the previous installment.

SCTV's originality continues to impress, particularly in this episode's "Lone Ranger Show," a *Tonight Show* parody featuring Moranis as a combination of Johnny Carson and the Lone Ranger with Flaherty as his sidekick, a mixture of Tonto and Ed McMahon. Many Carson elements are given unique twists here, particularly the interplay between host and sidekick, which focuses on Tonto being mocked for his drinking (as McMahon often was). Also well done is a variation on Carson's Carnac the Magnificent routine ("Colt 45." "What do you call a 45-year-old colt?"). Note also Tony Rosato's outlandishly dressed bandleader and the closing walk-on by *Tonight Show* executive producer Fred DeCordova.

One of the season's strongest Guy Caballero spots is also featured here, as the SCTV president makes a hysterical plea for money so the station can raise the orbit of the SCTV satellite, which is currently circling the earth at a height of only 15 feet, causing injury and panic. This sketch marks the first of many pieces in which Caballero asks for viewer contributions (previously Caballero had only asked for help from "wealthy Arabs" in show 33). Also note that Thomas's announcement mistakenly refers to Caballero as the SCTV station manager, a position held by Martin's Edith Prickley.

Dave Thomas has his best moment in the episode as Phil Donahue, admonishing the Pope (Rosato) for being "out of touch with the modern world" because he hasn't seen a male go-go dancer. Look closely (*very* closely) at the sketch's last shot — there in the otherwise all-female audience is Rick Moranis's Guy Friday character — a joke so underplayed and easily missed that it's odd Moranis even bothered.

Show 59 *(SCTV Television Network)*

1. Edith Prickley: Play It Again, Bob
2. The Trial of Oscar Wilde promo
3. SCTV News teaser

4. Great White North: How to make a guy go when he's sleeping
5. Roto-Rooster commercial
6. SCTV News: Travel Tips with Earl
7. Play It Again, Bob

What to watch for: Play It Again, Bob.

Hailed as one of SCTV's most successful—if not the most successful—sketches of all time, this piece was singled out by TV Guide as the sixth funniest "moment" in television history, beating out I Love Lucy's "Vitameatavegamin" episode and Monty Python's "dead parrot" sketch, among other substantial achievements in television comedy.

While not a straight parody of the film Play It Again, Sam (based on Woody Allen's play of the same name), there are clear nods to that movie throughout the piece, most obviously as the sketch opens on Moranis's Allen sitting in a movie theater watching a Bob Hope picture. This mirrors Sam, which opens with Allen watching Casablanca and showing the same awe for Bogart that Moranis's Allen has for Hope.

After this opening, the plot of "Bob" takes a decidedly different turn from that of Sam. Since Humphrey Bogart is deceased, Allen's character in Sam is limited from having a relationship with his idol anywhere except in his fertile imagination. However, in "Bob," Hope is still alive and just a phone call away from Woody, and soon the two are working together on a motion picture script. Here Thomas's Hope takes on aspects of both the Tony Roberts and Diane Keaton characters from Sam: Like Roberts, Hope brims with confidence, and as Woody Allen in Sam tries to forge a personal relationship with Keaton, here Moranis's Allen tries to forge a professional relationship with Hope.

Another element lifted from Sam is that Woody gets advice from a ghost; in Sam, it's Humphrey Bogart, while in "Bob" it's Hope's old partner Bing Crosby, played by Joe Flaherty. As Bogart helped Woody to court Keaton, Crosby, who knew Hope as well as anyone, helps Allen to court Hope. (Note how one of Moranis's line readings causes Flaherty to briefly but obviously break character.) One difference is that in Sam, Bogart is unseen by everyone but Allen; in "Bob," the recently-deceased Crosby can interact with the outside world and has a brief telephone interaction with Hope, with Hope left to wonder why the voice on the phone sounds so familiar.

Besides a wickedly funny script that is written on the same inspired level as the best of Allen's comedies (Hope wants the curvaceous Anita Ekberg to co-star in their movie; when he cups his hands to describe her, Moranis responds, "What, you want an actress with arthritis?"), "Play It Again, Bob" features two of the finest performances in SCTV's history. Thomas's Hope is particularly interesting, as he brings a cruelty and obsoleteness to Hope not found in his other appearances as the legendary comedian. On-stage, Hope's act is unfunny and outdated; off-stage, Hope is calculating, uncreative ("in New York, you give them [the audience] the Big Apple thing, in Chicago, you give them the Windy City stuff"), sexist, cheap, and Anti-Semitic (he fears Woody will try to "hustle" him off to "some deli" for lunch).

The final shot of "Play It Again, Bob" echoes the final shot in Casablanca, showing Allen and Hope walking away discussing what could be the beginning of a beautiful friendship but which appears more likely to be the beginning of a tumultuous working *relationship. Here Hope has clearly gotten the better of Woody, as not only has Hope talked Allen into performing stand-up for the first time in years, but for one of Hope's favorite types of audiences — members of the military. Hope is even shown to be in charge of Allen's material, commenting on some lame bits that will, in Hope's words, "slay 'em."*

With Allen crossing over into Hope's world, SCTV *gives us an ending in which the artist (Allen, then still at the peak of his creative powers) has sold out to the hack (Hope, decades past his prime and marking time by starring in insufferable television specials). A bittersweet ending of the type that Woody Allen often excels at in his films and which* SCTV *perfectly applies to the end of this masterful sketch.*

Although dwarfed by "Play It Again, Bob," this episode is aided by some brief pieces, in particular a fine "SCTV News" segment in which Earl Camembert shows film of his St. Lucia vacation. His unlikely traveling companion, a shapely blonde, all but ruins his trip by encouraging the numerous passes made on her by the locals. For once Camembert doesn't take the ribbing from Robertson ("she wasn't exactly fighting them off") lightly, even referring to Robertson's wife Edie as "Easy" Robertson.

Show 60 *(SCTV Television Network)*

1. Sunrise Semester with Angus Crock: Conversational Scottish
2. Chick Monk: Roadie Marriage Counsellor promo
3. Great White North: Back packing with beer on ski trips
4. The Dick Cavett Show: Dick Cavett
5. Gaslight
6. Sermonette: "Father" Raoul Wilson

What to watch for: The Dick Cavett Show.
Rick Moranis's premiere of his Dick Cavett impression stands out as one of the most celebrated pieces of the season. Attacking Cavett's narcissism while putting an inspired twist on his Woody Allen sketch from show 53, here Moranis plays Dick Cavett interviewing Dick Cavett, also played by Rick.

Why is Cavett interviewing himself? Because, as Moranis puts it, for years Cavett has been searching to interview someone with "the intelligence of John Kenneth Galbraith, the wit of Woody Allen, the irreverence of Mort Sahl, the charm of Sir Laurence Oliver, and the looks of Cary Grant." In Cavett's eyes, that person could only be himself. Although the premise and Moranis's uncanny impression are the obvious strengths of the sketch, it wouldn't be nearly so successful had the technical aspects of it — particularly the nearly undetectable split-screen effect and the seamless editing — not been handled so remarkably well.

Fortunately, Moranis is smart enough to keep the sketch brief, and once the joke has been told — that two Cavetts are even more pompous and irritating than one — he ends the piece. Despite Moranis's obvious ability to play Cavett, Moranis would only perform the impression in three more episodes.

While ultimately not successful, show 57's "Death Motel" sketch makes sense in that it attempts to determine whether Levy's Bruno character could survive without Candy's Dr. Tongue. (It couldn't.) However, this episode's lengthy parody of the 1944 film *Gaslight*—basically a rewrite of show 40's "Murder Is Bad for Your Health"—seems to contain no such reason for existence. Subtitled "A chilling suspense story," the piece provides neither suspense nor chills nor, more importantly, many laughs. While Flaherty is appropriately sleazy as the husband attempting to drive his wife (Martin) insane and Robin Duke is fine in her biggest role to date as an adulterous maid, there is simply nothing of interest happening here. Only by pulling out one of its favorite comedic devices—the abuse of dummies—does *SCTV* score any laughs.

Thomas doesn't fare much better in another lazy "Sunrise Semester" piece, the third one in a row to mock phrases or mannerisms supposedly common to a particular population group. (Although it is here that we discover that Thomas's Angus Crock is in fact a "famous Scottish blues singer," and probably the only one at that.) Vastly superior is the debut of Tony Rosato's best character, roadie Chick Monk, who, after suffering a hernia, becomes a marriage counselor. Rosato's Monk still insists on running his sessions as if he is putting on a stadium rock concert, complete with a dry ice machine and a complex system of lights, microphones (which he exhaustively checks and re-checks), cables, and speakers. Rosato's character is a spoof on legendary rock stage manager Chip Monck, who counts among his credits the Monterey International Pop Music Festival and extensive work with the Rolling Stones.

Finally, Levy's outrageously perverted Raoul Wilson makes his third appearance. Though not as depraved as the character's previous sketch, Wilson still finds time to espouse the virtues of porn magazines (not just the pictures, but the "good reading," like the "stories about young girls moving into new apartment buildings") while also confessing to enjoying girls whether they're "sixty or fourteen." As the sketch ends, Wilson is still trying to back out of that last statement, as even he realizes that prepubescent girls should not be noted as objects of desire. Even if he thinks they are.

Show 61 *(SCTV Television Network)*

1. Sunrise Semester: Man's Ability to Imitate
2. CCTA / NORCA commercial
3. SCTV News teaser
4. Great White North: Using snowshoes for spatulas
5. Monster Chiller Horror Theatre: The Odd Couple
6. Sea Talk promo
7. SCTV News: Products plugged
8. Comment with David Brinkley: The Viletones at CBGB
9. The Invisible Man promo
10. Cooking with Marcello: Lobster Cacciatore

What to watch for: SCTV News.
Levy's Earl Camembert has previously bent his journalistic standards (if indeed he

ever had any) in the face of sponsorship pressure (show 48), but never before has he so blatantly made an effort to ingratiate himself to corporate America as in this segment. Here Camembert's news items are no more than thinly veiled commercials for Tootsie Rolls ("guaranteed goodness") and Hertz ("friendly and helpful"). Although pretending to be offended, Robertson unabashedly mimics his partner by quickly plugging several agencies and products related to his upcoming vacation. An incisive take on the ever-worsening commercialization of local news that plays even better more than two decades after it originally aired.

One of the most nondescript episodes of SCTV's third season, featuring several average pieces. Most notably are two sketch premieres — Moranis's David Brinkley (first seen in show 54) gets his first "Comment" segment, while Tony Rosato's Marcello Sebastiano (first seen in show 57) has his first "Cooking with Marcello" sketch.

The "Marcello" piece is the deadlier of the two — it says something about the blandness of Rosato's supposedly signature character that this isn't even the worst of the "Marcello" bunch (that sketch is in show 67). Here Rosato attempts to cook Lobster Cacciatore while inadvertently conjuring up more memories of the lobster scene in Woody Allen's Annie Hall than anything resembling laughter. This weak segment unfortunately wouldn't stop Rosato from doing a similar sketch involving Chicken Cacciatore in show 76.

Conversely, Moranis's premiere "Comment" piece works wonderfully, as a beat-up David Brinkley shares his thoughts on, of all things, a recent concert by Toronto punk band The Viletones. Calling punk "the only decent current force in popular music," Brinkley is disgusted at the behavior of those who attend punk shows, although not because his expectations are unrealistic: "I don't mind getting wet, or for that matter, bleeding," he remarks. Already shredding Brinkley's image as a distinguished and reserved newscaster, Moranis would top this outing with his "quality smoke" editorial in show 74.

While no debut, Flaherty has a strong "Monster Chiller Horror Theatre" segment, as the show has inexplicably scheduled the Jack Lemmon/Walter Matthau film *The Odd Couple*. Clearly thinking on his feet, Count Floyd proceeds to lie about the movie's plot, claiming that the film is about a "real clean" guy and another guy who "drinks blood and kills people." Partly because of the absence of Candy's Dr. Tongue, Flaherty's Count Floyd did not have a strong third season; this sketch is his best of the year.

Show 62 *(SCTV Television Network)*

1. Shakespeare in the Park with Norman Gorman promo
2. Cheryl Kinsey: Traveling Sexologist
3. Great White North: Stuff that bugs us
4. The Merv Griffin Show promo
5. Guy Caballero: SCTV coin
6. Participaction PSA

7. Flashing Eyes promo
8. Mel's Rock Pile: Speed of Light

What to watch for: The Merv Griffin Show.
Rick Moranis debuts yet another impression in this parody of the long running talk show. What makes Moranis's Merv Griffin different from his other impressions is Moranis takes liberties with Griffin; specifically, he plays him as a cross between the actual Merv and his own flamboyantly gay Guy Friday character. His Griffin was never more flamboyant than in this sketch, largely due to his interaction with the openly gay Liberace (Thomas). Here Griffin and Liberace delight in examining their jacket linings while also fawning over the bare chest of Incredible Hulk *star Lou Ferrigno (Rosato).*

Most notable in this episode is the completion of the long evolution of the program hosted by Eugene Levy's Rockin' Mel Slirrup, which is finally called "Mel's Rock Pile," the third (after "SCTV Boogie" and "SCTV Disco") and final name for the program. Not only has the program evolved, so has Levy's Slirrup, a creation that has become sharper each time out. In this sketch, Levy puts the finishing touches on Mel's trademark dance while also solidifying the character's status as a nerd who continually falls prey to tricks and abuse from the show's teenaged dancers. Here Rosato, Moranis, Flaherty, and writer Dick Blasucci all pretend to have the surname "Blough" while claiming to come from a school (Greenback High) that obviously doesn't exist.

After some mixed appearances in supporting roles, Andrea's repressed sexologist Cheryl Kinsey gets her best sketch to date as she gives free sex advice to a couple (Thomas and Duke) whom she unashamedly spies upon. Recognizing her obsession with the couple, Thomas finally invites Kinsey to join them, which leads Martin to revive one of Kinsey's favorite bedroom lines — "Make me a woman, big boy"— from her first appearance in show 5.

Elsewhere, Joe Flaherty shines in three sketches: First, his New Yorker Norman Gorman stars in a very low-rent version of "Shakespeare in the Park," where he plays Hamlet with an embarrassingly thick New York accent. Then Guy Caballero (still erroneously being referred to as "station manager and owner") delivers a message about a gold SCTV anniversary coin that can be purchased in two different sizes — a $35,000 size or a smaller one for just seven dollars. (Also in the Caballero sketch, *SCTV* acknowledges on-air the long delay between seasons two and three, while also making an indirect reference to Dr. Charles Allard, the businessman helping to finance *SCTV*'s third season.) Finally, Flaherty's "Flashing Eyes" sketch brings back cruel interviewer Chuck Clark from show 38's "4th Degree."

Lost on most American viewers is this show's PSA for Participaction, an actual Canadian agency founded in 1971 that encouraged citizens to become physically fit. *SCTV*'s parody shows the agency's advice being followed in somewhat questionable ways: Two bums (Moranis and Thomas) fight over a bottle of booze while a young man runs away from police after snatching an old lady's purse. Probably not the physical activity the folks at Participaction had in mind.

Show 63 *(SCTV Television Network)*
1. Sunrise Semester with Veronica Swansong: Glamour
2. Edith Prickley: The Sammy Maudlin Show
3. Great White North: Miracle of back bacon
4. Stretch Your Arm promo
5. Ronny Barrett's Sports
6. Taxi Driver with Gregory Peck promo
7. Totacontrol commercial
8. Guy Caballero: Announcer flubs name
9. The Sammy Maudlin Show: Bobby Bittman and Bob Hope

What to watch for: The Sammy Maudlin Show.
Though not as sharp as most "Sammy Maudlin" sketches, this is still the finest piece on what is one of the season's weakest shows. Featuring a walk-on by Thomas's Bob Hope, the majority of the segment deals with Hope promoting a mini-series entitled "I Owe Peking Two Thousand Dollars" as well as a behind-the-scenes "making of" special. This premise spoofs an actual performance Hope gave in China in 1979 during which censorship and interpretation problems were dwarfed by the challenge of concocting a monologue with references that the Chinese would understand.

Hope's outtakes from the making of special—guests often bring outtakes to "Maudlin"—imagines what it must have been like backstage as Hope and his writers tried to brainstorm jokes that a Chinese audience would appreciate. Though apparently an accurate depiction of the situation—when Thomas showed Hope the piece, Hope told him, "That's exactly what it was like"—as well as being Thomas's favorite Bob Hope sketch, the outtakes run on far too long.

Another problem with the sketch is the unspoken absence of Maudlin's sidekick, William B. Williams, played by John Candy. With the previous "Maudlin" sketch (show 45), Williams's thinly veiled contempt for Levy's Bobby Bittman was beginning to add comedic tension to the proceedings. Fortunately, there is an interesting dynamic in the sketch between Hope and Bittman: Bittman barely bothers to hide his disgust when his pedestrian stand-up routine is interrupted by Hope's walk-on.

A disappointing episode, not only featuring an overlong "Maudlin" sketch, but also several forgettable shorter pieces. Newcomers Robin Duke and Tony Rosato are responsible for two of the worst segments; in one, Rosato lamely envisions gossip columnist Rona Barrett as a male sports reporter, while elsewhere Duke portrays an old Hollywood actress (a combination of Veronica Lake and Gloria Swanson) struggling to still look glamorous with the assistance of an effeminate director (Moranis).

This episode isn't helped by a weak Guy Caballero segment consisting only of the announcer botching Caballero's name. What's left, then, is a typically funny "Great White North," in which Doug delivers a feverishly paced monologue about how he and his brother Bob were raised by wolves. Even better is the first of several *Taxi Driver* parodies featuring unlikely celebrities — here Flaherty's exaggerated take on Gregory Peck — performing the celebrated "Are you talking to me?" scene from the Martin Scorsese film.

Show 64 *(SCTV Television Network)*

1. Crazy Crafts with Molly Earl: Bingo drop cans
2. SCTV News teaser
3. Great White North: Name that smoke
4. Tom Snyder M.D. promo
5. SCTV News: Earl disco roller skates
6. Grizzly Abrams
7. Hugh Betcha's Night Gallery
8. Mel Torme and Bob and Doug McKenzie anthems

What to watch for: Grizzly Abrams.
This parody of the wilderness show The Life and Times of Grizzly Adams *contains two of SCTV's most satisfying visual gags: First, Abrams (Thomas) tries to create fire by rubbing two sticks together but succeeds only in blowing himself up; then Abrams tries to send his pet turtle (in the original series, Adams's pet was a bear) to get help from some dim-witted locals. But in a shockingly funny conclusion, by the time the sluggish turtle leads the group to Abrams, all that remains is a very hairy skeleton.*

A very strong episode thanks in no small part to Robin Duke and Tony Rosato. Duke contributes the quintessential "Crazy Crafts" sketch as Molly Earl spotlights a contraption known as the "bingo drop can" that allows wearers to hands-free put out a cigarette while simultaneously playing several Bingo cards.

Not to be outdone, Rosato gives a fine performance in a parody of the Rod Serling TV series *Night Gallery*. The sketch, about a loser who buys a "date record," strikes a fine balance between creepy and comedy as the recorded date slowly becomes eerily realistic. In an unexpected twist, Thomas portrays a jealous husband who kills Rosato to the obvious delight of host Hugh Betcha (Flaherty).

The old guard of *SCTV* is also in fine form here: Eugene and Joe connect for a news segment that has Earl Camembert roller-skating onto the set. (In one of *SCTV*'s most dated references, Floyd Robertson calls Earl's skates "cheap Jimmy McNichol hand-me-downs," a reference to the short-lived TV series *California Fever*.) Far from letting Robertson get the best of him, this piece features Earl as his most confident, chiding his co-anchor for having "no concept of the times we're living in," and cheerfully pointing out that he is younger than the curmudgeonly Robertson. No doubt Levy intended this as a good-natured jab at his partner Flaherty, who is in fact more than five years older than Levy.

All of this material barely makes room for one of the best "Great White North" segments (during which Bob and Doug play a variation on "Name that Tune" called "Name that Smoke"), in addition to Rick Moranis's classic take on Mel Torme performing the American national anthem.

Show 65 *(SCTV Television Network)*

1. Sunrise Semester with Phil: Do-It-Yourself Advertising
2. Chick Monk: Roadie for the Defense promo
3. SCTV News teaser
4. Great White North: Star Wars
5. SCTV News: Mr. Earl Doll
6. Joni Mitchell "For Dogs Only" commercial
7. Bill Needle's Mailbag: Celebrities
8. SCTV Premiere: Return to the Planet of Empires (with VideoTech commercial)
9. Dialing for Dollars: The Fly Returns from Beneath the Planet of the Apes part 19

What to watch for: SCTV News.
Not since the "SCTV News" segment in show 42, in which Floyd Robertson mocked Earl Camembert for getting knifed in prison, has Robertson's contempt for his colleague been so wickedly evident. Here Robertson introduces the "Mr. Earl" doll, that, like Saturday Night Live*'s Mr. Bill, is abused and tortured strictly for laughs. Levy's reaction to the doll is a priceless look of horror, hatred, disgust, and embarrassment. Meanwhile, Flaherty's Robertson is beautifully smug.*

Somewhat of a throwback to the second season shows that had a running theme — this episode features two sketches concerning the *Star Wars* films (at which time there were only two). First up is "Great White North," which sees Doug unveiling his not-so-uncanny Darth Vader impression ("Good day, eh? You got any beer?"); besides being very funny, the sketch is notably dated, as the brothers fear that by the time the thirtieth *Star Wars* is released, "movies will be, what, six bucks?" The sketch is also prophetic in that Bob worries that they will soon be kicked out of the studio, which is exactly what happens in show 74.

Better still is a scene in which Flaherty's Guy Caballero introduces a pirated copy of the latest *Star Wars* picture (part 34). The film, premiering on SCTV before being released in theatres (because as Caballero lamely explains, "they wanted to see how it would look on TV"), is quickly ruined by a huge copyright infringement notice and the sound of police knocking on Caballero's door. Despite its unlikely premise — the stingy Caballero would never pay the large sum necessary to acquire such a counterfeit tape — the piece works and is also visionary about the very real problem that video piracy would soon become.

This episode also features the debut of Dave Thomas's self-described "SCTV critic-at- large" Bill Needle. First seen in a series of "Mailbag" segments (an improvement over a show 43 sketch that featured a similar Thomas character named Bob Clark), Needle would soon become Thomas's best original character and the source of some of *SCTV*'s most vicious attacks both on real celebrities (show 95's "Shoot for the Stars") and other *SCTV* characters (show 89's "Theatre Beat").

And, thanks to Eugene Levy, this episode features the first worthwhile "Sunrise Semester" of the third season as Levy's manic pitchman Phil delivers a lecture on do-it-yourself advertising. This appearance by Phil is a bit of an oddity in that in Phil's first and last sketches, he is the owner of Phil's Nails; here he christens himself "the Garment King." Perhaps his garment business didn't work out (could his commercials be to blame?) and he was forced to return to selling nails.

Show 66 *(SCTV Television Network)*

1. Edith Prickley: Hollywood Salutes Its Extras
2. Mamorex commercial: David Seville
3. Bill Needle's Mailbag: Show cut in half
4. Taxi Driver with Dick Cavett promo
5. Great White North: Exercise
6. Howard's Bristol Cream commercial
7. Sneak Previews
8. Hawaii Five-Ho promo
9. An SCTV Special Presentation: Hollywood Salutes Its Extras part 1
10. Tri-promo 1
11. An SCTV Special Presentation: Hollywood Salutes Its Extras part 2

What to watch for: Sneak Previews.
This classic sketch parodies the now-retired PBS movie review show initially hosted by Roger Ebert and the late Gene Siskel. Though Thomas (Ebert) and Flaherty (Siskel) don't look like their real-life counterparts nor do they try very hard to imitate the critics' voices or mannerisms, the piece works thanks to its silliness.

In the sketch, Roger and Gene look at the latest Star Wars *film (perhaps this sketch was pulled from the previous show to improve this weaker episode?), which amounts to nothing more than an astonishingly cheap sequence of toys being blown up good. Robert Altman's* Popeye *is also skewered, as Gene and Roger dub Altman's fictional "Henry" (also based on the comic strip of the same name) the "dog of the week." Here (in a scene reminiscent of show 28's "House of Cats") a small but savage dog attacks both Gene and Roger, leaving them barely able to continue the show. Cultural icons-in-the-making Siskel and Ebert would go on to be parodied countless times, on innumerable programs, but never with more success than here.*

Much of the time on this episode is devoted to an uninspired salute to movie extras. The tales told by "actors" played by Rick Moranis, Andrea Martin, and Tony Rosato should be funny because they have deluded themselves into thinking they are on par with "co-stars" like Elizabeth Taylor and Charlton Heston. Instead, their stories are just sadly pathetic. The only notable aspect of the lengthy sketch is Flaherty's turn as host Kirk Douglas. Contrary to the tribute theme of the piece, Douglas regards extras as cattle, claiming that when working on a movie, he likes to see how close he can get to them without acknowledging their presence. Flaherty himself acknowledges the tediousness of the sketch by yawning excessively before mercifully ending the piece.

Elsewhere, Tony Rosato scores as Hawaiian crooner Don Ho in a parody of the cop show *Hawaii Five-O*. (The catchphrase "Book 'em, Danno," is replaced by "Danno, book me," when Ho discovers that Frank Sinatra needs an opening act.) Rosato's parody of Ella Fitzgerald's Memorex commercials is less successful, though this doesn't stop him from doing a sequel in show 71.

Rick and Dave's "Great White North" provides this show with another highlight, as the topic of fitness causes Doug to demonstrate one of his favorite exercises — bending a wolf pelt. "I can feel it in my triceps and in my cornea," Doug claims. By this point in season three, viewers could feel Bob and Doug's value to *SCTV*— the characters could always deliver, even when surrounding sketches could not.

Show 67 *(SCTV Television Network)*

1. Men On Women
2. Guy Caballero: Men On Women
3. Great White North: How to roll your own when you got mitts on
4. Cooking with Marcello: Stuntwoman
5. Taxi Driver with Woody Allen promo
6. Bill Needle's Mailbag: Cut to thirty seconds
7. Guy Caballero: The Irwin Allen Show
8. The Irwin Allen Show

What to watch for: Men On Women.
The final sketch to feature Eugene Levy's Raoul Wilson, possibly the most oversexed male on the planet, is an offensive delight. A talk show in which men discuss women and women's bikinis in strictly the crudest terms, this is one of Levy's best performances from season three. But Levy is almost upstaged by Dave Thomas, who plays (along with Rick Moranis) one of two "real guys" who share Wilson's obsession with sex. Thomas's oafish character gets so overcome by the erotic nature of the discussion that he eventually loses the ability to speak and can only muster guttural cries of "yeah, yeah, yeah."

In a follow-up to the piece, Flaherty's Guy Caballero is forced to cancel "Men On Women" after receiving an angry call from his wife, the never-seen Googie. The fact that Guy is so quickly intimidated by his wife is reminiscent of a similar encounter with Edith Prickley in show 36 and serves as further evidence that Guy is easily threatened by headstrong women. Indeed, Guy is so threatened by Googie that not only does he cancel "Men on Women," he also apparently fires Raoul Wilson, who is never seen nor heard from again on SCTV.

A fine episode marred by a lousy "Cooking with Marcello" sketch featuring a nonsensical guest appearance by a stuntwoman (Duke). As the weak sketch unfolds, the question of "Why would a cooking show feature an interview with a stuntwoman?" is eventually replaced by "Is it too late to bring back John Candy and Catherine O'Hara?"

Fortunately, the episode also features "Men on Women" as well as "The Irwin Allen Show." Reminiscent of show 58's "The Lone Ranger Show," "The Irwin Allen Show" is a talk show parody hosted by "Master of Disaster" film producer and director Irwin Allen (Moranis), who was so nicknamed because of his run of successful disaster movies in the 1970s. During the talk show (and mirroring what happens in his films), his array of stars meet with various horrific deaths, most memorably Red Buttons (Thomas), who gets viciously attacked by a swarm of stuffed bees. Although funny, the guest appearance of Flaherty as Charlton Heston is a bit of a cheat, since Allen had nothing to do with *Earthquake*, the disaster film being alluded to with Heston's presence.

This episode is also notable for the most extensive Moe Green references since the Harold Ramis character was kidnapped by the Leutonian Liberation Front in show 29. During a set-up piece for the "Irwin Allen" sketch, Caballero is interrupted by a phone call from Green's kidnappers, who reiterate their ransom demands. Because they have obviously tired of Green, their asking price quickly decreases from one million dollars to "send a cab." To the perverse delight of Caballero, the call is punctuated by sounds of Green being beaten. Obviously Caballero felt the station was doing fine without Green, as *SCTV* was doing fine without Harold Ramis.

Show 68 *(SCTV Television Network)*

1. Got a Minute?
2. Great White North: Mystery Guest
3. Taxi Driver with Bob Hope promo
4. Big Brother wraparound: Guy Caballero and Edith Prickley messages
5. Big Brother wraparound: New Year's Eve 1983 party
6. Big Brother wraparound: Comrade Kangaroo
7. Big Brother wraparound: Comrade Allen
8. Big Brother wraparound: Doublethink promo
9. Big Brother wraparound: The Praise Big Brother Show
10. Big Brother wraparound: Edith Prickley and Guy Caballero conclusions

What to watch for: Doublethink.
As part of a wraparound exposing what television programming would look like in George Orwell's vision of 1984, this sketch takes Orwell's concept of "doublethink" and places it into the context of an inane game show. In Orwell's novel, through brainwashing known as "doublethink," citizens come to believe what the totalitarian party tells them even though they know the opposite to be true. Here beliefs are tested in a quiz show that rewards razor blades and shoelaces (necessities in Orwell's novel) to contestants who answer as the party wants, while simultaneously sentencing truthful contestants to death. By taking one of the most chilling aspects of Orwell's novel and turning it into an upbeat game show (hosted by an unctuous Eugene Levy), SCTV *creates the perfect mesh of tortuous television in a tortuous society.*

In the clearest foreshadowing yet of the complex wraparounds that were to become commonplace in the forthcoming NBC episodes, *SCTV* here presents what could be called their first high-concept episode: As the clock strikes midnight on New Year's Eve 1983, the SCTV network suddenly surrenders to

Telescreen, the name given to the only network television available in an Orwellian society that never ceases to remind its viewers that "Big Brother (who bears an uncanny resemblance to Orson Welles) is watching you."

The skill in this episode lies not only in the very real sense of disquiet that pervades the show (particularly alarming is the sign-on of Telescreen, complete with various disturbing sound effects and ominous warnings such as "it is a crime to adjust Telescreen"), but also in the lameness that is Telescreen programming, which is strikingly similar in form to programming in the pre–Orwellian world. Apparently Big Brother's totalitarian party can succeed in brainwashing its citizens and constructing the technology to monitor their each and every move, but they can't do anything substantial about TV programming. Perhaps *SCTV*'s point is that then-current television executives are as oppressive, tyrannical, suffocating, and uncreative as the people responsible for Telescreen.

Whatever the message, the Telescreen shows include content unlike anything ever presented on *SCTV*. Dave Thomas revives his Bob "Captain Kangaroo" Keeshan impression (formerly used for "Captain Combat") for an appearance as "Comrade Kangaroo," who instructs his child viewers to turn in their parents should they hear them having sex, an act forbidden (as in *1984*) under Big Brother. Late in the sketch, Thomas cracks while reading a promotion for the next installment, when "we'll watch Bunny Rabbit get vaporized and stuffed to make decorations for Hate Week"; the emotional line reading could be interpreted to mean either Keeshan is too compassionate to host such a hateful program or even that Keeshan's new role has made him viciously bloodthirsty.

Also memorable is Rick Moranis and Robin Duke's parody of Jim and Tammy Faye Bakker's *PTL Club* called "The Praise Big Brother Show." After Jim Bakker's sex scandal in the late eighties, parodies of the two would become commonplace, but *SCTV*'s satire of the two was among the first. (Still ahead of its time, *SCTV* would again feature a parody of Tammy Faye — then portrayed by Catherine O'Hara — in show 88.)

SCTV squeezes in a lot in this half hour episode: Besides the Telescreen programming, there is also a scene set at a SCTV New Year's Eve party that is notable for the first shot of Bill Needle (Thomas) and Guy Caballero (Flaherty) having a confidential conversation; later *SCTV* storylines (shows 84 and 85) would find these two characters as improbable but compatible partners in crime. Dave Thomas also scores as Bob Hope in the best of the running "Taxi Driver" promos ("I didn't let Darryl Zanuck talk to me that way") and as Doug McKenzie in a "Great White North" segment in which Doug tries to disguise himself as a "mystery guest."

Show 69 *(SCTV Television Network)*

1. Sunrise Semester with Angus Crock: Astrology
2. Monster Chiller Horror Theatre: Georgy Girl

3. Great White North: Best groups
4. SCTV News: Earl at Pit Bull Fight part 1
5. Comment with David Brinkley: What the hell is wrong with my barber?
6. SCTV News: Earl at Pit Bull Fight part 2
7. Cruisin' Gourmet promo
8. Two Way TV
9. Bill Needle's Mailbag: Show cut to 15 seconds
10. Crazy Crafts with Molly Earl promo
11. Sermonette: Rabbi Karlov

What to watch for: Comment.
As good as Earl Camembert's failed "undercover" report from a pit bull fight is — Floyd Robertson succinctly describes the disaster as "another awful report from a mediocre journalist" — the David Brinkley (Rick Moranis) commentary placed in the middle of the segment is better. While Dave Thomas was busy deflating the image of storied newsman Walter Cronkite, Moranis was more mean-spirited in turning journalist David Brinkley into a complete moron. Sporting a head of hair that looks like it had been cut and styled by a hedge trimmer, here Moranis's Brinkley simply grouses about the incompetence of his barber. While Levy's Camembert had previously shown a lack of professionalism in using an editorial to voice a personal vendetta (show 36), Moranis tops him here.

The experimentation of the previous episode reverts to a solid if underwhelming series of stand-alone sketches. Most notable here is Dave Thomas's outrageous "Cruisin' Gourmet" promo, a distasteful cross-pollination of a cooking program with the gay-themed Al Pacino thriller *Cruising*. (The piece also includes a nod to Pacino's *And Justice for All*). As Thomas mentions in his book, the fact that he got away with simulating a homosexual sex act on a chained-up turkey is remarkable. Perhaps the sketch's fairly clear reference to a crude sexual practice was lost on censors, as not only did the sketch air here, it was also (partially) repeated on show 88. (Contrary to Thomas's book, the sketch did not air during a NBC "best of" episode.)

In the third season, Rick Moranis wrote a few sketches that made clear his fascination with technology. One of the cleverest of these sketches, a demonstration of a product that through "gizmo communication" allows viewers to bank, shop, or pay bills through their TV, appears here. Not only does Moranis foreshadow the Internet with this piece, he also predicts the success of pay-per-view television. The difference between Moranis's "Two Way TV" and pay-per-view is that Moranis's technology only offers a limited variety of programs that the viewer can vote to watch. Agreeing with those who would argue that television programmers are obsessed with sex, Moranis forces his obvious favorite — *The Happy Hooker Goes to Hollywood* — on the home audience, going so far as to escort the film's title character onto the set of the clear audience favorite, *Leave It to Beaver*.

Show 70 *(SCTV Television Network)*

1. Gordon Lightfoot Sings Every Song Ever Written commercial
2. Cooking with Marcello: Live from the Vatican
3. Great White North: Sports
4. Crazy Crafts with Molly Earl: Bob
5. Guy Caballero: Alpha Channel
6. Alpha Channel
7. Bill Needle's Mailbag: Show cut to 7.5 seconds
8. Dialing for Dollars: The Partridge Family Goes to Mars

What to watch for: Alpha Channel.
With the advent of DVDs and the proliferation of their so-called "bonus features," behind-the-scenes segments on even the worst movies are now commonplace. Because of this, the Alpha Channel sketch, which introduces a new network that presents "movies while they're being made," is more dated than most SCTV sketches.

But the piece still holds up due to the cast's impressions, including three done here for the first time: Dave Thomas and Andrea Martin are Neil Simon and Marsha Mason; the autobiographical slant of Simon's films is mocked as he simply types whatever irrelevant musing comes out of Mason's mouth, while Martin skews Mason's tendency to cry uncontrollably in films. Joe Flaherty spoofs Alan Alda's "nice guy" reputation — here Alda complains vehemently about a "punk" fellow actor trying to "upstage" him. But the best gag in the sketch may be the sight of the "Alpha Channel De-Scrambler," an enormous and ugly box positioned on a TV set a third its size.

The second episode in a row to feature a sub-par series of brief sketches. But some do stand out: One of the best in a long line of record album commercials is here, as one of Canada's favorite sons, Gordon Lightfoot, gets mocked in a spot for a 379(!) album set that boldly features Lightfoot performing "Every Song Ever Written." Lightfoot's easy-listening folk style (heard in hits like "Sundown" and "If You Could Read My Mind") is mocked as Lightfoot (Moranis) turns in similar-sounding versions of songs as diverse as "Good King Wenceslas" and "Happy Birthday to You." Note the juxtaposition between Harvey K-Tel's manic pitch and Lightfoot's delicate blandness.

Not seen on-camera during the Lightfoot spot, Moranis has another off-screen role here: He plays a deranged man who calls into Walter Cronkite's "Dialing for Dollars" program because he has been driven insane by the program's logo. Noting that the dollar sign in front of the logo doesn't substitute for a letter like the dollar sign at the end of the logo does, he angrily asserts that the logo actually reads "SDIALING FOR DOLLARS." In retaliation, he threatens to put Cronkite's head in a vise, tightening it until the veteran newsman's mustache comes off.

While rookie Moranis already had countless characters under his belt, the other *SCTV* newcomers weren't as lucky. While his roadie Chick Monk was a more interesting persona, Tony Rosato obviously felt his Marcello character was his strongest. Robin Duke meanwhile basically created one recurring character, "Crazy Crafts" host Molly Earl. This being the first episode to feature full Marcello and Molly Earl sketches, it becomes clearer that Duke's creation is much more satisfying than Rosato's. While "Cooking with Marcello" meanders, Duke's piece — featuring a hungover Molly Earl with her "boyfriend" Bob (writer Dick Blasucci) — is very sharp. Based on their work on *SCTV*, it's not surprising that on their subsequent tour of duty on *Saturday Night Live*, Duke lasted three seasons while Rosato was fired after just one.

Show 71 *(SCTV Television Network)*

1. Sunrise Semester with Edith Prickley: Basic Photography
2. Mamorex commercial: Tom Waits and Rickie Lee Jones
3. Great White North: Going bowling loaded
4. Tri-promo 2
5. Bill Needle's Mailbag: Show cut to three seconds
6. Guy Caballero: Midnight Express Special
7. Midnight Express Special

What to watch for: Midnight Express Special.
One of the more ambitious pieces of the third season, this sketch combines not only the film Midnight Express *and the television show* Midnight Special — *resulting in musical acts performing from a Turkish prison — but also fine impressions from Levy and Rosato of the show's unlikely hosts, Bud Abbott and Lou Costello.*

The Abbott and Costello material, broadcast in grainy black and white, features uncanny replications of the physical comedy and classic wordplay of the comedy team. Only this time the pair find themselves in "the hassle of their lives" after Lou is discovered holding a package of hashish at a Turkish airport. A highlight is a spoof of the famous "Who's on First?" routine, as Levy's Abbott struggles to get Rosato's Costello to introduce the Robbie Robertson–led group of musicians known simply as The Band. Not knowing that the name of the band is actually The Band, Costello asks, "Who's the band?" "No, The Who's on next week," Abbott replies.

The musical portions of the sketch — here the cast members lip-synch to the actual performer's recordings — are reminiscent of "Rock Concert" from show 43, except that this time the musicians don't get blown up, they get busted for suspicion of drug use based on interpretations of the songs performed (e.g., John Denver's "Rocky Mountain High," Anne Murray's "Snowbird"). Rick Moranis also appears as Wolfman Jack (looking like an actual wolfman) alongside drug enforcer Dave Thomas: The two freely smoke from a huge hookah pipe even while they are busy busting others for drug use with little or no evidence. There are a lot of elements in this complex sketch, but they are woven together skillfully.

SCTV has little problem nailing this episode's complicated (and lengthy) "Midnight Express Special" piece, but it misses with the more straightforward sketches that open the show. A sketch on photography with Edith Prickley is further proof that the "Sunrise Semester" segments were brought back not because they worked, but because they were easy and cheap to produce.

Meanwhile, the second of two Ella Fitzgerald (Rosato) commercial parodies is no improvement on the first (show 66). Only the McKenzie brothers make the first third of the episode worthwhile, with a segment featuring the debut of their ventriloquism act.

Show 72 *(SCTV Television Network)*

1. Sunrise Semester with Edith Prickley: Disasters in the Home
2. Nasex Nasal Deodorant commercial
3. Bill Needle's Mailbag: Muffled at top
4. Great White North: Stuff that really bugs us
5. The Freddie de Cordova Show promo
6. Cookery Crock with Angus Crock
7. Quincy: Cartoon Coroner

What to watch for: *Quincy: Cartoon Coroner.*
A parody of the then-current series Quincy, *this sketch is most notable for featuring the premiere of Joe Flaherty's exasperated Jack Klugman impression. Here Flaherty embellishes Klugman's tendency to speak* very loudly *to contribute one of season three's most intense and memorable performances.*

The original Quincy character was a coroner who investigated suspicious cases that often led to murder charges; Flaherty's Quincy is a "cartoon coroner" who investigates the so-called "natural causes" death of Sylvester the Cat ("I've got a hunch there's more to this case than meets the eye, and I'm gonna prove it!"). Flaherty interrogates Tweety Bird and Spike the Dog, but it's his lengthy and detailed summation of the case that is a wonder. Ranting on a long list of horrible accidents that eventually befell Sylvester ("Tweety went up to him and he stuck some dynamite right in his ears!"), Flaherty exhausts himself. Perhaps the physical exertion involved in playing the role is the reason Flaherty appeared as Klugman only two more times.

This fine episode is anchored by two pieces: Flaherty's "Quincy" sketch and Thomas's "Cookery Crock" piece. While Thomas's surly Angus Crock character was a smart season three creation, Thomas had problems finding a good forum for him. After appearing in two weak "Sunrise Semester" pieces, Thomas finally gives the character a funny if unfocused sketch with — oddly enough — his own cooking show.

The strongest element of "Cookery Crock" is an appearance by Joe Flaherty as Gregory Peck as Dr. Josef Mengele from *The Boys from Brazil*. Why an actor would appear (on a cooking show, no less) not as himself but rather as a character from a film is unimportant; what's notable here is how Thomas and Flaherty work in a tasteless joke based on Dr. Mengele's human experiments and then quickly dispense of Peck, as he is scared off by the same breed of dogs that mauled his character in *Brazil*. Thomas (who calls this sketch a "personal favorite") later claimed that the dogs were indeed dangerous and that Joe "barely made it to safety" before they were subdued. Although slightly anarchic, the Peck material is bizarre enough to work, as do seemingly disparate sections in which Crock flirts with a 15-year-old audience member, gets drunk on scotch, and plays a blues song called "Edinburgh Town" with Tony Rosato and Rick Moranis.

Also strong in this show are two short pieces: A commercial parody for a nasal deodorant is reminiscent of the brief pieces done in the show's first year — note how Levy just happens to have a large graphic of the inner workings of the human nose framed and hung in his bedroom. Equally clever is a promo for a talk show hosted by Johnny Carson's executive producer Freddie de Cordova, in which de Cordova attempts to interview guests from his producer's post far off-screen.

Show 73 *(SCTV Television Network)*

1. Starting Out with Bill Needle promo
2. Eskimo Arts commercial
3. Edith Prickley: The Mating Game
4. SCTV News teaser
5. Great White North: Why are parking lots so small at donut places
6. Taxi Driver with Sid Dithers promo
7. SCTV News: Walter Cronkite
8. The Mating Game

What to watch for: SCTV News.
An inspired remake of the introductory "SCTV News" segment from SCTV's very first show. On that premiere, Floyd Robertson had all of the important news items while Earl Camembert was stuck with uninteresting local stories; to balance out the discrepancy, Earl concocted a false story about a pack of rabies-carrying caribou run amok. Here Walter Cronkite (Thomas) makes a surprise appearance on the "SCTV News" set and agrees to sit in for an awe-struck Camembert. Disgusted by Camembert's "chintzy" local items, Cronkite, as Earl had done before him, resorts to making up a sensational story of his own. In response, Robertson hands Cronkite the cruelest insult he can muster — "You're worse than Earl" — sending an embarrassed Cronkite slinking off the set. Seems Earl's rotten journalism is a plague that can bring down all who come near it — even Walter Cronkite.

Here Dave Thomas's Bill Needle character gets his best sketch yet as he hosts a program featuring performers on the rise. Foreshadowing "Shoot for the Stars" (show 95), Needle is an impossibly cruel host, relentlessly badgering optimistic young stars (Rosato and Duke) with stories about the difficulty of show business until the two guests are reduced to tears.

Thomas also stands out in this episode's longest sketch, a parody of the game show *The Dating Game* that brings together a trio of season three characters — Thomas' Angus Crock, Rosato's Marcello Sebastiano, and Moranis's Rabbi Karlov — as the show's eligible bachelors. Crock is outrageously cruel to both host Edith Prickley and the bachelorette (a grotesque Robin Duke), referring to Prickley as an "old cow" and Duke as a "big fat hog." Oddly enough, after strong appearances in this sketch and last episode's "Cookery Crock," Thomas would all but retire Angus Crock, reviving him just once more for an uninteresting "Sunrise Semester" in show 96.

Two characters with much more life left in them are Bob and Doug McKenzie; this episode features one of their strongest segments as the two lament about the size of parking lots at donut stores. Note Doug's story of waiting two-and-a-half hours to be served at Donut World, a wait endured in vain, notes Bob, because there are no waiters at Donut World. It's in exchanges like this that we realize that Bob, however minimally, is the smarter of the two McKenzie brothers. This sketch is referenced on the McKenzies' first album: The track "Peter's Donuts" ends with Bob and Doug getting a ticket for illegally parking in the street because — surprise — the lot at the donut store was too small.

Show 74 *(SCTV Television Network)*
1. Sunrise Semester with Norman Gorman: Societal Behavior
2. American Express with Henry Moore commercial
3. SCTV Special Report with Cassie Mackeral
4. SCTV News teaser
5. Great White North: Hosehead got us booted out of the studio
6. SCTV News: WASASL
7. Comment with David Brinkley: When will the street dealer be able to consistently provide quality smoke?
8. Gene Shalit's America
9. Dialing for Dollars: Space Week

What to watch for: Comment.
Twenty episodes earlier, Rick Moranis introduced his impression of David Brinkley, portraying the veteran newsman as a boozer. To top that, here Moranis does Brinkley as a stoner, spouting off about the poor quality of street drugs and bemoaning the lack of research into why dope makes its users so hungry. This classic piece is remarkable not only for the lack of respect it affords one of the most celebrated journalists of the 20th century, but also for being one of the few SCTV *sketches to experiment in drug humor.*

A series of mostly average sketches, highlighted by the Brinkley piece and the final solid "SCTV News" segment of season three. After being disgraced five episodes ago at a pit bull fight, Earl Camembert is further embarrassed when a masculine woman (Duke), representing a group known as Women Against Stereotypical Alternative Sexual Lifestyles, easily beats him at arm-wrestling. Floyd Robertson also takes down Earl, whose humiliation is complete when Robertson invites a small child ("Hey, kid!") to arm-wrestle Earl. Not surprisingly, Earl loses to the boy several times in a row.

This episode marks the last "SCTV News" sketch for some time in which Camembert is embarrassed, injured, disgraced, or otherwise mortified. While Levy's Camembert will continue his streak of horrid journalism, he will from here on out do so in other forums, such as "One on the Town" or "Nightline Melonville." Appropriately enough, though, his final humiliation, coming on the day of his retirement, will again happen on the "SCTV News" set (show 134).

While "SCTV News" goes into semi-retirement, Levy here introduces his impression of Gene Shalit in a funny if cruelly sophomoric sketch exposing an exclusive Malibu restaurant that caters to three overweight and affluent celebrities: Orson Welles (without John Candy, Dave Thomas takes the role), William Conrad (Rosato), and Shelley Winters (Duke). The piece features some of *SCTV*'s most extended physical humor to date, including an ending in which the three weighty stars and Shalit pounce on a huge cake. Their thrashing about on the delicacy sends the establishment toppling over the seaside cliff upon which it is built.

An amusing four-episode arc in which Bob and Doug are thrown out of their SCTV studio because Bob broke a camera starts here: While it doesn't make sense that the two would have an outdoor show (it costs more to go on location and equipment is even more in danger), the pieces are a welcome change of pace for the brothers while also foreshadowing more ambitious McKenzie segments (shows 87 and 97).

This show is ultimately dragged down by the deadly appearance of Andrea Martin's Cassie Mackeral character, a creation that hadn't been seen in the previous 65 shows. Her fashion segment on this episode is one of the most interminable sketches of the season.

Show 75 *(SCTV Television Network)*

1. Sunrise Semester: Greek Travel with Alki Stereopolis
2. Edith Prickley: Mel's Rock Pile
3. Wide World of High Voices promo
4. Exercise is Easy with Lucky Ibsen
5. Great White North: Stolen Car
6. Mel's Rock Pile: Richard Harris

What to watch for: Mel's Rock Pile.
The finest sketch with Levy's Rockin' Mel Slirrup. The last of season three's lengthy music-oriented sketches (which also include "Lee A. Iococca's Rock Concert" and "Midnight Express Special"), this piece is broken up into two sections: A dance contest and an outrageous appearance by Dave Thomas as actor/singer Richard Harris.

The dance finals are obviously rigged, as Mel first awards the cash prize to Jerome Slirrup (Moranis), who not only shares Mel's last name but also bears a striking resemblance to the host. A near revolt of the show's dancers—including a 32-year-old Tony Rosato who is still in high school just to meet girls—forces Mel to change his mind. Note this is the first—but not the last—time Moranis would play a younger brother to one of Levy's creations; in later episodes, Rick would appear as Skip Bittman, struggling comedian and sibling to funnyman Bobby Bittman.

The highlight of the sketch is Dave Thomas's return as Richard Harris, a devastating impression that Thomas later referred to as "the hardest edge I ever took at anybody." This time out, Thomas skewers Harris's 1968 hit "MacArthur Park," a track that he summarized as "a non-singer singing the longest [over seven minutes], most pompous song in the world." Thomas's performance satirizes not only the original, but also the more pretentious late seventies remake by Donna Summer, which clocked in at nearly eighteen *minutes. Thomas's performance of the tune features a spastic dance that he performs during the long—very long—instrumental breaks.*

The end of the song, signaled by the music building to a crescendo and a guest "artist" helping Harris with the final high notes, obviously comes as a great relief to an exhausted Harris; the relief is unfortunately short-lived as an unruly audience member hurls a brick right at Harris's stomach. This sight gag (combined with Mel's blasé "Hey, who threw that brick?") is one of the biggest laughs of the season.

While "Mel's Rock Pile" takes up the majority of the episode, there are other notable sketches here: Robin Duke gets one of her lengthiest solo spots with an exercise show focusing on the importance of head expansion. Pieces like "Exercise is Easy" make it apparent that Duke wasted her time on *Saturday Night Live*; it is regrettable that *SCTV* couldn't cajole her back to the show after Catherine O'Hara left *again* after show 105.

Elsewhere, Thomas's appearance as high-voiced Richard Harris is nearly matched by his turn as high-voiced racing legend Jackie Stewart in a promo for a show called "Wide World of High Voices." As good as Thomas is, Moranis steals the piece with a new rendition of "The Needle and the Damage Done" performed by a "'luded up" Neil Young: "I phoned up Crosby and I phoned up Nash / Just to see if they wanted to buy some hash."

Andrea Martin's Edith Prickley, though overused by this point in the season, does have her best moment of the year here, as she is seen giving a back massage to a stressed-out (and aroused) Walter Cronkite (Thomas again). The only weak segment of the episode is "Sunrise Semester," which is an unnecessary re-shoot of a piece from show 4. "Sunrise Semester" is the only sign in this episode that *SCTV* was reaching the end of a long (but artistically satisfying) season.

Show 76 *(SCTV Television Network)*

1. Cooking with Marcello: Chicken Cacciatore
2. Great White North: Cops and where to look out for them
3. Fish 'n Chips promo
4. Logos Galore commercial
5. Monster Chiller Horror Theatre: The Dick Cavett Show with Bobby Bittman

What to watch for: The Dick Cavett Show.
Strong though SCTV*'s third season was, the year wasn't great for some of the show's best recurring characters: "The Sammy Maudlin Show" only appeared once in the twenty-six episodes, as some of the sketch's supporting cast—John Candy (William B.*

Williams) and Catherine O'Hara (Lola Heatherton)—were absent. This situation left Eugene Levy searching for new environments for his Bobby Bittman character, and in this episode an inspired one was discovered as the oily funnyman is paired up with Rick Moranis's pompous Dick Cavett.

Note that the Cavett talk show sketch is presented as the feature film on Count Floyd's "Monster Chiller Horror Theatre." Unlike the host's alter ego (anchorman Floyd Robertson), Flaherty's Count Floyd was also having a distinctly sub-par season, missing the presence of Candy's Dr. Tongue character. However, the nonsensical use of Count Floyd in this piece only serves to emphasize what a disappointment the persona was this year. Flaherty's Count Floyd would bounce back in seasons to come.

As for this episode's "Cavett" sketch, what's most immediately obvious about Bittman's appearance is that the insincere compliments that go over so well on Maudlin's show don't fly with the intellectual Cavett. "How wonderfully inane," Moranis's Cavett plainly states after Bittman tries to pay Cavett some bogus respects. Even deadlier is Cavett's response to Bittman's outtakes from his new movie "Funny Stuff"; instead of the laughter and the drying of eyes from Sammy and William B., Cavett says that the clips, which demonstrate Bittman's cruelty to his co-workers, were "appallingly crude" and had a "facist tone." Bittman, for his part, manages to maintain a little pride by walking off the show.

Before leaving, Bittman's appearance draws some interesting parallels to the work of Jerry Lewis, most directly in Bittman's promotion of his new book "The Complete Film-Maker," which is a parody of Lewis's 1971 tome The Total Film-Maker. Also, Bittman's somber portrayal of a clown in "Funny Stuff" is a nod to Lewis's role in what is one of the best-known unreleased films ever, The Day the Clown Cried. The idea of a clown as a figure of melodramatic pathos also interested Levy enough to have Bittman don clown makeup again for a disastrous film called "The Poor Slob," which was depicted in Levy's Cinemax special The Enigma of Bobby Bittman.

Despite the unnecessary Count Floyd material, Bittman on "Cavett" is a brilliant meeting of two completely unlike minds. Although Maudlin is missed throughout the third season, this is a most worthwhile change of pace for Levy's Bobby Bittman character.

What little time there is left on this episode is taken up with a wholly unfunny "Cooking with Marcello" segment that sees the chef fighting with an unruly chicken. Never on *SCTV* was so much time squandered on such an unworthy character as was wasted on Rosato's Marcello in the third season. Elsewhere, a brief promo touts a new sitcom starring Abe Vigoda and Erik Estrada, and Rick Moranis scores as a woefully inappropriate spokesperson for a logo company.

Show 77 *(SCTV Television Network)*

1. Edith Prickley: The Cisco Kid
2. Marlon Perkins' Wildlife Dinner Restaurant commercial
3. Neil Jung: Psychiatrist promo
4. The Love Boat promo

5. Great White North: New studio
6. The Cisco Kid

What to watch for: Neil Jung: Psychiatrist.
A very funny promo featuring Rick Moranis as a combination of Canadian rock legend Neil Young and famed psychologist (not psychiatrist) Carl Jung. In the spot, he offers treatment to depressed performer Tony Orlando (Rosato) in two forms: Quaaludes and a deliciously high-pitched rendition of Orlando's hit "Tie a Yellow Ribbon 'Round the Ole Oak Tree."

One of the most bizarre of all *SCTV* shows, this program is mostly devoted to an old episode of *The Cisco Kid* ("Sleeping Gas") that has been completely re-dubbed with fitfully humorous dialogue. Adding to the strangeness of the proceedings is that the material hasn't been re-dubbed by *SCTV* cast members, but rather by members of the Second City Toronto stage show, including Don Dickinson, Steven Kampmann, Peter Torokvei, and most notably, future *SCTV* cast member Martin Short, who supplies the dialogue for sidekick Pancho.

This reinvention of a *Cisco Kid* episode was obviously undertaken with the hope of giving the cast, crew, and writers — an "additional material" credit indicates that the re-dubbed dialogue was either written or improvised by the four members of the stage company — a break at the end of a long season. And though a break may have been earned, the concept nevertheless results in season three's worst episode.

Most of the problem here has to do with the length of the "sketch." While some of the new dialogue — the revamped plot concerns a "Canadian Liberation Army" attempting to annex Nevada — is funny, the piece simply goes on far too long. If shortening "The Cisco Kid" was not an option, it should have been broken up into shorter and more easily digestible sections, with the show's other four sketches arranged between segments. (This tactic was chosen when *SCTV* decided to repeat this concept in its very last show.)

Show 78 *(SCTV Television Network)*

1. Guy Caballero: Model Satellite
2. Sunrise Semester with Phil: Do-It-Yourself Advertising (repeat from show 65)
3. The Merv Griffin Show promo (repeat from show 62)
4. Great White North: Star Wars (repeat from show 65)
5. Taxi Driver with Bob Hope promo (repeat from show 68)
6. The Dick Cavett Show: Dick Cavett (repeat from show 60)
7. Elvis 'n Costello promo (repeat from show 55)
8. K-Tel's Fast Talking Playhouse: Who's Afraid of Virginia Woolf? (repeat from show 54)
9. Tri-promo 1 (repeat from show 66)
10. My Fair Lady promo (repeat from show 53)
11. My Life One More Time promo (repeat from show 53)
12. Mamorex commercial: Tom Waits and Rickie Lee Jones (repeat from show 71)
13. Mel Torme National Anthem (repeat from show 64)

Concluding *SCTV*'s strongest season to date is a well-chosen "best of" show; with the highest number of sketches of any episode this season, preference is obviously given to brief sketches over more longer pieces such as "Lee A. Iococca's Rock Concert," "Play It Again, Bob," or "Mel's Rock Pile." Little matter, since all three of those sketches were repeated during the first few shows of *SCTV Network 90*, a new NBC program that debuted just two months after this episode originally aired.

PART TWO

The Ninety-Minute Shows (1981–1983)

By early 1981, *SCTV* was earning solid ratings in the U.S. markets in which it aired. The show was also being noticed for its quality — several critics not only praised the show, but also noted how much better it was than NBC's *Saturday Night Live*, which was struggling through its first season without creator Lorne Michaels. With the thought that *SNL* could be in a state of permanent decline, NBC announced the cancellation of the late-night music program *The Midnight Special* and the pickup of a ninety-minute version of *SCTV*, which was christened *SCTV Network 90* (simplified beginning at show 88 to *SCTV Network*). The program aired after *The Tonight Show with Johnny Carson* on Friday nights beginning May 15, 1981. Even though *SCTV* never replaced *SNL* (except on a few scattered and poorly promoted occasions), NBC needed quality programming — the night of *SCTV*'s premiere, NBC's primetime lineup included the movie *The Harlem Globetrotters on Gilligan's Island*.

The cast that assembled for the NBC programs was *SCTV*'s best yet: While Tony Rosato and Robin Duke were hired by *SNL*, John Candy and Catherine O'Hara returned to join relative newcomer Rick Moranis and veterans Joe Flaherty, Eugene Levy, Andrea Martin, and Dave Thomas. Despite this unprecedented collection of talent, the show was slow to get off the ground — as executive producer Andrew Alexander remembered, "everyone was reluctant to do it," while the cast lamented "biting off more than we could chew." Partly due to this trepidation, the first few NBC episodes leaned heavily on repeat sketches from the show's first three seasons. The cast also had to learn to juggle their own ideas with those of the network; some NBC ideas, like the inclusion of musical guests, were incorporated, but most others, such as a request to include more youth-oriented drug humor, were largely ignored.

Once the cast became comfortable with the longer format, the results were largely remarkable. Not content to simply fill the extra time with more sketches, *SCTV* soon began presenting shows with intricate wraparounds; while storylines had been used as far back as the very first show, the NBC episodes presented behind-the-scenes stories much more complex than anything attempted in the half-hours. Though the wraparounds occasionally amounted to filler (show 85's "Pledge Week" or show 92's "Doorway to Hell"), they also resulted in some of *SCTV*'s finest episodes, such as show 84's "Moral Majority" installment, show 93's *Godfather*-inspired broadcast, and show 106's Canadian Broadcasting Corporation parody.

While critics raved (*Time* called *SCTV* "the funniest show on the air and maybe the best too"; Canada's *Macleans* said the show was "one of the most successful pieces of television art ever made") and the industry noticed (the show received two Emmys for writing), all was not always well at *SCTV* during this period. The disappointing ratings reflected the show's very late Friday night time period (12:30–2 AM EST), while the popularity of Bob and Doug McKenzie led to cast resentment and the eventual departure of Moranis and Thomas as well as O'Hara. But even with a cast of just five regular players — Martin Short joined just as those three defected — *SCTV* presented twelve 90-minute episodes of surprisingly high quality. But with continuing low ratings and the imminent departure of burgeoning star John Candy inevitable, NBC cancelled *SCTV* in the spring of 1983, a move that ended a run of 39 network episodes and cleared the way for the show's final year on the pay cable channel Cinemax.

Show 79 *(SCTV Network 90)*

1. Guy Caballero: Introduction
2. High Q (repeat from show 35)
3. The Merv Griffin Show promo (repeat from show 62)
4. English for Beginners
5. Dr Benson: The Credit Psychiatrist commercial (repeat from show 19)
6. Edith Prickley: Introduction
7. Leave it to Beaver 25th Anniversary Party (repeat from show 15)
8. Great White North: Best groups (repeat from show 69)
9. Dan Money promo (repeat from show 24)
10. One on the Town: Music part 1
11. Hal Waxberg & Nikki: Introduction
12. The Millionaire (repeat from show 33)
13. 20 Depressing Hits by Connie Franklin commercial (repeat from show 12)
14. Guy Caballero: SCTV Mystic
15. Half Legs commercial (repeat from show 54)
16. Masterpiece Theatre: All the Long-Leggedy Beasties (repeat from show 24)
17. Spray On Socks commercial (repeat from show 4)
18. One on the Town: Music part 2
19. Play It Again, Bob (repeat from show 59)

What to watch for: Play It Again, Bob (see show 59).

This premiere NBC episode, besides containing twelve repeat sketches and a re-shoot of another ("English for Beginners"), also consisted of two types of new sketches that had to accomplish two different goals: First the program had to re-establish the world of the SCTV network, including its staff and on-air talent, for the audience unfamiliar with SCTV's premise. Then the cast had to incorporate musical guests into the show after producing 78 half-hour shows without them. Both goals were met here.

Of the five new sketches, four are simple pieces that use station personnel to welcome new viewers to *SCTV*. (Because of their specific contextual relevance to this episode, none of these sketches would be included in the later thirty-minute syndication versions.) Two of the four new pieces feature SCTV president and owner Guy Caballero (Flaherty), the most memorable of which opens the program. Here Guy is introduced with a sight gag that involves his wheelchair careening wildly off a ramp (the fact that Caballero uses a wheelchair just for "respect" is re-introduced). He then invites the audience to "sit back, *shut up*, and watch the show," admitting in the process that what viewers are in for is a night of "golden classics."

The initial Caballero message overshadows the second, in which Guy introduces a mystic (Thomas) that he has brought in as an outside consultant. Most interesting about the sketch is the appearance of Johnny LaRue (John Candy), who new viewers can already recognize as gullible, often drunk (he swills from a brown paper bag), and easily ridiculed (Thomas refers to him as a "pathetic little wretch"). This minor sketch corresponds with the minor role Candy has in the episode, a situation that couldn't have pleased NBC as many at the network initially viewed *SCTV* as a show with Candy and a cast of secondary supporting players.

Earlier in the episode we are re-introduced to SCTV station manager Edith Prickley (Andrea Martin). As opposed to Guy's fumbling appearance at the top of the show, Prickley comes across as confident, likable, and the brains behind the network, bragging of her "shrewd negotiations" that resulted in the return of SCTV "stars" Bobby Bittman, Lola Heatherton, and Sammy Maudlin. Meaningless names to any *SCTV* newcomer, but a holy trinity for longtime viewers.

The last "introduction" piece, featuring Rick Moranis as crew chief Hal Waxberg and Catherine O'Hara as *SCTV*'s first female crew member, is forgettable. The sketch appears to be included just to get Catherine and Rick in some new material; unfortunately, they are playing dull characters whose future appearances will be wisely kept to a minimum.

Levon Helm, the drummer from The Band, debuts as *SCTV*'s first musical guest in the only remaining new sketch, the premiere of the news magazine show "One on the Town," hosted by Earl Camembert (Levy). This sketch is significant not only for Helm's appearance (he performs two songs, "Sweet

Georgia Wine," which was edited out of off-net syndication, and "Summertime Blues"), but also because it is the first time that NBC viewers see the cameras of SCTV, the fictional television station, get turned off, and *SCTV Network 90*, the NBC series, continue to broadcast. This shift from SCTV programming to behind-the-scenes at SCTV will soon play a much larger role in the on-going evolution of *SCTV* from a half-hour to a 90-minute program.

The sketches rerun in this episode are well-chosen and spotlight most of the different types of pieces — promos, commercials, genre parodies, show-specific parodies, movie parodies, original character pieces — that new viewers would become accustomed to seeing. One of the smartest choices made was to bookend the show with two of the show's all-time best: The game show "High Q" and the movie parody "Play It, Again, Bob." Unfortunately, many viewers probably had already fallen asleep by the time the latter aired (approximately 1:45–2:00 AM Eastern Standard Time). This episode would not be the last time that *SCTV* would save some of its best material for the very end of the show, which helped to make it a must-tape program at a time when the home video cassette recorder market was quickly growing.

The biggest oddity of the show is a re-shot version of "English for Beginners," which originally appeared in show 2. Perhaps O'Hara and/or Martin wanted to upgrade their performances or the decision was made to give the sketch better production values. Regardless, either version would still count as one of the weaker points of the episode. Viewers of *SCTV* in off-net syndication would see both versions.

Almost as puzzling is the choice of the "Great White North" segment, which is far from the best of the many available. Maybe Moranis and Thomas wanted to introduce Bob and Doug to new viewers in a particularly pointless "GWN," since the McKenzie brothers were overall pointless characters that hosted a pointless show. This early misstep would not prevent Bob and Doug from soon becoming a phenomenon.

One rerun sketch presented here — the promo for "The Merv Griffin Show" — was significantly cut to eliminate much of the performances of third season cast members Tony Rosato and Robin Duke as *The Incredible Hulk* star Lou Ferrigno and his makeup woman.

Show 80 *(SCTV Network 90)*

1. 5 Neat Guys Neatest Hits! commercial
2. The Tim Ishimuni Show
3. Kwallada commercial
4. Edith Prickley: On the set with Johnny LaRue
5. SCTV Movie of the Week: Polynesiantown part 1
6. The Larry Seigel Show promo
7. Indira commercial
8. Great White North: Traveling

9. Bren's GenfemProctezePons commercial
10. The Sammy Maudlin Show: Outtakes from congressional hearings on drug abuse
11. The Rosemans promo
12. Yuri: Getting To Know You promo
13. Will: The Movie promo
14. SCTV Movie of the Week: Polynesiantown part 2
15. British Film Festival promo
16. The Gerry Todd Show 1

What to watch for: The Sammy Maudlin Show.
Returning to form after sitting most of the third season out, this installment is classic "Maudlin": Here guest Bobby Bittman (Levy) again brings outtakes, only this time they aren't from one of his movies or television specials, but from a congressional hearing on drug abuse in Hollywood. Despite their lameness — Bittman spills a glass of water, Bittman names Elmer Fudd as a drug user — the clips invoke hysterical reactions from Maudlin, William B. Williams, and Lola Heatherton. Best is one of Bittman's most heartfelt "as a comic in all seriousness" moments: "When I get paid, I get paid with the green stuff, I don't get paid with the white stuff!"

Note that in the sketch's fade-out, Heatherton chats with guest Mother Teresa (Martin), a conversation that foreshadows Mother Teresa's appearance on Heatherton's "Way to Go, Woman" (show 88).

The best-known sketch from this episode is the *Chinatown* parody "Polynesiantown," which features Candy's Johnny LaRue, Joe Flaherty's Vic Hedges (the character's first appearance), and musical guest Dr. John. The piece's clearest parallel to the similarly titled Roman Polanski film is its last shot, which is precisely what makes the sketch notable in *SCTV* lore. Like *Chinatown*, "Polynesiantown" ends with a slow crane shot that zooms out from a city street where a death has occurred. Although the shot is a crucial element to the parody, it was reportedly expensive and Candy and Flaherty (the main writers of the piece) were criticized for it, both inside and outside (Marvin Kitman wrote disparagingly of the piece in *Newsday*) the show. But *SCTV* was able to mine the controversy for material in later episodes (show 83 and both NBC Christmas broadcasts).

Setting aside the backstage turmoil, "Polynesiantown" features some fine slapstick humor, a solid supporting turn by writer Dick Blasucci (as Chuck, the *extremely* white-haired piano player at Johnny LaRue's Luau Room), a silly plot involving poisoned ribs and some mysterious "gems," and two performances by Dr. John ("Iko Iko" and "Such A Night"). Ultimately, though, the highlight of "Polynesiantown" isn't in the sketch itself, but rather in the introduction given by Edith Prickley (Martin) on the set of LaRue's latest movie, titled "Chicks in Their Underwear." Here we see LaRue, in full movie mogul mode, directing a brief sex scene with a shady looking group of yes-men who look more like members of the Corleone family than a film crew. LaRue is clearly enjoying his power at SCTV, yelling at Prickley and demanding that women on the set take their clothes off. (Prickley is upset that LaRue doesn't include her in this demand.) The failure of "Polynesiantown" within the fictional world of SCTV will soon have a crippling effect on LaRue's stature.

This episode is also notable for featuring the debuts of singing group 5 Neat Guys and *SCTV*'s resident VJ Gerry Todd. A commercial for the 5 Neat Guys' album *Neatest Hits!* opens the show but doesn't quite live up to later appearances from the group, particularly after the alcohol problems of the singer portrayed by Flaherty (he's the neat guy in the "N" sweater) become more apparent. Still, the juxtaposition of these five decidedly unhip guys crooning suggestive tunes like "Patsy Has The Largest Breasts In Town" and "She Does It" is inspired.

Concluding the show is the debut of "The Gerry Todd Show," a sketch (predating by several months the birth of MTV) featuring Todd introducing diverse clips ("video") that comprise his late night program. Two of the segments feature Moranis doubling as a lounge singer who does easy-listening versions of "Turning Japanese" and "Da Doo Doo Da Da"; also featured are commercials for Crazy Hy's, an electronics store run by two Orthodox Jews (Levy and his silent partner Moranis). The inspiration for the spots are then-current ads run by Crazy Joe's Drapery, a Toronto business owned by an Orthodox Jew who popularized the slogan "If You Don't Shop at Crazy Joe You Pay Too Much."

In addition to the first new *Network 90* "Great White North" (in which Doug is upset because of finding out Bob makes more money), most of the remainder of this episode is filled by a large amount of promos and commercials, many of which feature some new impressions. Thomas nails G. Gordon Liddy in a promo for "Will: The Movie," which includes nods to Liddy's admissions that he has threatened to string people up with piano wire and that he once captured and ate a rat to cure himself of his fear of rodents. Andrea Martin satirizes then-current tampon commercials featuring a wheezing Brenda Vaccaro. ("She sounds like a seal in heat," says a member of the crew.) Finally, Moranis is manic producer Larry Seigel, an impression of film producer Joel Silver, whom he and Thomas had recently met. The spot depicts Seigel fronting a new talk show that features nothing but the producer screaming at writers and executives, which is how Moranis claimed Silver actually behaved.

Of the other parody commercials, the most notable has to be "Indira," a spot for an *Evita*-inspired musical on the life of Indira Gandhi, featuring Martin as Gandhi and Flaherty as Slim Whitman playing Pungi Goabarra. This piece is one of the most repeated sketches in *SCTV*'s history, a fact that the show comments on in a later episode (show 97). Also, a commercial for a skin ointment called Kwallada features Donny and Marie (Thomas and O'Hara) in a skewering of the siblings' spots for Hawaiian Punch. Instead of the cry to "go Hawaiian," Donny and Marie here urge viewers to "go Kwallada" to clear up any aftereffects of sexual encounters.

Absent from the third season was Dave Thomas's Lin Ye Tang character; Tang's absence seemed to indicate that Thomas was getting uncomfortable playing an Asian role. But not only does Thomas eventually bring Tang back, here he actually introduces a *second* Asian character named Tim Ishimuni, who hosts a talk show featuring Candy as a Godzilla-type movie monster named Grogan. The broader Ishimuni character is even more racially insensitive than Lin Ye Tang; despite a fine performance by Candy, the sketch remains uncomfortable viewing.

One segment from this episode — a long promo for a "British Film Festival," consisting of clips from movies featuring Thomas's so-called "Angry Young Man" character — was deemed unworthy for off-net syndication. (The three films parodied here are *Look Back in Anger*, *The Loneliness of the Long Distance Runner*, and *A Clockwork Orange*.) The piece is an interesting failure, notable more so for Flaherty's choice to substitute a one-off character named Ben Bumme for his usual Alistair Cooke impression.

Show 81 *(SCTV Network 90)*

1. Sunrise Semester with Norman Gorman: Conversational New Yorkese (repeat from show 58)
2. Lola Heatherton in Concert promo (repeat from show 27)
3. Yellow Belly promo (repeat from show 37)
4. Speaking of Talk with Lou Jaffe (repeat from show 33)
5. Guy Caballero: Pirini Sclereso part 1
6. Melvin and Howards promo part 1
7. Sneak Previews (repeat from show 66)
8. The Point Shave and Haircut System commercial (repeat from show 19)
9. The Dick Cavett Show: Dick Cavett (repeat from show 60)
10. Melvin and Howards promo part 2
11. The Fracases part 1
12. Melvin and Howards promo part 3
13. Only for Women (repeat from show 40)
14. Great White North: How to make a guy go when he's sleeping (repeat from show 59)
15. The Babe Ruth Story promo (repeat from show 26)
16. Guy Caballero: Pirini Sclereso part 2
17. The Fracases part 2
18. Guy Caballero: Pirini Sclereso part 3
19. Sid Dithers Private Eye (repeat from show 39)
20. Monster Chiller Horror Theatre: Whispers of the Wolf (repeat from show 38)

What to watch for: Whispers of the Wolf (see show 38).

The second 90-minute show to consist mainly of repeats, though there is new material of interest. Among the original sketches, the lengthy "The Fracases" is the most noteworthy, thanks largely to Southside Johnny and the Asbury Jukes, who turn in arguably the finest musical performances ever on *SCTV*. (Look for future E Street Band member and Mrs. Bruce Springsteen, Patti Scialfa, as one of the band's back-up singers.)

Although the characters in "The Fracases" would never be repeated (save for Rick Moranis's Cole), viewers will recognize Dave and Catherine's hostile husband-and-wife routine from other sketches, most notably "The Millionaire" (repeated just two shows earlier). Here Andrea Martin joins them as their pregnant daughter Bunny, who is soon to be married to her boyfriend Cole. Bunny is not safe from her father's scathing abuse, as her dad calls her "lumpy" and refers to the man who impregnated her as "trigger-happy." These insults come so easily to Thomas and O'Hara that the material has an improvisational feel, particularly when O'Hara attempts to bite Thomas's finger when he threateningly points in her face.

In the first part of "The Fracases," the family attends a Southside Johnny gig to determine if the band is right for Bunny and Cole's wedding reception; the second part features the reception itself and is interesting in that much of it is done in the style of *Laugh-In*, with many brief joke-heavy conversations linked by the music of the Asbury Jukes. Among the characters at the reception, Flaherty plays a womanizer similar to his Alki Stereopolis character, Levy plays a wedding caterer similar to the wedding coordinator Martin Short would later play in the *Father of the Bride* remakes, and Candy has a bit part as a guest who charmingly informs Thomas that the event is "the finest shotgun wedding I have ever attended."

There are two new wraparound elements in this episode of distinctly different quality: Three "Melvin and Howards" spots parody the Jonathan Demme movie *Melvin and Howard*, which was based on the story of Melvin Dummar, a Utah gas station owner who claimed to have once picked up reclusive billionaire Howard Hughes on a deserted highway. *SCTV*'s Dummar (Moranis) is joined not just by Hughes, but also by Howard Cosell (Levy), Senator Howard Baker (Thomas), and Curly Howard (Candy) of the Three Stooges. The parody targets Dummar's assertions that Hughes didn't like music; here Moranis forces all of his passengers to croon, most notably a Cosell-led rendition of The Silhouettes classic "Get A Job."

The other new bits, involving SCTV president Guy Caballero and Martin's tired Pirini Sclereso character, are less successful. Here Guy has hired Pirini as his "vice president in charge of coordination," even though it's obvious that she is a cleaning woman given an important title to make it appear as if SCTV employs minorities in positions of power. The three segments are an excuse for Martin to do Sclereso's butchering of the English language shtick, a joke already familiar to new viewers thanks to the "English for Beginners" piece on show 79.

Of the repeat sketches on the episode, only a promo for "Yellow Belly" doesn't translate well. The sketch features Johnny LaRue as a stumbling coward of the old west who shoots and kills a defenseless mother and child. "Yellow Belly" plays much better in its original context as part of *SCTV*'s "30th

Anniversary Show" (show 37), in which LaRue introduces the program as one that was cancelled due to "something about violence and kids." The set-up makes the payoff funnier; without it, the piece is limited to the shock value of an innocent mother and child being gunned down by "the biggest coward in the west."

Show 82 *(SCTV Network 90)*

1. Comment with David Brinkley: When will the street dealer be able to consistently provide quality smoke? (repeat from show 74)
2. Cooking with Edith Prickley part 1 (repeat from show 43)
3. Tex and Edna Boil's Organ Emporium commercial (repeat from show 43)
4. Cooking with Edith Prickley part 2 (repeat from show 43)
5. Matchbook Advertising commercial (repeat from show 32)
6. Mr. Science (repeat from show 6)
7. The Sammy Maudlin Show: Bobby Bittman and Bob Hope (repeat from show 63)
8. Taxi Driver with Woody Allen promo (repeat from show 67)
9. What's My Shoe Size? (repeat from show 37)
10. Great White North: Why are parking lots so small at donut places (repeat from show 73)
11. Taxi Driver with Gregory Peck promo (repeat from show 63)
12. Lee A. Iacocca's Rock Concert (repeat from show 53)
13. Extreme Close-Up promo (repeat from show 8)
14. The Man Who Would Be King of the Popes preview (repeat from show 25)
15. Taxi Driver with Sid Dithers promo (repeat from show 73)
16. The Love Boat promo (repeat from show 77)
17. Dr. Chet Vet the Dead Pet Remover commercial (repeat from show 45)
18. My Fair Lady promo (repeat from show 53)
19. Harlett Romances commercial (repeat from show 31)
20. Mel's Rock Pile: Richard Harris (repeat from show 75)
21. Shock Theatre (repeat from show 8)

What to watch for: Mel's Rock Pile (see show 75).

The only NBC episode to feature all repeats, this compilation betters other "Best of *SCTV*" specials (see Appendix A).

Compensating for the lack of new material, this episode contains elements that are designed to make connections among sketches where no connections exist, the most ubiquitous being voiceovers at the end of several sketches that promote upcoming pieces. Also, for the first and only time, the show uses bizarre stock footage to promote non-existent sketches, such as film of a horse eating from a plate to advertise the program "A Horse Called Richard Harris."

Also, this is the only time that the cast succumbed to NBC's supposed demand for youth-oriented drug material at the top of the show, as the David Brinkley (Moranis) commentary on "quality smoke" runs before the opening credits, the first time that a sketch appeared before the titles.

This is also the first (but not the last) NBC episode to lack a musical guest; *SCTV* compensates by including two long musical sketches: "Mel's Rock Pile" (with Richard Harris) and "Lee A. Iacocca's Rock Concert," the latter of which is severely and poorly edited from its original version as seen on show 53. Lost is Moranis's George Carlin routine as well as any trace of performances by Robin Duke (who played Lee's daughter Imogene Iacocca) and Tony Rosato (who played crooner Tony Orlando).

The end credits of this episode also present a problem. In the original "Sammy Maudlin Show" as seen on show 63, surprise guest Danny Thomas does a spit-take that leaves Bobby Bittman drenched. A shot of Bittman's reaction is freeze-framed under the show credits, over which is heard a Bittman phone call to SCTV complaining about the unflattering shot. In the version of the sketch on this episode, the sketch fades out after the spit-take and an hour later, over the *SCTV Network 90* end credits, the same phone call is heard. But here Bittman's complaint is nonsensical, since the shot held is of him doing his stand-up routine and not of him taking the spit-take from Danny Thomas.

One of the advantages of watching *SCTV* from its inception on Global Television is the opportunity to see the evolution of the show's many characters. One of the dangers of presenting sketches out of chronological order on *Network 90* is that this evolution is lost on new viewers who are likely to be confused. For example, this episode's rerun of "Mr. Science": That Candy's Johnny LaRue would host such an extraordinarily cheap children's program is illogical considering he was most recently seen as the director, producer, and star of the big-budget movie "Polynesiantown."

Show 83 *(SCTV Network 90)*

1. Tri-promo 2 (repeat from show 71)
2. Fillips Milk of Amnesia commercial (repeat from show 18)
3. Johnny LaRue wraparound part 1: LaRue signs in
4. Sunrise Semester: Man's Ability to Imitate (repeat from show 61)
5. Johnny LaRue wraparound part 2: LaRue waits for Caballero
6. My Life One More Time promo (repeat from show 53)
7. Johnny LaRue wraparound part 3: LaRue gets one last shot
8. SCTV Special Report: The Space Shuttle
9. Johnny LaRue wraparound part 4: LaRue with Earl Camembert and William Morris
10. Phil's Nails commercial (repeat from show 42)
11. Great White North: Back bacon and snow chains (repeat from show 58)
12. Bad Acting In Hollywood (repeat from show 39)
13. Biller Hi-Lite commercial (repeat from show 39)
14. Johnny LaRue wraparound part 5: LaRue talks with Larry Seigel
15. Long Distance commercial (repeat from show 40)
16. Johnny LaRue wraparound part 6: Lunch Time Street Beef
17. SCTV Movie of the Week: The Grapes of Mud (repeat from show 23)
18. Words to Live By: Rabbi Karlov and Angus Crock (repeat from show 55)
19. Sunrise Semester with Dr. Cheryl Kinsey: The Inability to Fake Orgasms (repeat from show 5)

What to watch for: Phil's Nails (see show 42).

This episode is significant for containing *SCTV Network 90*'s first plot-driven "wraparound." For the remainder of *SCTV*'s NBC run, episodes that do *not* contain a linking plot device are less and less common as the show moves further away from being a collection of single unrelated pieces.

Many times the NBC-era storylines work extremely well: For instance, this episode's plot involving Johnny LaRue and the fallout from his expensive flop "Polynesiantown" holds up better than many of the show's stand-alone (and mostly repeat) sketches. The fact that the story elements here take up approximately just one-third of the episode indicates that *SCTV* introduced wraparounds rather cautiously into *Network 90*. Designating most of the time in the episode for more traditional sketches means the story elements do not overwhelm the show. (This highlights one of the problems with the half-hour off-net syndicated shows: By running the wraparounds in long, uninterrupted blocks and not in shorter segments as often intended, the careful structure of the ninety-minute shows is undermined.)

The real-life detractors of "Polynesiantown" inspired this episode's story: Johnny LaRue (Candy), faced with the prospect of having all of his station projects cancelled by Guy Caballero due to "Polynesiantown" cost overruns, agrees to host a live community talkback show. The program, "Lunch Time Street Beef" (reminiscent of show 31's "LaRue By Night"), is an embarrassment for LaRue — the show has no budget and the only resources Caballero will allocate for the program are "one camera, one microphone, and that's it!"

However much "Street Beef" disgraces LaRue, it is clear from the beginning of the episode that no one, from maintenance workers to security guard Gus Gusstofferson (Levy, reprising the character for the first time since show 2), treats LaRue with any degree of respect. This contempt is shared by Caballero, who grants LaRue "Street Beef" only after a tear-filled plea made more humiliating by the fact that LaRue was kept waiting for several hours while Caballero took meetings with anyone —*anyone*— who had ideas for new programs.

Despite promising to keep "Street Beef" cheap, LaRue instead outdoes "Polynesiantown" by ordering an indulgent *helicopter* shot that closes out the show. As the lengthy shot progresses, *SCTV* introduces an effective cliffhanger element as Caballero promises via voiceover that viewers have seen the last of Johnny LaRue. But not only would LaRue return, show 94 would also see the return of "Street Beef."

Besides the script, what makes this wraparound work is the fact that LaRue and Caballero are such interesting and multi-dimensional creations; these personas do not rely on shtick to get laughs. *SCTV* also plays on our curiosity surrounding the SCTV network itself; it is gratifying to get the first extended behind-the-scenes look at the operation. Providing that look at SCTV through the eyes of LaRue was wise, because even though he at first appears to be an unrelatable figure (he has his own limo), Candy succeeds at infusing LaRue with other, more relatable traits; for example, he too has to deal with annoying co-workers (Earl Camembert, Gusstofferson, Caballero's secretary) and a difficult boss. And his ultimate affection for SCTV — expressed best in his sniveling plea to Caballero — surely matches many viewers' pride in their workplaces as well. Finally, the rebelliousness of the final helicopter shot is satisfying for anyone who has ever dreamed of defying his or her superiors. Which is pretty much everyone.

The only new material outside of the LaRue wraparound is the "SCTV Special Report: The Space Shuttle" sketch, featuring Thomas as Walter Cronkite, Moranis as David Brinkley, and musical guest Robert Gordon performing Marshall Crenshaw's "Some Day, Some Way." Thomas and Moranis began their debasement of Cronkite and Brinkley in season three and wisely carry the impressions over to NBC. But overall, the NBC sketches don't work as well as the earlier ones, and this piece launches that trend. Cronkite missing camera cues and Brinkley getting a heat-resistant tile stuck to his hand is dull to begin with, and particularly deadly when the material is stretched out as long as it is here. The highlight of the sketch is Gordon, but even his appearance is weakened by a lame introduction from Cronkite, during which he confuses Robert Gordon with astronaut Gordon Cooper. Not to mention that Gordon appearing on a news report is awkward and lacks *SCTV*'s usual flair for seamlessly inserting musical performances into sketches.

The rest of this episode consists of repeat sketches; it is interesting to note that the rundown of the show is a throwback to the earliest days of *SCTV*, with a "Sunrise Semester" at the top and a "Words to Live By" at the bottom of the broadcast.

Show 84 *(SCTV Network 90)*

1. Sunrise Semester: Post Natal Exercises promo
2. Poocharé commercial
3. Moral Majority wraparound part 1: Guy Caballero
4. The Merv Griffith Show promo
5. Moral Majority wraparound part 2: Critic's Corner with Bill Needle
6. Mrs. Falbo's Tiny Town: Premiere show
7. National Midnight Star
8. The Brooke Shields Show promo
9. Moral Majority wraparound part 3: Needle and Caballero
10. Indira commercial (repeat from show 80)
11. Doorway To Hell: The Man Who Lived in a Box
12. Monster Chiller Horror Theatre: Dr. Tongue's 3-D House of Stewardesses
13. Great White North: Stuff that really bugs us (repeat from show 72)
14. Moral Majority wraparound part 4: Sunbright pullout
15. Rolling Hills Alcoholic Rehabilitation Center commercial

16. SCTV News: Floyd back from rehab
17. The Gerry Todd Show: Michael McDonald
18. Moral Majority wraparound part 5: Caballero's new plan

What to watch for: *National Midnight Star*.
In what is arguably SCTV's *finest hour (or sixty-six minutes sans commercials), "National Midnight Star"—a newsmagazine show born from a sleazy tabloid newspaper—stands out for being hilariously prescient, foreshadowing the rise of a genre of television still years away in 1981.*

Almost every cast member makes a significant contribution to the piece: Candy is the "top researcher" who has discovered ways that both your dreams and your underwear can kill you; Flaherty is a bizarre reverend with proof of an afterlife (not life after death, but a great party that goes on for six to eight weeks); Levy is both National Midnight Star *chairman Rawl Withers (an overhaul of his retired Raoul Wilson character) and Henry Kissinger on a drunken rampage. And anchors Moranis, O'Hara, and Thomas are there to remind skeptics that no matter how strange the story (such as "Slim Whitman Boasts: I Was the First Man to Yodel on the Moon"), the* National Midnight Star *would only report it if "It's True."*

This quintessential episode of *SCTV* was awarded the 1982 Emmy Award for Outstanding Writing in a Variety or Music Program.

As in the last episode, this show's wraparound takes up about a third of the program. But here *SCTV* takes on an issue weightier than Johnny LaRue. To begin at the beginning: This episode of *SCTV Network 90* was originally broadcast on NBC on July 10, 1981. In February of that year, the Reverend Donald E. Wildmon, in conjunction with the Reverend Jerry Falwell's Moral Majority group, created the Coalition for Better Television. Wildmon's tactics were simple—he, along with thousands of members of his coalition, planned to monitor television shows and then rank them based on sex, violence, and profanity. Then, after deciding which shows were most offensive, he would retaliate—not against the producers of the offending shows or against the networks that aired them, but against the advertisers who sponsored them.

Wildmon's methods had already proven successful without the support of Falwell's Moral Majority: In the late seventies, after facing pressure from Wildmon and his followers, Sears cancelled its ads on the ABC programs *Three's Company* and *Charlie's Angels*. And not long before this *SCTV* episode aired, advertisers were again beginning to crack under the pressure of Wildmon's group—on June 16, 1981, the chairman of Procter and Gamble—the leading television advertiser at the time with annual expenditures estimated at $500 million—gave a speech announcing that, because of program content, his company had withdrawn advertising from 50 television shows in just the past year.

One of Proctor and Gamble's largest product categories at the time was household cleansers, including laundry products. So it's no coincidence that this *SCTV* episode attacking the tactics of Wildmon and Falwell involves a new SCTV advertiser named Sunbright that manufactures cleaning supplies. The two *SCTV* characters that are asked to compromise themselves the most in order to placate Sunbright are the morally questionable duo of Guy Caballero and Dave Thomas's Bill Needle, the latter making his first *Network 90* appearance. The reasons for wanting to keep Sunbright happy are simple: Guy claims the company has agreed to invest $25 million annually in advertising.

It's no surprise that of the two, the money-hungry Guy is most willing to do whatever it takes to make Sunbright — or any advertiser — happy. In the first wraparound segment, his desk littered with Sunbright products, Flaherty sums up the issue at stake — that there are outside pressure groups trying to "make television more acceptable to you and me as fine Americans." Guy's opinion of such pressure groups? "Everyone has a right," Guy says, "to his or her opinion as long as they've allied themselves with any of our sponsors." This eagerness to put programming decisions into the hands of advertisers and the pressure groups they fear is made clearer when Guy is asked by two Sunbright executives (O'Hara and Moranis, parodying two NBC executives assigned to *SCTV*), "if certain pressure groups decided to stop buying Sunbright, would you drop certain programs?" Guy of course readily agrees, suggesting that producer Norman Lear — who had founded a group opposed to Falwell and Wildmon called the People for the American Way in 1980 — should worry about such things. "I'm in business," Guy states, succinctly summarizing his priorities as a broadcaster.

Of course Lear was just one of the many critics of the Moral Majority, and Bill Needle represents their opinions on his new program, "Critic's Corner." In a vociferous diatribe, Thomas's Needle screams about the insanity of "a small group of people" who "dictate the private and personal choices of the nation by holding a gun to the corporations that do the sponsoring." Needle is entitled to his opinion, but Sunbright is also entitled to not pay for his forum, and a Sunbright commercial scheduled for Needle's show is pulled in progress. Thomas's Needle then immediately switches gears, stating that if a small group of Nielsen families can decide what America watches, why not the Moral Majority? Never mind that a randomly selected group of Nielsen families don't have an organized political or moral agenda, but the about-face saves his job thanks to a stamp of approval given by Sunbright executives.

The approval even extends to a Sunbright spokesperson job for Needle, but his convictions get the better of him and he storms off the set of a live commercial, leaving Sunbright to ultimately pull their lucrative advertising off SCTV for good. Of course once the money is off the table, Guy indignantly lashes out at the Moral Majority: "We here at SCTV feel strongly that television should not be subject to the whims of any pressure group; nor should they be subject to the whims of any sponsor!" Unfortunately for Caballero, insult is added to injury as a major "alternative" sponsor — Harry's Sex Shop — also cancels its advertising since the programs on SCTV are not "violent or sexy enough." This turn of events leads Caballero to decide on a "pledge week," which plays a major role in the next episode of *SCTV Network 90*.

What makes this wraparound most effective is how *SCTV* combines a story involving its fictional characters with a real life subject no doubt unfamiliar to many of its viewers. Because even new viewers already recognize Guy Caballero as someone who acts with profit as his only motive, his embrace of these pressure groups and the advertisers that bow to them is immediately suspicious. And because Bill Needle is at the same time both less familiar but more relatable, viewers can identify with Needle's disgust and agree with his choice to ultimately rebel against Sunbright and their money. As seen through Needle's eyes, viewers reject the idea of pressure groups and advertisers dictating programming choices.

But the story ends on a cautionary note: Since the full impact that Wildmon and Falwell would have on television programming remained to be seen, *SCTV* had to guess at their success rate. The show ends up taking the view that the Moral Majority and the Coalition for Better Television would indeed have a major impact; if SCTV is to be an example of what would happen to the "real" networks, then the show prophesizes that pullout from advertisers would leave networks with unsold time and greatly diminished profits. Of course no "real" network would or could make the immediate decision to have a "pledge week," so the end result as *SCTV* sees it would be for the networks to ultimately have to cave in to advertiser boycotts, allowing the pressure groups to emerge victorious.

The real-life version played itself out very differently; Wildmon and Falwell eventually had a falling-out, and Wildmon's most ambitious boycott — of RCA, the then-owner of NBC — proved unsuccessful. Wildmon's power then greatly eroded (his Coalition for Better Television crumbled in 1982, seven years before the Moral Majority disbanded), although he has returned many times since with successful advertiser boycotts of shows such as *Married ... with Children* and *Saturday Night Live*. Despite keeping his name in the newspapers, Wildmon's mission to "clean up" television has been largely unsuccessful. But even decades after this episode of *SCTV* originally aired, pressure groups (such as the Parents Television Council) continue to exist, forever hoping to, in the words of Guy Caballero, "Make television more acceptable to you and me as fine Americans."

Aside from the wraparound, there is much impressive material in this episode. One sketch that the Reverend Wildmon wouldn't approve of (since it features women in states of partial undress) is "Dr. Tongue's 3-D House of Stewardesses." The "3-D" series of sketches is familiar to veteran *SCTV* viewers, but this is the preeminent "3-D" piece. Note that this is the first "Monster Chiller Horror Theatre" in which host Count Floyd doesn't mind that the movie isn't scary — after all, it features attractive women cavorting around in their underwear (including Catherine, who cannot control her laughter). "Did you get a good look at those chicks?" is Floyd's immediate response to the film, a line only improved by remembering that Floyd's target audience is children.

Network 90 viewers discover in this episode that Count Floyd is actually played by "SCTV News" co-anchor Floyd Robertson, who we learn has been away taking care of a drinking problem — a problem that had been heretofore hinted at several times in the first three seasons of *SCTV*. In reality, it doesn't appear that Robertson has entirely sobered up, a fact that could be the fault of a lackadaisical policy at his rehab center; in an ad for the treatment facility, Floyd claims that "they may not help you stop drinking, but maybe you can cut down."

Even with longtime characters like Floyd Robertson and Dr. Tongue to work with, cast members were busy churning out new personas that would play big roles in the show's future. Here Andrea Martin's Mrs. Falbo, the host of the children's show "Mrs. Falbo's Tiny Town," makes her debut. The idea behind the sketch, that a children's show would feature material wildly inappropriate for children, is not original, but the gentle execution is unique and certainly a far cry from kids' show parodies such as seen in the film *The Groove Tube*, in which a clown reads excerpts from *Fanny Hill*. Mrs. Falbo intends to be educational, but she's not very bright; for example, she kills a goldfish while attempting to explain how fish breathe. She's also the victim of bad timing — while looking at the king and queen through her "magic telescope," she inadvertently catches them (in a scene censored for off-net syndication) engaging in some bizarre sexual activity.

Although an argument could be made that making fun of kids' shows is typical fare for a comedy show, there's nothing typical about "The Merv Griffith Show" sketch. Another example of the multi-layered style of parody that *SCTV* excelled in, this sketch is an ingenious parody of both *The Merv Griffin Show* and *The Andy Griffith Show*, with Moranis playing Merv as Andy. Joe Flaherty summed up the sketch's genesis: "We were bored doing straight-on parodies. Why do just Merv Griffin? Why not do Merv Griffin doing 'The Andy Griffith Show?'" Flaherty contributes a mean Barney Fife to the piece, but as good as he and Moranis are, it is Levy's wonderfully uncanny Floyd the Barber impression that steals the piece. This sketch would become one of *SCTV*'s most celebrated pieces.

Besides "Merv Griffith," Rick's other showcase piece on this episode is the second (and last) "Gerry Todd Show." This sketch repeats some elements from the first installment (show 80), but Rick includes one original thread — a memorable impression of notoriously deep-throated singer Michael McDonald — that makes this "Gerry Todd Show" an improvement on the first. Moranis as McDonald is everywhere in this sketch — doing back-up vocals for a Tom Monroe (see show 79) version of "Downtown," providing the vocals for a low-rent carpet commercial, and, in the most inspired twist, starring in a video for Christopher Cross's then-hit "Ride Like the Wind." The video shows McDonald frantically driving to the studio to record his backup vocals for the Cross track; when the track is complete, McDonald's only spoken words — a ridiculously cavernous line reading of "OK. See ya" — provide a great punchline.

Show 85 *(SCTV Network 90)*

1. SCTV Pledge Week part 1: Guy Caballero
2. Dr. Shekter commercial
3. Farm Film Report: Favorite movies
4. The Expert from Kovak commercial
5. SCTV Pledge Week part 2: Maureen Wallace tour
6. Mel's Rock Pile: 20th Anniversary Special
7. Tracking the Unknown with Edith Prickley
8. SCTV Pledge Week part 3: Bobby Bittman & The Elephant Man
9. SCTV Pledge Week part 4: Lola Heatherton & Count Floyd
10. Critic's Corner with Bill Needle: NBC and the RCA satellite
11. Roy Orbison: "Working for the Man"
12. SCTV Pledge Week part 5: Dr. Tongue and Bruno with the Elephant Man
13. Fireside Chat with Mayor Tommy Shanks: Gun Control
14. Pit Stop commercial (repeat from show 34)
15. Great White North: Kids being able to use calculators in school (repeat from show 56)
16. Hugh Betcha's Short Story Playhouse: O'Henry
17. Daylea Yogurt commercial (repeat from show 41)
18. SCTV Pledge Week part 6: Happy endings and cute elephants

What to watch for: Hugh Betcha's Short Story Playhouse.
Thanks to a smart mix of the sophisticated and the sophomoric, this literary parody stands out in SCTV's weakest 90-minute episode so far. The piece begins in fine highbrow fashion, as Candy and Thomas do their best dramatic acting in bringing to life a non-existent piece that was supposedly penned by the American short story writer O. Henry. The story, entitled "The Private Booth," involves a Duke (Candy) who retreats to a private table at an exclusive club in order to get drunk and kill himself. The piece is quite somber, and SCTV *lets it proceed just long enough for the viewer to become engrossed in the solemnity of the story. And then an actor in a very cheap lion suit attacks and kills the waiter (Thomas).*

Host Hugh Betcha (Flaherty) then takes us into another reenactment, this one of the story behind "The Private Booth." In this section, John plays the author O. Henry, whose penchant for surprise endings angers his wife and publisher. Note here how SCTV *doesn't play down to its audience; the script includes arcane references to O. Henry's life, such as O. Henry's claim that "In the penitentiary, they could appreciate a good surprise ending." That line means nothing unless you know that the real O. Henry was once imprisoned for embezzlement.*

Although a show that is supposed to be parodying television may not seem like the right forum for this literary material, SCTV *makes it work by framing the second half of the piece as a* Night Gallery *parody that recalls Betcha's last appearance (show 64), when he hosted—what else—a parody of* Night Gallery. *"Short Story Playhouse" is a complicated and cerebral sketch that succeeds in redefining what could pass as "late night comedy." However, this segment surely alienated viewers and was noticeably absent when* SCTV *episodes were repackaged for syndication in the mid–1980s.*

A significant step back for *SCTV*. Despite some highlights, this episode's "Pledge Week" wraparound feels like filler and, not surprisingly, was completely excised from later syndication. Worse is the sketch "Tracking the Unknown with Edith Prickley," which is the first truly horrible sketch produced for NBC.

Another installment of "Mel's Rock Pile" not surprisingly fares much better. This time out, Rockin' Mel (Levy) is celebrating the show's 20th anniversary, complete with clips, appearances by some of the show's original dancers, and an appearance by Roy Orbison. The sketch is a bit of a cheat, since longtime *SCTV* viewers know that "Mel's Rock Pile" is predated by "SCTV Boogie" and "SCTV Disco" and couldn't have been around as long as it claims to have been, but such details are irrelevant. Giving the best performances in the sketch are Candy and O'Hara as a husband and wife who met on the first episode of "Mel's Rock Pile" but who are now miserably unhappy together; O'Hara tells Mel that she curses the day they met. This installment suggests that "Mel's Rock Pile" is itself cursed, as most of its former dancers have grown up to be social outcasts.

Finally, "Mel's Rock Pile" welcomes Roy Orbison to do solid versions of "Oh Pretty Woman" and (later) "Working for the Man." This appearance by Orbison is noteworthy because, although he was always a rock and roll icon, Orbison was not at a great point in his career, being as he was decades removed from his original glory days and several years away from his comeback with The Traveling Wilburys and his *Mystery Girl* album (shortly followed by his untimely passing). Maybe enthused just to get the gig, he is a good sport as he puts up with silly questions from Levy's Mel such as "Did you get the idea for those sunglasses from the Blues Brothers?"

Two other highlights of this episode come early. A commercial parody for a camera called the Expert parodies not only the then-ubiquitous James Garner and Mariette Hartley Polaroid ads, but also the film *Ordinary People*. (Playing Mary Tyler Moore, O'Hara sports a shirt that states, "I Am Not Donald Sutherland's Wife"; in real life, Mariette Hartley had a shirt made that read, "I Am Not James Garner's Wife.") The parody recalls a moment in the Oscar-winning film where the relationships among Sutherland, Moore, and Timothy Hutton become so dysfunctional that the three family members can't even pose for pictures together. The Expert camera is programmed to only capture "extraordinary" moments, and therefore refuses to operate until Hutton (Moranis) loses his temper. Note this concept borrows heavily from the "Polordak Camera" commercial from show 50.

The subject of *Ordinary People* also arises in the sketch "Farm Film Report," featuring film reviews from the long-lost characters of Big Jim McBob (Flaherty) and Billy Sol Hurok (Candy), who finally make their *Network 90* debut in this piece. The sketch represents a bit of a regression for these characters, since in the second season, the two had already evolved from farmers to farmers interested in movies to farmers interested in movies where things blow up to — in the "Rock Concert" sketch — hosts who blow celebrity guests up. Despite the backtracking, this is still a solid re-introduction to these characters, as well as being the first time the sign-off of "May the Good Lord take a liking to you and blow you up real soon!" is used.

Nothing gets blown up in the sketch "Tracking the Unknown," but perhaps the tape of this disjointed and humorless segment should have been. Supposedly a cross between the programs *Wild Kingdom* and *In Search Of*, the piece has something to do with host Edith Prickley going to the Gir Forest of India to search for a jungle boy who talks to the animals. What the sketch actually consists of is a lot of stock footage of trains, jeeps, foreigners, and animals, all with "humorous" voiceovers that are supposed to represent Edith's trip. It's never clear if the jokes are supposed to come out of the material itself or out of the fact that the show is trying to pass others' explorations off as their own. In the end, it doesn't matter, because neither aspect of the sketch works.

The rest of this *Network 90* episode is largely taken up with "SCTV Pledge Week," a continuation of last episode's storyline in which Guy Caballero decides to raise public funds after losing the support of many of the station's advertisers. Lacking in many different respects, the wraparound seems to exist solely as an easy way for the cast to bring out some of their characters, including Caballero, Lola Heatherton, Count Floyd, and Bobby Bittman. For his part, this is Bittman's second SCTV telethon sketch, having first appeared in the superior "Solid Gold Telethon" on show 30.

Despite some laughs involving Dave Thomas as The Elephant Man (he is the first to respond to Heatherton's pledge to sleep with the first caller to donate $5,000; later he stumbles upon a rehearsal with Candy and Levy as Dr. Tongue and Bruno) the "SCTV Pledge Week" resembles real PBS pledge breaks in one unfortunate way: Watching either, you are likely to find yourself thinking: "We get the idea, now please, can you get on with the real show?"

Show 86 *(SCTV Network 90)*

1. Gene Shalit Critics' Special promo
2. Lola Heatherton wraparound part 1: The Wrong Side of the Bed
3. John McEnroe coffee commercial
4. Lola Heatherton wraparound part 2: Lola's dressing room
5. Jake LaMotta's Raging Bull B-Que commercial
6. The Fishin' Musician: The Tubes part 1
7. K-Tel Ronco Popeli Product Crusher commercial

8. The Fishin' Musician: The Tubes part 2
9. Lola Heatherton wraparound part 3: SCTV News
10. You! With Libby Wolfson: Premiere
11. Lola Heatherton wraparound part 4: Lola! Bouncin' Back To You!
12. The Tubes: "Talk To Ya Later"
13. SCTV Movie of the Week: The Nobel
14. Lola Heatherton wraparound part 5: Conclusion

What to watch for: The Fishin' Musician.
Two new characters are introduced in this fine episode. But whereas Andrea Martin's Libby Wolfson would evolve and improve, John Candy's Gil Fisher—the host of the rock & roll outdoorsman show "The Fishin' Musician"—peaks with his first appearance.

"The Fishin' Musician" concept would become one of SCTV's favorite ways to incorporate musical guests into the program, and The Tubes were an inspired choice to be the first visitors to Gil Fisher's Scuttlebutt Lodge. The rock band was SCTV's first musical guest to seem relaxed and enthusiastic about performing comedy; one band member even dared a post-sneeze ad-lib ("I'm allergic to fish myself," he deadpanned).

After the first sub-par NBC episode, *SCTV* returns to form with this show that centers around events leading up to Lola Heatherton's first live prime-time special. This series of segments is darker than the usual *SCTV* fare, as Heatherton (O'Hara) struggles with drugs, personal and professional failures, a false suicide report, and a public breakdown. Only the weak *Wizard of Oz* conclusion — it is revealed that Heatherton dreamed many of the events — dilutes some otherwise strong material.

In the first segment of the wraparound, Dave Thomas's Bill Needle character is cast as the reluctant host of the early morning program "The Wrong Side of the Bed" (Needle claims his goal for the program is to "just get it over with as painlessly as possible"), and an obviously stoned Heatherton is his equally reluctant guest. When Heatherton reaches for a vial of pills, Needle brazenly attacks her for allowing viewers to see that entertainers use substances to "fake their way through performances," an anti-drug tirade that contradicts NBC's wishes to feature drug *humor* in the show's opening minutes. Because Heatherton reacts to Needle's disdain by walking off the show and ruining the program, the developing joke that Needle can't keep a show on the air is allowed to continue.

A most surprising character revelation comes in the story's next segment, when Flaherty's Guy Caballero tells Lola that, because she's "high," he's canceling her special. Although Flaherty softened Caballero's tone significantly after the character's first few appearances, here for the first time Caballero is almost *compassionate* as his concerns about Lola become evident. As if the fact that Caballero has a heart wasn't a big enough surprise, next we discover that Guy and Lola used to be lovers, a fact visualized in a soft-focus flashback in which the cliché of two lovers running together is tweaked by placing Guy in his wheelchair *wheeling* toward Lola. Apparently even during a time of intense passion, Guy still demands respect.

Guy's sudden cancellation causes Lola to loudly proclaim, "Now I don't want to live anymore," a statement that foreshadows "SCTV News" anchor Earl Camembert airing a false report that Lola has committed suicide. The continuing unprofessionalism of Camembert and his competition with Floyd Robertson motivate this lengthy scene, as Earl bases his decision to run the story of Lola's passing not because he's convinced that it's true, but because he wants to have a better story than Robertson. (Again, this internal competition is at the heart of these characters, serving as the basis for their first appearance on show 1.) But because the fraudulent nature of the story is not quickly revealed, the scene succeeds in creating real tension—maybe she *did* kill herself—that is not released until Floyd happily embarrasses Earl by retracting the news of Lola's death and forcing him to apologize for the false report. During his apology, note that Camembert states that the Lola story *would* have been great had it only been true—a sly commentary on journalists who seemingly take a perverse glee in reporting tragic news. While feeling disgust toward Camembert, again sympathies go out to Caballero, who is forced to rebuff questions about Lola's health by reinstating her special.

The live airing of Lola's special, which amounts to an aborted musical number, is a tour de force performance by O'Hara, as Heatherton has a nervous breakdown in front of what is presumably a large television audience. In fact, without the overwrought lyrics—"No one cares / No one loves me / You're all just parasites draining me of love"—the segment would work as drama, as a stumbling, squinting, and trembling Heatherton vainly tries to hide behind drugs but instead embarrassingly reveals too much of herself.

Embarrassing would describe the roll call of SCTV staff members that Lola has bedded, which she without warning begins to recite before being dragged out of the studio: "Mr. Guy Caballero! Johnny 'Why don't you just suffocate me' LaRue! Bobby 'How was I?' Bittman! Count Floyd, you're so bad it's scary! Bob and Doug, you hosers!" Heatherton's exit leaves time for The Tubes to re-appear for a performance of their semi-hit "Talk to Ya Later."

The Heatherton special is also notable for the premiere of the Juul Haalmayer Dancers. O'Hara drafted Haalmayer, the show's costume designer, to head up a team of dancers because he could not dance and therefore possessed the amateurism that Catherine was seeking. The Juul Haalmayer Dancers evolved throughout the rest of *SCTV*'s run; part of the pleasure of their appearances became noticing which cast member was joining them in each sketch. Here Eugene Levy is front and center, with writers Doug Steckler, Mort Rich, Dick Blasucci, Bob Dolman, and Haalmayer himself. Note, however, that the original idea that evolved into the Juul Haalmayer Dancers was hatched long before but again in connection with Lola Heatherton: In a spot from show 27 (and repeated on show 81), Levy, Thomas, and Flaherty all incompetently dance behind Lola.

Unfortunately, a strong storyline comes to a weak finish, as Heatherton wakes up in her dressing room only to realize that much of what had happened was a dream and that she actually slept through the time during which her special was to air. As if the connection to *The Wizard of Oz* wasn't obvious enough, the strains of "Over the Rainbow" are heard, with Lola concluding a soliloquy by exclaiming, "There's no place like SCTV!" Fortunately, the similarities to *Oz* end here as those gathered become embarrassed by Heatherton's show of emotion and quickly disperse, bringing to a close one of *SCTV*'s greatest single character explorations.

One cast member who was not involved with the Heatherton wraparound was Andrea Martin. Looking at the early NBC shows, it's noticeable that Martin's contributions tended to be solo or two-person pieces (the Edith Prickley and Pirini Sclereso segments, Mrs. Falbo's premiere). Dave Thomas suggests in his book that Martin's insecurities were perhaps to blame for isolating her a bit from the rest of the cast. If Thomas's suggestion is to be believed, then what Andrea did with her Libby Wolfson character was to take those insecurities and fashion her best character out of them.

As host of the "You!" talk show, Martin's Wolfson is a creature wallowing in self-doubt; she obsesses about her weight, her appearance, and her body odor. She is particularly fixated on the latter, constantly sniffing her fingers, smelling her armpits, or wondering aloud whether her breath smells bad. She poses the breath question to her first guest, a psychiatrist (Moranis), along with other inane queries as "Why can I not stop eating?" and "Do I have something in my eye?" Wolfson also gleefully informs the horrified doctor that she would "kill" to be anorexic for one week.

With Wolfson, Martin encapsulates smart and ambitious career women who nevertheless insist on obsessing over purely shallow matters as if they were back at their first high school dance. This first appearance by Wolfson is tantalizingly brief; there will be more of her to come.

Oddly, "You!" is Andrea's only appearance in this episode, for not only is she missing from the Heatherton wraparound, she is also absent from the show's longest stand-alone sketch, the "SCTV Movie of the Week" entitled "The Nobel." Not included in off-net syndication, "The Nobel" is one of the strangest of all *SCTV* sketches. Why the cast decided to embark on a lengthy and complex parody of an obscure camp classic—1966's *The Oscar* (with shades of 1963's *The Prize*)—is a bit of a mystery. This long sketch is likely to appeal only to those who have seen *The Oscar*, which starred Stephen Boyd, Tony Bennett (yes, that Tony Bennett), and Elke Sommer. Even that small segment of the audience was probably left wondering the point of parodying a movie so bad that it is already guilty of being a parody of itself.

Both "The Nobel" and *The Oscar* center around a ruthless and selfish individual who is relentless in his drive to succeed; in *The Oscar*, Frankie Faine (Stephen Boyd) abuses his friends to become a popular actor, while in "The Nobel," Mike Maxwell (Dave Thomas) abuses his friends to become a successful doctor. Suffering most in both pieces is singer Tony Bennett, who chose *The Oscar* for his first and only dramatic role. In "The Nobel," Joe Flaherty gives a wicked impression of Bennett's truly awful *Oscar* performance, but in fairness to Bennett, his lines were so ridiculous that *SCTV* saw little need to change them for their parody.

Also featured is Eugene Levy as Milton Berle, the legendary comedian who portrayed Faine's agent in *The Oscar* and who in "The Nobel" is Maxwell's lawyer, whom Maxwell employs to handle his rising number of malpractice cases. While Levy would later perfect his Berle impression (show 112's "A Star is Born"), here he does capture, with every raised eyebrow and wave of his enormous cigar, the ridiculousness of a recognizable comedian with no acting skills trying to create a dramatic character.

Levy's key scene is overshadowed by the surprising display of the most overt drug humor ever performed on *SCTV*, which has no parallel in *The Oscar*. The segment is courtesy of John Candy's second and final appearance as Dr. Braino, introduced here as a hippie who agrees to allow Maxwell to practice in a free clinic that he runs (this downfall of Maxwell's parallels Faine's, whose *Oscar* character has to take a lowly television job). To thank Braino, Berle pulls out a huge mirror and a large bag of cocaine, a tremendous amount of which Braino proceeds to snort through an enormous straw. The drug use is played strictly for laughs; unlike the earlier Bill Needle-Lola Heatherton sketch, there is no anti-drug message here. The existence of this scene surely has much to do with "The Nobel" being excluded from off-net syndication.

There are countless moments when *SCTV* very cleverly parodies *The Oscar* within "The Nobel," but the piece, though inarguably a successful parody, is unforgivably self-indulgent. It was either wonderfully subversive or just blatantly foolhardy for *SCTV* to mount such an alienating sketch when the program could have instead been trying to win over the large network audience it was now capable of reaching.

This is also the first *SCTV Network 90* program to lack an appearance by Bob and Doug McKenzie. The decision to not air a "Great White North" segment may have been made because the next episode features more than enough Bob and Doug to make up for their absence here.

Show 87 *(SCTV Network 90)*

1. Max Lax commercial (repeat from show 30)
2. Bob and Doug wraparound part 1: Brian Johns
3. Harry Filth preview (repeat from show 25)

4. Money Talks with Brian Johns: William E. Douglas (repeat from show 56)
5. The Johnny LaRue Show (repeat from show 1)
6. Shakespeare in the Park with Norman Gorman promo (repeat from show 62)
7. Bob and Doug wraparound part 2: Johnny LaRue
8. The Heys of Our Lives (repeat from show 42)
9. SCTV Afternoon Movie: Fantasy Island (repeat from show 44)
10. Bob and Doug wraparound part 3: The Ian Thomas Band
11. Bob and Doug wraparound part 4: Backstage with Ian Thomas
12. Anne Murray Super Special promo
13. Don Strom: Mental Illness PSA (repeat from show 50)
14. The David Susskind Show promo
15. La Rue-Tachi Concert on Wheels commercial
16. Bob and Doug wraparound part 5: Great White North
17. Mel Torme and Bob and Doug McKenzie anthems (repeat from show 64)

What to watch for: *Fantasy Island* (see show 44).

For the last time, *SCTV* allocates the majority of an episode to recycled material. Not coincidentally, this episode was also the final program in a production cycle; starting with the next cycle, *SCTV* would present all (well, *nearly* all) new sketches. About half of the airtime devoted to this episode's batch of repeats is taken up by the long "Fantasy Island" sketch, while almost all of the time devoted to new material is earmarked for a wraparound featuring Bob and Doug McKenzie (Rick Moranis and Dave Thomas) and Dave Thomas's real-life brother, musician Ian Thomas. It's a strong wraparound: Though less ambitious than others, it's noteworthy for giving Bob and Doug their first chance to interact with other station characters.

Like other successful wraparounds, this one works not only on a comedic level, but because it gives insight into the characters; as sophomoric as "Great White North" is, here we learn that Bob and Doug do actually *care* about their show and, when pressed, can work hard at the program, even if their limited intelligence prevents them from producing anything of merit. In addition, the shabby treatment they get from others makes them sympathetic characters — like dim, drunken children forced to live in an adult world.

In the first segment of the wraparound, the crew ridicules Bob and Doug for the inanity of their program. Noting that "Money Talks" host Brian Johns (Eugene Levy) is treated with respect by the crew, Bob and Doug decide that to be appreciated, they must improve their show, which to them means think of better topics. (The combination of the new Johns wraparound segment and the rerun "Money Talks" sketch is the most seamless way *SCTV Network 90* ever mixed old and new material. Note that the outro to "Money Talks," featuring Johns promoting a future show with an inventor who got rich by putting radios inside of toilet paper dispensers, is cut in the version seen here.)

The next time we see them, the McKenzies are meeting on the lawn outside of the SCTV studios (they apparently have no office) about the next day's show. Here we learn of the brothers' division of labor: Doug does the menial work of bringing cigarettes and beer, while Bob has the marginally headier task of creating topic ideas. Their meeting is interrupted by Johnny LaRue (John Candy), who regards Bob and Doug as children, albeit children who have beer and are willing to share. Conversely, Bob and Doug regard LaRue as children might a parent — they don't respect him, but they fear him, mainly because he might ask them to perform undesirable tasks. Although the two vow not to give in to LaRue's demands, they end up not only being talked into washing LaRue's limo, but also into investing what little money they have into a nightclub. Angered at being "hosed," Bob and Doug at least feel that they should be able to find some ideas for topics at the club.

After a long break for the "Fantasy Island" sketch (unless you're watching this episode on DVD, on which "Fantasy Island" has been inexplicably bumped to the end of the episode), the rest of the story plays out at the aforementioned nightclub. Flaherty's Vic Hedges returns as the nightclub owner, and, in an example of how *SCTV* feeds on itself, we suspect that LaRue's interest in investing has less to do with his belief in the club than to debts owed to Hedges that were spelled out in show 80's "Polynesiantown."

Next comes a performance from the Ian Thomas Band ("Hold On," a Thomas song that Santana later turned into a hit), who play well enough to have earned their spot on the show, even if their appearance has much to do with Ian Thomas being Dave Thomas's brother. Actually the elder Thomas by this point had recorded steadily for almost ten years while scoring several hit records in Canada as well as writing songs (like "Hold On") that would become hits for other artists. In fact, by Dave's own admittance, Dave owed Ian more than the other way around; in the mid-seventies, Ian had gotten Dave a job on a CBC Radio variety show, which allowed Dave to further hone his performing skills. Working on the radio show also gave Ian experience doing comedy — another good reason to have him on *SCTV*.

Ian Thomas's flair for comedy is most evident when Bob and Doug assume the identity of Brian Johns in order to gain entrance to the backstage area. (They introduce themselves as Brian Johns and — what else — his brother Doug.) Their obvious dim-wittedness causes Vic Hedges to be suspicious, but Ian is happy to find himself in the company of two "fellow hosers" and quickly agrees to appear on "Great White North."

The epilogue to the wraparound is a bit of a letdown and only exists as a way to work in another Ian Thomas performance. There is also a severe lapse of logic here: After Ian Thomas finishes his song, he goes to a room next door, which is revealed to be the "Great White North" studio. Perhaps this revelation is supposed to be a self-referential gag — look, we know there's no real nightclub and this is obviously a television show being shot on two interconnected sets — but if it is, the joke ruins the established reality of the scene. (The ending comes off even worse in the later off-net syndicated version, since the nightclub scene and the "Great White North" scene are connected by a tracking shot of the SCTV studios, which is meant to signify a change of locale. The locale change is rendered nonsensical by revealing that the sets are adjacent to each other.)

Two notes about the rerun material: "The Johnny LaRue Show" from *SCTV*'s very first episode is here, which is an odd choice in an episode that also features new footage of John Candy as LaRue. The obvious differernces in Candy's appearance is confusing. Also, due to the real-life assassination attempt on the Pope in May of 1981, the "Harry Filth" sketch was crudely edited to delete a reference to Candy's willingness to "off" His Holiness.

Show 88 *(SCTV Network)*

1. Perry Como: Still Alive commercial
2. Mayberline commercial
3. Benny Hill Street Blues promo
4. Great White North: Economics
5. Lola Heatherton's Way To Go, Woman! promo
6. Russian takeover wraparound part 1: Caesar part 1
7. CCCP1: Today Is Moscow
8. Russian takeover wraparound part 2: Caesar part 2
9. Russian takeover wraparound part 3: Guy Caballero & Johnny LaRue
10. CCCP1: Uposcrabblenyk
11. CCCP1: What Fits Into Russia
12. CCCP1: Mother Russia Cares PSA
13. Russian takeover wraparound part 4: Caballero calls NBC
14. SCTV Movie of the Week: The Jazz Singer
15. Russian takeover wraparound part 5: Cruisin' Gourmet promo (repeat from show 69)
16. CCCP1: Hey Giorgy! promo
17. CCCP1: Strelnokoff Vodka commercial
18. CCCP1: Tibor's Tractor promo
19. Russian takeover wraparound part 6: Caballero & Red Rooster
20. Wet Nurse promo
21. Russian takeover wraparound part 7: Caballero, Rooster, Dr. Tongue & Bruno
22. Eskimo Arts: Two Folon Sale commercial
23. Russian takeover wraparound part 8: Rooster, Dr. Tongue & Bruno fix satellite
24. Russian takeover wraparound part 9: Guy Caballero at Oval Office
25. Russian takeover wraparound part 10: Edith Prickley closing statement

What to watch for: Perry Como: Still Alive.
Undoubtedly one of the most popular SCTV *sketches and one of the pieces still most readily identified with the show. This inspired sketch features Eugene Levy looking and sounding uncannily like singer Perry Como, but with Como's "Mr. Relaxation" stage demeanor taken to an extreme: While singing bland versions of "Celebration," "Fame," "I Will Survive," and "What I Did for Love," Como is so relaxed that while singing he's lying motionless on a couch, lying motionless on the floor, or, best*

of all, lying motionless in a bed. Adding a comical juxtaposition to Levy's near-comatose Como are the very energetic Juul Haalmayer Dancers (featuring Rick Moranis) and two vivacious backup singers.

The sketch, which also features some testimonials from audience members ("I thought tonight's show was a little uptempo," one asserts), brought the house down at the 1982 Emmy Awards when it was shown. The segment also helped form a later partnership between Eugene Levy and Christopher Guest: When Guest was looking for a collaborator on the 1996 film Waiting for Guffman, *it was "Still Alive" that prompted Guest to call Levy: "I think that made me laugh harder than anything I've ever seen in my life," Guest claimed. But the surest sign of the piece's success is that it became linked to Como for the rest of his life, even meriting a mention in the Associated Press's obituary of the entertainer when he passed away in May of 2001.*

One of the most ambitious of all *SCTV* episodes, this show features a wraparound involving a Russian television station (CCCP1) that takes over SCTV's signal, resulting in Russian programming (and its philosophies and ideologies) being broadcast on SCTV.

While one of *SCTV*'s best-known storylines, it is not one of their most successful. While the parodies of Russian programming are solid — Thomas's "What Fits Into Russia" being particularly strong — the show bogs down in its interminable third act, as Flaherty's Guy Caballero sends Dr. Tongue (Candy), Woody Tobias, Jr. (Levy), and "satellite troubleshooter" Red Rooster (Thomas), into space to affix a "scrambler" on the SCTV satellite. The finale of the episode is especially problematic, as the storyline degenerates into a muddled mixture of *Dr. Strangelove* and *Fail-Safe*, complete with Rooster riding the CCCP1 satellite toward Russia a la Slim Pickens in *Strangelove*, while Guy Caballero speaks to the President, played by Henry Fonda (also Flaherty), who assumed the role in *Fail-Safe*.

Worse is the conflicting closing statement by Edith Prickley (Martin): Played over stock atomic bomb footage while Vera Lynn's version of *We'll Meet Again* is heard (a juxtaposition also used in *Dr. Strangelove*), Prickley tells President Reagan not to get too "trigger happy with that button" while also warning him not to let the "Ruskies get away with anything." This presumably illustrates the ambiguities of fighting a Cold War, an obvious fact unnecessarily underscored with heavy-handed commentary.

Infinitely better are the CCCP1 programs found in the middle third of this episode: "Today Is Moscow" is a cross between a "happy talk" morning program and SCTV's own "Great White North," as hosts Moranis and Thomas delight in such inanities as Moranis's new shoes, just as Bob and Doug had previously delighted in such inanities as their new boots. Also noteworthy is the Soviet technology used to record the program — Moranis and Thomas are both weighted down with enormous microphones hung around their necks, while a half dozen crew members struggle to move a gigantic camera referred to as a "new Soviet mini-cam."

Elsewhere, the brilliant "What Fits into Russia" fulfills Thomas's wish that the Russian parodies not just be Russian versions of North American shows. Here Thomas plays a host who simply stands in front of a map of Russia and ridicules other countries, continents, and U.S. states for being tiny in comparison to "the vast colossal size of Mother Russia." No matter that life in Russia was miserable for most; this show empowers its citizens by telling them that at least they live in a country bigger than Texas.

The look of the Russian sketches adds much to the material: By programming a device known as a Digital Video Exchange, every second frame was frozen *for* a frame. This effect gave the sketches the appearance of having been transferred from the Soviet video standard known as SECAM to the North American standard known as NTSC. An achievement that secured this episode a 1982 Emmy nomination in the category of Creative Special Achievement (*SCTV* lost out to a Shirley MacLaine special).

In addition to Eugene Levy's Perry Como sketch, much of the strongest material on this show has nothing to do with the wraparound. Nearly as memorable as Levy's Como is Andrea Martin's appearance as Lynn Redgrave in a parody of Redgrave's dispute with Universal Studios over her insistence on breast-feeding her baby between takes of her television series *House Calls*. Martin's enormously busty Redgrave stars as the title character in a show called "Wet Nurse," where she's called upon to feed not only her abnormally large infant son (Candy) but an entire hospital after a power failure cripples the cafeteria.

Equally outlandish is a piece reminiscent of the dual parody model perfected by show 84's "The Merv Griffith Show." Here Dave Thomas stars as the broad British comedian Benny Hill in a promo for "Benny Hill Street Blues." The sketch combines much of Hill's lowbrow shtick (dirty limericks, men in drag) with the serious day-to-day routine at a police precinct.

Catherine O'Hara also contributes two fine pieces: While Robin Duke was the first *SCTV* cast member to impersonate *The PTL Club*'s Tammy Faye Bakker (show 68), here O'Hara makes the impression her own with a commercial parody that savages Bakker for two of her most identifying characteristics: Her affinity for tears and her inclination to wear far too much makeup. O'Hara also partners with Martin for a Lola Heatherton promo in which the entertainer interviews Mother Teresa as part of a series of profiles on the "five most influential women of our time" (somehow, *Dallas*'s Charlene Tilton made the short list). Heatherton is at her most shallow here, having more sympathy for a sick young man because of his lack of show-biz knowledge than for his lack of food or medicine.

Out of all the stand-alone sketches, the weakest piece — a parody of the 1980 remake of *The Jazz Singer* that starred Neil Diamond and Laurence Olivier — is also the longest. That remake was about a conflict between a father and son over the son's future; the father (Olivier) wanted the son to become a Jewish cantor, while the son (Diamond) wanted to become a rock star. *SCTV* predictably reverses the plot, with the son (played by musical guest Al Jarreau) wishing to become a cantor while his adoptive father (Levy's Sid Dithers, in cornrows!) wants his son to be a great soul singer. The piece isn't awful, but a dull musical interlude ("We're in This Love Together") coupled with the singer's dull acting results in a mostly dull sketch. Thankfully, Levy's Dithers has several moments, particularly when he laments that he "should have adopted Barry White," and when he ridicules O'Hara's Linda McCartney ("I know why the band's on the run," Dithers tells her. "They've been running away from you!"). Note that the temple that Jarreau sings at is named Temple Beth Blasucci, a nod to writer Dick Blasucci.

Show 89 *(SCTV Network)*

1. Ricardo Montalban School of Fine Acting commercial
2. Sunrise Semester: Ventriloquism
3. Night School Hi-Q
4. Perma Lacque commercial
5. Great White North: How to stuff a mouse into a beer bottle
6. Libby Wolfson wraparound part 1: You!
7. Videotech video dinners commercial
8. Libby Wolfson wraparound part 2: Seth Dick III
9. Libby Wolfson wraparound part 3: Critic's Corner
10. Libby Wolfson wraparound part 4: Lenny Schechtman
11. The Fishin' Musician: Wendy O. Williams and the Plasmatics part 1
12. Pitchman commercial 1
13. The Fishin' Musician: Wendy O. Williams and the Plasmatics part 2
14. Pitchman commercial 2
15. Libby Wolfson wraparound part 5: Theatre Beat
16. Libby Wolfson wraparound part 6: You! promo
17. Dusty Towne commercial
18. My Bloody Hand promo
19. The Cow commercial
20. SCTV Movie of the Week: Power Play

What to watch for: Dusty Towne.
Although Andrea Martin is undoubtedly the star of this episode, it is Catherine O'Hara who stars in the show's funniest standalone piece, a commercial for an appearance by her bawdy nightclub comedienne Dusty Towne. Based on real-life performer Rusty Warren, the self-proclaimed "Knockers Up Gal," Catherine's debut of Towne is full of bad dirty jokes and filthy songs. (Note Rick Moranis playing drums in Towne's band.) The sketch also finds time to parody Warren's seemingly endless output of albums; the cover of Towne's Keep 'Em Sunnyside Up *is a dead ringer for the* Rusty Warren Bounces Back *album sleeve.*

Back on show 86, Andrea Martin premiered Libby Wolfson, the host of the women's program "You!" As successful as that debut was, here Martin delivers her finest work as the character, as Libby and her friend Sue Bopper-Simpson (O'Hara) stage a feminist play. The production fails miserably — and not just because of its exasperating title of "I'm Taking My Own Head, Screwing It On Right, and No Guy's Gonna Tell Me That It Ain't."

As with many other *SCTV* behind-the-scenes wraparounds, this one begins on-air, as Libby and Sue discuss the play on Wolfson's talk show. The importance of the play to Libby is obvious, as she grandly describes it as "the culmination of our life's work," yet at the same time neither Libby nor Sue know what their play is actually about, as Wolfson vaguely describes the material as involving "women, their tears, their fears, relationship, sex, mothers, careers ..." Throughout the sketch, Martin undercuts Wolfson's credibility by making her just as focused on picking her teeth or smelling her armpits as she is on discussing the "culmination of our life's work."

Making matters worse, neither Libby nor Sue knows who their audience is; specifically, they can't decide whether they want to try to appeal to men. This confusion becomes evident as Libby meets with their lone male co-star, Seth Dick III (Flaherty), who realizes that the play is so badly written he can't understand why he even makes an entrance. Flaherty portrays Seth Dick III to first seem hopelessly dim, but then slowly we realize that he is an actor simply in need of a coherent script, which he has clearly not been given. While fighting against sexism, here Wolfson is sexist herself— she treats Seth as an infant, even telling him that just because he performs in it, he doesn't have to understand the play.

Following a scene between Libby and her boyfriend Lenny Schechtman (Moranis disguised as *SCTV* producer Barry Sand with the last name of makeup artist Beverley Schechtman), *SCTV* brings the events back to the television station, using Dave Thomas's Bill Needle character to review Wolfson's play on his new show, "Theatre Beat." Before he even sees the play, Wolfson is in trouble: Needle readily admits that he "hates" theatre, declaring it "artistically inferior to movies and television." Needle then wastes no time lashing into the two hours of "drivel" that is Libby's play, pausing only to add that he doesn't want to prejudice us (far too late for that) and that we should make up our own minds by watching clips of the performance.

The clips from the play are terrifically horrid: Libby and Sue are incredibly unlikable women (really just thinly-veiled versions of themselves; note how Libby refers to her partner as "Benny") who spew gloriously bad dialogue ("I'm only truly fulfilled when I work 21 hours a day. Except when I have cramps, of course"). Best of all is the hack job they've done with Flaherty's Seth Dick III, who is supposed, we guess, to represent all men. Bad news for all men is that in the world created by Wolfson and Bopper-Simpson, Seth Dick III is hung at the play's end.

Despite the disaster she has created, our sympathies soon return to Wolfson: Her boyfriend Lenny is interviewed and he is appallingly callous about the play, remarking that the meal served was "a good piece of meat" and that the price was OK for "a bite to eat and something to look at." We also feel for Wolfson due to Needle's inexplicable praise of Seth Dick III; clearly Needle was prejudiced against Libby and Sue.

Finally, after Needle walks out on "Theatre Beat," the wraparound ends with a startling promo for the next edition of "You!" What's shocking about the piece is how awful Martin is made to look, as the failure of Libby's play has reduced her to a quivering mess. Instead of simply smelling her fingers, she is now chewing on her fingernails and sobbing to a psychiatrist (Levy), who is there to discuss the topic of "women, the arts, and coping with failure." In the end, then, after enjoying her colossal and deserved failure, we can't help but have total empathy for Wolfson. This episode represents Martin's finest *SCTV* work.

The two major stand-alone sketches in this show, "The Fishin' Musician" with guests Wendy O. Williams and the Plasmatics, and the movie "Power Play," were excised from off-net syndication. Like "The Nobel" from Show 86, "Power Play" was likely removed for being a lengthy parody of an obscure film. Meanwhile, the Wendy O. Williams "Fishin' Musician" sketch is the first of five Gil Fisher pieces to be cut from syndication; a recurring edit that makes sense since the inclusion of musical performances resulted in only fifteen minutes of comedy in the half-hour syndication versions.

The idea of having punk rockers Williams and the Plasmatics on the outdoorsman show "The Fishin' Musician" may have seemed too good to pass up; while it is humorous to see the band in this context, the sketch doesn't go anywhere. Williams is the only one who interacts with Gil and what little interaction there is between her and Candy is forced, resulting in the joke of the band not fitting in on "The Fishin' Musician" giving way to the reality of the band not fitting in on *SCTV*. The sketch does become decidedly livelier with the band's explosive (literally) performance of "The Doom Song," a cut from their then-current album *Metal Priestess*. (Although it may have seemed radical for *SCTV* to book the Plasmatics, it must be noted that *Fridays*, the *SNL* knock-off on ABC, had the band on several months earlier.)

More potentially dangerous than booking a punk band is parodying a film unfamiliar to nearly all of your audience. But that's what *SCTV* does with the sketch "Power Play," which is a spoof of a 1971 Canadian film entitled *Face-Off*. Both pieces are about a hockey player and his conflicting commitments to the sport and his girlfriend, but most of the similarities stop there. Unlike show 86's "The Nobel," which referenced the film *The Oscar* sometimes *too* closely, "Power Play" (with Candy as real-life Toronto Maple Leaf star Darryl Sittler playing a dim-witted and overly violent hockey player), is enjoyable even without knowledge of the film being parodied. But ultimately "Power Play's" satirizing of *Face-Off*'s heavyhanded indictment of hockey as a dangerous and violent sport will be more satisfying to those who have sat through the melodramatic original.

One highlight of this episode that did make it to off-net syndication is "Night School Hi-Q," a follow-up to the "High Q" game show parody from show 35. Returning here from that sketch is fastest fingered contestant Margaret Meehan, who once again insists on answering before questions or even categories are given ("Computers?" "ABBA?"). Her exchanges with host Alex Trebel (Levy), who is driven more and more insane with every incorrect premature guess, are again the highlights of the segment. While missing the originality of the first "High Q" sketch, this version is a little more balanced, with Flaherty's contestant in particular wrestling a few good lines away from O'Hara and Levy. A worthy companion to the original "High Q," this franchise was retired to make way for the later "Half Wits" sketches.

Not so quickly retired is "Great White North," featured here in one of its most notable segments, as the McKenzies discuss how to stuff a mouse in a beer bottle in order to acquire free beers. The concept here is so intriguing that Rick and Dave would reintroduce the topic in their Bob and Doug movie *Strange Brew*. And because of the link to the film, this sketch was included on the *Strange Brew* DVD that was released in October 2002.

While Bob and Doug were still going strong, this *SCTV* episode signaled the beginning of the downfall of Moranis's Gerry Todd. After only two "Gerry Todd Show" pieces, Moranis apparently felt that he had taken that concept as far as it could go and from here on only uses Todd in other, usually less amusing, contexts. His sketch here for Video Dinners (including "Shogun Sushi" and "Meatballs Meatballs") is an example of the mediocre pieces that marred the remainder of Gerry Todd's appearances.

Two other commercial parodies are notable largely for their cruelty: The more vicious of the two is a parody of Schlitz Malt Liquor commercials that replace that product's Bull mascot with actress Shelley Winters, who is referred to as "the Cow." Candy is unforgettable as Winters, as he runs after a crew member ("She's loose!"), gets transported via heavy machinery, and finally storms through a brick wall. (Note the appearance by then-current *SCTV* and future *Late Night with David Letterman* producer Barry Sand, parodied earlier in the episode by Rick Moranis.)

Opening the episode is a commercial parody for the Ricardo Montalban School of Fine Acting. Here Eugene Levy savages Montalban's acting skills, as he takes potentially promising actors and teaches them to speak and sing in ridiculously accentuated English while using inappropriately exaggerated gestures. A solid start to an episode nominated for a 1982 Emmy for Outstanding Writing (it lost to *SCTV* show 84).

Show 90 *(SCTV Network)*

1. American Orthodontal Group PSA
2. Mrs. Falbo's Tiny Town: G. Gordon Liddy
3. Zontar wraparound part 1: Hank Bain
4. Great White North: Shortcuts
5. George Carlin's Reel Love preview
6. Zontar wraparound part 2: Gusstofferson & LaRue
7. For Lifers Only commercial
8. Farm Film Celebrity Blow-Up: Meryl Streep
9. Don Rickles's Love is the Greatest Gift God Gave Us preview
10. Zontar wraparound part 3: SCTV News
11. Zontar wraparound part 4: Diff'rent Folks
12. Ted Gordon: Overbooked Attorney promo
13. Zontar wraparound part 5: The Sammy Maudlin Show part 1
14. Tex & Edna Boil's Prairie Warehouse & Curio Emporium commercial
15. Poocharé commercial (repeat from show 84)
16. Zontar wraparound part 6: The Sammy Maudlin Show part 2
17. Money Talks with Brian Johns: Henna Claire Graham
18. American Express with Henry Moore commercial (repeat from show 74)
19. Zontar wraparound part 7: Caballero & DeForest Kelley
20. Dr. Shekter commercial (repeat from show 85)
21. Zontar wraparound part 8: Zontar defeated

What to watch for: *The Sammy Maudlin Show.*
Even though this sketch is part of a wraparound, it is in actuality a stand-alone piece until its final few seconds. Indeed, the fact that SCTV *is able to turn this piece into part of the larger narrative shows that the cast was still experimenting with different ways to tell stories.*

Before the "Zontar" story intrudes, this "Sammy Maudlin" sketch proves itself as one of the darker pieces in SCTV's *oeuvre. The comedic target for the sketch is Joan Embry (O'Hara) who, as the former director of the San Diego Zoo, became famous for guesting on* The Tonight Show *with animals that either terrified Johnny or pooped on him. With Carson, Embry was always softspoken; here O'Hara's Embry is outrageously profane and even abusive to her animals. The appearance ends on an especially sinister note when Candy's William B. Williams accidentally shoots and kills Embry.*

Sandwiched between Embry and Dave Thomas's manic DeForest "Bones" Kelley (who, as in show 55, seems to think he's still on the Starship Enterprise) *is musical guest Natalie Cole. She and Flaherty and Candy have some sycophantic lines of the type normally reserved for Lola Heatherton or Bobby Bittman (William B.: "I have never seen a better chemistry than you [Maudlin] and Natalie Cole on a talk show in my life and I think the audience is going to back me up on this!"), but ultimately her musical appearance is the least satisfying of any* SCTV *guest to this point. Her performance of the song "Nothin' But a Fool" from her* Happy Love *album is the only time* SCTV *crossed paths with the eighties variety show* Solid Gold, *as Cole tediously lip-synchs on a dark and non-descript set.*

This episode is dominated by one of the silliest of all *SCTV* wraparounds, as SCTV is targeted for an alien takeover by the fictional planet Zontar. The takeover is assisted by insider Hank Bain (guest star Bonar Bain, the real-life twin brother of *Diff'rent Strokes* star Conrad Bain), an agent of Zontar who comes to SCTV under the guise of starring in a "rip-off" of his brother's hit sitcom. The "Zontar" story draws on 1950s sci-fi films like *Invasion of the Body Snatchers*, but it is most closely related to the 1966 remake of *It Conquered the World*, not coincidentally titled *Zontar, The Thing from Venus*.

In the film *Zontar*, a disgruntled scientist communicates with a being named Zontar via a communications system that looks like an elaborate ham radio. The cinematic Zontar speaks unintelligibly (the scientist explains his understanding of the creature as "hyperspace hypnotism"), while *SCTV*'s Zontar (Candy) speaks clear English. Using a scaled-down version of a similar communications system, Bain first speaks to Zontar after leaving a meeting with Guy Caballero, during which we learn that Caballero demands his new employees work for free their first couple of weeks, a stipulation to which Bain readily agrees. After all, acting is not the reason Bain has infiltrated SCTV.

In a sequence that parallels the glaring cheapness of *Zontar*'s special effects, Bain gives the orders for Zontar to send down its spaceship, which is nothing more than a Frisbee moving through a cheaply-constructed solar system (a piece of which is obviously a golf ball). Upon landing on the roof of SCTV, the Frisbee is surrounded by sprouting cabbages, which then enter the station via the heating and cooling system. These innocent-looking cabbages bear a strong resemblance to the seedpods seen in *Invasion of the Body Snatchers*; both turn out to be active beings that the aliens use to penetrate people's minds and bodies. When an unsuspecting person picks up one of these cabbages, he or she quickly becomes controlled by Zontar; Zontar's victims at SCTV are discernible by the appearance of huge cabbage leafs on the back of their necks, a send-up of the electrode that emanates from the neck of the victims in the movie *Zontar*.

As in the film, the Zontar that infiltrates SCTV concentrates on powerful people (although the rules of the sci-fi genre dictate that someone substantial must always survive to fight the invasion; here it will be Guy Caballero), including security guard Gus Gusstofferson (Levy) and newscaster Floyd Robertson (Flaherty). A scene in which Gus needlessly shoots at Costume Designer Juul Haalmayer mirrors an early segment in *Zontar* where a brainwashed police officer shoots and kills a defenseless citizen.

After the aforementioned "Maudlin" sketch, *SCTV* concludes the storyline as Kelley and Caballero begin to unravel the mystery of Zontar's takeover. Using a former *Star Trek* cast member in this story is a nod to the 1978 remake of *Body Snatchers*, in which Leonard Nimoy badly played a psychiatrist eventually brainwashed by aliens. The joke here is that these actors aren't able to occupy characters other than their *Star Trek* personas; not only does Guy refer to DeForest as "Bones," but Kelley refers to Guy as "Jim," referencing William

Shatner's *Trek* character. No world outside of *Star Trek* exists for Kelley, just as there is no acceptance of him outside that world either.

In a scene involving an interplanetary transmission from Zontar, all three parts crucial to most sci-fi movie conclusions appear: The unbelievable conquest of good over evil, the revelation of the alien's motivation for takeover, and the moral. In *Body Snatchers* and *Zontar*, the alien's motivation was simple — world domination. *SCTV*'s Zontar, however, has less lofty goals — their planet needs entertainment and wants to bring the inhabitants of SCTV to Zontar for a nine-show cycle and three "best-ofs." (Possibly the cast's way of saying they were overworked and were turning into zombies? Perhaps they felt they were under the control of a power-crazed leader?) The conquest of good over evil comes when Kelley reads in an interplanetary almanac that the planet Zontar is set to be destroyed by a giant asteroid, which then happens along with the instantaneous awakening of all of those at SCTV who had fallen under Zontar's spell.

The highlight of the segment is the melodramatic speech given by Caballero at the very end. The lecture, in which Caballero draws a parallel between Zontar's obsession with television and our own fascination with TV, is a wry send-up of the silly monologues given at the end of *It Conquered the World* and *Zontar*. Perhaps feeling guilty for providing nothing more than 80 minutes of low-budget thrills, the makers of these movies felt the need to have one of their characters pontificate on how "man is the greatest creature in the universe" and that despite the prevalence of human suffering, life's answers lie not in an alien race, but they "must be found from within ... the very heart of man himself" (two examples from *Zontar*). The final shot of a hoagie-shaped planet that mirrors Zontar's cabbage planet is a twist on the cautionary ending found in the original *Invasion of the Body Snatchers*, which hinted that alien-controlled zombies were living among us.

Although the Zontar wraparound does not equal the previous episode's Libby Wolfson storyline, the surrounding standalone sketches in this episode are more successful. Two of the most memorable are complementary sketches featuring Rick Moranis as both George Carlin and Don Rickles in parodies of Woody Allen's *Annie Hall* and Albert Brooks's *Modern Romance*, two movies in which a comedian tries to perform familiar shtick while playing a romantic lead. The Carlin segment works the best, as Moranis awkwardly and desperately tries to work in solo monologues ("Why do they call it a fix-up? Am I broken? Maybe I need a repairman, not a date"). This would be Moranis's last appearance as the comedian. (Regarding the Rickles piece, note that John Candy previously impersonated Don Rickles in show 39. Both Candy and Moranis did the impression exactly one time.)

Another impression that returns here for the last time is Dave Thomas's G. Gordon Liddy, who appears as an inappropriate guest on the children's show

"Mrs. Falbo's Tiny Town." Thomas seems to enjoy attacking one aspect of Liddy at a time; last time out (show 80) it was Liddy's penchant for piano wire; this time Liddy's love for firearms provides the grist for Thomas's mill. The centerpiece of the sketch, a "corrected" version of *Goldilocks* that turns the story from a fairy tale to an instructional account of how to employ firearms when coming across an abandoned cottage in the woods, is wickedly sharp, making this not only the funniest of the "Falbo" pieces, but also as good an indictment of America's gun culture as anything in Michael Moore's 2002 movie *Bowling for Columbine*.

Besides Mrs. Falbo and Mr. Messenger, two other returning favorites, farmers and film fans Big Jim McBob (Flaherty) and Billy Sol Hurok (Candy) are featured in the premiere of "Farm Film Celebrity Blow-Up" (note the sign still reads "Farm Film Report"). This series of sketches would carry these characters until the end of John Candy's run on *SCTV*. Everything is in place for this premiere — a celebrity guest (in this case O'Hara as Meryl Streep) enters, Candy and Flaherty focus on one aspect of the guest's personality (here it's Streep's penchant for crying in movies), and it is through exploiting this aspect that the guest is "blown up good." With this premiere, the "Farm Film" sketches become more of a showcase for the cast's impressions than anything having to do with Big Jim or Billy Sol. And even though the conclusions to these pieces are never a surprise, the glee that Candy and Flaherty project by seeing their guests explode is always infectious.

Several shorter pieces round out this episode, the best of which features Dave Thomas in a triumphant return as attorney Ted Gordon, a character first seen in *SCTV*'s very first episode. Elsewhere, Thomas and Moranis contribute one of the most directionless "Great White North" episodes yet, the topic of which — shortcuts — Bob and Doug never get around to addressing.

Not as successful is the opening sketch in the show, which is a limp satire of how sex is used to sell everything on television: The piece is a public service spot promoting the use of dental floss while visually only using shots of anonymous people's backsides. Note that this episode also includes three short repeat sketches.

Show 91 *(SCTV Network)*

1. Five Neat Guys Gold commercial
2. Emergency Caterers promo
3. Walter Cronkite's Brain
4. Tylenex commercial with Pirini Sclereso
5. Monster Chiller Horror Theatre: Slinky ... Toy from Hell
6. Small Town Dick promo
7. SCTV Movie of the Week: Gangway for Miracles
8. Great White North: Carpets
9. The Merv Griffin Show: Back to the sixties promo

10. Pepsi Challenge commercial with Pirini Sclereso
11. Pre-Teen World: Rough Trade
12. Carl's Cuts: Headcheese
13. Slappy 2000 Home Comedy Center commercial
14. Steeplechase
15. Shine Detergent commercial with Pirini Sclereso
16. Screen Acting with Dr. Tongue and Woody Tobias, Jr.
17. Video Dating commercial

What to watch for: The Merv Griffin Show.
Although this sketch is a step backward after the "Merv Griffith" piece in show 84, it is the highlight of this below-average episode. In the piece, Rick Moranis's Merv Griffin interviews such sixties icons as talk show host Virginia Graham (O'Hara) and transcendental meditation guru Maharishi Mahesh Yogi (Levy), but the sketch centers on its "on location" segments, which bring Merv into some of the revolutions—countercultural, racial, and sexual—of the 1960s.

The countercultural segment, featuring Easy Rider's *Dennis Hopper (Thomas) and Peter Fonda (Flaherty) with Griffin on a chopper trip to New Orleans, is the strongest, particularly when Merv gets a brutal, but cheerfully narrated, lesson in how hippies were sometimes treated: "Later on when we're all sound asleep, some local rednecks will beat us up, forever tainting our perceptions of the rural south!"*

For only the second episode of new material and only the fifth NBC show overall, this *SCTV* episode is devoid of any wraparound elements. Unfortunately, from the mediocre quality of much of the material presented here, it appears that the cast and writers had begun to rely on the wraparounds and weren't wholly confident in presenting sixty-six minutes of unrelated sketches.

One infamous sketch given a prime slot in the episode is "Walter Cronkite's Brain," featuring Thomas and Moranis again as Walter Cronkite and David Brinkley. Dave Thomas includes quite a bit about this sketch in his book, and much of it is apologetic: "If someone else had written it, I probably would have rejected it," Thomas claims. The post-production supervisor on the piece, Marc Giacomelli, is quoted as saying of the sketch that "no one knew what to make of it." Thomas also calls it "self-indulgent" and admits, "We had reached the limits of audience tolerance with sketches like that."

Loosely structured on a summer television series entitled *Walter Cronkite's Universe,* "Brain" ultimately fails because the piece is more about special effects than the script. There are a couple of laughs, however, most notably when an adult Brinkley visits the planet Krypton to stop Jor-El Cronkite from sending his son Wal-Tor to the planet Earth to become "the greatest reporter of them all." Noting prophetically that "the planet Earth is cluttered with too many reporters turning Earth into a media wasteland," Brinkley then admits that if he can stop the young Cronkite, "*I* will be the greatest reporter of them all." This last comment crystallizes the competitive nature between Rick and Dave's characterizations, which is at the heart of all of *SCTV*'s Cronkite and Brinkley pieces.

More notable than the "Walter Cronkite's Brain" sketch itself is the fact that Thomas broke his finger during the shooting of the sketch. The injury is obvious in just one piece in this show, a commercial for the "Slappy 2000 Home Comedy Center." If the indulgences of "Brain" made some think that Thomas was becoming bored with the format of *SCTV*, the "Slappy 2000" sketch confirms those suspicions. Featuring Dave as a rather generic "hip" spokesperson (noticeably *not* Harvey K-Tel), he begins his pitch for the product by commenting that late night comedy is as "common and predictable" as the "prime time drivel it's supposed to be superior to." After quickly finishing the intentionally lame bit, Thomas exhaustedly and self-critically groans "commercial parody ... satire ... TV ... oh brother."

Another sub-par sketch on the show is the "SCTV Movie of the Week," entitled "Gangway for Miracles." Shot in black and white, this is a parody of the 1962 version of *The Miracle Worker*, with Martin's Edith Prickley character in the Annie Sullivan role and Catherine O'Hara playing not Patty Duke Astin's Helen Keller, but a more violent character named Mad Dog who is loosely based on Regan, the possessed child from *The Exorcist* (in the credits she is billed as "Regan Duke Astin."). Unfortunately, this idea is not fully explored — Catherine's character is violent, but not possessed — and therefore this sketch fails at becoming another of the show's celebrated multi-layer parodies.

"Gangway for Miracles" ultimately boils down to a parody of one aspect of *The Miracle Worker*: The violent methods used by Sullivan on Keller. *SCTV* takes this idea to the extreme, as Sullivan discards her other teaching methods to take on Mad Dog in a closed-door, bare-knuckle fistfight, which has the end result of turning Mad Dog into an Edith Prickley clone. (Turning the child into the teacher could be read as a comment on the 1979 remake of *The Miracle Worker*, in which Patty Duke Astin switched from the role of Helen Keller to that of Annie Sullivan.) Despite the gritty performances by Martin and O'Hara, this sketch never gels. The practice of putting Prickley into movie parodies would continue, however, with later sketches such as "Prickley Heat" and "Prickley Business."

Some of the shorter sketches in this episode work much better, particularly a promo for a program called "Emergency Caterers." A parody of the 1970s program *Emergency!*, this piece follows a team of caterers especially experienced at dealing with crises ("They were French Chefs in Vietnam. When they came home, nobody wanted them. Now everybody wants them!"). In the promo, we see the caterers speed (thanks to footage from *The French Connection*) to a party that has run out of food, pickaxing and blowtorching their way inside to shovel beverages, Twinkies, and other hors d'doeuvres into the mouths of unconscious party guests. As in *Emergency!*, everything is played as if life and death hung in the balance, from the hosts' discovery of the problem ("We ran out fifteen minutes ago! The sardines were the last to go!"), to the revival of the guests ("He's coming to! He's coming to!").

Of the six remaining sketches, most notable is the first installment of *Carl's Cuts*. Dave Thomas notes in his book that the characters of meat-cutters Carl and Fred Scutz were designed to be Executive Producers Andrew Alexander and Len Stuart. If imitation is the sincerest form of flattery, this must be the exception to that rule, since Carl and Fred are pigs. Not pigs in a sexist or violent way, but pigs in a swine way. Literally. This is a bit confusing, however, since the premiere sketch only features Rick. So is he Andrew or Len? Basically, it doesn't matter, since the sketch (a brief monologue about headcheese), isn't funny, and if it is intended as an inside joke, it only offers more proof of how much Moranis and Thomas were starting to test the audience's patience.

Fortunately, the two still had Bob and Doug McKenzie, and the "Great White North" on this episode is a highlight of the show, if only for this memorable line from Bob: "We're real hungry today because our topic is, like, carpets." Elsewhere, Andrea Martin's Pirini Sclereso is featured in three commercial parodies that prove nothing other than the character deserved an early retirement.

This episode features three interesting sketches that were cut from later syndication. The most successful is "Pre-Teen World," a kids' educational show that recalls the PBS program *Zoom!*, which featured loads of precocious but hardly TV-savvy kids attempting to teach a young audience about a variety of topics. Here the *SCTV* cast tries to play about 20–25 years younger than they really are, and part of the joke is how they don't look even close to pre-teen age. With co-host Stephen Sealy, Candy creates another character with an inspired quirk—his throat seems to be perpetually dry, and he takes obviously painful swallows after about every third word. Dave Thomas also stands out as a boy named Glen who reads a letter from a young viewer named Darren who wants to know how to be on "Pre-Teen World." In a sight gag that recalls some of the early *SNL* monologues, an on-screen graphic is shown requesting that Darren send in his picture and resume, since things aren't working with Glen. In a clever follow-through to this scenario, Dave's character would be re-named Darren on all subsequent "Pre-Teen World" sketches.

As part of a segment called "Rock Rap," the controversial Canadian group Rough Trade performs a censored (the words "screwing" and "cream" are skipped by lead singer Carole Pope, while the word "bitch" is generously left in) version of their single "High School Confidential." (Note that years later, Carole Pope wrote in her autobiography that she and Andrea Martin were once lovers.)

SCTV's game show parodies almost always worked, but one that missed the mark is "Steeplechase," a lengthy sketch also excised from later syndication. According to Thomas's book (in which Thomas erroneously claims that the sketch was never produced), the sketch was conceived by Candy, who wanted to lay the game out on the same scale as a racetrack and use real horses as game pieces. In place of a real racetrack, the sketch instead uses a small game board, although the show did splurge for a "starter's gate" for the four contestants. Thomas can be forgiven for forgetting the immensely forgettable "Steeplechase"; specifically, the sketch moves at an agonizingly slow pace that foreshadows many of the pieces on the show's final Cinemax season.

The last sketch from this show that didn't make it to syndication is "Screen Acting" with Dr. Tongue (Candy) and Woody Tobias, Jr. (Levy). Here Candy and Levy begin by giving a nod to their Second City colleagues Dan Aykroyd and John Belushi by performing a scene from *The Blues Brothers* (a movie that Candy appears in). From there the sketch becomes similar to a Bob and Doug piece, as the two dance around the topic of acting in a big budget movie without discussing it with any real knowledge or divulging any useful information. In all, this sketch is an improvement on the "Death Motel" interview from show 57 while being a precursor to later behind-the-scenes Dr. Tongue and Bruno pieces such as "3-D Firing Line" (show 117) and "3-D Stake from the Heart" (show 100).

Show 92 *(SCTV Network)*

1. Double Love preview
2. Great White North: Microwave ovens
3. SCTV After School Special: Pepi Longsocks
4. Harry's Library of Distinction commercial
5. The Sammy Maudlin Show: Bobby and Skip Bittman
6. SCTV Movie of the Week: New York Rhapsody
7. Al's Sanitone Drycleaners commercial
8. Doorway to Hell wraparound part 1: Story of Wooden Man
9. Hollywood Squares Home Game commercial
10. Doorway to Hell wraparound part 2: Return to Hell
11. Doorway to Hell wraparound part 3: Elevator
12. The Nana Mouskouri Story promo
13. Mayor Tommy Shanks: Crime blotter
14. Doorway to Hell wraparound part 4: Caligula and Centurions
15. Gordon Lightfoot Sings Every Song Ever Written commercial (repeat from show 70)
16. Half Legs commercial (repeat from show 54)
17. Doorway to Hell wraparound part 5: Caballero's office

What to watch for: Pepi Longsocks.
A masculine take on the popular Swedish character Pippi Longstockings, this sketch (presented as a Bulgarian children's "classic" complete with horribly bad English dubbing), features a memorable lead performance by Candy as a boy who possesses "super powers and super strengths." Unfortunately, unlike Pippi Longstockings, Pepi cannot find any positive uses for his strengths, electing instead to use his brute force to kill his mother and his schoolmates.

What's distinctive about this sketch from the outset is the location work—the tiny schoolhouse, the fields (complete with windmill), the barns with stacks of hay—that somehow brings to mind Bulgaria, even to those wholly unaware of how Bulgaria actually looks.

Apart from Candy and Flaherty (who plays Pepi's potato-loving father), the cast creates generic variations on their "Pre-Teen World" characters for their roles as Pepi's classmates. That is until Pepi picks them up and hurls them through the air, killing them instantly. As if this violent ending wasn't questionable enough for a children's film, Pepi is completely satisfied with his sudden burst of violence, delighted that he finally has "no one to anger" him.

This episode—arguably the worst of the 39 NBC episodes—can be divided into three segments: First up is a strong opening third that includes "Pepi Longsocks" and the debut of Skip Bittman (Moranis as Bobby's younger brother) on "The Sammy Maudlin Show." The second third of the show is dominated by a dull parody of the 1946 Joan Crawford film *Humoresque*, which is somewhat redeemed by a fine guest appearance by violinist Eugene Fodor. The last third of the episode is reserved for a sloppy and underwhelming "Doorway to Hell" wraparound.

Before the show's descent into "Hell," *SCTV* presents another fine "Sammy Maudlin Show." The inspired premise for this sketch sees comedian Bobby Bittman (Levy) bringing out his younger brother Skip (Moranis), also a comedian, to make his network debut. This introduction into Bittman's family is an example of how *SCTV* was able to add textures and layers to even its most perfectly realized characters. From the moment Skip steps on Maudlin's stage—towing an embarrassingly huge reel-to-reel machine to tape his act—Moranis is arresting.

Once Skip starts interacting with Maudlin and William B. Williams, the sketch only improves. First the younger Bittman commits the show-biz mistake of prematurely trying out new material (an impression of George C. Scott), a mistake that Bobby does not hesitate to correct. As a big brother trying to assist his little brother, Levy is very convincing—he makes it clear that he believes in Skip's act, even though Skip does nothing but drop one bomb after another. The brotherly love stops, however, when Skip mentions Bobby's real name—Herschel Slansky—which brings about all sorts of reactions: Since it results in his first laugh on network television, Skip loves the revelation; Bobby is totally horrified; William B. plays the good sidekick and goes along with the positive audience reaction; while Flaherty's response as Sammy is most interesting. Maudlin laughs, but when he realizes how upset Bobby is, he shows concern and embarrassment for his friend, although that could be just concern for his show, which is slowly spinning out of his control.

After a tearful William B. speech in which Candy shamelessly turns the brothers' fight into a celebration of the United States as a land where people are free to disagree—"That's the great thing about democracy. And, damn it, that's the great thing about America"— it seems things are patched up between the Bittmans. Until Skip musses his brother's hair, sending Bobby into a fit.

On to the middle third of the episode: In his book, Dave Thomas references how Joe Flaherty wanted to have classical violinist Itzhak Perlman on *SCTV*. Whether the movie sketch "New York Rhapsody" was written with Perlman in mind is unclear; for whatever reason, Perlman never guested on *SCTV*, leaving violinist Eugene Fodor to star in the parody of *Humoresque*, the 1946 film that starred Joan Crawford as socialite Helen Wright and John Garfield as violinist Paul Boray. Not overlooking Perlman's musical abilities, it's hard to imagine him improving upon Fodor's work in the sketch; not only does Fodor perform a piece entitled "Dance of the Goblins" superbly, he also does a fine job as Paul Boray, surely the most demanding acting role required of any *SCTV* musical guest to this point.

Unfortunately, Fodor's work could not escape later editing — the off-network syndication version of "New York Rhapsody" cuts approximately one minute out of "Dance of the Goblins." Not only is the cut disrespectful, it is also ironic: In the film *Humoresque*, violinist Paul Boray complains when a radio station attempts to edit a concerto being played by his orchestra. Perhaps the *SCTV* syndicators were making their own (misguided) attempts at parodying the original movie.

But Fodor's acting and musical prowess are largely wasted in this overlong sketch, which features nice set and costume work (note the outrageously exaggerated shoulder pads O'Hara sports to play Crawford), but little in the way of actual humor. The piece (and the original film) examines a stormy, self-destructive, and ultimately tragic relationship between Crawford and the violinist. The sketch also features Martin and Flaherty as Boray's parents; particularly Paul's mother makes a significant impact, as it is her disapproval of Crawford that leads (on *SCTV* more directly than in the film) to Crawford's death.

The most direct parallel between "New York Rhapsody" and *Humoresque* is the scene in which Crawford meets Boray; in fact, the segments are so similar that the *SCTV* version goes beyond parody to near plagiarism (to use Guy Caballero's words from an earlier episode, "It's not really a spin-off; it's more of a rip-off"). In both, Crawford has a posse of young hangers-on who are all quick to offer her a light for her cigarette and a laugh for one of her unfunny jokes. In both, she verbally spars with Boray. In both, verbal fireworks turn to romantic fireworks, which eventually results in a loss of musical focus for Boray. For reasons of time, *SCTV* shorthands this career downfall as a montage of bars and nightclubs, the last of which is a shot of Johnny LaRue's Luau Room from show 80's "Polynesiantown." The self-referential gag is the biggest laugh of the sketch.

Both versions of the story end with the suicide of the Joan Crawford character; in "New York Rhapsody," O'Hara gives a fine physical performance as her Crawford drowns herself in a hot tub, while in *Humoresque*, the Crawford character commits suicide by drowning herself in the ocean. The scene works more in *Humoresque* because of the significance created in the film for the ocean and for her house on the water: The house was where Crawford went to escape; her drowning was the ultimate escape. One final common link between *Humoresque* (124 minutes) and "New York Rhapsody": They both overstay their welcome.

In fact, perhaps *SCTV* should have just turned the last third of this episode over to Fodor and his violin — anything to eliminate the five segments that make up the "Doorway to Hell" wraparound. Another Moranis and Thomas experiment in stretching the boundaries of *SCTV*, the pieces succeed only in being wholly different than anything that had come before on the show. Unfortunately, the segments are also humorless, incoherent, and insulting, a result perhaps inevitable given the sketches' inauspicious inception, of which Flaherty once revealingly said, "What was the premise? The fact that we were in Edmonton working our asses off and the show was hell to do."

As in "Walter Cronkite's Brain," the strength of the "Hell" wraparound is its look; Hell itself is particularly intriguing — lacking fire, it is instead designed to be dark, foggy, cold, and thoroughly unsettling. Also unsettling is the script, including a surprisingly self-referential message from Guy Caballero that follows the first false ending of "Doorway to Hell": For the first and only time, *SCTV* overtly acknowledges its wraparound devices, or as Guy calls them, a "topical or relevant story interwoven through the course of a programming day." More surprising is the acknowledgment of the *SCTV* cast not as a group of characters, but as performers who "began their careers in the school of improvisation." This misguided admission of *SCTV* as a comedy show and not as an actual television network belied the premise that the show had spent years fostering and indicated that the minds behind the program for once really didn't know (or maybe didn't care) what they were doing.

Looking to extend the "Hell" piece but lacking ideas, Caballero turns to the crew for inspiration, and the piece begins to resemble a night at The Second City theatre when the cast asks the audience for help in sparking some improvisation. After being told to "go to hell" by *SCTV*'s lighting director, Des Spence, and lacking any other suggestions, Guy returns to the "Doorway to Hell" set and forces host Lin Ye Tang (Thomas) and his two "actors," Mr. Wilcox (Moranis) and Wilcox's dummy, back through the door and onto the same cold and barren set as before.

After a couple more meandering scenes in Hell, the three walk through another door and are surprised to find themselves in Guy Caballero's office. As if the implication that *SCTV* is the final and most vile stage of hell isn't clear enough, the dummy sums it up by simply stating, "This place *is* Hell!" After Tang and Wilcox leave in disgust for going through "a maze of low-budget sets with no ideas and no cast" (a nod to the fact that Martin and O'Hara did not participate in the segments), the wraparound and the show stumble to a merciful end.

Not surprisingly, the "Doorway to Hell" wraparound was cut from off-net syndication. Also cut was a promo for "The Nana Mouskouri Story," an unfunny sketch with Martin as the famous Greek singer. The joke of the sketch is that a biography of Mouskouri would have less to do with her music and more to do with her ubiquitous eyewear. Moranis and especially Flaherty (playing a role very much like his Alki Stereopolis character) get a few laughs as Mouskouri's traitorous musicians.

Show 93 *(SCTV Network)*

1. My First Time commercial
2. The Godfather wraparound part 1: Connie's Wedding
3. The Godfather wraparound part 2: Tom Hagen & Leonard Bernstein
4. The Godfather wraparound part 3: Meeting of heads of five networks
5. The Godfather wraparound part 4: Caballero assassination attempt
6. The Godfather wraparound part 5: Networks hit
7. The Godfather wraparound part 6: Conclusion
8. Great White North: Back bacon and long underwear
9. SCTV Special Presentation: 3-D House of Beef
10. Birkney's Diamonds commercial
11. SCTV Movie of the Week: The Vikings and the Beekeepers

What to watch for: The Godfather.
Although this parody of the film classic could be considered a wraparound, it's significant that it doesn't actually "wraparound" anything other than actual commercials — a wise decision since the material is strong enough to stand as one solid piece. It seems even a shame to disturb the piece with ads, although after countless airings of Francis Ford Coppola's original Godfather *on television, the commercial breaks almost seem like part of the experience. In any event, this material is why this episode is easily one of* SCTV's *best 90-minute episodes.*

To label SCTV's *lengthy and ambitious "Godfather" piece a parody is to not give this material its proper due: The production is so rich in plot, direction, lighting, mood, character, impersonation, and (lest we forget) humor, that it should be considered an achievement all its own, albeit one obviously inspired by the 1972 classic.*

In order to orient the audience, the piece does begin with a spoof of The Godfather's *memorable opening. After some brief exposition with Johnny LaRue and Edith Prickley that serves to explain that Guy Caballero is attending his daughter's wedding, the implausible but unmistakable mixture of* The Godfather *theme music and the voice of* Andy Griffith's *Floyd the Barber is heard. Levy as Floyd performs an oddly arresting monologue about Opie breaking his barber pole, which is shot very similarly to Coppola's opening of the funeral director Bonasera recounting the story of the night his daughter was violently attacked. As in the original, SCTV's version is done in one take that zooms out from a close-up to an over-the shoulder shot of the Don (here "Don Caballero") listening. The first shot of Flaherty as Don*

Caballero mirrors the first shot of Marlon Brando as Don Corleone, though Caballero is far clumsier than Corleone with his feline friend.

SCTV *tries to replicate* The Godfather's *contrast of the quiet seriousness of the Don's office with the gaiety and extravagance of the wedding outside, but because of budget limitations, can't really pull it off. To hide this shortcoming, the wedding scene is played mostly as slapstick, as Connie (Martin) gets a painful lesson in how hotheaded her husband is, while godson and opera star Johnny Pavarotti (Candy, replacing the original's Johnny Fontaine) nearly passes out after holding a note for a ridiculous duration. Note also the presence of numerous mafia men, who are even more ubiquitous here than in the original's wedding scene.*

More interesting are scenes in Don Caballero's office that begin to expand the material beyond mere parody. The entrance of Sonny (Levy, in the James Caan role) and cool Michael (Moranis, subbing for Al Pacino), also introduces the character of Turk Ugazzo, a shady figure who wants Caballero to be involved in his pay television venture; Ugazzo becomes SCTV's *Sollozzo, the* Godfather *character who wanted the Corleones to get active in the drug trade. Moranis and Levy both exaggerate their individual characters' personalities: Levy as Sonny is in perpetual motion, while Moranis's Michael is passive to the extreme, losing his temper only to yell "You're out of order!" to Sonny—a reference to the later Al Pacino movie ...* And Justice for All.

The introduction of Moranis as Michael reminds us that although this character has never been seen, he has been heard introducing his dad several times in season three. (The fact that Caballero then referred to the character as "Ricky" connects those earlier pieces to this episode; here Caballero continues to call his son "Ricky" while others refer to him as Michael.) Note also that Moranis's "You're out of order!" reference was previously used when Thomas played Pacino in the "Cruisin' Gourmet" *promo (show 69). Finally, Levy and Moranis as the Caballero brothers continues the tradition of the two playing brothers, first in "Mel's Rock Pile" (show 75), then in the previous episode's "Sammy Maudlin Show."*

Another memorable scene (one shown by Candy and Flaherty during a visit to Late Night with David Letterman *during the talk show's first week) is between Pavarotti and Caballero during which Pavarotti asks the Don for help in securing a part in a war opera, just as Fontaine asked Corleone for help in securing a part in a war picture in* The Godfather. *This scene is perhaps too similar to its* Godfather *inspiration, except here the piece is played out as the overweight Pavarotti selfishly chokes down a huge wheel of provolone cheese. This scene concludes the material's first uninterrupted segment, mimicking how* The Godfather *used the wedding backdrop as a lengthy first act to open its story and introduce its family.*

One character not introduced in the first part of SCTV's *"Godfather" story is Tom Hagen, the Corleone lawyer played in the original by Robert Duvall. The second segment features Hagen (Dave Thomas), who is dispatched by Caballero to persuade the conductor Leonard Bernstein to give Pavarotti the aforementioned part, just as Duvall in the original was dispatched by Corleone to persuade producer Jack Woltz to hire Johnny Fontaine. Here the* SCTV *version intertwines most closely with Coppola's, as actor John Marley, who played Jack Woltz in* The Godfather, *guests as the conductor Bernstein.*

Marley's most memorable scene in The Godfather *is, of course, when he awakes* to find the decapitated head of his prized horse in his bed. This is restaged in the SCTV *version*, except there is no blood and the dying horse urges Bernstein to hire Pavarotti. Yes, the horse talks, but only to Bernstein, whose character is much more eccentric than The Godfather's Woltz: Besides being the only person who is able to hear the horse speak, Bernstein also labors under the false impression that he possesses a singing zucchini, which falls predictably silent in the presence of Hagen. Although his screen time is brief, Marley's presence adds an invaluable layer of authenticity to the proceedings.

After his performance as Hagen, Dave Thomas then plays the crucial role of Turk Ugazzo, a swarthy man who wishes to begin a pay TV channel with the help of the five networks — SCTV, NBC, ABC, CBS, and PBS. (Granting SCTV independence from NBC is in contrast to other 90-minute episodes in which SCTV is referred to as being partnered with NBC. The autonomy of the network shown here is truer to SCTV's original premise.) This scene, in which Ugazzo pitches his idea to the heads of the five networks, mirrors a similar "five families" meeting in The Godfather; in another tip to the movie, all network heads are Italian-Americans with names from the film such as Barzini and Tattaglia.

Just as Don Corleone decided against the narcotics business in The Godfather, so does Don Caballero decide against Turk Ugazzo's pay channel (dubbed "Ugazzo Home Vision"). This decision angers Sonny, who is excited about Ugazzo's extensive soccer coverage; Caballero firmly reminds Sonny not to "let anyone outside the family know what your favorite sport is!" This exchange is a spoof on the Godfather *scene* in which Don reprimands Sonny by telling him to "never let anybody outside the family know what you're thinking again."

Next comes perhaps the wraparound's most memorable scene: Wickedly ridiculing The Godfather *scene in which Don Corleone is riddled with bullets yet somehow survives*, SCTV *presents a lengthy scene in which Caballero is shot literally dozens of times as Ugazzo watches from a waiting car. The hit on Caballero and a subsequent armed attack on the set of "SCTV News" transforms SCTV into a heavily guarded compound reminiscent of the Corleone home. This sequence climaxes with the shift in power as Moranis's Michael declares a hit on all networks in retaliation for the hits on Caballero and SCTV.*

SCTV *next takes us to a hospital where Caballero is making an unlikely recovery* ("It will take a lot more than 600 bullets to slow me down"). After a cheap sight gag involving a drink of water and the countless holes those 600 bullets put in Caballero's body, Guy takes an FCC broadcast oath while the hits on ABC, CBS, and NBC ordered by Michael are delivered. This is a remarkable sequence, as it not only evokes the baptism segment in The Godfather, *but also presents an efficient condemnation of network television, as the broadcast oath recited by Guy (which calls for "innovative" and "creative" programs) is juxtaposed against examples of the medium (*Three's Company, *the infamous Jimmy "the Greek" Snyder/Brent Musburger feud on* The NFL Today*) that fall far short of the lofty standards called for by the FCC.*

If it seems unbelievable that the greedy Caballero would pass on the possible profits of Ugazzo Home Vision, the brief conclusion to SCTV's "Godfather" story rectifies any behaviorial inconsistencies. After negotiating a truce among the heads of the five networks, Caballero and Ugazzo privately bargain a 50–50 split on Ugazzo

Home Vision, thereby squeezing those "network jerks right out of the picture." This scene has no parallel in The Godfather *(although the final shot of Guy mirrors the final shot of Pacino in* The Godfather Part II*), but it serves to provide a satisfying conclusion to one of SCTV's finest achievements. (Although the character of Turk Ugazzo would never again appear, observant viewers will note future mentions of his name, suggesting that he and Guy did actually broker a deal.)*

After "The Godfather" is a behind-the-scenes look at the opening night of the "3-D House of Beef," a restaurant run by recurring favorites Count Floyd, Bruno, and Dr. Tongue, in what amounts to another attempt to release these characters from the limitations of "Monster Chiller Horror Theatre." The sketch works, thanks in no small part to musical guest James Ingram, who good-naturedly agrees to perform his hit romantic ballad "Just Once" to a silly-looking group of people wearing 3-D glasses.

Next comes "The Vikings and the Beekeepers," one of the better sketches to be edited out for off-network syndication. The difficult production of the piece — clothed in very heavy costumes, the cast was forced to spend hours in a hot studio while standing on an unsteady boat built on a hydraulic driver — is offset by the simplicity of the sketch's premise.

At the sketch's outset, we are informed that out of sheer boredom, the Vikings added the use of bees to their attacks of the English. Unfortunately for the Vikings, they couldn't get along with the beekeepers that were necessary to carry out these attacks. What is captivating about the sketch is that once the unbelievable premise has been set up, everything follows very logically from that idea. For instance, the Vikings (including Thomas, Levy, Candy, and Moranis) get frustrated with the beekeepers' demands — particularly the one about how bees cannot travel west by night — but the Vikings refrain from simply killing the beekeepers because they don't want to be left alone with the bees. The beekeepers (headed by Flaherty) are meanwhile fed up with the Vikings, but don't want to release their bees to kill the Vikings because they do not want to have to row.

Show 94 *(SCTV Network)*

1. Liberace's Musical Salute to the Holidays promo
2. Christmas wraparound part 1: Caballero kicks out LaRue
3. Great White North: Christmas show
4. Christmas wraparound part 2: Gerry Todd gets stedicam
5. A Christmas Message from Mayor Tommy Shanks
6. The Sammy Maudlin Show with Neil Simon & Marsha Mason part 1
7. Frank Incense commercial
8. The Sammy Maudlin Show with Neil Simon & Marsha Mason part 2
9. Neil Simon's Nutcracker Suite
10. Christmas wraparound part 3: Earl's Christmas Message
11. Christmas wraparound part 4: Johnny LaRue's Street Beef

12. The Dusty Towne Sexy Holiday Special
13. Christmas wraparound part 5: "White Christmas"
14. Christmas wraparound part 6: Bob and Doug arrive late

What to watch for: The Dusty Towne Sexy Holiday Special.
Back on show 89, Catherine introduced her take on bawdy nightclub performer Rusty Warren; here she takes the character to another level by making her the unlikely host of a traditional holiday program. More memorable than O'Hara's Towne, though, is John Candy's outrageous impression of B-movie star Divine, who features (with the Juul Haalmayer Dancers) in a music video of "Santa Bring My Baby Back To Me." Candy takes this wholesome Christmas ditty and, singing in an octave lower than Lou Reed and never pausing from fondling his humungous fake breasts, turns it into something disturbing.

Note that one of Towne's songs, "I'll Be a Homo for Christmas," was censored by NBC—the word "homo" was bleeped—but later restored for off-net syndication. Perhaps partly due to censorship issues with this character (which also possibly befell Levy's Raoul Wilson), O'Hara would not appear as Towne again.

After the complexity of "The Godfather" episode, *SCTV* delivers a loosely structured wraparound: A staff holiday party with appearances from many of the show's best-known characters. Though the segments lack focus, there is joy to be had in seeing characters that would otherwise have no reason to appear together (i.e., Bobby Bittman and Flaherty's Norman Gorman) interacting. In fact, this episode only goes awry with its most ambitious sketch—"Neil Simon's Nutcracker Suite."

As the wraparound begins, we enter the party with a group of SCTV staff members (including an undisguised Dave Thomas); once inside, the show takes us from conversation to conversation, including one in which Flaherty's "N" from the Five Neat Guys group drunkenly complains that "they're nothing without me." Although hinted at in previous sketches, this is the first real evidence that Joe's "N" neat guy has a drinking problem; his alcoholism will resurface once more before the Five Neat Guys characters are laid to rest.

During these pieces, there are various party guests milling around in the background, most notably a Viking, a beekeeper, and a waitress from the 3-D House of Beef. Obviously *SCTV* was making use of whatever costumes happened to be around, correctly assuming that if wouldn't really matter if their use made the gathering look at times more like a Halloween party than a Christmas party.

The loose structure of this wraparound made it easy to edit for off-net syndication. Several segments of the party were lifted from their original placement and dropped in elsewhere, while other bits were removed entirely. The excised segments include: Dr. Tongue (Candy) using a hot dog to show Norman Gorman (Flaherty) how 3-D works, and Earl Camembert obliging Gerry Todd's request for a video Christmas message. Surprisingly untouched in off-net syndication is the sight of Thomas's Lin Ye Tang and O'Hara's little-seen Nikki character smoking an enormous joint.

Not surprisingly included in the off-net syndication package are the "Street Beef" segments, in which John Candy (as Johnny LaRue) gives arguably the performance of his career. Outside in frigid weather and woefully underdressed for the elements, Candy performs solo for two remarkable segments. After finding no one on the street and no businesses open (shades of "Street Beef" from show 83), a frustrated LaRue argues with and finally dismisses his cameraman and soundman. Once LaRue is completely alone, Candy unleashes a rambling, disjointed, and often-hilarious soliloquy somehow done in one take.

The "Street Beef" finale is equally well-done: Santa Claus appears and presents LaRue with his Christmas wish — his own camera crane, which is yet another reference to the "Polynesiantown" sketch from show 80 where we first learned of LaRue's love for crane shots. Another example of *SCTV* not simply repeating characters or situations, but reflecting back onto itself to create layered, intricate scripts. Only O'Hara's meltdown as Lola Heatherton in show 86 does a SCTV performance came close to equaling Candy's work here.

Also solid are the wraparound's final two scenes: In the first, Guy Caballero and Bill Needle prophetically discuss the future syndication of *SCTV*— Guy claims he's going to take the ninety-minute shows and cut them up into thirty-minute segments, which of course is exactly what was done to *SCTV* a few years later. After Guy receives an explosive (literally) gift from Big Jim McBob and Billy Sol Hurok that sends him flying out of his wheelchair ("Every year they blow me up and every year I fall for it"), *SCTV* allows itself to wallow in a little sentimentality. Beginning with Lola Heatherton singing along to a backing track of "White Christmas," the shot soon cranes up and out (thanks to Johnny LaRue and his new camera) as Edith Prickley, Guy Caballero, Gerry Todd, Bill Needle, Earl Camembert, and Dr. Tongue join Lola in song. Eventually the shot freezes, the words "Merry Christmas" are added to the bottom of the screen, and the cast is heard shouting out holiday wishes. Fortunately, Bob and Doug McKenzie soon arrive to exorcise any possible maudlin aftereffects.

Speaking of maudlin aftereffects, this episode of *SCTV* is noteworthy not only for being the first Christmas show, but also for containing one of the few weak "Sammy Maudlin Show" sketches. Too bad, because what ultimately drags this sketch down is not Flaherty or Candy; indeed, their interplay is as mawkish as ever (Sammy: "Being a performer in this business of ours, we feel this warmth, this love, this fellowship, all year round. But you people out there only experience this stuff at Christmas"). What makes the piece forgettable is the appearance of Dave Thomas and Andrea Martin as Neil Simon and Marsha Mason, on the show to promote "Neil Simon's Nutcracker Suite," a film that follows "Maudlin."

Before Neil and Marsha, "Maudlin" starts out strong, as Sammy has an intense and prolonged coughing jag as he opens the show with "Here Comes

Santa Claus." Nicotine addiction has never been funnier, particularly when Sammy makes a solemn vow to quit cigarettes — just as he lights up another one. What he soon realizes is that not only are the smokes affecting his health, they also cause an on-set Christmas tree to ignite, bringing about a panic in the studio and an abrupt end to the segment.

As for "Neil Simon's Nutcracker Suite," the sketch is a parody of Simon's oeuvre more than a send-up of any particular film; specifically *SCTV* mocks Simon's willingness to turn seemingly every detail of his life into fodder for his screenplays. His autobiographical bent hit its peak in *Chapter Two*, the 1979 movie based on Simon's 1977 play that involved an author who, after the death of his wife, courts an actress played by Marsha Mason. *Chapter Two* has many parallels to Simon's life, as he *did* court Marsha Mason (they were married by the time of the film's release) after the death of his real-life first wife.

In *SCTV*'s "Nutcracker Suite," a playwright composes a play for his wife to star in as a Christmas present. Along the way, the author and wife meet a colorful cast of characters played by actors who had previously appeared in Neil Simon projects. Judd Hirsch (Eugene Levy) plays the playwright; Hirsch had previously played the playwright role in the Broadway production of *Chapter Two*. Marsha Mason (Martin) had by this point been in several Simon movies, while Alan Alda (Flaherty), Maggie Smith (O'Hara), and Michael Cain [sic] (Thomas) all appeared in *California Suite*. Also, Richard Dreyfuss (Rick Moranis) won a Best Actor Oscar for *The Goodbye Girl*, and James Coco (Candy) was in *Only When I Laugh*. These impressions (particularly Moranis's take on Dreyfuss), along with the opening titles that mock the number of credits Simon claims in his movies (the music is attributed to "Simon & Tchaikovsky"), provide the highlights to the largely lifeless sketch.

The rest of this episode is made up of shorter holiday-themed sketches. The best may be the "Great White North" Christmas episode, which features the McKenzies each giving each other a prized pack of smokes, an exchange that results in the only moment of affection on the "Great White North" set. Dave Thomas and Rick Moranis also feature prominently in the show's first sketch, a promo for a Liberace special entitled "Liberace's Musical Salute to the Holidays." Despite its seemingly can't-miss premise, the sketch falls flat, thanks in large part to Liberace's (Thomas) and Elton John's (Moranis) dueling pianos routine, which slowly goes nowhere. Far more interesting is John Candy's appearance as Orson Welles. Parodying some well-known outtakes of Welles badgering commercial directors, Candy mercilessly attacks the crew, whom he undeservedly blames for mistakes made during a dramatic reading of the lyrics to "Good King Wenceslas." Disgusted, Welles walks off the set — though not before grabbing an entire cooked turkey on his way out.

Show 95 *(SCTV Network)*

1. Monster Chiller Horror Theatre: Dr. Tongue's Evil House of Pancakes
2. Edith Prickley: Give 'Em Hell, Bess
3. Farm Film Report: Brooke Shields & The Boomtown Rats
4. Video: Use It Don't Abuse It PSA
5. Great White North: Great White North
6. Bill Needle's Shoot for the Stars
7. SCTV Movie of the Week: Teacher's Pet
8. Ben-Hur (repeat from show 13)
9. The Lone Ranger Show (repeat from show 58)

What to watch for: Bill Needle's Shoot for the Stars.
With this segment, Dave Thomas creates the perfect showcase for his finest creation, SCTV critic-at-large Bill Needle. Here the crude and abrasive Needle takes what would in any other hands be a fluff talk show and turns it into an evisceration of show business — an even crueler version of "The Sammy Maudlin Show."

Instead of chatting to his guests about their latest projects, Needle wastes no time crucifying the two celebrities unfortunate enough to be on his panel: Singer Rupert ("The Pina Colada Song") Holmes (Levy) and musician Chuck ("Feels So Good") Mangione (Moranis). Needle's hatchet job on Holmes is the more brutal of the two, as not only does he ridicule Holmes's claim that the singer had other hits after "Pina Colada" ("It was your only big hit, wasn't it?"), but he recklessly accuses Holmes and his ode to tropical drinks for turning "millions of helpless little teenagers" into "hopeless alcoholics." (For the record, Holmes did have one more Top Ten hit with the song "Him.") A wonderfully mean sketch.

With this episode and the one following, *SCTV* returns to mixing new material with repeat sketches from its first three seasons. Unlike the earlier *Network 90* shows, however, this time *SCTV* makes no effort to disguise the repeats; in fact, the show blatantly draws attention to them by announcing them as "SCTV Classics." These episodes also abandon the wraparound structure seen in most of the recent installments.

The first of these shows starts with a preview of "Dr. Tongue's Evil House of Pancakes" on "Monster Chiller Horror Theatre." Even though it is not indicated by the title, the movie promoted is a 3-D extravaganza, with clips featuring Dr. Tongue offering pancakes and syrup with the requisite cheap effect. Host Count Floyd (Flaherty) is visibly disturbed by the lack of horror in the clips, but he soon composes himself to discuss the fright appeal of different kinds of pancakes.

Candy and Flaherty, with the considerable assistance of Catherine O'Hara, appear elsewhere in another sketch with recurring characters. "Farm Film Report" is not quite yet officially "Farm Film Celebrity Blow-Up" (both an on-set sign and the introduction reference "Farm Film Report," while Flaherty calls the program "Farm Celebrity Report"), but the routine of the sketch is by now set. O'Hara makes her second straight appearance as the celebrity — this time as Brooke Shields — to be blown up by Big Jim McBob and Billy Sol Hurok.

O'Hara's tripping and falling upon her entrance as Shields is inspired by a then-recent *Tonight Show* appearance in which she stumbled into Johnny Carson's desk. She claimed it was a joke, but nobody knew for sure. The highlight of the sketch is undoubtedly Shields's putrid performance of the Rod Stewart hit "Young Turks," which is so bad that Big Jim and Billy Sol break their word to Brooke's mom Teri and blow Brooke up real good.

Following the merciful explosion of Shields, Big Jim and Billy Sol introduce the episode's musical guests, The Boomtown Rats, who perform their song "Never in a Million Years" before taking a bow and — what else — blowing up. The entire performance and subsequent explosion was removed from off-network syndication, with Big Jim and Billy Sol signing off right after Shields. Though the decision to edit the song was made probably because of time, the performance is remarkably dull. Bob Geldof is particularly disinterested; only on occasion does he bother to direct his lip-synching toward a microphone.

The weakest sketch on this episode is a promo for "Give 'Em Hell, Bess," in which Edith Prickley (Martin) plays Queen Elizabeth I. The inspiration for the sketch comes from the fact that Queen Elizabeth I was often referred to as Bess, which was also the name of Harry Truman's wife; Truman was the President who was immortalized in the piece *Give 'Em Hell, Harry*. Whatever the reason, the sloppy sketch is a confusing combination of Benny Hill (an oversexed Flaherty tries to molest the Queen), the Three Stooges and Abbott & Costello (both teams used the "slowly I turn, step by step, inch by inch" routine which this piece lifts), and Monty Python (the comedy group that could best pull off this decidedly British material). The best line of the sketch comes during Prickley's introduction, where she notes that her highness was "a woman, a queen, a virgin." Comparing herself to Her Majesty, Prickley then remarks, "two out of three ain't bad."

The longest sketch of this episode — a parody of the film *To Sir, with Love* entitled "Teacher's Pet"— is also the last new piece before "SCTV Classics" concludes the show. (In a rare move, the show specifically states the film being parodied, as "Teacher's Pet" is introduced as a "British classic on par with *To Sir, with Love*.) "Teacher's Pet" features Eugene Levy as Ricardo Montablan in the lead role of Zachary, who fills in for the original Sidney Poitier character of Thackery. Both men play new teachers in a school of "problem children" who, through some unorthodox teaching methods, become a major positive influence on their pupils' lives. As the main female students, Martin and O'Hara look remarkably like the young actresses in the original (Lulu and Judy Geeson), while the members of The Boomtown Rats, and lead singer Bob Geldof in particular, do a fine job as the male pupils.

Several key moments in *To Sir, with Love* are cleverly spoofed in *SCTV*'s version, all of which involve Montablan and his students (the film's dynamic that *SCTV* wisely focuses on). A scene from the original that featured the character Denham (played here by Bob Geldof) caught playing with a very small female squeaky doll is transformed into a scene in which Geldof is caught blowing up a life-size female sex doll. After dealing with this distraction, Montalban turns around to see a series of bras strung up on a line across his classroom, an impossibly constructed prank that mirrors a scene in the original in which Thackery comes across a sanitary pad being burned in a small stove. Each display repulses the teacher, but in each version the prank serves as the catalyst for drawing the teacher and the students closer.

In a nod to Ricardo Montalban's character of Mr. Roarke from *Fantasy Island*, *SCTV* has his "Teacher's Pet" character note a newspaper ad for a masseur in a Carribean [sic] resort, just as Sidney Poitier's Thackery takes note of an engineering position in a newspaper ad. Connecting a *To Sir, with Love* parody with *Fantasy Island* is another notable example of *SCTV*'s multi-layered scripts, which by this point in the show's history were coming so frequently that they seemed to be second nature. Of course Montalban accepts the position (as Thackery in *To Sir, with Love* accepts the engineering position), and Zachary's resignation leads to a going-away party that smartly parallels the final scene in Poitier's original.

The centerpiece of this scene is a full-length Boomtown Rats performance of the song "The Elephants Graveyard," a lively performance that easily bests their lackluster appearance in the earlier "Farm Film Report" sketch. (The idea that the students just happen to have a band is also straight out of *To Sir, with Love*.) In a parody of the lengthy dance segment in *To Sir, with Love*, O'Hara encourages Montalban to dance, which he does impressively (thanks to some obvious stand-in help), even though Poitier's Thackery had only unconvincing moves. "Teacher's Pet" lacks belly laughs, but succeeds at being accessible to everyone while also containing enough *To Sir, with Love* references to please fans of the original film.

Another pleasing touch in "Teacher's Pet" is the use of the same score as heard in *To Sir, with Love*, including the Mindbenders song "Off and Running." Two odd cases of censorship in the sketch are also worth mentioning: References about Zachary's masculinity are bleeped, while chalkboard graffiti that clearly reads "Einstein Was A Wanker" is inexplicably censored in later shots.

Show 96 *(SCTV Network)*

1. Norman White and the White Scat Chorale commercial
2. Comment with David Brinkley: Classic Rock Acts' Charlatan Counterparts
3. Rent-A-Retort / Hire-A-Harpie commercial
4. Sunrise Semester with Angus Crock: Lake Monsters

5. Midnight Video Special
6. All-Girl Friday Night Pajama Party part 1
7. K-I-L Target Leads commercial
8. All-Girl Friday Night Pajama Party part 2
9. Al's Garage commercial
10. All-Girl Friday Night Pajama Party part 3: LaRue picketed
11. One on the Town: Singles Bars part 1
12. SCTV Special Announcement: Mayor Tommy Shanks
13. One on the Town: Singles Bars part 2
14. Monster Chiller Horror Theatre: Blood-Sucking Monkeys from West Mifflin, Pennsylvania
15. Great White North: Space and snow routes
16. Lust for Paint part 1 (repeat from show 26)
17. Fish Police promo (repeat from show 39)
18. Lust for Paint parts 2 & 3 (repeat from show 26)
19. Logos Galore commercial (repeat from show 76)
21. Lust for Paint part 4 (repeat from show 26)
22. Alfred Hitchcock Presents: Murder Is Bad for Your Health (repeat from show 40)

What to watch for: *All-Girl Friday Night Pajama Party.*
A sketch unwisely cut from off-net syndication, "Pajama Party" features three of SCTV's best characters (Johnny LaRue, Dr. Cheryl Kinsey, Bill Needle) in a wholly original sketch with an inspired premise and several unexpected twists. The only lacking element may be the absence of Raoul Wilson, the sex-obsessed Levy character who would have really enjoyed this bawdy "Pajama Party."

Making a fine substitute for Wilson is Candy's Johnny LaRue, who is at his sleaziest here. Whether insincerely hawking the jigglefest as a nostalgia piece aimed at a female audience or instructing the pajama-clad women to engage in a waterfight (what Bill Needle praises as a "clever variation" of the catfight), it's thankfully obvious that the visit from Santa Claus in show 94 hasn't softened LaRue. But his "Party" doesn't last: LaRue is pelted with garbage by female protesters outside the SCTV studio, a comeuppance that continues on the next episode as Guy Caballero cancels all of LaRue's projects to clear airtime for new stars Bob and Doug McKenzie.

Despite the fact that most of this episode was eliminated from off-network syndication, this is a fine installment, featuring a number of notable stand-alone sketches. This show is also a study in contradictions: For every recurring piece revived from a long absence ("Comment with David Brinkley," "One on the Town," "Sunrise Semester"), there's something original ("All-Girl All Night Pajama Party," "Midnight Video Special," an unique appearance from Count Floyd).

The longest sketch from this episode to be included in syndication is "Midnight Video Special." As the program that ended *The Midnight Special*'s run, *SCTV* had earned the right to satirize the music-variety show, but that's not the point of this piece. Airing a few months after the launch of MTV, this sketch foreshadows a time when TV guest appearances by musicians will be in the form of music videos instead of live performances. Years later, shows like MTV's *Total Request Live* have made this a reality. "Midnight Video Special" also predicted the increase in the number of programs that relied almost entirely on music videos for content, such as USA's *Night Flight*, TBS's *Night Tracks*, and, most ironically, NBC's *Friday Night Videos*, for which the network cancelled *SCTV*.

Holding true to its premise, most of "Midnight Video Special" consists of two music videos — the Talking Heads' "Once in a Lifetime," and "Top Secret Man" from The Plastics, a Japanese B-52's–like band that failed to attain stardom in North America. It is unclear how the videos were chosen, but both, particularly the Talking Heads' selection, are innovative clips, especially considering how creatively bankrupt the music video art form was in 1982.

The clips are introduced by Moranis's Gerry Todd and Thomas's Tim Ishimuni who exchange some friendly banter that quickly turns heated after Todd makes a politically charged statement about the importance of buying "domestically-produced products" because of the "different kind of war going on today." Soon the two are using technological means to fight for control of the show, which sends the program off the air and the confused studio audience shuffling for the exit. The piece concludes like a bad science-fiction movie of the type *SCTV* parodied in show 90: A narrator reads a heavy-handed moral about how the U.S. and Japan should combine their technology to defeat "the silent enemy," which is revealed (through a clip from show 88) to be the Soviet Union. The recall of a funnier sketch doesn't disguise an awkward conclusion; "Midnight Video Special" is most notable as a prophetic look at music on television as well as a showcase for two fine early music videos.

In contrast to "Midnight Video Special," many of the new sketches on this show consist of recognizable characters in recognizable formats, and, with the exception of the two-person "Great White North," are one-person, one-camera pieces, proving that *SCTV* didn't have to be ambitious to work — the sketches are well-acted, tightly scripted, and, most important, funny.

One of the most interesting of the show's pieces is yet another "Monster Chiller Horror Theatre." What's notable about the sketch is that it was produced for the third season but unused until this NBC episode. During that earlier season, Joe Flaherty took an impromptu "mental health" trip to Italy; upon his return, he taped a large number of solo pieces to help fill the remaining shows, one of which was this sketch, in which Count Floyd thoroughly summarizes a film called "Blood-Sucking Monkeys of West Mifflin, Pennsylvania" (West Mifflin being an area near Flaherty's hometown of Pittsburgh).

The summary is so thorough because the film of "Blood-Sucking Monkeys" doesn't arrive on time and "Monster Chiller Horror Theatre" has no movie to run. So Count Floyd passionately tells the story in exhaustive detail, from the initial otherworldly arrival of the monkeys, to their devouring of farmers

("The bones would just fly all over the place like chicken. That's right, chicken!"), to the final scene of the Air Force dropping a bomb on Pittsburgh to eradicate the monkeys. What's most impressive about this piece is that it was, by all accounts, completely improvised.

Earl Camembert (Levy) returns in this episode with the second edition of his solo franchise, "One on the Town." Last time out (show 79), the sketch — including two numbers from musical guest Levon Helm — was the focal point of the episode. This time the sketch is far less ambitious, as Earl goes undercover to examine the singles bar scene. Basically, this means that Camembert tries and fails to pick up several women, has interview requests denied by bar employees, and gets drunk. Finally, after a bout with his cameraman, the sketch ends with Earl deciding that women in singles bars don't want to be picked up, even as new couples are seen making out behind him. Another job of lousy reporting, but another in a long line of good sketches for Levy's Camembert.

Another newsman making a return to an earlier format is Moranis's interpretation of David Brinkley, who returns to "Comment" after having been last seen in the ambitious "Walter Cronkite's Brain" (show 91). Here Moranis delivers a diatribe against "tribute" bands, or, as he refers to them, "charlatan counterparts ripping off the nostalgic music lover in every town in this country." Moranis's detail is remarkable; for example, Brinkley doesn't just meet the drink minimum, he has "three margaritas and a stinger." (In another example of this episode's no-frills approach, the previously used "Comment" set is no more; Moranis delivers his lines in front of a blank wall.)

Yet another character brought back to life on this show is Dave Thomas's Scotsman Angus Crock, making his first — and last — appearance in a new NBC sketch. For this "Sunrise Semester" piece, Thomas has altered Crock's appearance quite a bit, making him look older and more refined. Thankfully, Thomas has not allowed Crock himself to mellow, as he turns what at first appears to be an informative talk on "Lake Monsters" into a lesson on running a get-rich-quick scam that involves selling Loch Ness Monster "garbage" or "souvenirs" (they're the same to Crock) to unsuspecting tourists. Unfortunately, as Crock points out, this scam only works if you live on a lake. A very brief but amusing final sketch for Thomas's overlooked Angus Crock character.

Two creations that did not go overlooked — Bob and Doug McKenzie — appear here in (what else) "Great White North," which is strangely buried here as the final new sketch of the episode. This is a particularly strong and fast-paced "GWN," as each brother has his own topic: Bob examines snow routes, while Doug discusses the Space Shuttle arm that was manufactured in Canada. Doug easily wins this battle of the topics, as his visualizations of astronauts using the space arm to open beers and have a "beauty time" beats out Bob's brain teaser of how snowplows are allowed to park for lunch along snow routes that do not allow parking. Note that at the end of the sketch, Doug baits Bob by suggesting that the two "talk to Caballero" to see which topic *SCTV*'s president preferred; as the next episode would make clear, neither had to worry about Caballero's blessing. Caballero, along with growing numbers of North American TV viewers, had already decided that they liked these McKenzie brothers very much.

Show 97 *(SCTV Network)*

1. Guy Caballero: Reruns
2. Fancy Free Undershields commercial
3. Bob and Doug wraparound part 1: Carl and Fred Scutz
4. Al Peck's Used Cars commercial
5. Bob and Doug wraparound part 2: Caballero gives Bob and Doug their own special
6. The Days of the Week preview
7. Bob and Doug wraparound part 3: Lola Heatherton & Tony Bennett
8. You! with Libby Wolfson: Fitness
9. Nightline Melonville: Unemployment
10. Bob and Doug wraparound part 4: Dressing room / Prickley / LaRue & Bittman / Hair
11. Bob and Doug wraparound part 5: Great White North Palace A
12. Bob and Doug wraparound part 6: Great White North Palace B
13. Be My Friend commercial
14. Bob and Doug wraparound part 7: Bob and Doug clean up
15. John Belushi tribute

What to watch for: Great White North Palace.

The television disaster that is Bob and Doug McKenzie's first live prime time special represents Rick Moranis's and Dave Thomas's finest work as the brothers and one of the funniest NBC-era SCTV *pieces.*

The special is misguided in every imaginable way, but the problems can all be traced to the wrongheaded decision to take Bob and Doug out of their "Great White North" comfort zone and into the center of an overproduced and overbudgeted spectacle. Note how the special opens, as the over-dressed, over-coiffed, and completely clueless brothers bring the live proceedings to a crashing halt by painfully butchering their monologue. The brothers' on-air presentation is not much worse than it is on "Great White North," but wasting time arguing over cue cards and picking threads from clothes is not the stuff of most expensive prime-time network broadcasts.

After musical guest Tony Bennett is mercifully rushed onstage to liven up the deadly proceedings with a fine version of "I Wish I Were in Love Again," the McKenzie brothers join Morgan Fairchild (O'Hara) and favorite SCTV *target Joyce DeWitt (Martin) for a wonderfully terrible comedy sketch. A playful jab at the famous* Saturday Night Live *Czech Brothers sketches with Dan Aykroyd and Steve Martin (or as Bob says, "He's Steve Martin, I'm Conehead"), Moranis and Thomas "swing" through this sketch with unbelievable incompetence. This piece could be read as a vicious parody of the Czech Brothers sketches, particularly in light of the competitiveness between* SNL *and* SCTV *and how predictable the Aykroyd and Martin sketches quickly became (the characters were never allowed to branch out the way Bob and Doug were here). But Moranis and Thomas likely chose the Czech brothers because the characters were so familiar that the ineptness that Bob and Doug bring to the roles would be glaringly obvious. The sketch brings the special to an abrupt close as Caballero exasperatedly pulls Bob and Doug off the air.*

One of the many differences between *SCTV* and the original run of *Saturday Night Live* lies in where each program found inspiration for material: *Saturday Night Live*, where the cast often appeared as themselves, was easily able to create comedy out of backstage drama. In contrast, *SCTV* had a stricter concept to adhere to that usually didn't allow for off-air happenings within the cast to translate into usable on-air pieces. A notable exception exists in this episode.

This show aired in April 1982, as Bob and Doug McKenzie were at the height of their popularity. The *Great White North* album had been released in late 1981 and had peaked at number nine on the Billboard charts in March. Bob and Doug had spawned several popular catchphrases. And the media, when reporting on *SCTV*, invariably singled out Bob and Doug — the most notorious example being the February 4, 1982, *Rolling Stone* cover headline that named the McKenzies "*SCTV*'s Best Joke." Moranis and Thomas were getting more exposure and more money from outside projects than the other cast members, who, according to Thomas, "resented" the attention lavished on the two characters.

It is no surprise that during this period, NBC asked for more Bob and Doug McKenzie material. The network got its wish with this episode's fine wraparound, which smartly translates to the fictional world of SCTV no less than four real-life backstage storylines:

- NBC's desire to give the McKenzie brothers more time on *SCTV*, depicted here as Guy Caballero's desire to give the McKenzie brothers more time on *SCTV*.
- Pressures on Moranis and Thomas to market and promote the McKenzies, depicted here as pressure from the entrepreneurial team of Fred and Carl Scutz.
- Resentment from fellow cast members concerning Bob and Doug's popularity, depicted here as resentment from characters Johnny LaRue, Bobby Bittman, and Lola Heatherton concerning Bob and Doug's popularity.
- A possible growing indifference toward the characters by Moranis and Thomas themselves, depicted here as the failure of Bob and Doug to succeed beyond the "Great White North" program, suggesting that Rick and Dave felt that the characters were ultimately limited.

More proof of Moranis and Thomas's increasing apathy toward Bob and Doug is that they weren't afraid to ridicule their popularity; note this episode's depiction of the McKenzies as unlikely cover subjects for *Ebony, Paris Match,* and *Road & Track* magazines. Promoters Fred and Carl Scutz (also played by Moranis and Thomas) display these periodicals during their attempt to convince Guy Caballero to partner with them for a potentially lucrative Bob and Doug event; the Scutzes' pitch was undoubtedly similar to dozens heard by Moranis and Thomas by this point. The Scutzes were not so much "men" as "pigs" (Moranis had played his character already in show 91), complete with squealing voices and pig noses; in his book, Thomas claims the characters were ridiculing *SCTV* producers who tried to sell Moranis and Thomas on a profitable "Bob and Doug concert."

The devious Caballero, being more money-hungry than even Fred and Carl, throws them out in order to make his own merchandising contacts; he then embarks on the process of expanding Bob and Doug's air time, a choice that comes at the expense of shows fronted by Johnny LaRue, Bobby Bittman, and Lola Heatherton. Since those most hurt are all signature characters — those cast members' most readily identified *SCTV* persona — it is not hard to interpret these scenes as an expression of the perfomers' real-life outrage at not getting the attention afforded Moranis and Thomas.

As usual, Johnny LaRue is the biggest loser: In a scene that takes place in Bob and Doug's "dressing room" (which is actually a converted linen closet), Caballero relieves LaRue of his latest special, his limo (the same one that LaRue used to trick Bob and Doug into washing), his dressing room, and his per diem, handing them all over to Bob and Doug. This scene crystallizes the changing of the guards among the *SCTV* cast: Before Bob and Doug "took off," John Candy was the understood "star" of *SCTV*. With Moranis and Thomas's ascension, Candy lost the most power, so it follows that his Johnny LaRue character would lose the most as well.

Catherine's Lola Heatherton gets a funny scene as she interrupts a private meeting between Guy and Tony Bennett, who has agreed to guest on the "Great White North Palace." Here Lola blames her failed affair with Guy (previously discussed in show 86) for the ill-timed interruption of one of her shows for a Bob and Doug promo. This very personal discussion unfolds much to the embarrassment of Bennett, who tries in vain to sneak out of the office. Note that Bennett has not improved much as an actor since 1966's *The Oscar*.

Bennett also figures heavily in the wraparound's finale, as he consoles the McKenzies after their disastrous special by favoring them with a brief version of "The Best Is Yet to Come." This ending is particularly well done, as Moranis and Thomas afford Bob and Doug emotions — notably sadness and regret — not heretofore granted these characters. Having the traditionally refined Bennett hoist beers with the brothers is a winning final touch to an episode that represents a peak for Bob and Doug McKenzie; after this show, Moranis and Thomas would only do three more "Great White North" sketches before leaving *SCTV* to star in, write, and direct the disappointing McKenzie movie *Strange Brew*.

Some of the wraparound sketches in this episode were trimmed for off-net syndication, while the opening message from Guy Caballero was completely excised. In the message, Caballero insists that the show is a brand new episode; he then proceeds to discuss his preference for reruns, even saying, "If you're watching a rerun for the first time, you might not even know it's a rerun." (This logic was lifted by NBC several years later for their "It's New to You" campaign.) The highlight of the sketch comes after Caballero has finished his promise of new material when the sketch "Indira" begins playing. By this point, "Indira" had already aired on *SCTV* three times.

This *SCTV* episode, the first to air following the March 5, 1982, death of John Belushi, closes with a still photograph and film clip montage of the Second City alum. The brief piece is a tasteful, understated tribute to Belushi, whom most of the *SCTV* cast knew or had worked with on the Second City stage. In fact, at the time of his death, Belushi was scheduled to do a guest appearance on *SCTV*, described by Candy as a series of sketches involving Guy Caballero giving Belushi a chance on SCTV after a string of film failures had tagged him with the nickname "Box Office Poison."

Two stand-alone sketches featuring recurring characters take up most of the time in this episode not devoted to Bob and Doug. The first is the third installment of Libby Wolfson's "You!" talk show. While not the definitive appearance of this character — that would be the wraparound back in show 89 — this is Wolfson's finest stand-alone sketch. The strength of the fitness-centered piece is a video of her and a friend (O'Hara, playing a different character than show 89's Sue Bopper-Simpson) at a health club, barely participating in anything even remotely resembling exercise. Libby's inspirational talk show for women has never been more hopelessly non-inspirational.

Floyd Robertson (Flaherty) and Earl Camembert (Levy), whose appearances had been heretofore limited since *SCTV*'s move to NBC, return in the premiere of "Nightline Melonville," a solid new format that almost completely replaces "SCTV News" for the remainder of *SCTV*'s run. The premise of the sketch is similar to ABC's *Nightline*, in that it supposedly allows the co-anchors the opportunity to focus on the "major news event of the day." In reality, it provides a new format for the shoddy journalism that Floyd and (particularly) Earl practice. Levy is particularly good here, as technical problems (similar to those experienced in shows 19 and 55) get in the way of Earl's work: His reaction when flying geese appear on his oversized monitor is the sketch's best moment.

Show 98 *(SCTV Network)*

1. Hands Off Remote Control Converter commercial
2. National Midnight Star commercial
3. Pre-Teen World Telethon for Pre-Teen World part 1: Introduction

4. Turk Gruman: Police Dispatcher promo
5. SCTV Movie of the Week: Maudlin's Eleven
6. Pre-Teen World Telethon for Pre-Teen World part 2: Cathy Tutor
7. Prickley Heat commercial
8. The Adventures of Shake 'n' Bake
9. The Days of the Week preview
10. Nightline Melonville: Disappearance of Mayor Shanks's grandson
11. Pre-Teen World Telethon for Pre-Teen World part 3: The Recess Monkeys
12. Clinical Surgical Instruments commercial
13. Pre-Teen World Telethon for Pre-Teen World part 4: Cathy and Alexis
14. National Committee Against Noise Pollution PSA
15. Pre-Teen World Telethon for Pre-Teen World part 5: Guy Caballero extro

What to watch for: Turk Gruman: Police Dispatcher.
While "Maudlin's Eleven" is a triumph, nothing on this episode is as memorable as John Candy's Turk Gruman, a former limousine dispatcher now working for the police department in "the toughest precinct in New York City." Especially inspired in the purposefully overdramatic piece is Gruman's insistence on wearing slippers at work, a decision that leads to a memorable encounter with Flaherty's police chief. Note that this is the first sketch to feature Second City alum John Hemphill, who will make many more appearances on SCTV *on his way to eventually becoming a de facto cast member.*

After spotlighting Bob and Doug McKenzie — *SCTV*'s most popular characters — in the last show, *SCTV* reverses itself by setting aside much of this episode to a group of characters — the kids of "Pre-Teen World" — that had only appeared once before. Thanks to the freshness of the group and a unique musical guest (actually characters played by John, Eugene, and Rick), the wraparound thrives despite its tired telethon premise. Oddly enough, this entire wraparound was cut from off-net syndication, as was the only other previous "Pre-Teen World" sketch (show 91).

What sets this telethon apart from others previously featured on *SCTV* is that this one is staged not to fund the station as a whole, but only one show — "Pre-Teen World." The first segment of the telethon introduces its best gags: The exhaustion of the kids (O'Hara: "Is it light out yet?" John: "No, it's 11:30"), and the primitiveness of the show's tote board, which the "goofy-looking kid with the teeth" (Levy) presides over with chalk and eraser. Also notable is the wildly simplistic set for this wraparound; it's obvious that the budget for this episode was swallowed up by the more ambitious sketches "Maudlin's Eleven" and "The Adventures of Shake 'n' Bake."

The highlight of the telethon is the appearance of "guests" The Recess Monkeys: As opposed to musical turns by cast members Chevy Chase and Blues Brothers Dan Aykroyd and John Belushi on *Saturday Night Live*, Candy, Levy, and Moranis (all in character as their "Pre-Teen World" personas) were not afraid to have fun with their musical talents. Actually, the singing and guitar playing of Moranis comes off pretty well, but he is upstaged by the cotton-mouthed vocals of drummer Stephen Sealy (Candy) and the general goofiness of Levy's character. In a nod to some fellow countrymen, the "band" performs the song "My Girl" by Canada's own Chilliwack.

The telethon ends with an appearance by Guy Caballero, who arrives to make one last desperate plea for cash, probably because he plans to pilfer much of the money raised. Here Caballero warns viewers that if they don't donate, the "Pre-Teen World" kids will turn into "hardened criminals" upon losing their show, a prophetic statement given the many child TV stars from the era that would in fact turn into hardened criminals. Though it lacks ambition and polish, the "Pre-Teen World Telethon for Pre-Teen World" contains many moments of infectious silliness.

In contrast to the telethon segments, "Maudlin's Eleven," a lengthy "SCTV Movie of the Week" inspired by the 1960 Rat Pack film *Ocean's Eleven* in which eleven Army buddies attempt to pull a heist, is quite complex. "Maudlin's Eleven" is one of the better movie sketches of *SCTV*'s NBC years, particularly notable as a prime example of how *SCTV* allowed its characters to evolve and grow into different types of sketches.

Using the personas of Sammy Maudlin (Flaherty), William B. Williams (Candy), and Bobby Bittman (Levy) in a Rat Pack–inspired sketch is a logical step, since the *SCTV* characters originated from Sammy Davis Jr.'s short-lived talk show *Sammy and Company*. However, in transposing the personas to the film, the characters shift a bit: Sammy Maudlin, in essence a parody of Davis Jr., most resembles the leadership role that Frank Sinatra played in the original. Likewise, Bobby Bittman is arguably the closest to Dean Martin's character, although Bittman handles the duties of singing the sketch's version of "Eee-O-Eleven," the song Davis Jr. sings in the original. William B. Williams, here fulfilling the same sidekick function as on the "Maudlin" sketches, is closest to the Peter Lawford character of Jimmy Foster.

The rest of the "Maudlin's Eleven" cast are harder to trace back to *Ocean's Eleven*: Bill Needle (Thomas), a character who has never had anything to do with the "Maudlin" sketches, is here as a composite of the characters played in the original by Richard Conte (the electrician) and Buddy Lester (the burlesque club MC). In the "Maudlin's Eleven" scene that most closely parallels a scene from *Ocean's Eleven*, Needle punches an overly enthusiastic fan of his wife's burlesque routine. Needle is also responsible for the sketch's most darkly funny moment, when he is electrocuted while trying to cut power lines.

Despite being the antithesis of "cool," Skip Bittman (Moranis) is asked to help out with the heist, much to the displeasure of his brother Bobby. Skip's enlistment makes for a gang of five — in a bizarre recruitment, the other six members of "Maudlin's Eleven" are played by Johnny Puleo and his Harmonica Gang, a real-life group of musicians best known for their appearances on *The Ed Sullivan Show*. (Puleo passed away roughly a year after this episode aired.)

In *Ocean's Eleven*, Sinatra most definitely didn't have a "harmonica gang"; also vastly different in *SCTV*'s version is the heist itself: In *Ocean's Eleven*, the group plans on robbing five casinos in Las Vegas; in "Maudlin's Eleven," the plan is to rob sitcom star Danny Thomas. In a clever spoof on the complexity of the *Ocean's Eleven* heist, the "Maudlin" heist is at least as complicated, despite the relative simplicity of the crime. The most obvious nod to the original heist comes as the infrared paint used in *Ocean's Eleven* is substituted here for fluorescent skeleton costumes. (Skip, Bobby, and William B. claim their appearance in these skeleton costumes is due to their association with *The Red Skeleton Show*; Skeleton, not coincidentally, made a cameo appearance in *Ocean's Eleven*.) The group known as "Maudlin's Eleven" is even more unsuccessful at pulling off the heist than the group from *Ocean's Eleven*; more than half of the eleven die in their failed robbery, as compared to the single casualty in *Ocean's Eleven*.

Besides "Maudlin's Eleven," the most ambitious sketch here is "The Adventures of Shake 'n' Bake." This piece centers on the debate of whether William Shakespeare ("Shake") wrote the works attributed to him or if Lord Chancellor Francis Bacon ("Bake") penned them. Not exactly a premise from which hilarity would be expected to ensue, and indeed Thomas (who plays Shakespeare) wrote in his book that this sketch was another example of him running out of ideas and turning to unlikely places — in this case his Master's work in Shakespearean Literature — for inspiration. Writing fifteen years after the sketch aired, Thomas hints that he had strayed too far from the *SCTV* premise: "I pictured television sets turning off all across the country when 'Shake 'n' Bake' was on."

But perhaps Thomas is being too self-critical: While the sketch is hardly a laugh riot, it is still a smartly written piece that works its unique premise to its advantage. While it helps to have a minimal background in Shakespeare to appreciate the sketch, appreciation of *SCTV* has often meant bringing outside knowledge to the show. And more viewers (even late-night viewers) are likely to be familiar with Shakespeare than an obscure film like *The Oscar*, for example. Moranis and Thomas also wisely framed the sketch as an episode in a cartoon serial, which allows for several brief and disparate scenes.

The sharpest "Shake 'n' Bake" segment is the first, which finds Shakespeare backstage at the Globe Theatre still working on *Hamlet* even while it is being premiered. Here Joe makes a fetching Ophelia, while John and Eugene play Rosencrantz and Guildenstern as two flaming homosexuals. The second scene, showing Shakespeare and Bacon unwinding at a whorehouse, is almost as strong. (Bacon even has to apologize for a sexual faux pas from the previous night.) Although the final scene ends with a "to be continued" tease befitting a serial, Thomas and Moranis never presented more "Adventures of Shake 'n' Bake."

Speaking of recurring characters, Martin's overused Edith Prickley returns in "Prickley Heat," a *Body Heat* spoof that is one of the better NBC-era Prickley pieces. The sketch consists of a close recreation of the *Body Heat* trailer with some tweaking of the original's memorable dialogue ("You're not very bright, are you? I like that in a man" becomes "Boy, are you stupid! I like that in a man."). The piece is also notable for the return of Joe Flaherty's Charles Bronson (not the famous movie actor) character, last seen in "Steeplechase" (show 91).

Another returning character seen here is Rawl Withers, Editor of the *National Midnight Star* tabloid magazine, who is featured in a parody of a then-current *People Magazine* ad campaign. The point of the sketch is to tease the People's Global Golden Choice Awards, which will constitute the majority of the next episode. Not only are the awards themselves teased, but the plot is foreshadowed when Withers exclaims that he doesn't know who will win the awards because "it's not fixed." But, as it is revealed in the next episode, the awards show *is* fixed.

Show 99 *(SCTV Network)*

1. The People's Global Golden Choice Awards part 1: Lola and Lorna
2. Bob's Big Guy commercial
3. The People's Global Golden Choice Awards part 2: Guy & Rawl
4. Convert-A-Toup commercial
5. The People's Global Golden Choice Awards part 3: Bob Hope calls FBI
6. The People's Global Golden Choice Awards part 4: Five Neat Guys
7. The Merv Griffin Show: The Special Edition
8. The People's Global Golden Choice Awards part 5: FBI questions Guy
9. Great White North: 15 pin bowling
10. Tex and Edna's Prairie Warehouse and Curio Emporium commercial: Chuckie
11. The Fishin' Musician: Third World
12. The People's Global Golden Choice Awards part 6: Audience revolt
13. The People's Global Golden Choice Awards part 7: Epilogue

What to watch for: The Merv Griffin Show: The Special Edition.
Even though this show features a fine wraparound, the singular highlight of this episode is this inspired sketch, which improbably but successfully crosses sci-fi film classics 2001 *and* Close Encounters of the Third Kind *with Rick Moranis's Merv Griffin impression. As Dave Thomas wrote in his book, the segment, in which seven bonus minutes (directed by Thomas's Steven Spielberg) are added to the end of a Griffin episode, was a reaction to the 1980 release of the "special edition" of Spielberg's 1977* Close Encounters, *which Thomas viewed as selling "idiots the same thing again in a slightly different package."*

Little did Thomas and SCTV know that they were in fact ahead of their time with this sketch: Years later, the re-release of "special editions" of blockbuster movies was to become a common practice that would include new theatrical runs of George Lucas's original Star Wars *trilogy, Francis Ford Coppola's* Apocalypse Now, *and Spielberg's E.T. Also, NBC would introduce the notion of "supersizing" episodes, adding time to hits like* Friends *and* Will & Grace *in order to keep those shows' audiences tuned to the network for a few more minutes.*

This sketch alternates seamlessly between the actual "Special Edition" of The Merv Griffin Show *and Spielberg's "making of" the "Special Edition," which mirrors the television special produced about the making of the original* Close Encounters. *Most of the extended Griffin material takes place aboard a spaceship, just as the draw for the* Close Encounters *"Special Edition" was a new ending aboard the previously unseen alien mothership. Once aboard, the sketch becomes a more direct spoof of* 2001, *as the computer HAL 9000 attempts to wrest control of the show, much as the same computer tried to take over the spaceship in Kubrick's visionary film. Adding immense value to the piece is the fact that Douglas Rain, the actor who provided the voice for HAL in* 2001, *reprises his role for this piece.*

Dave Thomas claims that this sketch, seen by both Spielberg and Lucas, was partly responsible for Lucas's withdrawal from the public eye, a retreat Thomas speculates Lucas took in order to avoid becoming a further target for satire.

Nearly 100 episodes into its run, *SCTV* finally spoofs television's ever-growing reliance on award shows with "The People's Global Golden Choice Awards." Not satisfied to simply mock the inanities inherent in award programs, this solid wraparound also features backstage material involving the efforts by Guy Caballero and *National Midnight Star* editor Rawl Withers (Levy) to rig the awards in SCTV's favor.

Highlights within the context of the televised award show are many: The opening production number, featuring the Juul Haalmayer Dancers, Lola Heatherton (spelled "Lola Heatherington" to reflect the fact that Joey Heatherton's name was occasionally listed as "Heatherington") and Lorna Minnelli (Martin) is as lame as most award show opening numbers, but in a welcome surprise, *SCTV* has the live audience greet the number with the same complete indifference that most home viewers afford them. Poorly written award presentations are also dealt with, most perfectly in the exchange between unlikely co-presenters *Fantasy Island*'s Herve Villechaize (Candy) and *Quincy*'s Jack Klugman (Flaherty).

Speaking of impressions, Catherine O'Hara portrays Elizabeth Taylor as a doddering idiot with a food addiction (she stuffs her purse full of complimentary treats). Her confused appearance is eerily prescient of the real-life Taylor's equally confused presentation of the Best Picture award at the 2001 Golden Globes, during which producer Dick Clark had to appear onstage to remind her that the nominees are customarily read before the winner is revealed.

Dave Thomas's Richard Harris is once again the unlucky recipient of a thrown brick, just as he was on "Mel's Rock Pile" (show 75). Elsewhere, the Five Neat Guys give a terrible "tribute to the screen's best films" that is made even worse by one Neat Guy's (Flaherty) worsening alcoholism. Note this is the Five Neat Guys' last appearance on *SCTV*.

Much of the rest of the wraparound is story-driven, as SCTV's suspicious sweep of the awards ("Zontar" beats out *Raiders of the Lost Ark* for Best Special

Effects, while Skip Bittman beats out Timothy Hutton for Newcomer of the Year) prompts an upset Bob Hope (seeking revenge after being told by Caballero that there was no room for him in the awards telecast) to call the FBI. The inquiry leads to the incarceration of Withers, who takes the rap for Caballero. The episode ends in Rawl's cell at the Melonville State Penitentiary with Guy delivering yet another emotional speech, followed by an unexpected rendition of "Sometimes I Feel Like a Motherless Child," lip-synched by Guy, Rawl, the prison guard, and other prisoners. (A possible inspiration for this ending is the finale of *The Blues Brothers*, which also ended with a musical number set in prison.)

Two other aspects of the award show wraparound, both having to do with characters played by Dave Thomas, are notable. Thomas has never played Bob Hope as more evil and shallow—not only does Hope work deviously to discredit the award program, he then strains to steal one of the awards he succeeded in dishonoring. In his book, Thomas tries to distance himself from this performance, complaining that Hope was inserted as a "cheesy villain."

Note also that Dave's Bill Needle sparks the melee that closes the award show by publicly speaking out against Caballero's "lust for power." A hypocritical statement considering that Bill Needle was heavily involved with some of Caballero's earlier scams, such as the ones depicted in the "Pledge Week" episode (show 85) and the Moral Majority installment (show 84). Here Needle's outrage stems from jealousy over not being involved in the manipulation of the award show results. So he helps to bring it down.

Besides "The People's Global Golden Choice Awards" and "The Merv Griffin Show: Special Edition," the only sketch of significant length is the third installment of "The Fishin' Musician," featuring reggae band Third World. Beginning with this episode, *SCTV* begins to rely much too heavily on "The Fishin' Musician" as a vehicle for their musical guests: Three of the next six shows see musicians visit Gil Fisher's Scuttlebutt Lodge. Only the Carl Perkins sketch (show 101) is successful, and none of the three were included in off-network syndication.

Another sketch eliminated from off-net syndication is the "Great White North," which returns here for its first show since the "Great White North Palace" debacle of show 97. As the McKenzies explain, Guy Caballero would only give them back their show under the stipulation that they cut it from two minutes to a minute. After they explain this, they barely get around to mentioning their topic—15-pin bowling—before they run out of time. Though the return of Bob and Doug is welcome, ideas of what to do with the characters are running low—note that the premise of a show being trimmed for time is stolen from the "Bill Needle's Mail Bag" sketches of the third season.

Show 100 *(SCTV Network)*

1. Guy Caballero: Days of the Week
2. Bufferil commercial
3. House in a Box commercial
4. The Days of the Week episode 1
5. Just for Fun
6. Dr. X: An Old Friend Returns
7. Tex and Edna Boil's Prairie Warehouse and Curio Emporium commercial: Tex leaves
8. SCTV Special Presentation: The Making of 3-D Stake from the Heart
9. Boil's Warehouse and Curio Emporium commercial: Edith Prickley
10. Surprise Grab Bags commercial
11. __ and Edna Boil's Prairie Warehouse and Curio Emporium commercial: Auditions
12. The Irv Goldfarb Show
13. Boil's Emporium commercial: The Count
14. Sunrise Semester with Norman Gorman: Conversational New Yorkese II

What to watch for: Just for Fun.
By this episode—SCTV's 100th—it's clear that much of the show's humor comes from putting celebrities in the most unlikely of circumstances. While SCTV normally torments known entertainers, the results can be more bizarre when the cast targets other types of public figures. Case in point: This episode's "Just for Fun" talk show. This piece features Russian author Aleksandr Solzhenitsyn (Thomas), composer Aaron Copland (Flaherty), and feminist author Betty Friedan (Martin) as unlikely panelists on a show hosted by the unctuous and chauvinistic Stan Kanter (Levy).

Levy's Kanter is fiercely arrogant and self-absorbed, like Bobby Bittman with a better haircut and less jewelry. His lack of knowledge and respect for his esteemed panel is clear from his dubious introductions (on Aaron Copland: "Look out, Billy Joel!"), as well as his insistence that he interview them all at the same time. The comic highlight of the sketch comes as Kanter asks the group about his favorite subject: women. After surviving a near walk-out, Kanter somehow gets the three luminaries in a heated debate about the physical attributes of the day's most popular actresses: Betty Friedan admires Loni Anderson (big breasts), Solzhenitsyn prefers Mariel Hemingway (strong eyebrows), and Copland is infatuated with Paula Prentiss.

SCTV marks its 100th episode with a decided lack of fanfare—no mention of the milestone, no repeats of past sketches, no never-before-seen outtakes, not even a musical guest. Instead there is simply a collection of all-new stand-alone sketches free of any linking wraparound material. The show is a curious mix of fresh ideas ("Just for Fun," "Irv Goldfarb," "Dr. X") and not so fresh ideas (another appearance by Dr. Tongue and Woody Tobias, Jr., the return of Norman Gorman and Harvey K-Tel). Fortunately, the show could still find ways to present even the most oft-used characters in surprising formats.

The best example of well-worn characters in unique surroundings is in the longest sketch of the episode, "The Making of 3-D Stake from the Heart." The piece finds the cast skewering director Francis Ford Coppola (Moranis) just one episode after lampooning filmmakers Steven Spielberg and George Lucas. But unlike Spielberg and Lucas, Coppola's career was in poor shape when this sketch originally aired; his most recent flop, *One from the Heart*, bankrupted his Zoetrope Studios and fueled his growing reputation as a director who couldn't work within the confines of either a budget or a normal shooting schedule.

Like Spielberg and Lucas, though, Coppola had already begun the practice of reediting his finished movies; for example, he had already reworked the first two *Godfather* pictures extensively for television. Therefore the premise of this sketch — that Coppola would be so upset with the failure of *One from the Heart* that he would re-shoot, re-edit, and re-cast the picture — isn't implausible. Slightly less believable is that Coppola's remake would be a 3-D picture starring Dr. Tongue (Candy) and Bruno (Levy).

Joe Flaherty's Count Floyd serves as host for this behind-the-scenes special on "3-D Stake from the Heart"; unlike his hosting role on "Monster Chiller Horror Theatre," here he is relegated to a straight role. The laughs in the sketch are found elsewhere, particularly in the increasingly contentious interplay between Tongue and Bruno; the two continually bicker about irrelevant annoyances such as Tongue's use of the word "diffused."

More pointed are the sketch's attacks at Coppola and his recent tendency toward failed experimentation: For example, he decides to use a hidden camera to shoot his picture even though this horribly disorients his actors. And at one point he insists without explanation that all actors wear bags over their heads for a 24-hour period. But *SCTV* saves its sharpest jabs for Coppola's buffoonish efforts to secure financing for the film (including an inappropriate plea to the children who watch "Monster Chiller Horror Theatre"), efforts that, as revealed by a "for sale" sign on the movie set, ultimately fail.

While Candy, Flaherty, and Levy were relying on their most durable characters, Thomas and Moranis were creating new characters of varying success. Existing in the shadows of "Just for Fun," this episode's "The Irv Goldfarb Show" is a dark send-up of low-budget local talk shows. The look of the sketch particularly (with its minimal set, unstable camera movements, and bad audio) makes it more a spoof of a public access cable TV program than anything normally seen on SCTV. As Goldfarb, Thomas is an awkward bore with an over reliance on note cards.

As the president of a security company and Irv's only guest, Moranis's detail-oriented and fast-talking character stands in stark contrast to Goldfarb. After an appropriately slow start, the sketch takes a surprisingly quick turn into darkness after Rick's character is accidentally shot by Goldfarb, sending Rick's fierce attack dog in hot pursuit of the host. (Reminiscent of another Thomas sketch, "Cookery Crock" from show 72, in which dogs chase guest Gregory

Peck.) Despite Rick being unharmed, the police take Goldfarb away as the show's credits appear. Note also that this piece includes a cheap commercial for a Bali Indonesian restaurant that foreshadows later advertisements for The Driftwood Inn.

The other Thomas/Moranis sketch of note is "Dr. X," which is loosely based on the 1963 Roger Corman movie *X: The Man with the X-Ray Eyes*. Placing the character (Thomas) into the format of a classic television show, the sketch's style — the piece is shot in striking black and white — succeeds more than its substance. Everyone in the sketch (which includes Thomas, Moranis as The Invisible Man, and John Candy as Dr. X's boss) is a straight man looking for a comic foil; there simply aren't any laughs. The piece is watchable thanks to its unique look, but in the end it is another example of Thomas and Moranis forcing pieces that don't really fit into the *SCTV* puzzle.

This episode is ultimately most notable for the premiere of "The Days of the Week" serial, an ambitious soap opera parody that will stretch across several shows, becoming the first *SCTV* franchise since "Great White North" to be granted so much consistent airtime. Overall, "The Days of the Week" collapses under the weight of its own authenticity — the parody is simply too similar to actual daytime dramas to be a truly effective satire.

To its credit, *SCTV* does fill "The Days of the Week" with somewhat addictive plotlines, the majority of which are introduced in this premiere edition. Recognizing the frequent use of hospitals as settings for soap operas (a fact exploited back in show 27's "Restless Doctors" sketch), the first scene of "The Days of the Week" takes place in — where else — a hospital, where we first meet rock star Clay Collins (Moranis). Collins is there to receive some test results from his physician, Dr. Elliott Sabain (Levy), who is meeting with Dr. William Wainwright (Candy). Sabain is on edge — he's furious that Wainwright can't provide ice for his scotch on the rocks — because Collins's test results are grim.

As soap opera characters frequently feature in multiple storylines, we soon learn that Dr. Wainwright is involved in an embezzlement scheme with a particularly dumb hood known only as Rocco (Flaherty); here Rocco calls to make a demand for more of the profits from Wainwright. Despite the fact that he's doing most of the work and is taking on most of the risk, Rocco has only secured himself five percent of the haul, which he is now hoping to increase all the way to eight percent. After barely muzzling his laughter, Wainwright accepts the revised terms, much to Rocco's misguided satisfaction.

The plan that the two have hatched is to have Rocco portray a wealthy woman's long-lost son, then to kill her after she changes her will to leave the "son" her large fortune. The son, named Billy McKay, became lost after suffering a bout of amnesia — the most-used malady in soap opera history, and hence its appearance here. In another scene, we meet the wealthy mother, Violet McKay

(O'Hara) and her maid, Mojo (Martin), who are discussing Billy's imminent reappearance. Like the Rocco character, Mojo is outrageously stupid, particularly when she wonders if Violet will like Billy more than she likes her. (Violet: "He *is* my son." Mojo: "Am *I* your son?") As they are in this premiere, Mojo and Rocco will prove to be the most enjoyable characters in "The Days of the Week"; they provide the laughs that seem to be a secondary consideration of the serial.

The eventual departures of Rick Moranis, Catherine O'Hara, and Dave Thomas will lead to a big shake-up on "The Days of the Week"; their imminent exit is also the impetus for a series of hit-and-miss sketches in this episode involving Tex and Edna Boil. In the first and best in the series of ads, Dave Thomas is unpredictably cranky as he utters the previously unthinkable line "That's *wrong*, Edna" in response to Edna's "Right, Tex?" This shocking development hasn't even sunk in when Tex suddenly walks out of the shot, exclaiming, "You talk too much Edna. I'm gonna get the hell away from you!" This segment would in fact be the final Tex and Edna Boil piece (until a 1989 Andrea Martin Showtime special) and a fine way to end what had already become a tired series of sketches.

Unfortunately, instead of retiring the characters, Martin was determined to prove that there was life in Edna Boil without Tex, a theory that would turn out to be largely untrue. The three follow-up ads in this episode are highlighted by auditions held to replace Tex, which feature the welcome reappearance of Flaherty's Seth Dick III (Libby Wolfson's theatrical co-star in show 89), as well as the inspired use of Moranis as a rock musician playing The Band's "Chest Fever" and Procol Harum's "Whiter Shade of Pale" on a huge array of keyboards.

Show 101 *(SCTV Network)*

1. Annie commercial
2. Stairways to Heaven commercial
3. Donahue on Pornography promo
4. Pet Peeves of the Stars: Elizabeth Taylor
5. The Days of the Week episode 2
6. The Happy Wanderers
7. Second Nose Job promo
8. Nightline Melonville: Children's Milk Fund
9. Pet Peeves of the Stars: Bob Hope
10. Pet Peeves of the Stars: Luciano Pavarotti
11. Audiogames by Intellicoustic commercial
12. The Fishin' Musician: Carl Perkins part 1
13. K-I-L Target Leads commercial (repeat from show 96)
14. The Fishin' Musician: Carl Perkins part 2
15. Great White North: How to beat the Russians in the space race
16. Pet Peeves of the Stars: Morgan Fairchild

17. Fish Flakes and Frosted Fish Flakes commercial
18. Stand Up and Be Counted with Bill Needle

What to watch for: The Happy Wanderers.
It took a while, but with the creation of polka stars Yosh and Stan Shmenge, Candy and Levy were finally able to create a comedy partnership that rivaled the Moranis and Thomas duo of Bob and Doug McKenzie. Yosh (Candy) and Stan (Levy) never rivaled the McKenzies' popularity, but they could be just as entertaining and, more importantly, they never wore out their welcome. The final "Happy Wanderers" (on show 118) is the finest Shmenge sketch, but it was bettered by the post–SCTV telefilm The Last Polka. *In contrast, the major post–SCTV Bob and Doug project,* Strange Brew, *didn't improve on the SCTV McKenzie appearances, and the film fell far short of the characters' peak of the "Great White North Palace" material in show 97.*

This gradual improvement does not mean it took time for Yosh and Stan to develop. In fact, the characterizations are flawless in this premiere sketch, which features the Shmenges doing what they do best: Playing polka music to a studio of elderly people who alternate between dancing to The Happy Wanderers Band and consuming plenty of cabbage rolls and coffee. We learn early on that the lederhosen-clad Yosh and Stan are from the mythic country of Leutonia (the same country that spawned the political group that kidnapped Moe Green in season two); a fictional country was a wise choice for their homeland, since no recognizable country could have issued two brothers that look (including facial boils that appear as if they require immediate medical attention) and sound like the Shmenges. (Note that they also don't look or sound like Candy's "Leutonian Hour" host from show 3.)

Outside of Yosh and Stan, the premiere sketch also features an appearance by Rick Moranis as Linsk Minyk, a former member of The Happy Wanderers Band who left to start a solo career. Looking a bit like Slim Whitman, it appears that Linsk Minyk left because he was more interested in popular music than polka music (an interest confirmed in The Last Polka*). In his brief set, Minyk does Leutonian versions of "Stairway to Heaven" and The Monkees' "Last Train to Clarksville." This curiosity about popular music (and the revenue it garners) would later strike Yosh and Stan (show 118), but in this premiere sketch the brothers are all about playing traditional polka. Incidentally, it's obvious from the beginning that Eugene and John aren't actually playing their instruments, but this matters little to the success of the piece.*

For the second straight episode, *SCTV* goes wraparound-free, presenting an (almost) all-new show of stand-alone sketches. Whereas the previous show contained more experimentation, this episode just goes for the laughs and largely gets them, resulting in the last great show with the original NBC cast.

After two bland trips to the Scuttlebutt Lodge, this episode features a return to form for John Candy's Gil Fisher, better known as "The Fishin' Musician." To the show's credit, the Gil Fisher sketches continued to resist repetition; despite the fact that Fisher was to take rock legend Carl Perkins fishing, the piece avoids comparisons to the Tubes' appearance (show 86) simply because Gil, Carl, and Carl's musicians never get to their destination. Instead the group stops at a bar where Gil, exhausted from driving and wired on "700 cups of coffee and four cartons of cigarettes," proceeds to get drunk while groping waitresses, provoking a group of Nazis, and getting pummeled by a guy a fourth his size. During all of this, Candy unleashes a pathetically apologetic narrative.

"The Fishin' Musician" from this episode was once again edited from off-net syndication, as was a fine sketch with Dave Thomas's Bill Needle character that returns Needle to his unique strength of hosting failed programs. After busting up the awards broadcast in show 99, Needle's latest short-lived show, a 3 AM phone-in program called "Stand Up and Be Counted," is indicative of his decreased stature at the network. But Thomas doesn't let the late hour put Needle in a restful mood — if anything, he's more outrageous, labeling people who would call in at that hour as "losers, morons, pill poppers." He berates his callers, who improbably include Carl Sagan, Tip O'Neill, and Mr. Blackwell, telling the latter that he "looks like the head waiter at Stuckey's." As often happens, though, the last laugh is on Needle himself, as Guy Caballero phones in to cancel the program, barely five minutes after it has begun.

Of sketches not eliminated from off-net syndication, the lengthiest are two recurring pieces: The second "Days of the Week" episode and the third (in only five shows) "Nightline Melonville." The latter piece is notable due to Flaherty's Floyd Robertson, an alcoholic who had been in treatment (show 84), being completely drunk and antagonizing the usually passive Mayor Tommy Shanks (Candy). Predictably, Levy's bumbling Earl Camembert ends up making a bad situation worse, sending Shanks over the edge with a simple "shut up." This remark causes Candy's Shanks to go on a surprising profanity-laced tirade, which culminates in an in-person visit to the "Nightline Melonville" set where Shanks proceeds to beat up Earl as the show leaves the air.

The second installment of "The Days of the Week" sees the introduction of two more characters: Zach Harrington (Thomas), who has ambitious plans to topple the United States' government, and May Matlock (Martin), a wealthy socialite who is inadvertently standing in Harrington's way. This storyline gets credit for being the most original of the serial — it's difficult to imagine any daytime drama featuring a scene such as the one with Harrington flirting with Matlock while she stands on a table with a noose around her neck. Thomas is especially good in the role, using his charm (his character most resembles the charismatic Victor Newman from *The Young and the Restless*) to sweet talk Matlock without letting on that he finds anything odd about her present suicidal condition ("I trust I didn't come at a bad time," he says as she adjusts the tightness of her noose).

The remainder of this episode consists of successful shorter pieces, highlighted by a run of strong sketches that open the show. First up is a commercial for an original cast production of the musical *Annie*: Reminiscent of "Perry Como: Still Alive" from show 88, the joke here is that everyone is too old to be playing their roles, particularly a rough-looking, raspy-voiced, chain-smoking

Andrea McArdle (Martin) as the original Annie. The sight of a gravelly-voiced Annie choking out the vocals to "It's the Hard Knock Life" is inspired, as is the stuffed "original dog" Sandy being dragged across the stage. Rick Moranis also joins in as the original Daddy Warbucks, who needs a walker and an IV to reprise his role.

Foreshadowing the Linsk Minyk rendition of "Stairway to Heaven" on "The Happy Wanderers," the "Annie" sketch is followed by a commercial for the "Stairways to Heaven" album, a collection of 30 different versions of the Led Zeppelin classic. Narrated in typically frantic style by Thomas's Harvey K-Tel, the sketch features snippets of the track as sung by wildly dissimilar singers such as Barry White, Slim Whitman, Luciano Pavarotti, Buffy St. Marie, and the Five Neat Guys. In fact all of the singers have only one thing in common: They are all wholly inappropriate interpreters of the song.

Next Thomas dusts off his Phil Donahue impression in a promo for a *Donahue* show that examines the world of pornography. Viciously satirizing Donahue's status as a champion of women's causes, the sketch culminates in Donahue sitting naked in a peep show booth, imploring women to actively attend their own porno houses. The piece also mocks the audience of Donahue's show, a group of middle-aged women who come across as deeply offended by pornography yet obviously titillated by Donahue's saucy interview with a stripper (O'Hara) and by the sight of the talk show host's own nude body. Moranis steals the sketch as a sleazy porno shop proprietor whose uneasiness at being filmed causes him to unleash a remarkable flurry of profanity.

Despite the lack of any wraparound element in this episode, there does exist a continuing series of sketches entitled "Pet Peeves of the Stars." The segments are an easy way to get screen time for a few of the cast's impressions: O'Hara scores the best two segments, one featuring Elizabeth Taylor complaining about her reputation for having a strong handshake, the other as Morgan Fairchild lamenting the impossibility of locating cartridges for her collection of civil war and antebellum handguns. Dave Thomas's Bob Hope's pet peeve, however, is the most plausible, as he complains about the proliferation of "tell-all" books like *Mommie Dearest*. The complaint seems like one Bob Hope would have, or maybe it seems plausible because it's a complaint that Dave Thomas's interpretation of Bob Hope — which is so good that it all but replaces the real Bob Hope in the consciousness of *SCTV* viewers — would have.

Show 102 *(SCTV Network)*

1. Edison Gum commercial
2. The Sammy Maudlin Show: Chariots of Eggs
3. Johnny LaRue's Discount Deprive-A-Rama commercial
4. SCTV Special Live Presentation: Buzz Aldrin's Mercury III Players

5. The Days of the Week episode 3
6. Ethel Merman: Wake Up and Love Me commercial
7. Great White North: How come Americans have twist-off beer caps and Canadians don't
8. Mr. Boom Microphone commercial
9. Mrs. Falbo's Tiny Town: Melonville Maximum Security Prison
10. Wheelbarrow World commercial
11. Revenge
12. Carl's Cuts
13. Guy Caballero: Political stance of SCTV

What to watch for: Revenge.
This eerily prophetic sketch, hosted by Dave Thomas doing an impersonation of staff writer Eddy Gordetksy, is the funniest and timeliest piece in this episode's rundown. When "Revenge"—a game show that helps people get (what else) revenge—first aired in the spring of 1982, no one could have predicted the rise of confrontational "trash TV" programs like The Jerry Springer Show, Maury, *and* Cheaters *that would make this darkly comic sketch almost tame by comparison.*

The objective of "Revenge" is summed up by the appearance of the show's first guest: A woman (Kathy Laskey) with petty complaints about her garbage men is treated to home video of one of her sanitation workers suffering a hernia after being made a victim of a cruel joke perpetuated by "Revenge" staffers.

After Flaherty makes an appearance as a viewer who is arrested for arson after seeking revenge without the show's help, Moranis makes a startling appearance as an angry viewer (he has garbage piled up at his house because his garbage man has been incapacitated with a hernia) who proceeds to bomb the studio. While the ending remains funny, it now brings to mind the Jenny Jones *incident, in which guest Jonathan Schmitz shot and killed another guest, Scott Amedure, after Amedure revealed on Jones's show in 1995 that he had a crush on Schmitz. In that case, it was proven that "trash TV" shows such as* Jenny Jones *have real-life consequences that can lead to real-life tragedy, a lesson "Revenge" tried to teach fifteen years earlier. "Revenge" is* SCTV *at its darkest and prophetic best.*

SCTV blew it. This episode, which aired on June 5, 1982, represented *SCTV*'s best chance at finding success with a wider audience: Daryl Hall and John Oates (at the peak of their early-eighties commercial success) were the musical guests, and the episode was originally broadcast in the highly visible *Saturday Night Live* time period. After the previous episode featured somewhat broader material perfect for this larger audience, this show unwisely leads off with two sketches that are long, slowly paced, and — particularly to the younger *SNL* audience — largely inaccessible.

While it could be seen as admirable for *SCTV* to resist the urge to "sell out" to win over a larger audience, the early appearance of Hall and Oates — the best time slot a musical guest ever got on *SCTV*—indicates that the cast was not above making some concessions in hopes of hooking unfamiliar viewers. Unfortunately, most unfamiliar viewers probably lost patience with the episode somewhere during the lengthy "Buzz Aldrin's Mercury III Players" sketch, and NBC responded to the overall lack of public enthusiasm by never again giving *SCTV SNL*'s time period.

A prime example of where this episode errs is "The Sammy Maudlin Show" sketch, which takes up nearly the first third of the program. The sketch's comedic highlight is the clip of director Bobby Bittman's new film "Chariots of Eggs," which stars Hall and Oates as runners competing in a race in which they must balance eggs held on spoons placed in their mouths. It's an unforgettably silly scene, one that immediately deflates the grandeur of the Oscar-winning *Chariots of Fire*. Moreover, Hall and Oates are actually *funny*, and they deserve credit for performing comedy at a time in their careers when they didn't need to be taking any risks.

Unfortunately, the "Chariots of Eggs" clip comes so late in the sketch that the piece has already worn out its welcome. Not that there aren't scattered laughs, but far too much time is spent on the panel discussing the film and setting up the clip. Hall and Oates's performance of their single "Did It in a Minute" also slows the sketch: The song is not bad, but the rendition is too obviously mimed; note how off Hall is on the song's last chord. This "Maudlin" outing is a frustrating endeavor that requires far too much patience.

Also testing viewers' stamina is an equally overlong sketch featuring Walter Cronkite and David Brinkley (Thomas and Moranis) anchoring live opening night coverage of Buzz Aldrin's Mercury III Players, an event billed as "the first union of the American space program and the American theatre." The Cronkite and Brinkley sketches have always been hit-or-miss; here the idea is clever, but the execution is bland. The sketch features at its center an intriguing blend of a NASA space launch and a play's premiere, with Candy as Christopher Kraft (NASA's first flight director) directing a production of T.S. Eliot's *Murder In The Cathedral*. Most inspired is the decision to have the astronauts perform while in their suits and helmets; the decision to not expose the actors' faces eliminates any chance for the audience to become emotionally involved in the production.

But that emotional distance carries over to the sketch itself; indeed, much of the piece would be funny if it wasn't first and foremost so dull. The highlights of the sketch belong to Thomas and Moranis's takes on the legendary broadcasters; in particular, Moranis is particularly good as Brinkley, whether playing an illegal shell game in front of the theater or hitting on an "actress/model" at the theatre bar.

More purely entertaining is a solid edition of the children's program parody "Mrs. Falbo's Tiny Town," which here features Mrs. Falbo (Martin) and Mr. Messenger (Candy) on a tour of Melonville's Maximum Security Prison. Why would a children's show tour a prison? Well, it wouldn't, but that logic is second to a string of gags, beginning with Mrs. Falbo tricking Mr. Messenger into getting shot at by prison guards. The interaction between the jovial Falbo and Messenger and the hardened criminals provides much of the piece's humor, including an inappropriate concert that features Falbo and Messenger mixing Johnny Cash's "Folsum Prison Blues" with the children's ditty "The Little Skunk's Hole." After a prison break erupts, a massive prisoner corners Falbo with a decidedly non-musical request. Ending this children's show with a hint of prison rape is shocking but, thanks to the relentless perkiness from Martin's Falbo, somehow not distasteful.

Due to the length of the pieces already mentioned, the only other sketch of significance is the third installment of "The Days of the Week," which is notable for the introduction of Catherine's promiscuous Sue Ellen, the fiancée of Moranis's Clay Collins. Here she freely admits to Collins that she engages in sex with a group of bikers (including John Hemphill, in his second *SCTV* appearance), and she is somewhat relieved when she discovers that it's not her cheating that is bothering Collins, but rather his impending death. Catherine's false display of sadness at Clay's news is particularly memorable.

This episode also marks a brief return to form for Bob and Doug McKenzie; the characters had been largely missing in action since the "Great White North Palace" wraparound five shows earlier. The topic — why Americans have twist-off beer caps — is explored more seriously than most of their other subjects; Doug theorizes that American beer is less potent and drinkers in the states need to "whip 'em off and drink, whip 'em off and drink" fast in order to get a good buzz. Not only does he come up with a plausible hypothesis, but Doug also makes a valid suggestion to American beer makers: "Why not just put more alcohol in your beer?" A reminder of why Bob and Doug McKenzie were so popular in the eighties.

The two sketches that make up the last segment of the show are pure filler: Another "Carl's Cuts" show and a message from Guy Caballero in which he responds to viewer complaints that SCTV does not take enough of "a political stance on the issues of the day." Whether or not Caballero's commentary stems from any actual complaint about *SCTV* is unclear, but what is clear is that *SCTV*'s lack of political humor has helped to keep the show from showing its age in repeats and home video.

While this episode has many worthwhile segments (particularly "Revenge"), the broadcast undoubtedly failed to attract new viewers to *SCTV*. New viewers or not, the next episode would see a new cast member join *SCTV*, a Second City stage vet named Martin Short.

Show 103 *(SCTV Network)*

1. Bell Telephone commercial
2. The Battle of the PBS Stars part 1: Fred Rodgers [sic] and Julia Child boxing match
3. Wok on the Wild Side: The Case of the Stir-Fried Corpse
4. The Battle of the PBS Stars part 2: Beverly Sills and Joan Sutherland pole vault

5. The Days of the Week episode 4
6. The Battle of the PBS Stars part 3: Football
7. SCTV Movie of the Week: I Was A Teenage Communist
8. Harry's Sex Shop commercial: Small Businessman of the Year
9. Big Dude TV Dinner commercial
10. Charlie's Kitchen
11. Mean Joe Greene Playhouse: The Big Dude and the Kid
12. Love Slaves of the Southwest promo
13. Comment with David Brinkley: Brinkley quits

What to watch for: *The Battle of the PBS Stars*.
In one of the most successful examples of SCTV's *trademark multi-layered parodies, this series of sketches combines the inanity of* The Battle of the Network Stars *(a series of specials that featured prime-time personalities like Catherine Bach and Gabe Kaplan racing through obstacle courses) with the respected stars and programs of the Public Broadcasting System. Levy and Moranis host this crossover parody— Levy as the loquacious Howard Cosell (who actually did host the* Network Stars *specials) and Moranis as the equally verbose Dick Cavett. Throughout the piece's three segments, Levy's Cosell becomes increasingly annoyed with Cavett's rambling stories and lack of sports knowledge, until he finally delivers a brutal body check on Cavett just to shut him up.*

As fine as Levy and Moranis are, the series of pieces is best known for the boxing match between Fred Rodgers [sic] (Short) and Julia Child (Candy). Playing the lovable host of Mr. Rogers' Neighborhood, *Martin Short makes an immediate impact in his very first SCTV sketch, while the segment also foreshadows the broader physical humor that Short would bring to SCTV.*

Note that "The Battle of the PBS Stars" was thought strong enough to comprise the bulk of the first episode of SCTV's *mid-1980s non-chronological off-network syndication run.*

The fourth straight NBC show to lack a behind-the-scenes wraparound device, this episode is notable not only for its reliance on newcomer Martin Short, but also for its lack of reliance on established characters. The longest sketches — "Mean Joe Greene Playhouse," "I Was a Teenage Communist," and "Wok on the Wild Side" — are all unique items. Even "The Battle of the PBS Stars" features several impressions never before seen — Thomas's Carl Sagan, O'Hara's Jane Fonda and Joan Sutherland, and Martin's Beverly Sills. The close of the episode also features two strikingly strange pieces: Thomas's "Charlie's Kitchen" and O'Hara's "Love Slaves of the Southwest."

Speaking of strange, the same year that saw *SCTV*'s NBC premiere, the embattled network also broadcast *The Steeler and the Pittsburgh Kid*, a one-hour telemovie starring Pittsburgh Steeler legend "Mean" Joe Greene and based on, of all things, the wildly popular Coca-Cola commercial that featured Greene's touching post-game encounter with a young fan. It's a safe bet that Pittsburgh native Joe Flaherty, sensing a way to combine his love of the Steelers with *SCTV*, was behind the idea of doing a second Greene commercial/movie combo.

The commercial that "inspires" the movie is for a line of frozen meals called Big Dude TV Dinners, a series of gastronomical monstrosities that take up an entire kitchen table and feature enough food to feed the entire Steeler football team; for example, Greene's features a 24-pound turkey, eight ears of corn, five pounds of potatoes, and an entire pineapple upside-down cake. In an example of *SCTV* being ahead of its time, over twenty years later Swanson would introduce a line of so-called Hungry Man XXL TV Dinners. The Swanson meals feature over one pound of food each, well over one thousand calories per meal, and alarmingly high amounts of fat, cholesterol, and sodium.

The fact that Greene and co-star (former Steeler running back) Rocky Bleier had already retired by 1982 is key to the plot of "The Big Dude and the Kid," which is presented by an unusually excited Alistair Cooke (again, Flaherty channeling his personal enthusiasm for the Steelers) during an installment of "Mean Joe Greene Playhouse." The movie is in essence a parody of the scene in *The Babe Ruth Story* (itself already parodied by *SCTV* in show 26) in which the Babe pledges to hit a home run for a sick child; here Martin Short plays a hospitalized youngster who begs Greene to play the San Francisco 49ers and "make a lot of tackles." What ultimately makes this sketch work is the enthusiasm of Greene and Bleier, who seem to be greatly enjoying their first (and probably only) crack at sketch comedy. As the piece includes several thinly veiled cracks at his small stature, Bleier is especially good-natured.

Short also stars in "I Was a Teenage Communist," a passable cross between the 1957 horror movie *I Was a Teenage Werewolf*, anti-communist films produced by Hollywood during the "Red Scare" years of 1947–1954, and juvenile delinquency movies of the era such as *Blackboard Jungle*. Combining these genres is not as big a stretch as it might seem, since all three types of films were usually cheaply made schlock-fests with sensationalistic titles and attention-grabbing posters designed to turn a quick buck. Both Short and musical guest Dave Edmunds turn in fine performances in the sketch; while acting obviously isn't Edmunds's forte, he does deliver a memorable performance of the Bruce Springsteen–penned track "From Small Things (Big Things One Day Come)."

Clearly working overtime, Short is also featured in "Wok on the Wild Side," which stars John Candy as Jean-Pierre Yang as Harry Wok, a TV chef who does detective work on the side. The sketch looks great and boasts an intriguing story, but it's simply not funny. Apart from a couple of quick gags, it's hard to find even attempts at humor in the sketch. Most notable is how Candy plays an Asian character: In contrast to Dave Thomas's Lin Ye Tang or Tim Ishimuni, Candy wisely elects to let the makeup express the ethnicity of the character and does not use any exaggerated dialect or mannerisms.

Rick Moranis closes out not only the episode but also his *SCTV* appearances as David Brinkley with a funny "Comment" segment: Looking horribly unkempt, Moranis's Brinkley here announces his immediate retirement to

Florida in order to raise dew worms. Note the list of events that Brinkley claims to have covered, which includes Vietnam, the Battle of Hastings, and the Parting of the Red Sea. A knock on Brinkley's advanced age or his state of mind? A sketch inexplicably cut from off-net syndication.

In a strange promo supposedly set at a trailer park in Scottsdale, Arizona, O'Hara plays a middle-aged retiree lamenting the discovery of her husband in their motor home with a rubber ball in his mouth, his pants around his ankles, and his hands tied above his head. The piece, aptly titled "Love Slaves of the Southwest," is so striking in its look—shot on black-and-white film—and O'Hara's performance is so intriguing that the short segment is immediately unforgettable. A long-time writer of *SCTV*, Doug Steckler, has even gone on record as saying "Love Slaves" is his favorite piece.

And then there's "Charlie's Kitchen." Certainly one of the strangest pieces ever presented on *SCTV*, "Charlie's Kitchen" is nearly indescribable, although Dave Thomas did attempt to decipher it in his 1996 book. The character of Charlie, basically a grumpy old man (Thomas) who resembles an older Bill Needle, is a loosely based impression of Martin Short's father. Loosely based because Thomas had never met the man, who had passed away by the time this sketch was produced. In the segment, Thomas cooks sausages, berates the show's writers and director, pours himself a drink, and, after an obvious edit, lights a cigarette and ends the show. The edit is notable because Thomas angrily claims an NBC executive ordered the cut without his knowledge. Not that Thomas is himself overly fond of the sketch: He once referred to it as an example of "how perverse my work got towards the end of my run on *SCTV*."

Show 104 *(SCTV Network)*

1. "Mr. Know-It-All"—The Life of Nostradamus promo
2. Identical Bellhops promo
3. Money Talks with Brian Johns: Time-Sharing condominiums
4. Nightline Melonville: Nuclear Arms Buildup
5. Identical Cheese Hostesses promo
6. Martin Scorsese's Jerry Lewis Live on the Champs Elysees commercial
7. Great White North: Dog scoops
8. Identical Opec Oil Ministers promo
9. The Days of the Week episode 5
10. International House of Panties commercial
11. Rome, Italian Style
12. The Fishin' Musician: Jimmy Buffett
13. Frank Levine: One Stop Lifestyle Services promo
14. Mouse House promo
15. Tommy Shanks message: Chipped tooth
16. Norton Sheeff's The Making of Dr. X: The Man with the X-Ray Eyes promo
17. Insight with Skip Bittman promo
18. Sunrise Semester with Salvador Dali: Elementary Drawing

What to watch for: Rome, Italian Style.
One of the more complex and perhaps inaccessible pieces in the SCTV *canon*, "Rome, Italian Style" is an intricate parody of Italian surrealistic films, focusing most specifically on a masterpiece of that cinematic movement, Federico Fellini's 8½.

The first clues that the sketch is inspired by several films are revealed in the opening titles: The star of "Rome, Italian Style," Marcello Gassman (Flaherty), has a name derived from popular Italian leading men Vittorio Gassman and Marcello Mastroianni, while the director's name, Federico de Sica, is an homage to Italian filmmakers Federico Fellini (8½) and Vittorio De Sica *(*The Bicycle Thief*)*. The title of the piece, meanwhile, is a nod to a series of Italian films containing the words "Italian Style" in the title, such as Divorce, Italian Style and Adultery, Italian Style.

The bulk of the (purposefully poorly dubbed) sketch revolves around Angelo (Flaherty), a family man so bored with his life that he wastes much of his time fantasizing. Both Flaherty and Italian film expert Peter Bondanella (the author of The Cinema of Federico Fellini and Italian Cinema: From Neorealism to the Present*)* point to 8½ as the inspiration for Angelo's fantasy sequences. Of particular note is a sequence in the Fellini film in which the women in Guido's (Marcello Mastroianni) life revolt against him. That revolt is represented in "Rome, Italian Style" by Martin (his wife) and O'Hara (the object of his sexual fantasies)—the actresses give two of their most boldly sexual performances here.

The most obvious lift from 8½ comes at the sketch's end, when Angelo spots a parade consisting of himself, several clowns, and other characters from the sketch; the parade parallels one at the end of Fellini's film, in which Guido is confronted by a string of circus types, musicians, and characters from his life. In both cases, the parade signals a rebirth for the protagonist—freedom from the dreams that are holding both men back.

According to Bondanella, "some of the more surrealistic effects may also recall Fellini's first color film, The Temptations of Dr. Antonio. Ditto with the confession to the priest [Eugene Levy]. Some of the sixties costumes seem to recall some other films, such as Antonioni's Blowup or even Elio Petri's Tenth Victim or Joseph Losey's Modesty Blaise.*"* Not only does "Rome, Italian Style" open up a cinematic world to viewers unfamiliar with Italian film, it also exemplifies better than perhaps any other sketch SCTV*'s refusal to underestimate its audience.*

This episode of *SCTV* is most notable for being held back by NBC for several months in order to air as the show's "season premiere" in the fall of 1982. Coming at the end of a production cycle, the episode was delayed so NBC could begin *SCTV*'s fall season with an episode featuring a full cast and not the smaller cast (minus Moranis, O'Hara, and Thomas) of cycles four and five. But what the postponement of this episode meant was that an installment of lesser quality began the season instead of the far superior show 106. That episode, which involved Guy Caballero airing programming from the Canadian Broadcasting Corporation because of a strike at SCTV— would have made a far more promising beginning to the new season.

An oddity with this episode is how strongly it starts before it suddenly and completely falls apart. The batch of sketches making up the show's final half-hour are particularly flat, beginning with the worst of John Candy's "Fishin' Musician" sketches. (The piece — with musical guest Jimmy Buffett — does have one highlight: A shot of Candy's Gil Fisher stuffing an enormous steak into a pan of trout being cooked is a memorable continuation of the running gag that Gil — who hosts a televised fishing program! — can't stand the taste of fish.)

Despite a couple of disappointing Moranis and Thomas pieces near the end of the show — a follow-up to show 100's "Dr. X" is particularly unwelcome — the two do contribute a fine "Great White North," which is significant for being the final *SCTV* appearance of Bob and Doug McKenzie. For the segment, the brothers find something that they enjoy discussing that has nothing to do with beer, back bacon, or even donuts: Dog crap.

Thomas also contributes a solid opener for the episode in which he plays famed prophesier Nostradamus in a promo for a biographical film. As the movie's title — "Mr. Know-It-All" — indicates, the sketch takes the inspired notion that Nostradamus was indeed a terrific visionary, but was otherwise intolerable due to his extreme arrogance about knowing the future. The sketch's best moment is when Nostardamus tells a sexual partner that she will not become pregnant — a prediction, given its source, that the woman is quick to believe.

"Mr. Know-It-All" ends with an interesting bit of self-referential humor that again reflects Thomas's admitted boredom with the show: Two images of Nostradamus argue with each other over the length of the promo, the laughs generated by the promo, and the fact that as with most *SCTV* promo sketches, the movie will never actually air. While Thomas may have been trying to be subversive with only two *SCTV* episodes left on his contract, *SCTV* already had a long history of playing with its own reality: Not every one of those shows promoted as such could possibly all air Thursdays at Nine.

Three other sketches also promote programs to be broadcast during that Thursday hour: "Identical Bellhops," "Identical Cheese Hostesses," and "Identical OPEC Oil Ministers" all parody the premise and theme song of *The Patty Duke Show*, which ran for three seasons in the early 1960s. But instead of Patty Duke playing identical but behaviorally different cousins, *SCTV* gives us Joe Flaherty, Catherine O'Hara, and Eugene Levy playing dual roles, all of which feature a self-assured persona alongside a less worldly twin. The pieces are particularly noteworthy for being technically superb, bettering any special effect created for Patty Duke's program.

Also strong are several other pieces seen early in the episode: First, Eugene Levy's Brian Johns character makes his fourth and final appearance as the host of "Money Talks." On this episode he looks at the popularity of time-share condominiums with a series of clips supposedly shot at a resort in Turtle Bay, Florida. (The episode's credits give special thanks to a Holiday Inn, where the piece was actually filmed). These segments feature Johns buying in to the resort after receiving only the slightest pressure from a condo sales representative (Candy, playing an older take on Johnny LaRue). Then after writing out the check for $6,000, Johns is ignored by the beautiful types who populate the resort and ultimately humiliated by Candy after Johns's check bounces; Johns explains in the outro to the piece that he discovered that he had been recording his withdrawals as deposits for the last "couple of years." As funny as this line is, Levy is able to work in a touch of pathos as it becomes evident that Johns, who unabashedly worships rich people, is forever doomed to be excluded from their company.

Elsewhere, Martin Short premieres his savage Jerry Lewis impression in a commercial sketch for "Martin Scorsese's Jerry Lewis Live on the Champs Elysees." The Scorsese connection comes from the unlikely (but successful) collaboration the two had just achieved with the movie *The King of Comedy*, and the Champs Elysees setting references Lewis's sold-out run at Paris's Olympia Theatre in the 1970s. The heart of the piece is Short's skewering of Lewis as a truly schizophrenic performer, moving quickly from sophomoric comedian to pretentious lecturer on the shoddy state of the motion picture business. These wild shifts in tempo mirror Lewis's MDA telethons, during which he would often tell a joke, then suddenly make a tearful plea for donations. Short also touches on Lewis's reputation as a tyrant, as he completely eviscerates his conductor (Thomas) for blowing a musical cue.

Proving that there is still life in one of the oldest *SCTV* franchises, Flaherty does his rare Salvador Dali impression in a fine "Sunrise Semester" sketch that closes the episode. The topic is elementary drawing, but Flaherty's Dali cannot resist turning his simple sketch of a face into something surreal, using eggs (which he breaks right on his canvas) in place of eyes and covering the drawing with black ants. The use of the eggs in the drawing refers to two of Dali's most famous works: "Eggs on a Plate Without the Plate" and "Soft Self-Portrait with Bacon." The ants mirror Dali's real-life use of the insects in his drawings, including, significantly for this sketch, a drawing simply titled "Ant Face."

Stranger are the two shortest sketches on the show: A wildly frantic commercial for a business called the International House of Panties promises every possible type of panty imaginable — sheer, tiger-striped, even pre-owned. Eugene Levy's frenzied voiceover is combined with a lengthy shot of men in overcoats and dark sunglasses rifling through tables of panties to create something uniquely unforgettable. Not quite as successful is a commercial for the sequel to the mouse-packed horror films *Willard* and *Ben*: "Mouse House" seems to consist only of mice running around an intricately built miniature house. Both of these bizarre sketches were edited out of *SCTV*'s off-network syndication run.

Show 105 *(SCTV Network)*

1. DiMaggio's on the Wharf commercial
2. Street Beef wraparound part 1: Caballero's office
3. Tyde commercial
4. Talking Projector Adventure Serial
5. The Days of the Week episode 6
6. Street Beef wraparound part 2: Street Beef part 1
7. Lipschitz & Lipschitz commercial
8. Street Beef wraparound part 3: Street Beef part 2
9. TV Talk
10. Carl's Cuts: Deliverance
11. Street Beef wraparound part 4: Donny & Caballero introduced
12. Now "Nosy" the Short-Haired Terrier Dog Got His Name promo
13. The Wall Street Journal commercial
14. Finnian's Rainbow Meat commercial
15. Street Beef wraparound part 5: Donny & Caballero discuss schedule

What to watch for: The Days of the Week.
SCTV's daytime drama parody ends its first cycle of segments (it would return after a six episode hiatus) with its most satisfying installment. Featuring the wedding between the dying Clay Collins (Moranis) and the adulterous Sue Ellen (O'Hara), this installment parodies soap opera episodes in which a major event (usually a wedding, a funeral, or—see show 117—a trial) brings all of the show's characters—and all of the characters' storylines—together.

But this piece doesn't just parody soap operas: Guest Bill Murray makes a memorable appearance spoofing Dustin Hoffman's character from *The Graduate*. Just as Hoffman's Benjamin Braddock did, Murray is seen driving to the wedding, only to run out of gas and run the last few blocks to the church. Like in *The Graduate*, all of this is done to the tune of Simon and Garfunkel's "Mrs. Robinson"; though when Murray runs out of gas, he continues to hum and sing the tune, acutely aware of the movie he is emulating.

This episode could be referred to as SCTV's *Abbey Road*. Not because it's as artistically successful as that Beatles recording, but because it apes that album's construction: Whereas *Abbey Road* had one side produced to please John Lennon — the "song" side — and one side produced to please Paul McCartney — the "suite" side, this *SCTV* episode is also made up of two halves: The more ambitious Rick Moranis and Dave Thomas pieces sit not so comfortably alongside another John Candy and Joe Flaherty wraparound devoted to Johnny LaRue's *Street Beef*. While the Thomas and Moranis segments are more original, most of the material goes nowhere. It's no coincidence that the highlight of the show, *The Days of the Week*, is the only segment to shun cast alliances.

The talents of one of *SCTV*'s most high-profile guest stars, Second City theater alum Bill Murray, are largely wasted here. Besides *The Days of the Week*, his best moments come in the show's first sketch, a commercial for a restaurant owned by former baseball great Joe DiMaggio (Murray). While in real life Joe

DiMaggio did actually own an eatery on San Francisco's famed Fisherman's Wharf, he didn't promise a free meal to customers who could throw three strikes past him, and he certainly didn't physically abuse customers whose pitches he deemed too inside.

Unfortunately, Murray is saddled with a listless and unlikable role in no less than the third *Street Beef* wraparound, which was entirely cut from off-net syndication despite Murray's star power. In the sketches, Murray plays Donny, a neer-do-well who is able to charm Johnny LaRue and eventually Guy Caballero with implausible stories of female conquests and celebrity friendships. For Murray, the part is a cross between his deadbeat groundskeeper in *Caddyshack* and his celebrity reporter from *SNL*'s "Weekend Update" but without the laughs generated by either of those characters.

Though he appears for much of this episode as his signature character Johnny LaRue, John Candy makes a more memorable impact in an odd commercial parody for a brand of lunchmeat named after a 1968 Francis Ford Coppola film. The spot features Candy as an enormous leprechaun who violently coerces a mother and child to eat "Finnian's Rainbow Meats" despite the fact that the product is wholly unappetizing. The sketch is notable for featuring the *SCTV* debut of Mary Charlotte Wilcox, an actress who, with the imminent departure of Catherine O'Hara, would be seen much more frequently for the remainder of *SCTV*'s run.

In another short segment, Joe Flaherty is featured as a pompous spokesperson for *The Wall Street Journal* who is suddenly forced to beg for spare change when he gets his sportscoat caught in a newspaper box. The piece is interesting in that it stretches the limits of a normal commercial parody; unfortunately, as social commentary — the envied businessman put in the unenviable position of a beggar — it's crude. More effective is a promo for an after-school special called "How Nosy the Short-Haired Terrier Dog Got His Name." The sketch is one long shot of two elderly women (Martin and O'Hara in rather convincing makeup) rambling on (and on) about how many inappropriate places "Nosy" has placed his extremely curious snout. SCTV's children's programming has always been dubious; this show could be the network's worst offender yet.

Largely missing in this episode is Eugene Levy, though he is featured (as author Norman Mailer) in a memorable laundry detergent commercial. The spot, which depicts Mailer having a violent confrontation with fellow scribe Gore Vidal (Short), wickedly mocks not only Mailer's tumultuous real-life relationship with Vidal, but also an infamous 1960 incident between Mailer and his then-wife Adele: After drinking heavily at a party, Mailer stabbed Adele with a penknife, effectively ending their marriage (Adele wrote about the incident and her life with Mailer in the 1997 book *The Last Party*). Here partygoer Mailer breaks a glass on Vidal's head, covering his clothes in "blood and 80-proof bourbon."

Then there are the long Rick Moranis and Dave Thomas pieces: In the episode's most ambitious sketch, the two play the lead roles in an adventure serial inspired by the then-recent success of *Raiders of the Lost Ark*, itself a tribute to serial films popular in the first half of the 20th century. The sketch is skillfully constructed, with two false endings and assorted surprises like those found in the best of the classic serial films. The problem is that serial films weren't by and large *funny*, and neither is this very lengthy sketch. The most significant moment comes when Thomas's character — the serial's writer — exclaims, "I'm a comedy writer. I can't write this adventure stuff." If only Thomas himself would have remembered that he too was being paid as a *comedy* writer.

In another lengthy sketch, Thomas and Moranis team up for the final appearance of their "pig" characters, Carl and Fred Scutz. The piece at first seems to be just another brief "Carl's Cuts" sketch, but it instead becomes a fitfully funny parody of the film *Deliverance* with Carl and Fred transporting a shipment of film and headcheese. Surprisingly, the centerpiece of the parody is a reenactment of the film's infamous male rape scene.

Also getting a send-off in this final episode for Moranis, O'Hara, and Thomas is Thomas's Bill Needle character. It's fitting that Thomas allows this sketch to feature a sentimental (if mockingly so) farewell, since Needle is most like Thomas than any of his other characters. And despite feeling burned out from the show, surely Thomas had mixed feelings about leaving *SCTV*; after all, he, along with Flaherty, had been one of the show's two most dominant creative voices since Harold Ramis's departure. So Needle's extended walk off is (if a bit self-indulgent) well earned and even touching.

The farewell comes at the end of a Bill Needle show entitled "TV Talk." The sketch is not one of the character's best; it exists only to afford Thomas a chance to grouse off— and not humorously so — about the antiquated Nielsen ratings system. As valid as Needle's complaints may be, twenty-five years later the sketch is very dated, particularly when he pontificates about the VCR revolution.

The piece then turns into a retrospective of Dave Thomas's work as Bill Needle, with quick shots from several of his failed shows that he claims were short-lived by design because people can always be counted on to tune in to a new show at least once to see how bad it can be. Of course *SCTV* viewers know that some of Needle's sketches lasted longer than one outing (particularly "Critic's Corner" and "Bill Needle's Mailbag"), but the reasoning is true to Needle's cynical persona.

Bill Needle would be one of the most missed *SCTV* characters as the cast shrank from eight members to just five beginning with the next episode. The sight of Thomas as Needle walking off the set (while paraphrasing Tom Joad's famous speech from *The Grapes of Wrath*) is the most overt on-air indication that *SCTV* was at the end of an era. A different chapter in the show's convoluted history was about to begin.

Show 106 *(SCTV Network)*

1. The Penolta M-X commercial
2. The Sammy Maudlin 23rd Anniversary Show part 1: Lon Chaney, Jr.
3. SCTV Strike wraparound part 1: SCTV News Announcement
4. The Sammy Maudlin 23rd Anniversary Show part 2: Lorna Minnelli
5. The Sammy Maudlin 23rd Anniversary Show part 3: Bobby Bittman
6. SCTV Strike wraparound part 2: SCTV News Update
7. The Sammy Maudlin 23rd Anniversary Show part 4: Bobby Bittman part 2
8. SCTV Strike wraparound part 3: Dithers announcement / Caballero reaction
9. SCTV Strike wraparound part 4: Prickley & Trudeau at Studio 54
10. SCTV Strike wraparound part 5: Guy Caballero
11. CBC: Hinterland Who's Who
12. CBC: Monday Night Curling promo
13. CBC: It's A Canadian Fact: Thanksgiving
14. CBC: Moose Beer commercial
15. CBC: Headline Challenge part 1
16. CBC: Hinterland Who's Who repeat
17. CBC: It's A Canadian Fact: Niagara Falls
18. CBC: Headline Challenge part 2
19. CBC: The Journal
20. CBC: It's A Canadian Fact: Canadian Football
21. CBC: National Film Board of Canada: The Chair
22. CBC: Tri-promo
23. SCTV Strike wraparound part 6: Prickley & Dithers negotiate
24. CBC: It's A Canadian Fact: Pearl Harbor
25. CBC: Garth and Gord and Fiona and Alice
26. SCTV Strike wraparound part 7: SCTV Strike Update
27. SCTV Strike wraparound part 8: SCTV press conference
28. The Sammy Maudlin Show Anniversary Show part 5: Earthquake

What to watch for: Garth and Gord and Fiona and Alice.
Due to a work stoppage at SCTV, Guy Caballero is inspired to air programming from the Canadian Broadcasting Corporation in this memorable episode. The final sketch presented as CBC programming is a parody of the 1970 Canadian film classic Goin' Down the Road.

The original, which stars Doug McGrath and Paul Bradley as two uneducated blue-collar workers who leave the Maritimes in search of a better life in Toronto, is a fine film despite its lapses into melodrama. Yet it is these lapses that make the picture ripe for parody. In SCTV's version, lawyer Garth (Candy) and physician Gord (Flaherty) have successful practices in the Maritimes, yet the two still feel compelled to move to Toronto, along with a nuclear physicist named Fiona (Martin) they pick up along the way. The early scenes of the three driving to the big city are impressive recreations from scenes in Goin' Down the Road, *as is a pivotal scene where Candy receives bad news regarding employment in Toronto. Note that Jayne Eastwood plays Alice, a part based on her role in the original movie.*

Her connection to the 1970 film adds more than a touch of authenticity to the parody.

What is not authentic in the parody are some of the sketch's highlights, such as a scene in which Garth strikes a woodchuck with his car. Turns out the woodchuck is being filmed by the CBC for a "Hinterland Who's Who" vignette (parodied earlier in the episode); Levy, as the CBC director, makes a valiant and emotional attempt to bring the woodland creature back to life using mouth-to-mouth resuscitation before angrily discarding the woodchuck's lifeless body. Also funny is the frequency with which Candy and Flaherty hit Toronto's Yonge Street, the self-described "world's longest street"; had SCTV *been as popular as* Saturday Night Live, *it's not hard to imagine the rallying cry of "Yonge Street!" becoming a national catchphrase. Also unforgettable is the speed with which Gord gets Alice pregnant; in the original film, the characters of Betty and Joey have several dates before Betty's pregnancy; here Flaherty and Eastwood are alone for no more than a few seconds before Gord cries out in despair, "Garth, I got her pregnant!"*

Somewhat amazingly, the first episode of *SCTV* following the departures of Rick Moranis, Catherine O'Hara, and Dave Thomas is one of the show's finest. Although John Candy remarked to David Letterman that the remaining cast members were "getting real lonely," the abandonment seemed to at least initially rally the gang of five. This episode's premise allowed *SCTV* to present an original and inventive series of sketches, while the construction of the episode, with a "Sammy Maudlin Show" anniversary special serving as a wraparound to the CBC wraparound, is flawless.

Despite the substantial losses of Moranis, Thomas, and O'Hara, the cast members who remained left behind countless characters that could still be utilized. Chief among these were the core players in "The Sammy Maudlin Show," and it's no surprise that *SCTV* didn't wait to schedule another "Maudlin" sketch. The piece on this episode ridicules Johnny Carson's annual clip shows, which often forced celebrities and even colleagues (one oft-used *Tonight Show* clip featured an obviously drunk Ed McMahon pitifully bantering with his boss) to relive some of their most embarrassing moments. Here Maudlin presents clips that humiliate several of his supposed show-business friends, particularly William B. Williams, whose embarrassment leads to his on-air resignation.

Speaking of Carson, the first clip shown by Maudlin is a parody of one of The King of Late Night's most famous segments — the tomahawk throw by Ed Ames. Maudlin's version features a Native American actor (Levy) who, while demonstrating the art of rock throwing, hits William B. Williams in the groin with a large stone. The original Carson segment is meticulously reenacted here, right down to the endless laughter (Carson boasted that the Ames segment had one of the longest laughs in television history) and Maudlin's quip of "What is this, Frontier Nutcracker?" matching Carson's original "Welcome to Frontier Bris" ad-lib.

Lorna Minnelli, Andrea Martin's devastating parody of Liza Minnelli, enters next: Martin's Minnelli could be seen as substituting for the now-departed Catherine O'Hara's Lola Heatherton, but long-time viewers will remember that Minnelli appeared on the first "Sammy Maudlin" segment (show 4) before the character of Heatherton was even created. While a clip shown of Minnelli accidentally swallowing a fly during a musical number is enjoyable, it doesn't match the excerpt of Bobby Bittman jettisoning his scheduled comic performance upon learning of the Falkland Islands War. Bittman responds to the news by asking Sammy and William B. to join him in a horribly off-key version of Harry Belafonte's "Island in the Sun," which abruptly ends due to Bittman's inability to hold back his tears. (Although he does admirably muster the strength to plug an upcoming concert appearance.)

Viewers have already been tipped off to this episode's storyline by this point in the episode, as two of the "Maudlin" clips are interrupted with news of an impending strike at SCTV. Viewers of the later off-network syndicated version of *SCTV* actually saw the "Maudlin" sketch in its entirety without the two interruptions, marking the only instance where sketches edited for their original airing were presented intact for syndication.

Once Caballero gets the nod from Canadian Prime Minister Pierre Trudeau (Short) to begin airing CBC programming, the episode takes on an entirely unique tone, starting with an uncannily accurate spoof of the dreary Canadian Wildlife Service vignettes entitled "Hinterland Who's Who." Even though the narrator's voice is unmistakably John Candy's, the sketch (which spotlights the woodchuck) probably led many viewers to believe that *SCTV* actually *had* co-opted the CBC.

"Hinterland Who's Who" also plays a role in "Headline Challenge," a parody of the long-running Canadian game show *Front Page Challenge*. *SCTV*'s version makes a joke of the program's longevity — "Headline Challenge" is said to be celebrating its 35th anniversary, an impossible feat since in 1982 that would mean the program would have started in 1947, a full five years before CBC Television went on the air. *Front Page Challenge* would get the last laugh, however; it *would* eventually celebrate its 35th anniversary before being canceled in 1995 after 38 years on the air.

Similar to *What's My Line?*, *Front Page Challenge* invited panelists to quiz a mystery guest about his or her ties to a news headline. Though certainly a Canadian institution, author Peter Kenter, writing in his book *TV North: Everything You Wanted to Know About Canadian Television*, referred to *Front Page Challenge* as "slug-paced," which sounds positively speedy compared to the tempo of "Headline Challenge": From Eugene Levy's leisurely entrance as host Dougall Currie (he arrives at his podium long after the audience's tepid applause dies down) to the tedious interviewing of the show's incredibly dull celebrity panelists, the sketch maintains a remarkably slow pace. Instead of hampering the sketch, though, the pace somehow makes the piece better—

every character is so unbelievably boring that eventually their dullness becomes comedic.

Besides being unflattering to Canadian media figures, "Headline Challenge" bluntly states that Canada is no hotbed of activity — there is apparently so little news happening in the country that the first panelist (Flaherty) guesses the mystery headline immediately, revealing an embarrassed Canadian Mountie (John Hemphill) as the show's first guest. However, the second guest completely stumps the panel, largely because he is introduced as a "popular Canadian actor," and the panelists can't name any Canadian actors deserving of the description "popular." The guest (Candy) ultimately reveals himself as Morely Markle (Candy), the popular narrator of the aforementioned "Hinterland Who's Who" vignettes.

The dullness of Canadian life is also mocked in "The Journal," a newsmagazine show that parodies the then-new CBC program of the same name. The lack of respect granted *The Journal* and the CBC is best evident as host Barbara Frum (Martin) throws to a live satellite interview with Muammar Khaddafi (Levy), who reacts angrily to the interruption to his interview with Ted Koppel. (Sadly, the real-life Barbara Frum died in 1992 from complications of chronic leukemia. As a testament to Frum's importance to the program, *The Journal* could not survive without her; following her death, the show was transformed into *Primetime News*.)

"The Journal" was edited out of off-network syndication, as was the brief film "The Chair." The film features nothing more than a single chair moving via stop-motion animation around a barren set, a close parody of an actual 1957 National Film Board of Canada short called *A Chairy Tale*, about a chair that declines to be sat upon.

Yet more memorable pieces in this episode are a pair of CBC promos, which serve to make SCTV's normal lineup actually look compelling by comparison: First, Canada's obsession with curling is mocked in a spot for "Monday Night Curling," which features Candy, Levy, and Flaherty as the country's version of Don Meredith, Frank Gifford, and Howard Cosell. There is more truth behind this piece than most American viewers would likely recognize: Author Peter Kenter notes that in Canada, curling, first televised in the 1950's, "draws hundreds of thousands of loyal viewers." Later, Candy plays three roles in a promo for CBC's Sunday night lineup, including "The Rowdyman" (who is rowdy only until told to quiet down, at which point he is exceedingly polite), the Canadian version of *Magnum P.I.* ("Magnum P.E.I.," which stands for Prince Edward Island), a piece that sees Candy doing an early version of his Steve Roman character, and "Hello Metric, Au Revoir Avoirdupois," featuring Candy satirizing Canadian comedienne Luba Goy's appearances on the Canadian educational programs *W.O.W.* and *Just Ask, Inc.*

Once the strike has been settled (with SCTV management scoring a decisive victory), *SCTV* resumes programming with the finale of the "Maudlin" special. Since Lorna Minnelli is passed out drunk with an obviously inebriated William B. staring down her dress, we're led to believe that some time has passed since the first part of the show. How much time is uncertain, but it hardly matters; in fact, when this sketch aired in off-net syndication, this segment came immediately after the earlier Bobby Bittman clip. The sketch — and the episode — ends with William B. quitting the program, but not before falling into a huge cake marking Maudlin's anniversary. Although it's unclear at this point whether the resignation will stand, the stage is now set for a Williams-less "Maudlin," as well as Williams's embarrassingly awful solo talk show (show 114).

Just as Williams would find out he would need Maudlin (and vice versa), *SCTV* would soon find out they needed Moranis, O'Hara, and Thomas. But they were not missed for this episode.

Show 107 *(SCTV Network)*

1. Twelve Angry Men promo
2. Indecent Exposure wraparound part 1: Guy forges check
3. Indecent Exposure wraparound part 2: Underground garage
4. Krishna Sings Manilow commercial
5. Indecent Exposure wraparound part 3: SCTV News I
6. SCTV Movie of the Week: The Nutty Lab Assistant
7. Indecent Exposure wraparound part 4: Boardroom meeting
8. Indecent Exposure wraparound part 5: Caballero's estate
9. Mrs. Falbo's Tiny Town: What To Do On A Rainy Day
10. Indecent Expsoure wraparound part 6: Caballero's admission
11. Swinging with Mother Nature promo
12. Indecent Exposure wraparound part 7: SCTV News II
13. LaRue Tachi 1250A commercial
14. Indecent Exposure wraparound part 8: Willard & Caballero

What to watch for: Swinging with Mother Nature.
Martin Short introduces crooner Jackie Rogers and — more importantly — his son, Jackie Rogers, Jr., in this darkly comic promo. In an appearance on the TV program Second City Presents, *Short explained the genesis of Rogers, Jr.: He wanted to do a "lounge singer" character, but because Bill Murray had in his opinion perfected that persona on* Saturday Night Live, *he knew he had to create something different. So he created a character similar to Murray's, then immediately did away with him in order to focus on the character's less-talented (and unmistakably unattractive) son.*

Out of that brainstorm comes this promo for a special (supposedly filmed in 1970) featuring Rogers's tribute to the great outdoors, a tribute labeled by the announcer as a "musical extravaganza that was doomed from the start." And indeed it was, as a mountain lion fatally mauls Rogers while the cameras roll. The mountain lion footage leads into an iris shot of Rogers, Jr., who morbidly encourages viewers to tune in to this resurrected show, because his dad "gave his life for this special." Literally. Since Short's Rogers, Jr. character would forever live in the shadow of his deceased father, this sketch becomes not only a clever introduction but also necessary backstory for the character.

After getting along admirably without them in the previous episode, for this show *SCTV* tries to supplement the loss of Moranis, Thomas, and O'Hara by bringing on two comic guests: Fred Willard, an alumnus of The Second City stage and then-current co-host of the NBC program *Real People*, and, more significantly, Harold Ramis, returning to *SCTV* for the first and only time since leaving the show early in the second season. Unfortunately, the expanded cast doesn't translate to expanded laughs, as Willard and Ramis get stuck in one of *SCTV*'s least inspired wraparounds.

The storyline here involves SCTV president Guy Caballero getting himself embroiled in a check forging scandal after falsifying an endorsement on a company check made out for $499,975 to Fred Willard. (The amount just so happens to be the cost of Caballero's new east wing in his home — $500,000 — minus $25, the combined total in Caballero's bank account and SCTV petty cash.) When Willard realizes he is expected to pay thousands of dollars in income tax for a payment he never received for a SCTV show (supposedly "Farm Film Report") he never appeared on, he begins an investigation that eventually ends at the SCTV Board of Directors and its Chairman, "Crazy Legs" Hirschman (Ramis).

If the plot sounds familiar, it's because the story satirizes the real-life mess that engulfed former Columbia Pictures studio head David Begelman in the late seventies when he forged a studio check meant for actor Cliff Robertson. Like Willard in *SCTV*'s version, Robertson investigated and discovered that Begelman had forged two other checks for a total of $40,000. Begelman was suspended by Columbia with pay for a year but then completely reinstated by their Board of Directors. For his detective work, Robertson found himself ostracized from Hollywood and without motion picture work for three years. Begelman's career never fully bounced back after the scandal and he committed suicide in a hotel room in 1995. *The Wall Street Journal*'s David McClintick first reported the check-forgery story, and in 1982 McClintick expanded on those reports in his book *Indecent Exposure*.

Despite being overlong and plot-heavy, the wraparound has several memorable moments: The first comes while Caballero is deciding which person in his "wealthy celebrity" file is going to pay for his home addition. The first name he mentions — Cliff Robertson — he rejects because "he'd probably catch on," Robertson being the one responsible for blowing the whistle on the real-life scandal that inspired this *SCTV* episode. Also notable is Willard's disastrous decision to confide in Earl Camembert, which leads to a underground garage scene inspired by *All the President's Men*'s "Deep Throat" segments. But whereas Robert Redford and Hal Holbrook held secluded meetings, Camembert and Willard are continually interrupted, until their confidential conversation degenerates into the two of them screaming at each other over deafening car noise.

Also interesting in this wraparound is the fact that Caballero's home is shown for the first time (not counting show 93's *Godfather*-inspired compound). Here we have a scene in Caballero's private movie theater where he is watching, of all films, *The Oscar*, the movie so savagely parodied in show 86's "The Nobel." While viewing Tony Bennett's biggest scene, Caballero mutters to himself, "Damn fine performance. I don't care what they say." This is done to show Caballero's own personal bad taste, proclivities that surface time and time again with the type of programming with which he fills SCTV's schedule.

The longest respite from the wraparound elements in this episode comes with the presentation of the "SCTV Movie of the Week," a parody of Jerry Lewis's film *The Nutty Professor* called "The Nutty Lab Assistant." Even if this sketch failed (which it does not), it would still be notable as the first television appearance of Short's signature character Ed Grimley, one of the most instantly memorable characters ever featured on *SCTV* (though in this premiere Short plays him noticeably calmer than he will portray him in later episodes and certainly more so than he played Grimley on *Saturday Night Live*).

Almost equal to Grimley's premiere is musical guest John Cougar (not yet using his real surname Mellencamp), who, in the Buddy Love role, proves to be a great sport and a more than adequate actor. (Cougar would later direct and star in the more serious film *Falling from Grace*.) Cougar's best moment and arguably the most courageous bit of comedy ever performed by a musical guest on *SCTV* comes when Grimley's secret potion wears off, causing the cocksure rock star Cougar to slowly transform back into the social misfit Grimley. Cougar's appearance on *SCTV* is one of the show's most interesting guest spots: Never before nor never again would *SCTV* feature a performance by a musician whose popularity both critically and commercially was on such an upward trajectory. Not exactly The Beatles on *Ed Sullivan*, but as close as *SCTV* would ever come.

In addition to a fine "Mrs. Falbo's Tiny Town" sketch that spotlights a heretofore unexplored sexual chemistry between Falbo and Mr. Messenger (this being the final "Mrs. Falbo" sketch, this intriguing coupling never came to fruition), there are two other notable segments in this episode: The inspired "Krishna Sings Manilow" commercial is very strong, with Levy and Flaherty leading a group of Hare Krishnas in emotionless chanting versions of Barry Manilow hits like "Mandy," "I Write the Songs," "Can't Smile Without You," and "Copacabana." Hare Krishna jokes are as pedestrian as most of Manilow's music, but here *SCTV* pulls out an original variation on the material.

Also humorous if sophomorically so is the show's first sketch, a promo for a new film adaptation of the classic play *12 Angry Men* that stars twelve of the most effeminate males in show business. While the announcer very imposingly lists off the names of the "men" in the cast (including Richard Simmons, Rip Taylor, and Liberace's live-in lover Scott Thorson), a camera slowly pans toward the door of a jury room where a gaggle of very high voices can be heard. A different cast might have turned this idea into a longer scene with twelve prissy actors flamboyantly discussing a serious case, but *SCTV*'s cast was smart enough to score the laughs quick and to keep the piece short and simple. Too bad the same thinking wasn't applied to the episode's protracted wraparound material.

Show 108 *(SCTV Network)*

1. Melonvote: It's Your Decision promo
2. Vic Hedges for Mayor commercial: Because Nobody's Perfect
3. National Glassproducers Association commercial
4. Libby Wolfson for Councilperson commercial
5. The Happy Wanderers Salute Composer John Williams part 1: Superman
6. Vic Hedges for Mayor commercial: The Alternative
7. Troy Soren for Board of Education commercial
8. The Happy Wanderers Salute Composer John Williams part 2: Jaws
9. Shmenges PSA: Register, Then Vote
10. The Happy Wanderers Salute Composer John Williams part 3: Star Wars
11. Tommy Shanks commercial: Bathtub
12. You! with Libby Wolfson: Robert Wellesley
13. Vic Hedges for Mayor commercial: Because He's Saved A Lot of Lives
14. Stars In One: Linda Hopkins part 1
15. Mark Camden commercial: Actual Courtroom Footage
16. Stars In One: Linda Hopkins part 2
17. Proposition 12 commercial
18. Mark Camden commercial: Crime
19. Melonville Mayoral Debate
20. Tommy Shanks commercial: Hospital
21. Human Sexual Response with Dr. Cheryl Kinsey
22. Skip Shanks for Dogcatcher commercial
23. Melonvote Live
24. Sunrise Semester with Ed Grimly: Snakes

What to watch for: The Happy Wanderers Salute Composer John Williams.
Despite the strength of this episode's election material, it is the second appearance from the Shmenge Brothers that is most memorable. As if Leutonian polka stars Yosh (Candy) and Stan (Levy) weren't brainless and unhip enough, this piece does them the added injustice of placing the brothers in some of the silliest costumes imaginable. All the insulting outfits are inspired by movies with musical scores written by John Williams; the Shmenges' questionable idea of a salute to Williams is to play polka versions of his film scores while wearing attire related to the corresponding film. No matter the low demand for polka versions of the themes to Star Wars, Superman, *and* Jaws, *or that no one in his or her right mind would want to see either Shmenge brother in form-fitting Superman tights.*

On paper, this 90-minute *SCTV* episode looks like an exhaustively prolonged retread of the 30-minute show 32. But this election episode is so different (and in many ways preferable) to the previous one that the two shows are nearly beyond comparison. Note that both episodes feature election coverage from

"Election Central" anchored by Floyd Robertson and Earl Camembert, and that both installments smartly satirize political advertising and debates. But where show 32 centered mostly on Johnny LaRue's campaign for city council, this episode focuses on two key Melonville races as well as several smaller ones while mining sharper-edged humor from not only the election process but also from television's handling of election returns. Perhaps more than any other NBC-era installment, this episode is a testament to how well *SCTV* could take advantage of their expanded 90-minute format.

The races focused on here are the battle for Melonville mayor between incumbent Tommy Shanks (Candy) and challenger Vic Hedges (Flaherty), and the contest for a city council seat between incumbent Robert Wellesley (Second City stage grad David Rasche) and challenger and talk show host Libby Wolfson (Martin).

Of the two, the race for city council between Wolfson and Wellesley is the most interesting. Wolfson's candidacy is introduced in a political ad in which she claims to be "the voice of the people" which may be true as long as "the people" are defined as spoiled affluent women. The tone of the ad is best summarized by one well-dressed woman who enthusiastically says, "I wouldn't vote for anybody else even if I knew who the other person was."

That piece is followed by an edition of "You!" that Wolfson hosts from a makeshift studio in the "ghetto" in order to be closer to her possible constituents. Despite these noble efforts, Martin makes it clear that Wolfson is, at best, annoyed by her neighbors and, at worst, scared to death of them. In either case, her obliviousness to their problems is clear when she states that she got into politics after the rates for her manicures went up. But that inane declaration is nothing compared to the daft discussion she has with her guest, her opponent Robert Wellesley. While Wellesley speaks quite sensibly about his platform, Wolfson is distracted by smells in the studio, smells emanating from her body, and her own confusion about what constitutes a "municipal issue" after being told that "wars" isn't one.

Notable in this strong piece is the casting of David Rasche as Robert Wellesley; it's a wise move, as the straight role requires not only a seriousness of purpose but also chiseled good looks, qualities none of the male cast members could likely convey as well as Rasche. But Rasche doesn't just fill the role; his reactions to Wolfson's stupidity are priceless. Following this single appearance on *SCTV*, Rasche would go on to star as a Dirty Harry–esque cop in the cult comedy series *Sledge Hammer!*

Elsewhere, the silliness of small-town politics is mocked via two propositions that are given their own commercials: One is a confusing bill regarding disposable bottles versus returnable bottles that, judging by the spot's tagline ("Vote 'yes' on proposition 38. Or 'no,' depending on how it's worded"), even the sponsor of the ad doesn't understand. The other, even more bizarre, proposition asks

Melonville citizens to vote to keep English — and not Esperanto — the official language of the city. Why such a proposal would exist is unanswerable, much less why there would be any fear that such a proposal wouldn't pass. Nevertheless, not only is the idea funny, but so is the ad condemning a language change — the spot uses fear tactics to illustrate what could go wrong if a "stop" sign instead read "haltu," or if public restrooms were marked "viroj" and "virinoj." The actor in this scene is writer John McAndrew, another staff member who would help out on-camera for the remainder of *SCTV*'s cast-deficient run.

As in any election, the campaigning leads to the voting results, which are revealed in this episode in a lengthy sketch featuring Floyd Robertson and Earl Camembert. Although reading results of phony elections doesn't sound like classic comedy, *SCTV* is able to make it work in a piece that serves as both comedy and as a series of satisfying resolutions. A comedic thread that mocks news organizations' competitive need to declare winners as early as possible (which foreshadowed by nearly twenty years the 2000 Gore/Bush debacle) runs through the sketch and is the highlight of the piece. Levy's Camembert proceeds to blindly and enthusiastically accept the projections as guaranteed results, going so far as to say that viewers who haven't voted yet should save themselves the trouble. If the revelation that all of the projected results are wrong is predictable, the acrimony of Levy's Camembert is not, as he cruelly tells the alcoholic Robertson to "go have a drink" when Robertson mocks how seriously his partner took the projections.

SCTV breaks away from election material in this episode only four times, each time for a sketch involving a recurring, or in the case of the "Stars in One" piece, a new character destined to reappear several times. As the host of "Stars in One," Martin Short introduces a lousy interviewer who is prone to getting his facts wrong. The character is not, however, *Primetime Glick*'s Jiminy Glick, but a character named Brock Linahan who is based on Brian Linehan, a Canadian talk show host. Linehan, according to author Peter Kenter, "delighted in shocking celebrity guests" with a "broad knowledge of arcane biographical tidbits." In his debut appearance, Linahan likewise attempts to impress musical guest star Linda Hopkins with extraordinarily obscure details about her life. But instead of impressing Hopkins, his wholly inaccurate information only amuses her. Short does a wonderful slow burn as he launches into one detailed question after another, only to have all of his information refuted by a clearly amused Hopkins.

Elsewhere, Martin's sexologist Dr. Cheryl Kinsey returns for a program entitled "Human Sexual Response," which features as its topic "Teenage Sexuality." This sketch is fueled by an unremarkable idea — an old sex education movie is mocked — that somehow works, thanks mainly to the spirited reactions and questionable advice of Martin's randy Dr. Kinsey. Not only does Martin's Kinsey think that it's acceptable for teenagers to sleep around, she also strongly encourages teens to write her "in detail" about their problems. Martin's portrayal as Kinsey as not so much a doctor but as a pervert looking for a socially acceptable way to get her kicks was never better realized.

Besides introducing Brock Linahan and the fey Troy Soren in this show, Martin Short also brings back Ed Grimley for the episode's final sketch. It's odd now to see Grimley kept waiting so long; the producers of *SNL* would never have delayed a Grimley sketch to so late in the program. Ironically, Short's *SCTV* sketches as Grimley were almost all superior to the character's *SNL* appearances, including this one, a "Sunrise Semester" lecture on snakes. (Note how just as Short was breathing new life into *SCTV*, he was also breathing new life into the creaky "Sunrise Semester" franchise.) The sketch's highlight comes at the end, as Grimley tussles with a (remarkably fake-looking) king cobra snake that he inexplicably has on hand. While under the snake's supposed hypnotic trance, Grimley orders the credits rolled and this solid episode concludes.

Show 109 *(SCTV Network)*

1. Angel Cortez: FBI Jockey promo
2. Get Them Reading, Get Them To A Library PSA
3. Gus/Edith wraparound part 1: Security Desk
4. An Evening with John Houseman commercial
5. Farm Film Report: Denny Terrio
6. Gus/Edith wraparound part 2: America
7. SCTV Movie of the Week: The Bowery Boys in the Band
8. National Midnight Star
9. Harry's Scramble Days commercial
10. BBC Classics Presents: Jane Eyrehead
11. Reverend Gene Filler commercial 1
12. Monster Chiller Horror Theatre: Dr. Tongue's 3-D House of Slave Chicks
13. Curly Sings the Great Movie Love Themes commercial
14. Gus/Edith wraparound part 3: Bar
15. The People's Court
16. Reverend Gene Filler commercial 2

What to watch for: Angel Cortez: FBI Jockey.
Martin Short wasn't the only cast member introducing new characters during the latter NBC shows. Looking much like his "Magnum P.E.I." persona from show 106, here John Candy premieres Steve Roman, a wonderfully bad actor who is most notable for his inability to learn any of the innumerable accents he is inexplicably entrusted with mastering.

In his first appearance, Roman plays an undercover FBI agent posing as a Mexican jockey. A man of Roman's impressive girth trying to hide out as a jockey is implausible enough, but his cover is not nearly as ridiculous as the horrible Mexican accent he reveals at the end of the sketch. Not that Roman thought playing a Mexican would be easy: In introducing the character, he claims that the role is "hard," because "I play a Mexican and everything," while implying that his co-star has it easy because "she doesn't have to be a Mexican like I do." Following this auspicious debut, Candy would understandably milk Steve Roman for the remainder of his SCTV *tenure.*

For the third straight broadcast, *SCTV* turns to a non-musical guest to help fill out its reduced cast. But for the first and only time, the show features a visiting performer with no connection to The Second City: Robin Williams. Though not a graduate of the theater troupe, Williams had many credits to his name by the time this *SCTV* episode aired in November 1982: He had wrapped production on the fourth and final year of the hit TV series *Mork and Mindy*, and he was already well known for his unpredictable stream-of-consciousness stand-up comedy. As he would later prove in surprisingly varied film roles (including his Academy Award–winning supporting role in *Good Will Hunting*), Williams is a fine actor, and his stint on *SCTV* works well.

In fact, it seems a missed opportunity that Williams isn't in more of this episode, as the four sketches in which he appears (contrast this to *Saturday Night Live*, where the host is typically in the majority of the pieces) prove that Williams's comedic sensibilities meshed well with *SCTV*'s. The most successful of the group features Robin Williams as master thespian John Houseman proving the adage that a great actor can hold an audience simply by reading the telephone book. Williams studied under Houseman at Juilliard until Houseman supposedly told him that his talents lay in stand-up comedy. Surely indebted for the advice, Williams's impression of Houseman is accurate while maintaining a softer edge than many of *SCTV*'s most wicked celebrity parodies.

Williams also appears in two brief sketches as sleazy country gentleman preacher Reverend Gene Filler, whose sole purpose seems to be soliciting funds for a place of worship called the Church of Unlimited Credit. The first piece is handled by Williams alone, while the second also features Martin Short as Filler's son Biff, who claims that writing a check to the Church of Unlimited Credit cured him of a hideous skin affliction. These two pieces are humorous but slight: Perhaps the name given to Williams's clergyman — Filler — is less a moniker than the character's purpose in this episode.

The only sketch in which Williams interacts with multiple cast members is "The Bowery Boys in the Band," one of the most inspired multi-layered film parodies in *SCTV*'s canon. The sketch improbably manages to interweave the Leo Gorcey–led comedy team with *The Boys in the Band*, the groundbreaking 1970 film about gay life. The piece also includes parodic elements of the 1978 Vietnam War epic *The Deer Hunter*. While many of the gay characters in "The Bowery Boys in the Band" are broad and stereotypical (high voices and limp wrists abound), here the source material must be considered: *The Boys in the Band*, while certainly a seminal film (and play), not only had its share of stereotypes, but it was also so full of miserable, self-loathing characters that many interpreted the material as a denunciation, and not a celebration, of the homosexual lifestyle.

In *SCTV*'s "Band" sketch, which wisely steers clear of such misery, Robin Williams stars as a gay version of Slip, the Bowery Boy played by Leo Gorcey. As the piece opens, Slip is throwing a birthday party for one of his friends; those familiar with *The Boys in the Band* will recall that most of that film also takes place at a birthday party. As in the original film, trouble arises with the arrival of heterosexual party crashers, here the unplanned guests are Slip's fellow Bowery Boys Whitey (John Candy in the role played by Billy Benedict) and Sach (Huntz Hall's role played here by Martin Short).

While Slip tries to hide the orientation of every party guest (not to mention his own) from the "straight ahead" Whitey and Sach, the piece is saved from *Three's Company*–style silliness thanks to the sheer audacity of the sketch's premise and the performance of *SCTV*'s guest. Williams effortlessly shifts back and forth between a butch persona (when dealing with his old cronies) and an effeminate guise (when talking with his party guests). But Williams doesn't completely steal the piece: Note the appearance of Second City alumnus Don Lake (who would later be featured in all of the Christopher Guest/Eugene Levy films) as the birthday boy who accepts the gift of a duded-up cowboy in the scene most directly taken from *The Boys in the Band*.

Robin Williams does not appear in any of the remaining sketches in this episode, the most ambitious being an overly faithful retelling of the Charlotte Brontë classic *Jane Eyre*. Re-titled "Jane Eyrehead," the lengthy piece is founded on two comedic devices: Here the title character (Andrea Martin) is not only as innocent and plain as the original Jane Eyre, but also sorely lacking in intelligence. Unfortunately, the character isn't humorously dumb but rather irritatingly naïve. The second device, centering on Joe Flaherty's performance as Edward Rochester, is more maddening: Flaherty plays Rochester—the owner of the estate where Eyre(head) works as a governess—using the voice and mannerisms of Eddie "Rochester" Anderson, the African-American actor best known for playing Jack Benny's butler. This joke worked better when John Candy played Ben-Hur as Curly from The Three Stooges in show 13; the racial undertone of Flaherty's interpretation is unpleasant, while the broad acting style he employs is simply grating. The joke does pay off nicely at the sketch's end, when Eyrehead returns to find Rochester living in a black-and-white world and employed as Jack Benny's butler, but by then the long sketch has worn out its welcome.

One of the worthier additions to the string of "Monster Chiller Horror Theatre" sketches is in this episode—"3-D House of Slave Chicks," starring Dr. Tongue (Candy) and Woody Tobias, Jr. (Levy) as Bruno. What differentiates "Slave Chicks" from "3-D House of Stewardesses" (show 84) is the fact that "Slave Chicks" is presented in "Smell-O-Rama," Count Floyd's latest creation for defrauding (to the tune of $19.95 a can) his youthful audience. "Smell-O-Rama" promises the home viewer the ability to smell scents germane to the movie, all somehow accessible through the use of a single can of something that looks remarkably like spray deodorant.

Forget the fact that "Smell-O-Rama" could never work; the fun of the sketch is seeing Tongue and Bruno add effusive sniffing to the exaggerated bobbing and weaving of their familiar 3-D gimmick. The sketch even generates enough goodwill to withstand the final predictable joke of Bruno passing wind. (In a bit of self-deprecation, Flaherty responds to the scent by claiming, "I've got tears in my eyes, and I don't think that's from laughing.")

"3-D House of Slave Chicks" marked the return of Tongue, Bruno, and Count Floyd after an absence of eight shows; returning from an even longer sabbatical (13 shows) here are "Farm Film Celebrity Blow-Up" hosts Big Jim McBob (Flaherty) and Billy Sol Hurok (Candy), who in this episode victimize Denny Terrio (Short), host of the syndicated program *Dance Fever*. Short doesn't exactly impersonate Terrio, but rather a generic dance show host: With his leather pants, pink socks, pink leather tie, helmet of thick black hair, and cocky swagger, Short could just as easily be channeling Terrio's *Dance Fever* successor, Adrian Zmed.

Making an unwelcome return on this episode is the tabloid television program "National Midnight Star." A highlight on show 84, it's surprising that it took *SCTV* 25 shows to bring the sketch back for an encore. What's more remarkable is how disappointing this second piece is: Whereas the first "NMS" was an eerily hilarious foreshadowing of the rise of tabloid television, this piece is woefully flat, with nary a laugh to be found. Note that Andrea Martin is playing a toned-down version of her anchor from "Hollywood Dirt Tonite" (show 119), a piece that would later successfully revitalize this sketch format.

Finally, there is an interesting *People's Court* parody near the end of this episode that mocks those who would blame television for their own bad behavior. The piece centers on a wife (Martin), who becomes injured when she drives her car into her garage door that her husband (Flaherty) painted to appear open, an idea that he says he got from watching too many Road Runner cartoons. The judge (Short), tired of people unwilling to be accountable for their own actions, orders Flaherty to the cartoon-like death of being dropped into the Grand Canyon with a large boulder strapped around his stomach. Flaherty seems unfazed by the punishment, assuring a court reporter (Levy) that he can save his own life either by grabbing onto a twig on the way down or by using a package that he reveals as containing "one Acme parachute," two survival tactics undoubtedly learned from Warner Brothers cartoons.

The "People's Court" piece, with its usage of cartoon music and cartoon references, is somewhat reminiscent of "Quincy: Cartoon Coroner" (show 72), but it clearly has a serious agenda that the previous sketch did not. In fact, the social criticism of the sketch recalls most closely Dave Thomas's rants as SCTV's critic-at-large Bill Needle. Perhaps this evocation is no coincidence: Sharp-eyed viewers of this episode's credit crawl will note that Dave Thomas earns a writing credit for this show, possibly explaining the origin of this unique and thought-provoking piece.

Show 110 *(SCTV Network)*

1. Peter Pan commercial
2. Towering Inferno wraparound part 1: Paramutual News
3. Towering Inferno wraparound part 2: Studio tour
4. Al Peck's Used Fruit commercial
5. Towering Inferno wraparound part 3: Fire ignited
6. Kid Sister PSA
7. Towering Inferno wraparound part 4: Fire Department arrives
8. Monster Chiller Horror Theatre: Four for Texas
9. Towering Inferno wraparound part 5: Group plans escape
10. Towering Inferno wraparound part 6: Conclusion
11. One On The Town: Urban Transit of the Future
12. When Wives Look Older Than Their Husbands promo
13. Let's Find Jerzy promo
14. Shakespeare for College Credit
15. Melonville Calendar: Premiere
16. Words To Live By: Mr. Mambo and Band de Brava

What to watch for: Peter Pan.
In the history of SCTV, there are few impressions more memorable than John Candy's brutal take on Divine, the female impersonator who achieved notoriety through his starring roles in many of John Waters's films. And in the history of SCTV, there are few more memorable sights than John Candy playing Divine playing Peter Pan — a role that the weighty Divine was most certainly not born to play. *Presented as a commercial for a new Andy Warhol/John Waters stage production of the popular musical, Candy here gives one of the most inspired performances of his career. A strong contender for the flat-out funniest SCTV sketch produced after the departures of Moranis, O'Hara, and Thomas.*

Roughly half of this episode consists of a wraparound parody of the 1974 disaster film *The Towering Inferno*; the only other time *SCTV* devoted so much of an episode to a single film parody was the "Godfather" installment (show 93). The relative success of both episodes is akin to the relative success of both films–while *SCTV*'s "Godfather" episode and Coppola's original film are towering achievements, this show and the Irwin Allen movie are lighter (even sometimes mindless) entertainments.

The exposition of *SCTV*'s "Inferno" mirrors Allen's film; both present details of an opening night party at the world's tallest building while simultaneously introducing the building's architect. In the original, Paul Newman's character is a heroic figure, while *SCTV*'s architect (Levy) is an unkempt nitwit.

During an interview with Levy, we learn several key facts, including that there exists a combination *nuclear reactor* and revolving restaurant at the top of the skyscraper where the party will take place, and that the SCTV network is the only tenant to lease space in the building (it is hinted that the space was too cheap for Caballero to refuse). The 280-story structure itself is revealed, in a *very* lengthy upward pan shot, to be astonishingly chintzy in appearance.

After an intricately staged scene in which we are taken to one of SCTV's new studios—the facility is so tiny that nothing can be shot effectively, least of all an elaborate western helmed by an exasperated director (Candy)—the "Inferno" plot heats up. As in the original movie, the establishing party scene is shot as if the viewer is a mingling guest privy to several different conversations. We meet the owner of the restaurant, Johnny Nucleo (Martin Short), a man whose exposure to radioactivity has left him with a Bride of Frankenstein-esque hairstyle and a wildly protruding eyeball. We are also introduced to skyscraper owner Norma Rayburn, a Joan Crawford–esque character played by Andrea Martin. Unlike the original's ultimately sympathetic builder (William Holden), Rayburn clearly has a reckless disregard for safety, and in that respect recalls the villainous electrician played by Richard Chamberlain in *The Towering Inferno*. In an enlightening exchange between Martin and Levy, we learn that the entire building—all 280 stories—was built for the sum of $12,000, though even this pittance was too much for Martin's Rayburn: "You could have brought it in for under ten [thousand] if you hadn't insisted on windows!"

The highlights of *SCTV*'s *Towering Inferno* parody come courtesy of familiar characters Dr. Tongue (Candy) and Bruno (Levy), whose bickering reaches unparalleled heights in this episode. Much of their arguing concerns the occupation of a party guest (Mary Charlotte Wilcox in her biggest role to date) whom Bruno fancies; despite obvious clues (she is overly concerned that Bruno may be a cop since "in my line of work I can't be too careful"), Bruno doesn't see why Tongue insists that she is a hooker.

With the start of the actual fire, the "Inferno" wraparound becomes too plot-heavy, save for a few moments such as the sudden interruption of fire-induced panic for a performance of a saccharine song similar to the original's "We May Never Love Like This Again." Flaherty's arrival as Charlton Heston playing the bumbling Fire Chief is also solid, although why *SCTV* cast Heston in the role and not the original's Steve McQueen is unclear. Perhaps no one on the cast could perform an effective McQueen impression, or maybe *SCTV* simply thought it tasteless to parody an actor who had fairly recently died.

Besides Heston, another welcome late addition to the wraparound is an obvious body double for SCTV station manager Edith Prickley, seen earlier at the party being escorted by Dr. Tongue. Since Andrea Martin was already saddled with the role of Norma Rayburn, the decision was made to use a body double for Prickley. But instead of trying to hide the stand-in, *SCTV* cast a body double twice Andrea Martin's size while having the other characters continuously refer to her as "Prickley's double."

A later attempt to rescue Johnny Nucleo, who is trapped at the top of the building, is also inspired: A grappling hook is thrown — past all 280 stories, no less — up to the roof in an effort to physically pull the building down to the ground to save Nucleo. The grappling hook mirrors the rescue attempts in *Towering Inferno* that utilized a breeches buoy. Despite their best efforts, the fire fighters trip and send the nuclear reactor flying through the air, where it lands off the coast of Japan. Here *SCTV* suddenly switches from a parody of an *American* disaster movie to a *Japanese* disaster movie as Nucleo, made gargantuan by his exposure to nuclear waste, is seen unintentionally terrifying hordes of Asian people. With Nucleo in Japan, and with everyone else from the inferno — including a still-bickering Dr. Tongue and Bruno — safe on the ground in Melonville, the wraparound concludes.

While Dr. Tongue and Bruno play major roles in the "Towering Inferno" wraparound, their partner Count Floyd (Flaherty) is relegated to a solo "Monster Chiller Horror Theatre" sketch. This episode's piece sees Floyd futilely promoting the Rat Pack movie *Four for Texas* as a horror classic. Even though this premise has been utilized before (i.e., Count Floyd trying to sell *The Odd Couple* as frightening back on show 61), Flaherty is still able to wring laughs out of his attempts to scare viewers that not only does the movie feature a "pack of rats" but that it also *isn't* in 3-D: "Peter Lawford ... just standing there? You don't think that's scary?"

Eugene Levy's Earl Camembert gets his third and final "One on the Town" sketch here; this time the piece is made up of several disjointed jokes that are not overwhelmingly humorous on their own, but rise to a comic crescendo when strung together with Levy's bumbling Camembert as the linking comedic force. Levy is also strong in this episode as his sleazy pitchman Al Peck, seen in an amusing commercial selling — who knew there was a market for this — used fruit.

Three of *SCTV*'s oddest sketches make up the penultimate segment of the episode, all of which were deemed too strange for *SCTV*'s off-net syndication package. The funniest sketch is a promo for a game show entitled "Let's Find Jerzy," featuring Joe Flaherty doing a particularly manic interpretation of author Jerzy Kosinski. In the piece, Kosinski challenges contestants to a frenzied game of hide-and-seek, a practice that the real-life Kosinski enjoyed. (Sharp-eyed viewers will note the recycling of audience footage from show 102's "Revenge.")

Even more bizarre is a sketch entitled "Shakespeare for College Credit," which features a professor discussing what he considers to be the three main themes — entering, staying there, and leaving — common to all of Shakespeare's plays. What's most strange about the sketch is the fact that writer John McAndrew, and not one of the regular cast members, plays the professor, which happens to be the sketch's only part. Since *SCTV* had previously only used writers on-screen to play bit parts, the choice to cast McAndrew in a solo piece is curious, so much so that it distracts from the sketch.

The final two pieces in the episode are also solo sketches, though they are quite dissimilar from each other — one sketch introduces a new franchise, while the other is a new installment of a recurring sketch initially seen on *SCTV*'s very first show. The former piece is "Melonville Calendar," hosted by a new character of Andrea Martin's named Yolanda Divilbis. Technically, the sketch makes the "Sunrise Semester" pieces look complex — all that exists here is Andrea reciting a list of upcoming local events. Predictably, the joke is that all of the happenings in Melonville are painfully tedious, including a "clean up and fix up day" and two Victor Borge concerts.

The final sketch of the show is a new "Words to Live By" segment, the first and only new "WTLB" piece in the entire NBC run. For a segment entitled "Words to Live By," the piece features remarkably few words, since most of the sketch — following a brief message by Candy's Mr. Mambo — consists of a lively performance by the heretofore-unannounced musical guest Band de Brava.

Making the piece a joy to watch is Candy, who exuberantly mambos throughout the big band's performance. Watching a seemingly carefree Candy dance, particularly now with the knowledge of the health problems that would eventually take his life, is touching and symbolic of the joy that Candy brought to his work and to his fans. It's a shame that this footage isn't as well known as, for instance, the "Don't Look Back in Anger" *Saturday Night Live* segment that features an elderly John Belushi as the last living Not Ready for Prime Time Player. The segment's omission on the 1992 home video release *The Best of John Candy on SCTV* is unfortunate, as is the fact that the piece was cut short in syndication. Coupled with this episode's "Peter Pan" opening, "Words to Live By" brings to a close an episode bookmarked by Candy's unparalleled talents.

Show 111 *(SCTV Network)*

1. LaRue Christmas wraparound part 1: Christmas Carol from Guy Caballero
2. The Love Spirit promo
3. The Fella Who Couldn't Wait for Christmas promo
4. Rex and Edna Boil's Prairie Warehouse and Curio Emporium commercial
5. Count Floyd's Have Yourself a Scary Little Christmas promo
6. LaRue Christmas wraparound part 2: LaRue at construction site
7. The Driftwood Inn commercial: Christmas
8. The Lighting of the Melonville Christmas Tree
9. Christmas Day with the Shmenge Family
10. Pre-Teen World promo
11. LaRue Christmas wraparound part 3: Andrae Crouch
12. SCTV Super Special: Christmas — That's All
13. You! with Libby Wolfson: Chanukah

14. The Driftwood Inn commercial: New Year's
15. LaRue Christmas wraparound part 4: Caballero's bedroom

What to watch for: Christmas Day with the Shmenge Family.
Levy and Candy roll out the polka-playing duo of Yosh and Stan Shmenge again, but the choice to take the brothers out of "The Happy Wanderers" studio prevents the characters from becoming stale.

As the title of the piece suggests, this sketch introduces the Leutonian Christmas traditions celebrated annually by the families of Yosh and Stan. The bizarre holiday customs include "the exchanging of the socks," where the men trade footwear to commemorate the sharing of worldly possessions, and "the looking at the tree," which consists of partygoers engaging in a long and silent stare at the host's tree, no matter how pathetically sad the tree may be (and here is).

NBC promotion for this episode (had the network bothered to promote *SCTV*) might have read: "Tonight, a Very Special Episode: Johnny LaRue and Guy Caballero discover the true meaning of Christmas." This holiday installment of *SCTV*, which asks viewers to delight in the transformation of heretofore sleazy characters into lovable people, is an unfortunate misstep that rings untrue — the maturation of LaRue and Caballero is a nonsensical holiday episode ploy that doesn't connect with either the characters' prior appearances nor their future ones.

The telecast does get off to a rousing start as the pre-transformed Caballero and LaRue engage in an all-out fistfight. The fact that these two characters don't like each other is well documented, but to see them behaving so violently is a true surprise. Making the fight more sordid is the fact that it breaks out during Caballero's on-air Christmas message. (Seasonal cheeriness not being his strong suit, the "message" consists solely of Guy lipsynching poorly to a recording of "The First Noel.")

After this rousing opening, the story sadly becomes a pale sequel to the previous year's Christmas episode, even including a flashback to the segment in show 94 when Santa Claus gave LaRue the camera crane that LaRue had so desperately wanted. Seeing his crane taken away due to unrelated debts, LaRue decides to return to the site of last year's encounter with Santa in order to get more stuff. The idea eventually leads to a few dull moments with LaRue outside of a construction site waiting for Santa Claus's arrival, which mirrors last year's segment just repeated in flashback.

Unfortunately, the episode degenerates from there: Instead of Santa Claus awakening a drunk LaRue (as in last year's show), an unnamed angel played by musical guest Andrae Crouch awakens LaRue to teach him that there are people suffering greater setbacks than losing a camera. In what is undoubtedly the most saccharine scene in *SCTV* history, Crouch takes LaRue to the Melonville Men's Mission, where LaRue is horrified by the grotesque appearance of the bums seeking food and shelter. LaRue has been disgusted by bums before — most notably in show 4's outrageous "Cooking with LaRue" — but here his disgust is meant to trigger feelings of sympathy for those less fortunate. The fact that *SCTV* is attempting to teach compassion during what can be the worst time of the year for many is fine; the heavy-handed way in which the show delivers the message is not. Bringing a lighter touch to the proceedings is Crouch, who momentarily stops the bleeding with a fine performance of his song "Soon and Very Soon." The song, not coincidentally, refers to a meeting with one's Lord, sung just as LaRue realizes that he has met a messenger of God.

The schmaltz continues in the show's final scene, a *Christmas Carol*–inspired segment in Guy Caballero's bedroom with Guy as Scrooge. His slumber is interrupted by a steady procession of station characters — Gus Gusstofferson, Juul Haalmayer, Lola Heatherton, Edith Prickley, Ed Grimley — all professing to be worried about LaRue's whereabouts. Guy's initial resentment at being woken and his lack of concern for LaRue suddenly and awkwardly turns to worry, which is resolved by the sudden appearance of LaRue. As Scrooge does in *A Christmas Carol*, Caballero vows to change his misery and cruel ways, and LaRue in turn earnestly remarks that he is now amongst "my friends ... people who care about me." Why the writers forced such a despicable character to recite such treacle is a mystery. What's not a mystery is why this cloying wraparound was excised from off-net syndication.

Another sketch cut from syndication, a live bi-coastal special featuring Bobby Bittman (Levy) and Jackie Rogers, Jr. (Short), is more successful and free of such sentimentality; indeed, with its melodramatic reminders of the late Jackie Rogers, Sr. (he of the ill-fated special promoted in show 107), this sketch successfully skewers such holiday-induced corniness. The treat of this sketch is seeing the full flowering of Short's Rogers, Jr., which now includes his disturbing albino appearance, his grotesque tendency to giggle through his teeth, and his fey dance steps. Not to be outdone, Levy gives his more-seasoned Bittman character a particularly funny running joke involving a mishap with some jugglers.

This holiday episode is most notable for the first return appearance of Catherine O'Hara since her departure after show 105. Her return is fairly understated, as her only standout sketch is the "Love Spirit" promo that features her signature creation, Lola Heatherton. Here O'Hara looks and sounds great in several musical clips from the finished show, the strongest being an atrociously depressing song reminiscent of the selection Lola performed before her breakdown on show 86. Juul Haalmayer's Dancers (again featuring the agreeable Martin Short) are a welcome addition to the proceedings.

While Lola Heatherton is an obvious character for O'Hara to portray on this return appearance, she also takes a chance by playing a new role: A nasty impression of legendary comedienne Lucille Ball. As depicted by O'Hara, Ball is so creepy that she makes a perfect "scary" guest in a promo for a Count Floyd Christmas special; her gravelly singing voice and cruel asides being eons away from the familiar image of America's favorite TV redhead.

Still a relatively new character, Short's Ed Grimley gets his best sketch in a promo for an after school special entitled "The Fella Who Couldn't Wait for Christmas." Fans who only know the Ed Grimley character through Short's year on *SNL* will notice that this sketch in particular is the blueprint for his pieces on that program. Instead of trying to fit the scene-stealing Grimley into a collaborative sketch such as show 107's "The Nutty Lab Assistant," or into a restrictive franchise such as show 108's "Sunrise Semester," this piece was the first to feature Grimley as a manic, wordy, whirlwind of a character who couldn't keep his feet still or his mouth shut.

Of course Ed Grimley is not the first intellectually inferior character featured on *SCTV*; one favorite dimwit, Candy's Mayor Tommy Shanks, is featured here in one of his finest sketches, "The Lighting of the Melonville Christmas Tree." A title sequence hints that this lighting will be as impressive as the lighting of the Rockefeller Center Christmas Tree in New York City, but that hope is dashed as Shanks stoically flicks a switch and lights a tree reminiscent of the one from *A Charlie Brown Christmas*.

A pair of commercials for a sleazy motel called The Driftwood Inn are perhaps the oddest highlights of this episode: Consisting of a series of still shots and a voiceover from Levy (no other cast members are seen or heard), these commercials are clever parodies of local (and cheap) advertisements that foreshadowed the folksy Motel 6 "We'll leave the light on for you" campaign. (Their cheapness is also evocative of a spot seen during Dave Thomas's "Irv Goldfarb Show" in show 100.) The economy of the commercials is matched by their subtleness: Only those paying attention will catch the ads' selling points of a "three day and one night" package and a checkout time that has been "extended to 10 AM."

Show 112 *(SCTV Network)*

1. Chateau la Feet commercial
2. Half Wits
3. Scenes from an Idiot's Marriage preview
4. Monster Chiller Horror Theater: Tip O'Neill's 3-D House of Representatives
5. SCTV Feature Presentation: A Star Is Born
6. Farm Film Celebrity Blow-Up: Dustin Hoffman
7. Artisans and Their Art
8. The Days of the Week episode 7
9. Stars In One promo: Steve Roman
10. Melonville Calendar: Idella Voudry

What to watch for: Half Wits.
By this point, SCTV had presented a large number of game show sketches, most of which were successful. But one of its finest, "Half Wits," surprisingly came

about by tweaking one of the lesser entries in that genre — show 91's "Steeplechase."

Most of the scattered laughs in "Steeplechase" were born out of the contrast between the seemingly elementary categories ("Famous Whale Novels") and the unexpectedly difficult questions each contained. But in "Half Wits," the similarly simple categories instead lead to the easiest questions imaginable; for example, the choice of the "Clothes Found in Bedroom" category results in the question, "Name an article of clothing found in the bedroom." The joke here is that for the "Half Wits" contestants, such rudimentary questions are in fact unsolvable mysteries.

Martin Short's Lawrence Orbach character would soon become better known as the aquatically challenged half of a male synchronized swimming duo in a celebrated Saturday Night Live *sketch, but on "Half Wits," Orbach isn't even the most memorable contestant. That honor goes to the pig-nosed Arthur (Flaherty), who lies about his job ("medical research") because he wrongly believes it will make him appear smart. John Candy is also funny as a contestant who has a wife and "two boys named Frank." Rounding out the panel is Andrea Martin, whose best moment comes when she cites "cheese omelets" as an example of a dish from Italy.*

After a tepid Christmas show, *SCTV* returns to the top of its game with this episode, its finest set of stand-alone sketches since show 101.

Although not the episode's highlight, the reappearance of "The Days of the Week" is the program's most notable aspect. With the wedding of Sue Ellen and Clay Collins on show 105, it appeared that the serial had run its course. But six shows later, the sketch resumes here with a new storyline focusing on the trial of Dr. William Wainwright (Candy) and Rocco (Flaherty) for the fraud and embezzlement of Violet McKay (the departed O'Hara). The fact that O'Hara, Moranis, and Thomas have by now left *SCTV* and taken their "Days of the Week" characters with them actually works to *SCTV*'s advantage here, since the soap opera parody is able to incorporate another aspect of the daytime drama genre — the massive actor turnaround. To that effect, Mary Charlotte Wilcox joins the cast as Janet Halsey, a town gossip who is intent on profiting from the mental deterioration of rich socialite May Matlock (Martin).

While their characters on "The Days of the Week" would become more combative, Flaherty and Candy just kept getting more harmonious as Big Jim McBob and Billy Sol Hurok. Here their recurring sketch — the first of three segments over the last six NBC episodes — formally changes its name from "Farm Film Report" to "Farm Film Celebrity Blow-Up." Almost as funny as the appearance of Martin Short as Dustin Hoffman as his *Tootsie* persona is Candy and Flaherty's confused reaction to his feminine appearance — note Candy looking up Short's skirt as if to see to what lengths the actor committed himself to his latest part.

Short also shines with his Jerry Lewis impression, which is on display here in a preview for "Scenes from an Idiot's Marriage." While this spoof of Ingmar

Bergman (*Scenes from a Marriage*) isn't as memorable as *SCTV*'s first ("Whispers of the Wolf" from show 38), the piece is still strong. Credit Short, who is able to alternate between the "serious" Lewis (behavior befitting a Bergman film) and the "slapstick" Lewis (a pantomime set to "The Typewriter Song"— shades of *Who's Minding the Store?*) with remarkable ease.

"Whispers of the Wolf" originally appeared as a "Monster Chiller Horror Theatre" sketch; that show's host, Count Floyd, makes his fourth appearance in as many episodes here. Perhaps burned out on Dr. Tongue and Bruno shtick, here Flaherty's Floyd presents a preview of a "political thriller" called "Tip O'Neill's 3-D House of Representatives." Though predictable, the sight of John Candy as then Speaker-of-the-House O'Neill waving paper and pen is difficult to resist. So are Floyd's usual futile attempts to make the movie seem scary: "Democrat or Republican, I'd run from that guy," he states.

Another strong segment featuring Candy is a "Stars in One" promo that features his Steve Roman character. Already his third appearance, Candy wisely presents here an opportunity for viewers to learn the history of this wanna-be thespian who stars in a different *SCTV* show each week. (Wait, wasn't that Bill Needle's modus operandi?) Through the probing questions of Short's Brock Linahan, we learn that since being signed by Guy Caballero as SCTV's highest-paid performer, Roman has shrunk one-and-a-half inches and gained nearly two hundred pounds. This sketch raises the question that since Candy's Johnny LaRue was previously named as SCTV's highest-paid performer (show 93), was it Candy's intention to phase out LaRue and concentrate more on Roman?

The episode's most ambitious sketch is "A Star Is Born," a lengthy movie parody that mocks the widely panned 1976 remake that starred Barbra Streisand and Kris Kristofferson as two singers at decidedly different points in their career. Surprisingly, the sketch was excised from off-network syndication despite being one of *SCTV*'s most enjoyable movie parodies.

The sketch stars Joe Flaherty in the Kristofferson role of fading rock star John Norman Mane (the character was named John Norman Howard in the 1976 film); Flaherty's approach to the Kristofferson role is similar to his approach to the Tony Bennett role in *The Oscar* parody "The Nobel" (show 86)—he knows he doesn't have to exaggerate the performance being parodied much since the original was already so very bad. Instead the sketch mines comedy by making John Norman's songs more ridiculously putrid than they were in the original movie; the film's uninspired Paul Williams lyrics are replaced by simplistic "barnyard lyrics" that make children's music complex by comparison. The scene where Flaherty rasps these pointless lyrics to his band's redundant rock beat (similar to the sound of the John Norman Speedway band seen in the 1976 film) is a highlight.

Playing Streisand's Esther Hoffman role (redubbed Esther Blodgett here) is guest Crystal Gayle, who does an admirable job with one of the largest acting roles ever given to a musical guest on *SCTV*. Not having Andrea Martin perform her devastating Streisand impersonation seems at first odd, but ultimately makes sense; Martin's exaggerated take on the singer/actress, particularly when combined with the drunken antics of Flaherty's Kristofferson, may have proven to be an overly irritating combination (as indeed the real Streisand and Kristofferson became in the 1976 film).

Playing it mostly straight, Gayle provides a fine complement to Flaherty. And her role as an up-and-coming singer allows her the perfect opportunity to perform "Our Love Is on the Faultline," from her then-current album *True Love*. (The performance comes as Flaherty abruptly walks off a TV show and turns the stage over to Gayle; this scene closely resembles a segment in the film set at a charity concert during which Kristofferson surprisingly brings out Streisand. Both Gayle and Streisand are too coolly confident for unknown performers getting such a sudden and unexpected big break.)

Even though she doesn't play the lead, Andrea Martin does leave her mark; as Esther's singing partner Big Momma Maui, she figures prominently in the opening scene, which plays as another inside reference to show 80's "Polynesiantown." In that sketch, a customer hit Big Momma with a pineapple; here she takes a bowling ball to the head. Also, in both sketches, Big Momma exits with the identical line "Big Momma's hungry" and with the identical motivation — to eat ribs. Lastly, the song that Big Momma and Gayle perform is "Tiny Bubbles," the same song that "Polynesiantown" guest star Dr. John refused to perform.

Also memorable in the sketch is Eugene Levy as Milton Berle who, along with Mary Charlotte Wilcox as singer Deborah Harry, presents Esther Blodgett with a Grammy Award. Levy's appearance here as the legendary comedian, who annoyingly slows down the sketch's award presentation just to recite embarrassingly unfunny jokes, allows *SCTV* to exact revenge upon the real Berle for "Mr. Television"'s disrespectful behavior when he presented *SCTV* writers with an Emmy at the 1982 awards. Flaherty, who seemed most visibly annoyed with Uncle Milty when trying to accept *SCTV*'s first-ever Emmy, was probably gleeful to (albeit belatedly) tell Berle off ("Uncle Big Mouth, you've interrupted enough award shows with your cheap jokes") and then punch him out. [The original clip of Milton Berle and Martha Raye presenting *SCTV* with this Emmy is included as a bonus feature on the second volume of Shout! Factory's *SCTV* DVD box sets.]

Note that Gayle, in her Grammy acceptance speech, references "Ugazzo Records," a nod to show 93's Turk Ugazzo character, and Terry Gordica, who was in fact *SCTV*'s post audio supervisor. Note also that the sketch's final shot — Gayle standing triumphantly with her arms raised — is an image clearly intended to mock the final narcissistic shot of Streisand in the 1976 film. Arguably the finest *SCTV* sketch to be excised from off-network syndication.

Show 113 *(SCTV Network)*

1. Robin Williams for Taing commercial
2. I Want to Do My Own Commercial commercial
3. Stars in One: Oh, That Rusty!
4. SCTV Classifieds: Dwayne Millage's Dispenser Plans
5. Koffler and Meltzer promo
6. From Steve with Love promo
7. SCTV Special Presentation: Vic Arpeggio, Private Investigator
8. SCTV Classifieds: The Spam Dagger
9. The Sammy Maudlin Show: Sandler & Young and Luciano Pavarotti
10. The Days of the Week episode 8
11. SCTV Classifieds: Duard Weese
12. Building a Better House with Karl Bildenhausen
13. Philosophers at Work promo

What to watch for: Stars In One.

Back on show 15, SCTV suggested what Leave It to Beaver *might look like had it survived for 30 seasons; the memorable sketch depicted Beaver and Wally as grown-up pathetic losers. But what if the Beaver and Wally characters weren't allowed to grow up? What if the Beav was still a precocious kid, but one played by the same, though much older, actor? That's the premise behind this sketch. Hosted by Martin Short's Brock Linahan, the piece goes behind the scenes of a long-running Dennis-the-Menace–type sitcom entitled "Oh, That Rusty!"*

Besides Linahan, Short also plays the show's star, a middle-aged actor who has been playing an eight-year-old for 29 years. Seen in a writer's meeting devouring oysters, he is balding, heavy, coarse, profane, and unbearably narcissistic. Short's outrageous turn as the elder child star is one of SCTV*'s most contemptuous characterizations not portrayed by Dave Thomas; not surprisingly, Thomas has mentioned this sketch as one of his favorites. Arguably Martin Short's finest work on* SCTV.

Following a stellar episode, this show starts strong but — with a particularly weak middle third marred by a subpar "Sammy Maudlin Show" and an overlong Vic Hedges movie — quickly runs out of steam.

The tired middle of this episode is disappointing since the first half-hour is *SCTV* at its best. Besides "Oh, That Rusty!," this program includes the inspired notion of the network having a "sale" on its surplus advertising minutes (another sign of a financial crisis at SCTV), thereby allowing small businesses a rare chance to advertise on television. Eugene Levy's Phil, the proprietor of Phil's Nails who insists on doing his own commercials despite a nervous condition that causes him to flail his arms wildly, introduces the sale. Despite not having done the character for several seasons, Levy steps into Phil like he's been waving those arms for months.

Three other short pieces highlight the first third of the episode: Andrea Martin and Mary Charlotte Wilcox are strong in a funny *Cagney & Lacey* parody ("It's just like *Starsky & Hutch*, only with chicks.") Note that an identification tag on a corpse reads Val Stefoff, who was *SCTV*'s third assistant director at the time.

Better is Martin Short's devastating parody of comedian Robin Williams; here Williams is supposed to be doing a commercial for a breakfast drink, but instead goes from one unfunny tangent–a Richard Simmons impression to *The Wizard of Oz* to harassing a floor director — to another. Short doesn't look much like Williams, but he has his voice, his laugh, his mannerisms (i.e., he touches himself frequently), and the Williams shtick — the material doesn't have to be funny as long as it's done *real fast*— down cold.

Bad comedy also plays a role in another sketch featuring John Candy's Steve Roman character. Here Roman is starring in a Valentine's Day special entitled "From Steve with Love"; already a proven failure at handling drama or action, Roman decides to turn to musical variety — a form that he defensively claims "can be very difficult for a straight actor like myself" — in the hopes of earning those millions of dollars SCTV is paying him. The results are predictably awful: Not only does Roman blatantly read cue cards, he also reads funny lines over-dramatically and refuses to soil his good looks by taking a pie in the face.

Candy also figures in the final two sketches of the episode, the first of which, a home improvement show called "Building a Better House," is one of the more bizarre *SCTV* segments. Candy plays Karl Bildenhausen, a stern man with a heavy German accent, who is reminiscent of one of Candy's earlier characters, the bully Paul Fistinyourface. Bildenhausen differs mainly from Fistinyourface in how he intimidates people: Whereas Fistinyourface threatened people directly, Bildenhausen gets his way by utilizing his menacing Doberman Pincher named Prinz.

"The Days of the Week" is the brightest spot in the middle of this episode, which begins with a lengthy presentation of a "1960 black and white classic" entitled "Vic Arpeggio, Private Investigator." Vic Arpeggio, a lousy detective and even lousier saxophone player, is yet another role for Flaherty's versatile Vic Hedges character. Also featured are Eugene Levy, who plays two roles (a wealthy man who hires Arpeggio for protection as well as Arpeggio's bandleader), Andrea Martin as the wealthy man's daughter, John Candy as her boyfriend who bears an uncanny resemblance to comedian Buddy Hackett, and Martin Short as a police officer.

"Arpeggio" is another in an increasing line of sketches that work impressively stylistically but less impressively comedically. (Other examples being "Jane Eyrehead" from show 109 and show 105's "Talking Projector Adventure Serial.") Not that the script is fundamentally flawed: The characters are introduced well and the plot — Levy hires Arpeggio, the Levy and Candy characters are murdered, and Martin is captured and confesses to the crimes — unfolds nicely. But style, believable characters, and a logical plot do not make up for not being funny, which for remarkable stretches, this piece isn't. Interestingly enough, *SCTV* would try another "Arpeggio" sketch in its Cinemax season with greater success.

More disappointing is the return of "The Sammy Maudlin Show," seen here for the first time since the departure of sidekick William B. Williams (Candy). Here Candy is in the sketch, but his guest turn as Luciano Pavarotti is dull. It appears that no one bothered to write a script for the banter between Pavarotti and Maudlin, as nearly any unscripted talk show regularly features interviews more entertaining. The sketch even regurgitates the scene from *The Godfather* parody (show 93) that featured Candy's Pavarotti and Flaherty's Don Caballero fighting over a block of provolone cheese. The sketch ends badly with the cheap joke of the heavy Pavarotti falling through the stage.

One bright spot in the "Maudlin" sketch is Eugene Levy and Martin Short's obscure but successful impression of the vocal duo Sandler and Young. Singing a medley that incorporates "Three Blind Mice," "Frere Jacques," and Simon and Garfunkel's "The 59th Street Bridge Song (Feelin' Groovy)," Short and Levy perform with such an unbelievable lack of energy that it seems the sketch is being accidentally played in slow motion. The duo's tediousness extends to the interview segment, so much so that Maudlin rudely implores them to leave. In response, Levy (as Young) just smiles and says, "We get that all the time, Sam."

Show 114 *(SCTV Network)*

1. Shower in a Briefcase commercial
2. It's in the Kurds promo
3. Bobby Bittman wraparound part 1: Bittman and Ben Vereen in Vegas
4. Farm Film Celebrity Blow-Up: Bernadette Peters
5. The True Story of Billy the Kid preview
6. Bobby Bittman wraparound part 2: People and Things
7. Masterpiece Theatre: In Celebration of Alternatives promo
8. The William B. Show
9. The Days of the Week episode 10
10. Bobby Bittman wraparound part 3: Bobby's Back promo
11. Shirt Glue commercial
12. Sunrise Semester: Communicating with Extremities

What to watch for: The William B. Show.
One of SCTV*'s bravest sketches, "The William B. Show" is painfully unfunny, and that's what makes it so very funny. Though* SCTV *had previously featured pieces with characters suffering meltdowns (most notably the Lola Heatherton special on show 86), it had never before allowed a character—Earl Camembert included—to be as embarrassed and degraded as William B. Williams is here.*

To call "The William B. Show," the hosting debut of Sammy Maudlin's former sidekick (Candy), disastrous is a gross understatement. What makes this piece memorable is that SCTV *doesn't let William B. (or the viewers) off the hook easily—the debacle that is "The William B. Show" is allowed to unfold so excruciatingly slowly that the sketch becomes an endurance test, until the endlessness of the piece becomes the joke. With its dreadful jokes, guest and audience revolt, and physical and emotional damage suffered by its host, "The*

William B. Show" is the closest SCTV *ever came to the style of anti-humor perfected by the late Andy Kaufman.*

Lola Heatherton had one, Bob and Doug McKenzie had two, Johnny LaRue had *four*, and finally, with this episode, Levy's Bobby Bittman gets his first and only wraparound episode. Telling the story of his retirement and eventual comeback, the wraparound is one of *SCTV*'s most succinct, consisting of only two lengthy segments and one short promo. Besides their collective brevity, perhaps the most notable achievement of these pieces is that they craft Bittman into a sympathetic character without stooping to cheap sentimentality.

Bittman's retirement announcement arises from pride; he would rather quit the business than accept a demotion from headliner to opening act for guest star Ben Vereen. The proposed change in billing comes after Vereen's opening act — condensed here to a single performance of the Fats Waller classic "Joint Is Jumping" — completely eclipses Bittman's. But before the demotion, a yet-to-be-humbled Bittman embarrasses himself by claiming to have never met Vereen, despite several previous meetings between the two that Vereen remembers vividly. Here Levy excels at playing the shallow and egotistical Bittman familiar to *SCTV* viewers.

The instant that Bittman hears word of Vereen's promotion, however, Levy has our sympathies. Instead of throwing a tantrum (as the cowering hotel owner played by Short obviously expects), Bittman reluctantly agrees to the demotion, then, his ego obviously bruised, abruptly announces his decision to retire. Underlying the complexity of this long opening segment is a final shot of Vereen with a single tear running down his cheek — though obviously a clichéd effect used for laughs, the moment is also surprisingly touching.

Bittman's life in retirement is detailed in an interview done as part of a program unimaginatively titled "People and Things." For reasons unknown, Bittman decides to retire to a farm in Idaho, where he looks ridiculously out of place — his garish fur coat and several gaudy rings clashing with a pair of ill-fitting overalls. But Bittman not only *looks* lost, he *is* lost: His repetitive claims of being "at one with myself" and "at one with nature" are impossible to swallow. What's more convincing is his unintentionally self-deprecating remark that he is a "simple man" with a "simple mind."

But while Levy invites viewers to laugh at Bittman, he also invites sympathy by revealing quite clearly that Bittman knows he has made a mistake cutting himself off from his former life, most pointedly when the former funnyman pathetically asks the interview crew to stay over for a couple of days, a request spoken like a sad child who doesn't want his father to go away on a business trip. At the conclusion of the interview, co-host John Candy correctly reads Bittman as having second thoughts, but interviewer Mary Charlotte Wilcox, echoing the reasons that caused him to retire in the first place, claims that Bittman is too proud a man to change his mind and return to show business.

Wilcox was wrong. In the brief conclusion to this storyline, Bittman is seen in a promo for his comeback special, titled "Bobby's Back." Based on the material in the promo, Bittman didn't use the time away to improve his act, but it's heartening to see Bittman refusing to accept defeat by returning to show business, even if he hasn't grown as a performer. But however satisfying this storyline, the ending is predictable: Levy's Bittman needs an audience and *SCTV*'s audience needs Bobby Bittman. He's too good a character to lose.

What is lost after this episode is "Sunrise Semester": The long-running series of sketches that premiered in show 1 has its final installment here featuring Andrea Martin as an arrogant professional actress named Claire Warmel who gives a lecture on the importance of communicating with hands. The sketch is mildly amusing, but Warmel is too similar to Eugene Levy's spastic pitchman Phil. For this or perhaps other reasons, Claire Warmel's first appearance would also be her last.

Elsewhere, Martin debuts a stunningly accurate impression — actress Bernadette Peters — on this episode's "Farm Film Celebrity Blow-Up." While getting Peters's irritating schoolgirl voice down, Martin bravely pushes up her breasts in a fine effort to approximate the actress's generous bust line. (Big Jim and Billy Sol nod in approval of the revealing outfit.) Because of her attire and high-pitched voice, neither Candy nor Flaherty take her seriously, rudely rejecting her true claims of appearing in the films *The Jerk*, *Annie*, and *Pennies from Heaven*. This lack of respect causes Peters to cry, which becomes her catalyst for blowing up "real good."

Also real good are three solo Martin Short sketches, the most notable of these being a clever variation for his Ed Grimley character, as Short casts Grimley in the title role of "The True Story of Billy the Kid." While this piece is not of the "frantic" Grimley variety (see show 111's "The Fella Who Couldn't Wait for Christmas"), the sketch does show that Short was eager to experiment with his creation, something he couldn't or wouldn't do once Grimley became huge on *Saturday Night Live*.

Short is even better in two commercial parodies. Particularly memorable is a piece for a fictional contraption called Shower-In-A-Briefcase. Bettering even most of Dave Thomas's Harvey K-Tel sketches, Short's pitchman is unbelievably abused while displaying this new product. First he is completely caked in mud, then soaked with a violent stream of water, then forcefully hurled down the street (along with trees, street signs, and garbage cans) while using the "bonus attachment" Blow-Dryer-In-A-Briefcase. Some of *SCTV*'s finest physical humor.

Later in the episode is a commercial parody reminiscent of ones from earlier shows (show 72's "Nasex Nasal Deodorant," show 4's "Spray-On Socks") that highlighted particularly odd and useless products. Short stars as a man who is embarrassed by exposed shirttails, an affliction cured by the wonders of an item called "Shirt Glue." In a show heavy with recurring characters and long pieces, still-new cast member Short continues to prove his worth by contributing these two unique (and brief) commercial sketches to the episode.

Show 115 *(SCTV Network)*

1. Guy Caballero: Sweeps Week
2. Sweeps promo 1
3. Energy Ball wraparound part 1: Night of the Prime Time Stars rehearsal
4. SCTV News promo
5. Energy Ball wraparound part 2: Ed Grimley's disappearance
6. The Long Hard War promo 1
7. Energy Ball wraparound part 3: Arlene Francis & Gusstofferson
8. Sweeps promo 2
9. The Days of the Week episode 10
10. Energy Ball wraparound part 4: Police and Caballero
11. The Long Hard War promo 2
12. Murray's File: Sweeps Week
13. The Long Hard War promo 3
14. Energy Ball wraparound part 5: Caballero calls Pert
15. Energy Ball wraparound part 6: Night of the Prime Time Stars
16. Energy Ball wraparound part 7: Energy Ball explained
17. Energy Ball wraparound part 8: Energy Ball destroyed

What to watch for: Murray's File.
Although part of the "sweeps week" wraparound, this talk show sketch with Eugene Levy as host Murray Shulman—a send-up of Canadian talk show host Dr. Morton Shulman—stands on its own. The piece features a panel of TV programming executives disagreeing with Shulman's position that, during sweeps week, quality television programming "goes down the toilet." Levy's Shulman is a belligerent and obnoxious jerk, but he is arguing the same point that SCTV argues throughout most of this episode. Apparently when Shulman makes his case, he is supposed to be dismissed as a clueless blowhard, yet the same argument is supposed to be accepted when made in other areas of the episode.

One episode after delivering one of its briefest wraparounds, *SCTV* here delivers its lengthiest, a ponderous high-concept plot involving the schlock programming produced by SCTV for "sweeps week" and a concurrent attack by an energy ball that is supposedly the "subconscious of television" fighting back after "decades of lousy programming."

The story elements are so dominant in this episode that this is the only wraparound that needed to be broken up into *three* 30-minute shows for off-network syndication. Note that while the sketch order was changed, all of the segments seen here aired in full on the later syndicated version.

Inexplicably, this episode of *SCTV* won the 1983 Emmy for Outstanding

Writing in a Variety, Music, or Comedy Program. In winning the award, the show beat out four worthy contenders that all happened to be other episodes of *SCTV*: shows 109, 110, 111, and 117. By honoring this episode, the Academy erroneously praised *SCTV* for its ideas but not for its execution.

The episode's execution fails in two areas: Most unforgivably, *SCTV* turns the last third of the program into a laugh-free high-tech thriller, as a mysterious diminutive character named Pert (Andrea Martin) is called in by Guy Caballero to exorcise the energy ball haunting the SCTV studios. Pert is modeled on the character played by the actress Zelda Rubinstein in the movie *Poltergeist*, who is called upon to exorcise ghosts haunting the home of a middle-class family. Martin's role is not the only element lifted from that film: The energy ball's victims—including Ed Grimley (Short), Gus Gusstofferson (Levy), and an NBC executive—are not killed, but imprisoned by the ball. As in *Poltergeist*, the victims' cries for help can be heard through static-laden television transmissions.

Instead of boasting a swift and comical conclusion (akin to Zontar's defeat in show 90), this episode gets mired in a dizzying array of phony technical gibberish, from residue dust analyses to long explanations and even longer demonstrations of how the energy ball can be defeated. Most of this far-fetched activity takes place in an area called the "high-tech room," which, given Guy Caballero's penchant for cheapness, is remarkably modern, especially for a cellar-dwelling television network like SCTV. What only partially redeems these segments is the arresting visual effect work credited to Bill Goddard and Gary L. Smith, who were nominated for a 1983 Emmy for Outstanding Individual Achievement in Special Visual Effects. (The pair lost out to a segment of ABC's *The Winds of War*, ironically parodied elsewhere in this episode.)

In addition to the frustration inherent in losing minutes to gadgetry and special effects, this episode is also infuriatingly narrow-minded in its definition of "quality" television. When the energy ball—the supposed "subconscious of television"—takes human form, it morphs itself into various representations of television excellence, which then captures those it deems responsible for the supposed currently lousy state of television. *SCTV* uses three 1950s programs—*The Honeymooners*, *What's My Line?*, and *The Mickey Mouse Club*—to represent TV at its best. Considering how much groundbreaking and important television had been presented in the sixties and seventies, this glorification of fifties television only serves to make *SCTV* appear embarrassingly out of touch.

Not surprisingly, the episode works best when *SCTV* drops the energy ball to lampoon blockbuster shows of the type typically scheduled by the networks for "sweeps" periods. Best is *SCTV*'s stripped-down version of the 1982 celebrity cavalcade *Night of 100 Stars*, which here features only five stars under the title "Night of the Prime Time Stars." *Night of 100 Stars* was overdue to be ridiculed, particularly since the special beat out *SCTV* in the high profile Outstanding

Variety, Music, or Comedy Program category at the 1982 Emmys. *SCTV* gets its revenge by turning the special into a lame line-up of awful music, bad comedy, and hokey tributes (much of it seen here in rehearsal form) starring five of the dimmest TV stars of the day, including Linda Lavin (*Alice*), Gavin MacLeod (*The Love Boat*), Merlin Olsen (*Father Murphy*) and Jamie Farr (*M*A*S*H*). (Note that Linda Lavin and Gavin MacLeod were actually featured in the original *Night of 100 Stars* special.)

Each cast member does a fine job with his or her impression and each has at least one scathingly funny moment. Martin as Lavin rehearses a putrid version of "I Loves You, Porgy" from the musical *Porgy & Bess*. Candy and Short constitute what may be the worst comedy act of all time with Olsen and Farr doing a hapless version of the Abbott & Costello "Susquehanna Hat Company" routine. Candy's Olsen is a clueless actor — instead of reading lines, he punches out the irritatingly upbeat Farr.

Levy's Lorne Greene has a very good rehearsal scene in which he attempts to work his repertoire of dirty limericks into the show, but most memorable of all is Flaherty's Gavin MacLeod, who blabbers endlessly about his "luck" in show business. His talk of luck ends, though, after being captured by the energy ball while presenting a woeful tribute to TV's Bonnie Franklin (*One Day at a Time*) on the show's live broadcast. When the energy ball is defeated at the end of the episode, MacLeod is the one captive who is not saved. "I guess his luck ran out" is the explanation given.

Besides the "Night of the Prime Time Stars" material, the remainder of the sketches related to the "sweeps week" theme are quite good. Flaherty begins the episode with a Guy Caballero message concerning sweeps programming that is refreshingly honest in its promise of "programs with good-looking young women."

To prove Guy's point, his message is immediately followed by a fast and funny promo showcasing examples of *SCTV*'s "sweeps" shows including "Jumping for Dollars," a Johnny LaRue–hosted show that consists solely of braless women leaping in the air to grab dollar bills hung just out of reach. Significantly, this piece is the last *SCTV* appearance ever for John Candy's signature character, Johnny LaRue. Though he doesn't have any lines, the expression on Candy's face while his female contestants jiggle about is superior to anything in LaRue's previous appearance (the Christmas wraparound in show 111). Note that another program promoted, "Dallas Cowgirls Salute [composer Aaron] Copland," is extremely reminiscent of a previous promo, show 54's "Bittman Does Dallas."

Another piece that recalls an earlier sketch is a promo for "SCTV News" that brims with headlines about sex. This sketch tops the version from show 31, however, thanks to some raunchy video clips used to accompany such hard-hitting stories as "House of Prostitution Raided in Partytown," "Lingerie

Fashion Show," and, best of all, "Break-In Theft at Melonville Academy on Increase, Principal Retaliates with Strip Search."

Finally, to combat the ABC blockbuster miniseries *The Winds of War*, *SCTV* presents (innuendo certainly intended) "The Long Hard War," a miniseries consisting of no less than 28 parts. Fortunately, *SCTV* spares us the entire show and presents only three short promos, all of which center on the sexual exploits of the men fighting World War II.

"The Days of the Week" is the only segment that steers completely clear of the episode's "sweeps week" theme. It's not a particularly memorable installment, but the sketch does come as a welcome reprieve from the wraparound material that otherwise dominates this inexplicably celebrated episode.

Show 116 *(SCTV Network)*

1. The Women Who Donahue Forgot promo
2. Give 'Em Hell, Larry promo
3. Boil's Las Vegas Junket and Quickie Marriage Tour commercial
4. Western Redundancy Playhouse Theatre commercial
5. Catcher in the Rye Rye commercial
6. Jackie, We Hardly Knew Ye promo
7. The Sammy Maudlin Show: South Sea Sinner
8. The Driftwood Inn commercial: St. Patrick's Day
9. The Days of the Week episode 11
10. Miss Leutonia Pageant
11. SCTV Editorial Reply: Troy Soren

What to watch for: Western Redundancy Playhouse Theatre.
116 shows and countless sketches into its run, SCTV *could still come up with some terrifically original ideas, such as this understated piece consisting of three clips from three separate one-act plays. The common elements linking the plays are that all three are set in the American Old West, and all three feature dialogue in which words are needlessly embellished by synonyms. The line that the plays have "reviewer critics and audience patrons alike rising from their seat chairs in thunderous applause clapping" best sums up the joke. This piece was worth whatever effort was spent perusing the nearest thesaurus.*

With this episode, the second subpar outing in a row, cracks begin to show in *SCTV*'s armor. Not only is much of the material amateurish, some of the more tedious segments seem to have made it to air without being properly edited. As on the following year's *SCTV Channel*, pieces frequently run on far too long, giving the appearance that the cast and writers are desperate to fill the time between the opening titles and closing credits any way they can.

Much of this criticism can be directed at one sketch—a parody of an obscure 1949 film called *South Sea Sinner*—that consumes a third of this episode. Unfortunately for guest star Betty Thomas, her contribution is mostly limited to this piece; making matters worse for her is she has the sketch's dullest role, a whorish nightclub singer named Coral (played by Shelley Winters in the original). This amounts to a missed opportunity to showcase Thomas's comedic talents (honed on stage at The Second City), which at the time were overshadowed by her dramatic role as Sgt. Lucy Bates on NBC's *Hill Street Blues*.

"South Sea Sinner" is presented within the context of a "Sammy Maudlin" sketch, which provides the piece with a promising open. Notable here is that this sketch features the return of Candy's William B. Williams to the "Maudlin" show; Williams had left (show 106) to star in his own disastrous talk show (show 114). Even the normally complimentary Sammy has nothing good to say about Williams's solo outing: "You went right down the toilet with that one" is the most positive statement Maudlin can muster. Since the cancellation of his show, William B. has lost any trace of pride, tearfully nodding in agreement when Sammy says Williams's only value is in setting up the "more talented people like myself." Note that it was similar comments (made by Lorna Minnelli) that caused Williams to walk off Maudlin's show in the first place.

This exchange leads to the introduction of Betty Thomas, who is humorous playing herself as a talk show host's worst nightmare. She gets extremely angry when asked about her height — over six feet — or about her role on *Hill Street Blues*, lightening up only when speaking about her new film, "South Sea Sinner." Upon learning that the film co-stars singing duo Sandler and Young, Flaherty gives a horrified reaction as Maudlin remembers them as "those cats that were on the show a while back and kind of brought it down" (show 113). Maudlin then introduces what he thinks will be a "clip" of the movie, but unbeknownst to him or to Thomas, William B. has orchestrated with the staff to show the entire movie. This ploy stuns Maudlin ("You call that a clip?") and infuriates Thomas, who believes no one watching the show will pay for a movie they've already seen in its entirety. Thomas physically attacks Williams as the credits roll, while Sammy apologizes to the rest of the show's guests — including Paul McCartney, Vice President George Bush, and Soviet Premier Yuri Andropov — whom he has unintentionally bumped due to the length of Thomas's "clip."

This idea of sabotaging a film star's publicity tour by making the theatrical release of his or her movie irrelevant is a good one, but the execution is doomed to fail, as the "South Sea Sinner" sketch ultimately does. Because the anticipation is of a brief clip, patience is severely tested as the segment surprisingly drags on and on past any reasonable expectations. Not that it's unacceptable to play with viewers' expectations, but the experiment has to be entertaining to succeed. Otherwise the trick becomes — like "South Sea Sinner" — an excruciating endurance test.

Not much better is the first forgettable Shmenge Brothers piece: While Candy and Levy succeed in finding another unique context for the brothers, installing them as hosts for a beauty pageant doesn't work. Not that there aren't some laughs here, especially when Yosh and Stan show evidence for the first time of having strong libidos: Candy claims they are hosting because they "love to look at the women," and the brothers somehow get themselves into an awkward conversation about their favorite part of the female body. Despite these moments, this is the worst Shmenge sketch, and the only one to be eliminated from *SCTV*'s off-network syndication package.

Not all is lost here: The first third of this episode is remarkably strong, particularly a promo for a biopic on the life of Jackie Rogers, Sr., starring his son, albino performer Jackie Rogers, Jr. (Short).

Short is a marvel as both generations of Jackie Rogers, but he is best here at depicting the elder's show business comeback, coming while Rogers, Sr. was working as a boxer. Despite its regurgitation of jokes from "Battle of the PBS Stars" (show 103), this scene is worthwhile for the addition of Levy's impression of comedian Jack Carter, who helps Rogers, Sr. land his ill-fated comeback special (first seen in show 107). At the sketch's end, watch for a sly edit that allows Short to transform from the bronze Rogers, Sr. to the albino Rogers, Jr. with just a splash of water to the face.

An equally fine sketch featuring a recurring character is an advertisement for a Las Vegas trip/quickie wedding offered by Andrea Martin's Edna Boil and her new husband Stan (Candy). Much of the credit for this piece goes to Candy, who plays Stan as a deliciously foul slob. The slovenly Stan guzzles beer, belches, smokes, coughs, and even does an impression of a beer fountain while sitting at Tex's old spot at the organ. Besides Candy's grotesqueness, the sketch also gets laughs from the description of the trip: A bus ride, "ham spread and faucet-fresh water," and a side excursion to the fictional "Mustang Chicken Ranch" where "hubby will be serviced in a legal atmosphere."

Andrea Martin, along with guest star Betty Thomas, is also featured in the episode's opening sketch, a promo for the dramatic story of "The Women Who Donahue Forgot." The piece tells the story of two bowling partners who travel to Chicago to attend a *Donahue* taping, only to be falsely told by the show's producers that they will be asked a question by host Phil Donahue. What makes the sketch work (besides finding out that the women go on the trip because they had money left over from a "slave sale") is how the piece expertly builds tension to make the passing over by Donahue seem almost tragic. "You think that's something that happens to other people," Thomas wretchedly opines.

Show 117 *(SCTV Network)*

1. Edith Prickley: Live from the Melonville Baths promo
2. Whatever Happened to Baby Ed? commercial
3. Farm Film Celebrity Blow-Up: Neil Sedaka
4. The Fishin' Musician: Joe Walsh

5. 3-D Firing Line: Midnight Cowboy II
6. The Days of the Week episode 12
7. Mel's Rock Pile: Tribute to Punk Music
8. Snake Channel commercial
9. Stars In One: On Location promo

What to watch for: 3-D Firing Line.
For their final appearance together as Dr. Tongue and Bruno, John Candy and Eugene Levy deliver the characters' strongest sketch since "3-D House of Stewardesses" (show 84). The pair is imaginatively cast as Joe Buck (Tongue) and Enrico "Ratso" Rizzo (Bruno) in an ill-conceived 3-D remake of the 1969 film Midnight Cowboy. *Another fit of inspiration sees the scenes from the film contained not within yet another "Monster Chiller Horror Theatre" sketch, but rather a unique format called "3-D Firing Line" that allows for a panel discussion between Tongue, Bruno, host Count Floyd (Flaherty), film critic Pauline Kael (Wilcox), and a new character, the Pittsburgh Midget (Paul Flaherty).*

But the focus of the sketch are the clips from the remake; by choosing to parody only select scenes from Midnight Cowboy, *Candy and Levy are able to focus their spoof on the strengths of the John Schlesinger original— namely, the interplay between would-be Texan stud Buck and would-be manager Rizzo. Candy gets the most laughs by stealing shtick from his own Steve Roman character; Tongue's Joe Buck adopts a remarkably unauthentic Texas dialect, highlighted by his endless use of the phrase "y'all."*

Levy has his moments as well, particularly when mercilessly mocking Tongue's unbelievable accent. Note also how Levy combines Bruno's hunchbacked sway with "Ratso" Rizzo's limp to give his character a truly unique walk. Giving added authenticity to the parody is the fact that much of the clip footage is performed to the sounds of Harry Nilsson's "Everybody's Talkin'"— the song that did for Midnight Cowboy *what Simon and Garfunkel's "Mrs. Robinson" did for Hoffman's first film,* The Graduate. *"Midnight Cowboy II" marks a fine end to the long string of Dr. Tongue and Bruno sketches.*

Just when it seemed *SCTV*'s best days were behind it, the show responds with one of its finest episodes, a remarkable collection of stand-alone pieces. This 39th episode for NBC would be *SCTV*'s last for the peacock network.

As if the cast knew that this show was to be its last for NBC, every sketch involves some of *SCTV*'s most durable recurring characters. But by constructing pieces around underused characters (Rockin' Mel Slirrup), characters that hadn't been seen recently (Gil Fisher), and well-worn characters placed in original situations ("Midnight Cowboy II"), the sketches manage to come off as fresh.

The biggest surprise in this episode is the resurrection of "Mel's Rock Pile," the dance show parody that hadn't been seen since show 85. The most memorable element in this installment is the appearance of the entire cast as the fictional English punk band The Queen Haters, who perform a rip-off of the Sex Pistols song "God Save the Queen" entitled "I Hate the Bloody Queen."

"Mel's" punk tribute also includes a slam dance contest won quite handedly by a college football player, who delights in chasing down dancers of smaller stature (i.e., everyone else) and tossing them through the air. The winner is not too happy with his prize, however, which he is told will be an autographed picture of guest Stephen Sealy (Candy), the perpetually dehydrated co-host of "Pre-Teen World." Having Candy revive his Sealy character for a part in this sketch is a masterstroke, particularly since the other "Pre-Teen" characters aren't worth another look.

Also returning after a long absence (12 shows) is "The Fishin' Musician" and its host, Gil Fisher (Candy). Fisher's return is unexpected, since it seemed the character was exhausted after *SCTV* went through a run of six episodes (shows 99–104) during which Fisher appeared three times. That stretch was excessive, but the return of "The Fishin' Musician" for the final NBC show turns out to be a welcome one. Despite an awkwardly slow start during which Fisher discusses his book of poems ("Prose & Arrows"), the sketch picks up with the entrance of musical guest Joe Walsh and his band, which includes Joe Vitale, Waddy Wachtel, and George "Chocolate" Perry (a line-up that explains the "Joe Joe and the Chocolate Waddy" T-shirt that Walsh gives Candy). Although the piece — involving Walsh and his band sending Fisher on a fictional "snipe hunt" — is darkly funny, Walsh himself is so uncomfortable doing comedy that he reads his first few lines while staring at the floor. Those lines, which include Walsh's claims that he "hasn't really seen" *SCTV*, but has heard it's "supposed to be real funny," are lifted out of the "Fishin' Musician" segment with Carl Perkins (show 101). Most show business agents likely echoed this unawareness of *SCTV* when the program called to book their clients as guests.

Also notable in this final NBC episode is a commercial for "What Ever Happened to Baby Ed?," a parody of the 1962 Bette Davis/Joan Crawford vehicle *What Ever Happened to Baby Jane?* The "Ed" in the title is none other than Martin Short's Ed Grimley, who assumes the wheelchair-bound role of Blanche played by Crawford in the original. In Dave Thomas's book, Martin Short is quoted as saying that "What Ever Happened to Baby Ed?" is his "favorite Ed Grimley piece." This opinion probably comes out of affection for Candy, whose portrayal of Skip, Ed's maniacal brother, steals the scene.

While not quite as outwardly grotesque as Skip Grimley, the equally evil Dr. William Wainwright, also played by Candy, finally gets his comeuppance in the satisfying conclusion to "The Days of the Week" serial. Like the first season wedding finale, this climax brings most of the characters together, this time for the trial of Rocco (Flaherty) and Wainwright on charges of conspiring to murder Violet McKay. Notably missing is Andrea Martin's May Matlock; Matlock's is the only storyline that the show fails to bring to a close, an oversight that serves to render her earlier scenes rather pointless. Though lacking Matlock, the piece does feature cameos by Carol Burnett and former cast member Catherine O'Hara.

The exchanges between the characters played by Flaherty and Candy provided much of the highlights in "The Days of the Week," but an even more fruitful partnership between the two was their sketches as Big Jim McBob (Flaherty) and Billy Sol Hurok (Candy). Their last performance as the farmers/pop culture critics — here with singer/songwriter Neil Sedaka (Levy) — registers as one of their best pieces. Much of the credit has to go to Levy, who creates one of his sharpest impressions with a Sedaka that is at once uncannily accurate and laughably over-the-top. Candy and Flaherty are merciless as they mock Sedaka's high voice (Flaherty says he sounds "like a girl"), which proceeds to get higher as Sedaka gets angrier (Candy: "I bet when you get real mad, the only one that can hear you is your German Shepherd"). Although he threatens to leave, he eventually utilizes his high voice as the catalyst for blowing up during a special rendition of "Breaking Up Is Hard to Do" renamed "*Blowing* Up Is Hard to Do."

While Big Jim and Billy Sol appeared often on *SCTV*, they couldn't match the frequency of Andrea Martin's appearances as SCTV Station Manager Edith Prickley. But there was still life in the well-worn character, as here Martin delivers what may be her finest Prickley sketch, a promo for "Edith Prickley: Live from the Melonville Baths." This piece, modeled after Bette Midler's famous 1970s run at New York's Continental Baths, features Prickley doing a high-energy variety show in front of dozens of towel-clad gay men. Martin has never been funnier as Prickley, but what makes her performance more remarkable is the fact that she was seven months pregnant at the time of this shoot.

The final *SCTV Network* (the show would be re-christened *SCTV Channel* for its next and final season) sketch has an appropriately nostalgic tone, as Martin Short's Brock Linahan takes his "Stars In One" program on location to his hometown. Fittingly enough for his final sketch on his final show as a regular, John Candy snares the sketch's biggest laughs: He plays Linahan's high school physical education teacher, who bluntly reveals that Linahan's incompetence at basketball led Linahan's late father to wonder out loud, "Where did I go wrong? What did I do to deserve this?" Linahan also unwisely seeks out his first sexual partner (Andrea Martin), who, in stark contrast to Linahan's detailed account, has absolutely no recollection of him.

The final shot of the final NBC episode shows Short's Linahan behind the wheel of his car; unlike Linahan's trip to the past, *SCTV* was headed to the future this time with another different incarnation. Like Linahan's trip, the voyage would be rough.

PART THREE

The Forty-Five Minute Shows (1983–1984)

After NBC cancelled *SCTV*, Executive Producer Andrew Alexander signed an agreement with the burgeoning premium cable channel Cinemax to air what would turn out to be *SCTV*'s last season. Becoming Cinemax's first-ever original programming seemed to come as a surprise to the cast, as Martin Short later claimed that they thought they were going to air on HBO, the much larger corporate sister to Cinemax. Signing with Cinemax kept the show — now called *SCTV Channel* — alive, but only for a select few: In 1983, there were 83.3 million TV households in the United States, and only two million of them subscribed to Cinemax.

What those two million subscribers received was a weakened *SCTV*. For starters, John Candy's departure left only a cast of four regulars: Joe Flaherty, Eugene Levy, Andrea Martin, and Martin Short. Candy's exit proved more damaging than the previous departures of Rick Moranis, Catherine O'Hara, and Dave Thomas combined: Whereas the previous defections were of cast members whose boredom with the show was sometimes evident in the material they wrote and performed, Candy was still consistently making superior contributions when he left. The difference is clear by studying the season's guest appearances by former cast members: While John Candy's guest spot (show 118) was a highlight of the season, the returns of Thomas and O'Hara were bland and — particularly in the case of Thomas, who was barely seen performing with his former cast mates — awkward. (Rick Moranis did not return.)

Though assisted by guest appearances, the four full-time cast members were spread too thin and they in turn spread their ideas too thin — sketches were frequently, sometimes exasperatingly, overlong. While the 35-minute Christmas movie (show 120) was an interesting experiment, there were other lengthy pieces—"The Date Debate" (show 121), "Oliver Grimley" (show 129), and "2009" (show 130)—that dragged on long past their welcome. Worse were clip pieces thinly disguised as "new" promos that were often used to kill time.

However, the year was not without its successes: Show 118's "Happy Wanderers" sketch marked the best appearance from Yosh and Stan Shmenge, while the retirement of Earl Camembert in show 134 was a pitch-perfect send-off to one of *SCTV*'s finest and longest-running characters. Relative newcomer Martin Short in particular contributed some memorable pieces (the best of which is show 119's *Gimme Shelter* parody "Gimme Jackie"), while supporting players Mary Charlotte Wilcox and especially John Hemphill also breathed new life into the program. And the relative absence of wraparound material (shows 124 and 135 being the exceptions) was a welcome change of pace from the NBC shows that were occasionally plot-heavy.

Ultimately, writer Paul Flaherty was correct when he said of *SCTV Channel*: "It was a very erratic season." Ultimately, the strain of keeping the program going became too great, and after these 18 episodes and 135 overall, *SCTV* was no more.

Show 118 *(SCTV Channel)*

1. Guy Caballero: SCTV Channel
2. Maudlin O' The Night promo 1
3. The Soren-Weiss Report promo 1
4. Prickley Business preview
5. The Soren-Weiss Report promo 2
6. JFK My Way promo
7. The Soren-Weiss Report
8. Maudlin O' The Night promo 2
9. The Happy Wanderers: New Wave Salute part 1
10. Calvin Kline Jeans commercial
11. The Happy Wanderers: New Wave Salute part 2
12. Maudlin O' The Night promo 3
13. Melonville Calendar: School Fire
14. Maudlin O' The Night part 1
15. Moms Dearest commercial
16. Maudlin O' The Night part 2

What to watch for: The Happy Wanderers.
For this first Cinemax show, SCTV *relies heavily on recurring characters, and none of them are represented better than polka stars Yosh (now* guest star *John Candy) and Stan Shmenge (Levy). Their salute to new wave music (an overt plug for their record "New Wave Shmenge") is the funniest Shmenge sketch of all, as Yosh and Stan are painfully oblivious at how to appeal to the youthful "new wave" market.*

The highlight of the piece—and one of the highlights of the season—is the video ("That helps the sales," Yosh explains to their antediluvian studio audience) for something called the "Power to the Punk People Polka." A mix of cheesecake, alienated children playing with cabbages, and punk kids joining a Shmenge-led polka revolution, the segment was deservedly named by Time Magazine *as one of the year's best music videos.*

"Beaming its two cents worth across the nation," *SCTV* reinvents itself (again) as a cable service dubbed *SCTV Channel* with this premiere Cinemax episode. Aside from the lack of (real) commercials, the absence of musical guests, and the shortening of the program from 90 to 45 minutes, little about this new season of *SCTV* appears at first to be any different from the last. That continuity is thanks in large part to the guest appearance of John Candy, who unfortunately would return for only this one episode.

Appropriately enough, Joe Flaherty's Guy Caballero kicks off the new season by welcoming viewers to the new SCTV Channel. While claiming that "you can see it all" on SCTV, Caballero reviews other channels that are now supposedly obsolete thanks to the comprehensiveness of SCTV Channel. Despite a putdown of *SCTV*'s former network NBC — "That's the fluff network," Guy claims — the piece is pretty tame.

Where there's Guy Caballero, there's usually Edith Prickley; here Prickley appears in a *Risky Business* parody called "Prickley Business." Andrea Martin does double duty in the sketch as Prickley and her sister Edna Boil, who gets the sketch's only laughs. Otherwise this piece about a boy (Short) "tormented by his own churning adolescent juices" is actual torment. Much better is Andrea's spoof of a then-current Calvin Klein ad campaign in which she erotically relays a tale of getting a fish bone stuck in her throat.

Martin also manages to come across as both silly and sensual playing Jennifer Beals, the star of *Flashdance* and the first guest on "Maudlin O' the Night." A vicious parody of Alan Thicke's woeful talk show *Thicke of the Night*, this final appearance of Flaherty's Sammy Maudlin finds the sketch that began as a parody of *Sammy & Company* now parodying an entirely different talk show. The sketch is a fine if disjointed finale for one of the most celebrated characters in the *SCTV* canon.

The highlight of "Maudlin O' the Night" is the introduction of "Maudlin's Zanies," a cruel spoof of a similar group of comedians who regularly appeared on Thicke's program. Maudlin's group is embarrassingly awful, in particular a scathing interpretation of Howie Mandel (Short) who does some truly bad improvisation before being deservedly beaten by guest Henry Kissinger (Eugene Levy). Martin's Jennifer Beals makes a lasting impression by endlessly removing various pieces of underwear in a parody of a famous scene from *Flashdance*. In her interview promoting a remake of *Cat on a Hot Tin Roof*, Beals reveals that she used a stand-in for all the "tough" acting scenes, just as she used a double for the most demanding dancing scenes in *Flashdance*.

Finally, this premiere episode features the first pairing of effeminate newsmen Troy Soren (Martin Short) and new character Joel Weiss (Eugene Levy).

"The Soren-Weiss Report" is a current events precursor to *In Living Color*'s "Men on Film," in which Soren and Weiss superficially bitch about people and places making headlines. The joke gets old quickly and even this brief sketch drags. Short should have left this annoying character behind at NBC, but instead the addition of Levy as Weiss will result in more screen time for Soren as the Cinemax year continues.

Show 119 *(SCTV Channel)*

1. An Officer and a Gentile preview
2. Mel McElroy: Rooaway commercial
3. We Got A Maid promo 1
4. Hollywood Dirt Tonight part 1
5. Mel McElroy: Self Made Mel commercial
6. Hollywood Dirt Tonight part 2
7. We Got A Maid promo 2
8. Mel McElroy: Think Aussie commercial
9. SCTV News promo
10. We Got A Maid promo 3
11. Mel McElroy: Mel McElroy Film Festival promo
12. All Weather Talk Show promo
13. Gimme Jackie

What to watch for: Gimme Jackie.
Joe Flaherty once claimed that during this final season "no one took the show seriously except Marty." That statement begins to ring true with this episode, arguably the season's strongest, as Short's contributions start to transcend those of the other cast members. In "Gimme Jackie," a parody of The Rolling Stones documentary Gimme Shelter, Short provides some of the season's hardest laughs, often by resorting to lowbrow physical gags of the type rarely seen on SCTV *Channel*.

But there is subtlety here as well: The reactions of Jackie Rogers, Jr. while watching footage of a disastrous free concert closely mirror Mick Jagger quietly reliving the nightmare of Altamont in Gimme Shelter. But outrageousness prevails, particularly when a sweat-soaked Rogers, Jr. is forced to admit on a program called "Lie Detector" (hosted by Eugene Levy's F. Lee Bailey) that he staged a free concert just to "ball some ladies."

This episode of *SCTV Channel* is most notable for the return of founding cast member Dave Thomas, who had been absent from *SCTV* for over a year. Unfortunately, Thomas's return was reportedly uncomfortable ("I failed to connect with any of my old cronies," is how he described the situation), and his on-air material suggests that he felt isolated from his former colleagues: Only in "Gimme Jackie" does Thomas appear alongside any regular cast members.

To Thomas's credit, he doesn't settle for resting on past successes, instead choosing to introduce a new character named Mel McElroy, a self-described "star of Australian stage and screen." Unfortunately, he presents this same character in no less than five sketches, with each appearance becoming progressively more irritating.

The current cast members produce better material then Thomas. Particularly strong is a retooling of the "National Midnight Star" sketches (shows 84 and 109) as a more direct *Entertainment Tonight* spoof called "Hollywood Dirt Tonight." Hosted by seedy *National Midnight Star* chairman Dr. Rawl Withers (Levy) and a trashy new character of Andrea Martin's named Remy Martin, "HDT" is brazenly vicious. Particularly biting is an interview with Buddy Hackett's chauffeur (Short) who is suing Hackett, his so-called lover, for palimony. The interview plays on the 1982 suit filed against Liberace by his chauffeur Scott Thorson; note that Short's character says he now drives for Liberace since being fired by Hackett.

A sketch with less success is an unnecessary promo for the SCTV News team of Floyd Robertson (Flaherty) and Earl Camembert (Levy). This promo, depicting Robertson as a serious journalist full of contempt for the bumbling Camembert, offers nothing unique to longtime *SCTV* fans and is of little value to newer viewers since Floyd and Earl will only appear together once more.

A parody of the then-current NBC program *We Got It Made* is better. A critically reviled and short-lived rip-off of *Three's Company*, *Made* is reworked here as a Pirini Scleroso (Martin) vehicle called "We Got a Maid." One of the character's better sketches and a satisfying dig at *SCTV*'s former network.

Show 120 *(SCTV Channel)*

1. The Driftwood Inn commercial: Christmas
2. SCTV Special Presentation: It's A Wonderful Film
3. The Driftwood Inn commercial: New Year's

What to watch for: The Driftwood Inn commercials.
Done in the same monotonous style as previous Driftwood Inn advertisements (shows 111 and 116), these two commercials reveal what happens when the owners of the blandest motel in the universe go on a holiday cruise. First interim manager "Eddie" promotes his "battle of punk bands" as an attempt to bring "young swingers" to the motel; later the owners (upon returning from vacation) encourage viewers to visit "Eddie" at Melonville General Hospital. Seems "Eddie" suffered some injuries in the "fire, riot, and explosion" that broke out during the punk party and not only destroyed the Driftwood but also brought to an end this brief run of memorable commercials.

Christmas episodes were not *SCTV*'s forte. In the first (show 94), a dull movie sketch and a lazily structured (though fitfully funny) wraparound all but eclipsed one of Catherine O'Hara's best sketches ("The Dusty Towne Sexy Holiday Special"). And despite a fine Happy Wanderers segment and perhaps the definitive Ed Grimley piece, show 111 was even worse, as *SCTV* unwisely tried to turn two of its sleaziest characters, Johnny LaRue and Guy Caballero, into lovable softies.

This holiday episode, consisting almost entirely of the longest uninterrupted sketch in *SCTV*'s history, relies even more on sentimentality than the previous Christmas shows. Schmaltz combined with a sketch of unprecedented length seems like a bad mix, but somehow this show works, if only marginally so. Whereas the episode doesn't contain anything to match the highlights of previous Christmas shows, it also doesn't contain anything to match the lows of those shows: Recurring characters are absent in the 35-minute "It's a Wonderful Film," therefore the script's eventual decline into sappiness is less offensive than if favorite characters were being compromised for the sake of holiday-themed pablum (show 111).

"It's a Wonderful Film" relies on the structure of *It's a Wonderful Life* (with nods to *A Christmas Carol* and the Bing Crosby film *Going My Way*) to tell the story of movie producer Marty Simmons (Eugene Levy). Simmons has traveled to a fictional town in Vermont to fire elderly director Frank Bailey (actor Charles Palmer) because "Miracle at Holiday Lodge," an "old-fashioned" Christmas movie Bailey is helming, is unmarketable to teenagers. Simmons feels the film should be remade as a teenage sex romp entitled "All-Girls Private School Christmas Break" under the direction of a persistently coked-out Martin Short.

"It's a Wonderful Film" is at its worst when it allows Levy's character to humorlessly pontificate on the dumbed-down nature of the movie business. The piece makes its point much more succinctly during scenes of the sex comedy that is replacing Bailey's holiday movie. For example, the cast of the new film consists of: A group of attractive young women inexplicably dressed only in towels, a grandmother who exists solely for "hip" drug humor ("you know how Grandma likes to fry her brain at Christmas"), and someone referred to as simply "Booger Eater."

Note that the name of Levy's character — Marty Simmons — is virtually identical to Matty Simmons, the real-life producer of *National Lampoon's Animal House*, the godfather of modern teen sex comedies (co-written by *SCTV* alum Harold Ramis). It's also not a little ironic to see Levy criticize teen sex comedies now that many people know him mainly as "Jim's Dad" from the very successful and very raunchy *American Pie* films.

The funniest role in "It's a Wonderful Film" is Martin Short's young director, who snorts so much coke that it violently gushes out of his nose when he laughs. Not faring as well as Short is guest Catherine O'Hara, who is saddled with two humorless roles, or actor Charles Palmer, who is so wooden as Frank Bailey that he appears to be reading cue cards with lines that he's never seen before.

There are other problems with the sketch: The gimmick of the talking stars on the Hollywood Walk of Fame is a lame variation on *Wonderful Life*'s conversing angels. A scene with Levy, O'Hara, and Short driving to Vermont is unintentionally amusing as Levy raves about the scenery that is obviously a cheap special effect. And the final scene, during which luminaries (including the governor of New York and the Pope) suddenly appear on the "Miracle at Holiday Lodge" set, is an embarrassing example of *SCTV* trying to satirize cheap sentimentality while simultaneously wallowing in it.

Yet somehow "It's a Wonderful Film" is a minor success. The script is ambitious but tight, with even the most fantastical elements logically presented and resolved. Not surprisingly, the performances — except for Palmer — are excellent, and it is a pleasure to see O'Hara, even if she's not given very good material. And if nothing else, what other Christmas movie features both Jackie Rogers, Jr. *and* The Queen Haters on its soundtrack?

Show 121 *(SCTV Channel)*

1. Rich and Jealous preview
2. The Date Debate part 1
3. Calvin Kline Jeans commercial
4. Michael Caine in The Mousetrap commercial
5. The Date Debate part 2
6. The Lottery promo
7. Skidder Ridder commercial
8. Scary Previews

What to watch for: *Rich and Jealous*.
For the third time in four shows, SCTV Channel *features a movie parody with Andrea Martin at the top of the episode. "Rich and Jealous," a send-up of the 1981 Candice Bergen / Jacqueline Bisset vehicle* Rich and Famous, *is the best of the three. But instead of former college roommates Bergen and Bisset,* SCTV *presents the inspired duo of Barbra Streisand (Martin) and — apparently cast because director Streisand wanted to be the clearcut beauty of the two — Ruth Gordon (guest Valri Bromfield). (Although they never worked together, the two actresses do have something in common: They both won Oscars in 1969.) Unfortunately, this sketch is the only piece in which Bromfield and Martin showcase their noticeable chemistry.*

One of the excuses given for the relative weakness of the *SCTV Channel* season is that the show, as Joe Flaherty said, "didn't have the cast." This episode contradicts that argument as no fewer than seven players — the regular cast plus guest stars Dave Thomas, Catherine O'Hara, and Valri Bromfield — collaborate on one of the worst shows of the season.

The worst sketch in the episode is an amateurish game show piece called "The Date Debate." The piece meanders on for no less than fifteen minutes, a remarkable length for a sketch in which almost nothing happens. The nadir is reached when the host (Short) and a contestant (O'Hara) embark on an excruciatingly long walk in order to spin the "Wheel of Romance," a prop that is inexplicably located in another studio. A variation of this joke worked on *Monty Python's Flying Circus*, but here — inserted near the end of a sketch that has already *long* overstayed its welcome — the gag is odious.

Dave Thomas returns for the second time in four shows, but like his appearance in show 119, the results are mixed. It's not just that the material is hit-and-miss; the fact that he again doesn't appear with any other cast members is awkward. Thomas is at his best as Michael Caine arguing against complaints that his 1982 film *Deathtrap* is too similar to his 1972 picture *Sleuth*.

Worse are two bits Thomas performs alongside guest Valri Bromfield. In his book, Thomas claims he fought for Bromfield — who was hired to write for Andrea Martin — to act in the sketches because "they're not things that Andrea can do." Why Thomas felt that way is unclear; there is nothing in Bromfield's performances that the more versatile Martin couldn't have at least equaled and likely improved upon.

One of the Thomas and Bromfield sketches — an update on the horror film *Cujo* with Bromfield as a crazed wife stalking beleaguered husband Thomas — is included as part of "Scary Previews," arguably the weakest Count Floyd sketch ever. Coming so soon after show 117's classic *Midnight Cowboy* parody, this sketch underscores how badly John Candy was missed during the Cinemax season. Not only do film critics Count Floyd (Flaherty) and Bruno (Levy) make a poor attempt at recreating the hostile bickering perfected by Bruno and Candy's Dr. Tongue, but one of the movies reviewed is a direct comment on the hole left by Candy's exodus: Called "The Mysterious Disappearance of Dr. Tongue," the movie consists of nothing more than Bruno searching for his missing partner. Unfortunately for viewers, Levy's hunt for Candy proves unsuccessful.

The only worthwhile segment in the lengthy "Scary Previews" is a clip from a *Dr. Jekyll and Mr. Hyde* update starring Scott Baio (Short). The selling point for this version of the famous story is that Baio completes a wildly unbelievable transformation from Jekyll to Hyde *sans makeup*, which basically means that Short simply and hilariously grunts, puffs out his cheeks, and pulls on his shirt. It's a shame that the rest of "Scary Previews" wasn't discarded, leaving only this Short gem behind. Instead the sketch, like most of this episode, is left to meander aimlessly.

Show 122 *(SCTV Channel)*

1. Irving Cohen: Dustfree commercial
2. Stars In One promo: Senor Wences's hand puppet
3. You're On with Max Lansky part 1
4. Foreign Film Festival: Das Boobs part 1
5. Irving Cohen: Bojax commercial
6. Foreign Film Festival: Das Boobs part 2
7. Edna Boil's Prairie Warehouse and Curio Emporium commercial: Boil World
8. You're On with Max Lansky part 2
9. Irving Cohen: Tardy Cannon commercial
10. You're On with Max Lansky part 3

What to watch for: Das Boobs.
Although it comes a little too soon after the sex comedy jokes in show 120's "It's a Wonderful Film," "Das Boobs" is another fine example of SCTV's *unparalleled multi-layered style of parody. The piece is an unlikely mix of two notable films from 1981: The sex farce* Porky's *and the critically acclaimed German submarine WWII drama* Das Boot. *Note that the script is credited to Bob Clark (who wrote and directed* Porky's*), Wolfgang Peterson [sic] (who directed and co-wrote* Das Boot*), and, in a nod to his role in creating the grandfather of all modern teen sex comedies (*Animal House*), former cast member Harold "Von" Ramis.*

"Das Boobs" expertly recreates the look and feel of the claustrophobic Das Boot. *In the lead role, Flaherty is convincing as Jürgen Prochnow, maintaining that actor's unwavering intensity even after becoming immersed in the sketch's* Porky's*-inspired plot of getting a young virgin seaman named Peewee laid. (Addressing his crew, Flaherty morosely intones: "There are a few things I'd like to talk to you about. First and most ominous, the mission. Then, something even more critical ... plans for Peewee's birthday party.")*

"Das Boobs" represents the first SCTV *Channel piece to take advantage of the show's newfound freedom from NBC's standards and practices division. While the piece is nowhere as profane as* Porky's*, it does feature references to getting "laid," and, in a scene reminiscent of the infamous* Porky's *shower segment, Levy instructs one of the women to "nibble on this knockwurst." But some of the piece would have been right at home on NBC: The poor English dubbing recalls "Pepi Longsocks" (show 92) and "Rome, Italian Style" (show 104), while the bad special effects shots recall the "Zontar" wraparound (show 90).*

This strong episode — the first of the season to not feature an appearance by a former cast member — provides further proof that the incredibly shrinking cast was not the sole reason *SCTV Channel* didn't live up to past *SCTV* incarnations.

"Das Boobs" and the phone-in show "You're On" — featuring Levy as affluent Melonville councilman Max Lansky — anchor the program. Whereas "Das Boobs" is technically and comedically ambitious, "You're On" is strikingly simple, consisting of only Levy, a telephone, and a very bad hairpiece. But "You're On" works almost as well as "Das Boobs," thanks largely to the impeccable comedic timing of Levy.

The format of "You're On" recalls some of Dave Thomas's solo pieces as "critic-at-large" Bill Needle (most directly show 101's call-in program "Stand Up and Be Counted"), and in many ways Lansky is similar to Needle: Both are contemptuous snobs who seriously overestimate their level of power and influence. Both also have horrible tempers, but whereas Needle never made an attempt to hide his anger, Lansky wants us to believe that he's "not a man that gets upset." Levy lets Lansky's true colors show, though, when callers begin to taunt his hairpiece; soon a seething Lansky is referring to his audience as "snake scum," "snake dirt," and "scummy, snake vermin, pus-ridden," suggesting that one caller "should be put in prison and he should be tortured."

Taking a cue from Dave Thomas's series of Mel McElroy commercials in show 119, Martin Short features his songwriter character Irving Cohen in a trilogy of spots. Unlike Thomas, Short wisely ensures that each spot is funnier than the last: The final ad has Cohen shilling for a fictional product called the "Tardy Cannon" while being literally shot out of a cannon.

While Cohen is almost inherently funny, Short's talk show host Brock Linahan is only as good as his guests. Fortunately, Linahan has a memorable interview here with ventriloquist Senor Wences's dismembered hand. The highlight of the piece comes as both Linahan and the hand sob over his "breakup" with Wences, which tragically came while the hand was already having marital problems. Another example of Short's unapologetic silliness that was often so refreshing on *SCTV Channel*.

Show 123 *(SCTV Channel)*

1. Half Wits: The semi-finals
2. The New Pet preview
3. Commercials are Coming to Pay TV commercial
4. Happy Hour (Six Gun Justice episode 6: Going to Town)
5. Humanity: The Final Days / Bobby Bittman: My Wacky World promo
6. Stars In One: Bob Hope part 1
7. Johnny Adee: The Untold Story promo
8. Stars In One: Bob Hope part 2

What to watch for: Half Wits.
While not as memorable as the original (show 112), this piece is a worthy sequel to one of SCTV's *finest game show sketches. Though it brings back the same host (Levy's Alex Trebel) and the same intellectually challenged contestants — with John Hemphill substituting for John Candy — the format is markedly different. Here the four contestants are paired off in teams to play a variation of the game* Password, *in which one contestant gives clues to a secret word while his or her partner attempts to guess the word.*

As in the original, Flaherty gets the most laughs, playing so poorly that his incompetence defies description. And even with the straightest role, Levy is still very funny as Trebel, who once again slowly but surely loses his patience with his panel of slow contestants. The cast must have been pleased with this return of "Half Wits," as they would bring it back again later in the season (show 131).

After the highs and lows of the previous two episodes, this show is more typical *SCTV Channel* fare, with the majority of sketches being fairly average.

Most notable about this episode is the first installment of "Six Gun Justice," a parody of 1940s Western serials that is reminiscent of the soap opera parody "The Days of the Week." Superficially, the two have nothing in common, but both are genre parodies that feature ongoing stories told over a number of installments. Both franchises also suffer from emphasizing the accuracy of the parody at the expense of actual laughs. Unfortunately, "Six Gun Justice" has even fewer overall laughs than "The Days of the Week."

Fortunately, *SCTV* frames the "Six Gun Justice" pieces inside a children's show titled "Happy Hour," hosted by Happy Marsden (John Hemphill). Children's shows inappropriate for children are nothing new on *SCTV*, but here the show takes the concept to a new level by setting "Happy Hour" in — what else — a bar. Hemphill, whose pockmarked face makes him a questionable choice to host a children's show anyway, gets his first strong recurring character with Marsden. Happy is clearly an alcoholic, but instead of painting the character as an obnoxious and profane loudmouth, Hemphill brings a surprising subtlety to the role. Note, for example, how he fidgets while awaiting his refills from bartender (and *SCTV* writer) Mike Short or how he has an increasingly tougher time speaking clearly or simply staying awake the longer the show continues.

The other significant piece on this episode is undoubtedly the "Stars In One" interview with Bob Hope. Not only does this sketch signal the last *SCTV* appearance of Dave Thomas's signature impression, but it is also the final *SCTV* appearance of Thomas himself. The sketch makes clear Thomas's reverence for Hope, as neither before nor after has there been such a lengthy and straightforward interview with any of the cast members' celebrity impressions.

Thankfully, Thomas's reverence for Hope doesn't preclude him from being funny as Hope, and the interview is entertaining. One of the pleasures of the sketch is simply seeing Thomas interact with another cast member — here Martin Short (as Brock Linahan) — since nearly all of his other Cinemax contributions were either solo or with Valri Bromfield.

Thomas plays Hope as a proud man with no regrets, not even backing down when discussing his support of the Vietnam War. If there is an aspect of Hope that Thomas is contemptuous of, it is his lack of relevance in contemporary entertainment: He claims to not understand Mel Brooks and is disdainful of young comedians in general, who he dismisses as "National Lampoon kids." Hope's idea of a good movie is a remake of *The Greatest Story Ever Told*, which he claims to be currently directing. Thomas discusses Hope's wholly unmarketable plans for the film, including its cast: Phyllis Diller, Jack Klugman, and *Buck Rogers*'s Gil Gerard (as Jesus!). The sketch ends on a high note as well, with Thomas's Hope inexplicably insisting that the interview — which he thought was for Canadian TV — is "not to be shown in the States under any circumstances!" The Hope interview is without question Thomas's strongest contribution to *SCTV Channel*.

Show 124 *(SCTV Channel)*

1. Happy Hour promo
2. Spy wraparound part 1: The Great Escape
3. Lewis Sings Dylan commercial

4. Spy wraparound part 2: Fred Winston introduced
5. Al Peck's Hardware Store commercial
6. Spy wraparound part 3: Cafeteria
7. The Fred Winston Show promo
8. Spy wraparound part 4: The spy revealed
9. Spy wraparound part 5: Epilogue

What to watch for: The Fred Winston Show promo.
As part of this episode's wraparound, this piece demonstrates what might happen if an unknown and untalented non-performer, here guest Fred Willard as "Xerox Department" worker Fred Winston, was abruptly given a variety show (a nightly three-hour show, no less) simply for making nice with SCTV president Guy Caballero.

The sketch is highlighted by Winston's wrongheaded comedy ideas, including the copying of body parts on a Xerox machine. But note the repeats of two earlier SCTV jokes: The miming to "The Typewriter Song" was previously done in show 112's "Scenes from an Idiot's Marriage," and the appearance of a troupe of gaudy dancers is right out of show 86's "Gene Shalit's Critics Special." Fresh ideas were clearly at a premium by this point in SCTV*'s history.*

After six Cinemax shows of relatively straightforward sketches, a show dominated by a wraparound element — so common in the NBC shows — almost seems like a novelty. But this *Stalag 17*–inspired episode, with Caballero quarantining SCTV employees in POW-like barracks to capture a spy suspected of selling programming ideas, mostly falls flat.

What works in the wraparound is how well *SCTV* re-creates the claustrophobic feeling of the POW barracks as seen in Billy Wilder's 1952 film. The implausible plot is easier to accept due to the setting, which is complete with POW staples such as guards with dogs, sirens, and searchlights. Also impressive is the editing of the barracks scenes, which effectively gives the illusion that multiple characters from the same cast member (i.e., Short's Ed Grimley and Brock Linahan) can interact.

Unfortunately, laughs are scarce throughout the wraparound. The funniest moments come in the episode's introduction and epilogue — neither of which have anything to do with *Stalag 17*— as Caballero is seen trying to plan his evening: Caballero's private thoughts reveal that he fancies wet T-shirt contests, hanging out with a gang of young toughs at the local 7-Eleven, and Barbra Streisand. And as it becomes apparent that Caballero has no friends, Flaherty succeeds in earning some rare sympathy for Caballero.

The revelation of "Happy Hour" host Happy Marsden (Hemphill, by this point in the season practically a full-fledged cast member) as the spy is also handled well, particularly when Marsden reveals his reasoning for providing rival networks with SCTV ideas: He feared that SCTV's competitors were going to expose him as an alcoholic. The fact that Marsden would allow himself to be blackmailed over his drinking habits is treated with disbelief by the SCTV staff since, as Guy says, "There isn't a soul within 200 miles of Melonville that doesn't know you're a boozehound." (A surprisingly caustic Ed Grimley adds, "You think that cheap mouth spray works?")

Two sketches unrelated to the wraparound don't improve this episode: A sketch featuring Martin Short as Jerry Lewis promoting an album of Bob Dylan covers is funnier as an idea than as a sketch. The most interesting aspect of the piece is the obscure Dylan tracks chosen to appear on the fictitious album: Songs like "The Death of Emmett Till," "Only a Hobo," and "Seven Curses" were officially unreleased at the time the sketch aired. Worsening matters for Short was the injury he suffered while shooting the dissatisfying sketch, as he was accidentally yanked off a twelve-foot podium during the "Blowin' in the Wind" segment.

Another uninspiring sketch features Levy's pitchman Al Peck selling obsolete items such as used home computers, ancient radio headsets, 8-track players, and Pong video game machines for a "Dinosaur Daze" promotion. The sketch is passable, but too simple; it lacks the oddness of the Al Peck's Used Car ad (show 97) or the Used Fruit spot (show 110). After this pitch, Levy never performed as the character again on *SCTV*.

Show 125 *(SCTV Channel)*

1. Guy Caballero: Commemorative Plates
2. Stars In One: On Location with Libby Wolfson
3. Monster Chiller Horror Theatre: Modern Problems
4. Happy Hour (Six Gun Justice Episode Seven: A Date with Tojo) part 1
5. Friends of American Crooners and the Stop Julio Iglesias Committee PSA
6. Happy Hour (Six Gun Justice Episode Seven: A Date with Tojo) part 2

What to watch for: *Monster Chiller Horror Theatre*.
He had already failed many times to sell a non-scary film as a blood-curdling one, but Count Floyd's prior attempts had never been more unsuccessful than with this struggle to push Chevy Chase's 1981 bomb Modern Problems. *Surprisingly, Flaherty infuses the pitch with a cruelty about the Chase picture that adds to the sketch's appeal. Not that Flaherty isn't willing to admit to his own career failures: A connection between Chase's dwindling box office numbers and the poor sales of Count Floyd's 1982 mini–LP is gleefully made by the Pittsburgh Midget (Joe's brother Paul Flaherty). The last memorable Count Floyd sketch.*

An above-average Cinemax show distinguished by a fine behind-the-scenes look at Libby Wolfson's feminist film "L'Insignificance: Diary of a Female Person." While the piece isn't as satisfying as Wolfson's play (show 89) or her run for political office (show 108), the sketch is a solid showcase for Andrea Martin's best character. The segment is also noteworthy for its back-story; for instance, Martin reveals that Wolfson institutionalized herself after show 89's disastrous theatrical debut. Best is the sketch's epilogue in which an obese

Wolfson attempts to escape from a spa resort with food in one hand and her still-unfinished film in the other.

Also notable in this episode is a unique Guy Caballero piece in which Caballero goes to Cinemax's New York offices to secure a loan. In the sketch, certainly inspired by David Letterman's comedy remotes, Caballero is stunned to find that Cinemax's offices are located in the boiler room of the Time Life Building. He is equally flabbergasted when the slovenly president of Cinemax rudely attacks him with an enormous sub sandwich.

Elsewhere, a PSA smartly parodies the famous "crying Native American" Keep America Beautiful television spots that were introduced in the 1970s. The sketch features a Native American (Short) weeping over Julio Iglesias's rise to stardom, particularly as it has come at the expense of many Italian-American singers. Making the sketch prophetic are reports that surfaced years later that the actor who played the Native American originally was not Native American but Italian-American.

Finally, the continuation of "Six Gun Justice" offers little of interest beyond the continued inappropriateness of "Happy Hour" host Happy Marsden (Hemphill). Here he drunkenly informs his young audience about the embarrassing demise of serial hero Don Mills, who died after getting caught in his Murphy Bed.

Show 126 *(SCTV Channel)*

1. Nursery School Association of America commercial
2. Just for Fun
3. Vic Arpeggio Private Investigator: Black Like Vic part 1
4. Dumont Color TV commercial
5. Vic Arpeggio Private Investigator: Black Like Vic part 2
6. Old Gold Cigarettes commercial
7. Vic Arpeggio Private Investigator: Black Like Vic part 3

What to watch for: Just for Fun.

Eugene Levy's turn as unctuous daytime host Stan Kanter was a highlight of show 100; this return improves upon that original. While the format—three esteemed guests are forced to suffer through an inane interview—remains the same, this time the guests are put through the additional torture of having to concoct a comedic improvisational scene. Not only do the guests—Pierre Trudeau (Short), Indira Gandhi (Martin), and William F. Buckley (Flaherty)—begrudgingly perform the scene, but they are somehow well versed in improv pantomime such as wiping glasses and lighting cigarettes. An amusing nod to the cast's beginnings at Second City, where improvisation was a part of each night's performance.

The second solid Cinemax episode in a row. Not only does "Just for Fun" improve on its previous NBC appearance, but Joe Flaherty's second turn as "Vic Arpeggio: Private Investigator" also surpasses its predecessor. The improvement comes from not only a more creative storyline—inspired by the 1964 film *Black*

Like Me—but also a funnier script, with laughs courtesy of Arpeggio's ineptness in disguising himself as an African-American butler. Here *SCTV* treads into more material that may not have been allowed on NBC, as the show successfully dares to extract humor from the American South's treatment of African-Americans in the 1960s. Note that while Flaherty is playing Vic Hedges playing Vic Arpeggio, Martin Short's character, while not billed as such, bears more than a passing resemblance to Montgomery Clift.

The Arpeggio sketch also benefits from including the supposed original commercials from the show's initial 1962 broadcast. Both are strong: The first allows Levy another chance to ruthlessly impersonate Milton Berle. The second, an advertisement that touts the supposed health benefits of Old Gold cigarettes relative to other brands, reflects the fact that cigarette advertisements were commonplace on television until they were banned beginning in the late sixties. Note that in the ad Short plays runner Roger Bannister as a chain smoker; in reality, Bannister is said to have once walked out on a live taping of the television show *I've Got a Secret* when he realized the show was sponsored by a cigarette company.

The remaining sketch in the program sees the return of Martin Short's "child" star Rusty Van Reddick, who was previously featured in the classic "Oh, That Rusty!" piece on show 113. This forgettable segment unfortunately eliminates the best aspect of that sketch — the crass actor behind the character — and therefore only serves as a reminder of the superiority of that initial piece.

Show 127 *(SCTV Channel)*

1. Edith Prickley: Depression
2. Murray's File / Dialing for Dollars promo
3. Sophia's Bath Oil commercial
4. The Ramblers Greatest Hits commercial
5. SCTV News Special Report: Youth: Do They Give A Damn, or What?
6. Sophia's Meatball Hut commercial
7. Happy Hour (Six Gun Justice Episode Eight: Last Chance for the Allies) part 1
8. Sophia's Muffler Shop commercial
9. Happy Hour (Six Gun Justice Episode Eight: Last Chance for the Allies) part 2

What to watch for: Sophia's Bath Oil commercial.
Like Dave Thomas's Mel McElroy in show 119 and Martin Short's Irving Cohen in show 122, Andrea Martin's Sophia Loren impression is featured here in a trilogy of commercials. The final two are rather pedestrian (though the slogan for Sophia's Muffler Shop — "No Muff Too Tuff"— is a nice touch), but the first is a slapstick delight that improves on a similar sketch ("Oil of Oil") from show 46. The 100% olive oil that is Sophia's Bath Oil results in Loren slipping and sliding on the floor, struggling to maintain the level of style and glamour for which she is known. One of Martin's most memorable Cinemax contributions.

A typically weak Cinemax episode improved slightly by the best of the five "Happy Hour" sketches, notable for Happy Marsden's bloody run-in with some film editing equipment. Continuing his misguided exposure of the off-screen lives of the "Six Gun Justice" stars, Marsden also lets his young audience know about heroine Maggie Butterfield's real life problems with nymphomania and kleptomania. This serial's episode is also better than most: Highlights include Levy and Short's singing duet and the appearance of a ridiculously fake bear whose attack on our heroes (again, obvious dummy stand-ins) is the most memorable of the serial's cliffhangers.

Also strong is a commercial featuring a sixties folk group called The Ramblers. Note this piece predates by several years The Folksmen, the similar group created by Christopher Guest, Michael McKean, and Harry Shearer and seen in the 2003 film *A Mighty Wind*, co-written and co-starring Eugene Levy. Viewers listening closely will detect the unmistakable voice of announcer Lou Jaffe (Levy), unheard for countless episodes.

The other sketches are less successful: A message from Edith Prickley (Martin) about depression is pointless while a Soren and Weiss (Short and Levy) report is similarly uninspired. Flaherty's appearance as Floyd Robertson is the sole highlight of the latter sketch, as the newsman gets drunk (the character's drinking problem a long running thread) and queries Soren and Weiss about their sexual orientation.

Both "Murray's File" and "Dialing for Dollars" are promoted in this episode as returning soon, but only "Murray's File" does (show 128). The "Dialing for Dollars" footage (featuring new host Earl Camembert) therefore likely comes from a sketch that was deemed unsatisfactory for air.

Show 128 *(SCTV Channel)*

1. Bell Telephone commercial
2. Books in Brief with Rita Shubb I
3. Newsbreak with Earl Camembert
4. The New York Actors' Television Theatre Production of Harvey preview
5. Books in Brief with Rita Shubb II
6. Murray's File: Canadian Television in the American Market
7. Scrapco Presents: Artisans and their Art
8. Mel's Rock Pile: The psychedelic sixties part 1
9. Newsbreak with Rita Shubb
10. Mel's Rock Pile: The psychedelic sixties part 2

What to watch for: Artisans and their Art.
Here Martin Short's vulgar businessman Brad Allen is indicted on charges of bribery in relation to the construction of the new Melonville Art Dome. His feeble response to the charges includes playing a badly doctored FBI security tape to give the false impression that he actually turned down offers of money and prostitutes. Allen was not one of Short's better characters, but by this point even Short's weaker contributions were proving superior to the surrounding material.

A weak episode with a surprisingly high number of jokes that play across two or more sketches. While the Brad Allen bribery scandal works best, the others — involving a stammering character named Rita Shubb (Martin) and an artist (Hemphill) who unsuccessfully tries to promote his painting exhibit — are simply annoying.

Most surprising is the awfulness of the "Mel's Rock Pile" piece; most of the previous installments of the sketch were classic *SCTV*, but this one — a look back to psychedelic rock — is truly bad. The material is too obvious to be funny — a former peace-loving hippie played by Joe Flaherty is now a sales manager for Smith & Wesson, while a 1960s acid-rock band called The Tangerine Conspiracy has become a tame hotel act branded as Happiness Unlimited. (An uncredited Catherine O'Hara, plays the lead singer.) Elsewhere, jokes about host Mel Slirrup (Levy) having acid trips are embarrassing. Only Martin Short's appearance as the fried drummer of Happiness Unlimited works, but even that character is an imitation of his Lawrence Orbach creation.

Elsewhere, the return of abrasive host Murray Shulman (Eugene Levy) is a bigger treat than the return of his guests, the achingly dull host and panel of "Headline Challenge" (based on the long-running Canadian game show *Front Page Challenge*). Constructing a sketch about the tediousness of *Front Page Challenge* is itself tedious, as that point was made when the original "Headline Challenge" sketch aired on show 106.

Better is a long preview of a Martin Scorsese remake of the whimsical film classic *Harvey*; Short and Flaherty are impressively over-the-top as tough New York brothers whose relationship becomes strained after one brother (Short) begins to communicate with an invisible rabbit. The rabbit's appearance at the end of the sketch to kill Flaherty ("Suck on this, Carmine") is a true surprise and the biggest laugh in the episode.

Show 129 *(SCTV Channel)*

1. Cheryl Kinsey at the Statler Hilton Hotel promo
2. SCTV Family Classic: Oliver Grimley part 1
3. Edna Boil's Going Out of Business Sale commercial
4. SCTV Family Classic: Oliver Grimley part 2
5. Salt Buddy commercial
6. SCTV: We've Got It All! promo
7. Melonville Calendar: Sandler and Young
8. Sammy Maudlin promo

What to watch for: Melonville Calendar.
In their two previous appearances, Eugene Levy and Martin Short's take on the singing duo Tony Sandler (Short) and Ralph Young (Levy) highlighted otherwise dull sketches; here they are the focus of a very funny piece. Appearing to promote their upcoming performance at the Melonville Art Dome (apparently Julio Iglesias wasn't available), the two sleepwalk their way through the song "Real Live Girl."

Their duet occurs much to the dismay of host Yolanda Divilbis (Martin), who didn't know they were coming, has never heard of them, and (once she hears them), can't get rid of them fast enough.

Now past the halfway point in the season, *SCTV Channel* bottoms out just as *Second City Television* did at the end of its second season. This episode is in many ways a microcosm of the Cinemax season, featuring myriad examples of the show's ongoing problems.

The worst sketch is the overlong and maddeningly pointless "Oliver Grimley," an interpretation of the Charles Dickens classic *Oliver Twist* that stars Martin Short's Ed Grimley in the title role and Sid Dithers (Eugene Levy) as Fagin. This piece is a prime example of *SCTV*'s occasional tendency to expend a great deal of effort to ensure that a sketch is aesthetically accurate while putting forth no effort to ensure that anything in the sketch is remotely humorous. The sketch is impressively crafted to resemble David Lean's definitive 1948 filmed version, but outside of the opening — a humorous recreation of the famous "gruel" scene ("That certainly wasn't much gruel, I must say") — and the close, in which Ed's gay father (Flaherty) comes to take Ed to America, there is simply nothing interesting in "Oliver Grimley."

Also obvious in this show is the lack of new ideas, particularly in two sketches featuring Andrea Martin. Though Martin does what she can with Edna Boil's last *SCTV* appearance, she can't cover the fact that the script is devoid of humor. Also, while a sketch promoting a Dr. Cheryl Kinsey special has its moments (Kinsey as Johnny Carson's "Carnac"), overall it's a pale imitation of the much funnier "Edith Prickley: Live from the Melonville Baths" piece (show 117).

Beginning with this episode and continuing with most of the remaining shows, *SCTV* blatantly wastes time with promos that consist of clips of old sketches edited together with new voiceover copy touting the magnificence of the SCTV Channel. Though few *SCTV Channel* sketches are notable for their brevity, these "new" promos take the art of time killing to a new and unfortunate level.

Similar to a tease run in show 127, this episode oddly features a promo for a (seemingly finished) "Sammy Maudlin Show" that never aired.

Finally, this show includes a clever commercial parody for a shoe-soiling product called "Salt Buddy" that shamelessly promotes itself as an invention that helps men effectively cheat on their wives. "Salt Buddy" is a silly piece that carries on the tradition of *SCTV* commercials for odd products like "Spray-On Socks" (show 4) and "Shirt Glue" (show 114) and, in the process, proves that *SCTV* could still be funny. Just not as often.

Show 130 *(SCTV Channel)*

1. Guy Caballero: 2009
2. SCTV promo: We've Got It All! (movies)
3. 2009: Jupiter and Beyond

4. Which Way You Running, Johnny? Promo
5. The Making of 2009: Jupiter and Beyond

What to watch for: *The Making of 2009.*
Even though it's unnecessary, the behind-the-scenes look at the sci-fi film "2009" proves to be more entertaining than the movie sketch itself. What's interesting about this segment is that it is more timely decades after it aired, in large part due to the "making of" features that have become so commonplace on DVDs. More importantly, the behind-the-scenes look is simply funnier than the film, thanks to the presence of Levy's incompetent director Woody Tobias, Jr. and the shameful but appropriate displays of disrespect afforded to him by the cast and crew. A strong comeback for Levy's Woody Tobias, Jr., particularly after the dreadful "Scary Previews" sketch from show 121.

    SCTV's celebrated style of multi-layered parodies, in which several different works are satirized in one sketch, is again on display in this episode's main piece, the 22-minute movie "2009: Jupiter and Beyond." This sci-fi sketch, which encompasses *2001: A Space Odyssey*, 1950s "tribe of lost women" pictures such as *Queen of Outer Space* and *Cat Women of the Moon*, *The Wizard of Oz*, and even an old comedy routine done by everyone from the Marx Brothers to Charlie Chaplin to Lucille Ball, is perhaps *SCTV*'s most ambitious since the multi-layered form's apex, show 44's "Fantasy Island."

    Unfortunately, "2009" doesn't nearly match the dizzying heights of the classic "Fantasy Island" sketch, as it becomes yet another example of a piece that gets bogged down in aesthetics at the expense of laughs. This is most evident in the sketch's first few minutes, which painstakingly and tediously recreate the finale of *2001* with Martin Short's Irving Cohen taking the place of the character played by Dave Bowman in the original.

    "2009" improves as the piece segues into its main plot of three astronauts who accidentally land on a planet inhabited only by attractive (and armed) women and their man-hating Queen (Wilcox's Idella Voudry). When "2009" does work, it is thanks to the performances of Levy, Short, and Flaherty, as astronauts Ernest Borgnine, Paul Simon, and Art Garfunkel. All three of the impressions are outstanding; one of the more curious aspects of this sketch is that none of these pitch-perfect impersonations were ever performed on *SCTV* outside of this single piece.

    Besides the making of sketch, the time devoted to "2009" is further increased by a needless introduction to the movie from a very excited Guy Caballero. Elsewhere, another grating filler promo spotlighting SCTV's commitment to movies (including show 91's "Slinky" and show 98's "Prickley Heat") is shown. And finally, there is an odd sketch about a confused man (Hemphill) who leaves home only to find the world a complex and troubling place. These pieces provide some relief from "2009," but unfortunately not many laughs.

Show 131 *(SCTV Channel)*

1. 4th Annual Melonville Save the World Parade part 1
2. Half Wits: The Championship Round part 1
3. Shangri-La Dance Studio commercial
4. Half Wits: The Championship Round part 2
5. 4th Annual Melonville Save the World Parade part 2
6. Myra: Story of a Small Town Gypsy promo
7. 4th Annual Melonville Save the World Parade part 3
8. Monster Chiller Horror Theatre: Halloween Always Falls on Friday the 13th
9. 4th Annual Melonville Save the World Parade part 4

What to watch for: Shangri-La Dance Studio.
In this inspired spot, John Hemphill plays a sleazy spokesperson for a prostitution ring that covers as a dance studio. From the beginning of Hemphill's pitch — "Perhaps you haven't been getting enough [meaningful pause] dancing in your life*"— it is obvious that dance instruction is* not *the recreational activity being offered by Shangri-La. The joke is expertly played throughout the spot, as Hemphill creepily touts Shangri-La's "clean" instructors, as well as specials that allow customers to "dance" with two women at once. An appreciated added touch is the false eyeballs Hemphill sports, allowing him to refrain from blinking throughout the entire commercial. With this piece, Hemphill solidifies his status as one of the most vital members of the* SCTV *team during its Cinemax season.*

This mediocre episode is most notable for the final "Monster Chiller Horror Theatre" sketch. After years of failure, Count Floyd (Flaherty) excitedly believes that the Pittsburgh Midget (Joe's brother Paul) has come up with a scary film. Unfortunately, the movie is entirely made up of one very long POV shot of someone (or something) stalking a TV studio; literally nothing happens until the end when a security guard fatally shoots the unseen (and out of shape) predator. While it's a pleasure to see the Count excited (if only briefly) about a scary movie, the sketch — like the film shown — is tedious. But the Flaherty brothers do have chemistry together, making the Pittsburgh Midget a worthy late addition to the "MCHT" franchise.

The game show "Half Wits" also returns for the final time in this episode, and while this is the least worthy of its three appearances, Eugene Levy still provides laughs as the show's increasingly frustrated host Alex Trebel. This installment also serves as a logical conclusion to the "Half Wits" sketches as Trebel finally snaps; his attempt to strangle Arthur (Flaherty) is thwarted by two men in white coats who drag him off the set.

Levy also appears in this episode as Joel Weiss, who, along with his partner Troy Soren (Short), anchors coverage of a Melonville parade, an idea that allows *SCTV* to eat up loads of screen time by showing actual parade footage acquired from a Canadian TV station. The sketch, mercifully edited into four short segments, is largely a bust, despite the inspired idea of having Soren and Weiss's elevated broadcast booth accessible only via an unstable rope ladder.

The scene in which a frightened Soren is left precariously hanging from the ladder ("I have vertigo!") is particularly memorable.

After hardly appearing in the previous episode, this is another bad show for Andrea Martin. Besides "Half Wits," her only appearance is in an inexplicable promo for a show about a Southern woman who believes she is a gypsy. Martin deserved better.

Show 132 *(SCTV Channel)*

1. Philosophers at Work promo
2. Jackie Rogers, Jr. for President commercial: He Loves You
3. Melonville Calendar: Pre-Menstrual Syndrome Awareness Week
4. Jackie Rogers, Jr. for President commercial: At Least Sleep on It
5. Happy Hour (Six Gun Justice Episode Ten: East Meets West) part 1
6. Jackie Rogers, Jr. for President commercial: You Should Remember Him on November 6th, You Should
7. Happy Hour (Six Gun Justice Episode Ten: East Meets West) part 2
8. Manny's No-Frills Pentagon Surplus Stores / Sparey Corp. commercial
9. SCTV News Update: Jackie Rogers, Jr. withdraws
10. A Melonville Moment

What to watch for: Jackie Rogers, Jr. for President.
One of the best ideas of the second half of this season sees Martin Short's grotesque Jackie Rogers, Jr. declaring his Presidential candidacy. Short doesn't waste time explaining why the entertainer is running, he simply presents three funny campaign commercials, the best of which features Rogers, Jr. rapping with blue-collar workers. Rogers, Jr. can't believe people could lead such boring lives; he asks one woman if she dances in a club after hours a la Jennifer Beals in Flashdance. *In an equally strong final segment, Earl Camembert (Levy) interviews Rogers, Jr. about his sudden decision to withdraw. Besides angering women voters by referring to his common-law wife as his "whore lady," Rogers, Jr. simply got a better offer—eight weeks at Caesar's Palace in Las Vegas. Short had a knack for finding unique venues for Rogers, Jr. and these sketches are no different.*

One of the better Cinemax shows in some time, this episode is aided mightily not only by Short's Jackie Rogers, Jr. pieces, but by the unlikely return of Joe Flaherty's Duard Weese, a character last seen in show 113. Weese is featured in a "Melonville Calendar" segment that previews a week's worth of events devoted to the topic of pre-menstrual stress. Flaherty and Wilcox's Idella Voudry amateurishly act out some scenes dealing with this problem, which are made funnier by Weese's inability to take the subject matter seriously. Note that this sketch aired about seventeen months prior to a short comedy film about PMS that Martin and Catherine O'Hara did for *Late Night with David Letterman*. Martin later referred to the *Letterman* piece as having explored "unchartered comedic territory"; obviously she forgot about this earlier (and better) *SCTV* segment.

Flaherty's Duard Weese also appears (driving his drunk cab as advertised on show 113) in a musical number about the happiness of Melonville birds, one of the most embarrassingly bad sketches ever seen on *SCTV*. How this depressingly cheery number ever made it on air is a wonder. Two other short pieces, a sketch mocking the government's tendency to overpay for military supplies and another "Philosophers at Work" promo, work better. The latter features a group of deep thinkers pondering the question of who is the luckiest white man in the world. In a nod to show 115, Gavin MacLeod is ruled out.

That leaves "Happy Hour" and "Six Gun Justice." As happened with the soap opera parody "The Days of the Week," "Six Gun Justice" becomes better as it progresses simply because the storyline gets more engrossing. In this episode, our heroes travel to the White House, where President Franklin D. Roosevelt concocts a plan to stop the alliance of Slade Cantrell, Blackie, and Prime Minister Tojo. But through an unfortunate series of events, the plan leads to U.S. bombs being dropped on our heroes, resulting in a riotous cliffhanger. Speaking of Cantrell, John Hemphill continues to shine as Happy Marsden, who here updates his audience on the current whereabouts of the actor who played Slade Cantrell. Turns out he lives on a houseboat with his "companion" Phil.

Show 133 *(SCTV Channel)*

1. Guy Caballero: British programming
2. A Medical Minute 1
3. Grimley's Celebrity Fairie Tayles: The Fella Who Was the Size of Someone's Thumb
4. A Medical Minute 2
5. Canadian Gaffes and Practical Amusements
6. A Medical Minute 3
7. Melonville Calendar: Rotary Week

What to watch for: Canadian Gaffes and Practical Amusements.
Somehow this sketch, a Canadian version of TV's Bloopers and Practical Jokes, manages to be both tedious and humorous. In Dave Thomas's book, Joe Flaherty singles out this piece as an example of the cast doing "funny things that weren't really funny." But he's wrong; the piece is *really funny.*

Like show 106's "Headline Challenge," the sketch that marked the first appearance of Dougall Currie (Levy), Sondra Wicks (Martin, who at times lapses into Arlene Francis here), and Phillip Marks (Flaherty), much of the humor here lies in its (and the characters') monotony. The joke that these humorless characters are now attempting broad comedy works and makes this sketch stronger than "Headline Challenge" (and certainly better than show 128's "Murray's File").

More hilarious than the show's lame "practical amusements" is the Currie "gaffe": When a clip of him dropping a note card is shown, we expect that slight mishap to be the extent of the "gaffe." Surprisingly, an embarrassed Currie then sounds off with a loud and lengthy fart. In keeping with the sketch's sudden turn from reserved to raunch, Marks then lets loose with SCTV's first-ever use of the word "shit." An oddly effective sketch and a worthy addendum to the CBC episode (show 106).

Like the previous show, this episode is stronger than some recent installments. Besides the Canadians of "Canadian Gaffes," the British take a solidly funny hit from Joe Flaherty's Guy Caballero who here responds vehemently to viewers' suggestions that SCTV carry more British programming. To prove that PBS already carries all the worthwhile British shows, Caballero shows a clip from a fictitious British show that is matched only in dullness by, well, "Canadian Gaffes." Later, as if to acknowledge the current weakened state of *SCTV*, Caballero admits that programming on SCTV is "the good stuff, not the great stuff."

An example of that good, not great, stuff is "Grimley's Celebrity Fairie Tayles," a parody of the then-current Showtime series *Faerie Tale Theatre*. Here a version of *Tom Thumb* (starring Short's Ed Grimley) is fairly uninspired until Joe Flaherty appears as Alan Alda, who is also credited with writing this adaptation. Alda, who some felt used the latter years of the sitcom *M*A*S*H* as his personal political platform, makes the questionable decision to turn the conclusion of the children's story into a statement about horrible prison conditions. (Note the appearance of Martin Short's wife Nancy Dolman as Clarissa, the cobbler's daughter.)

The rest of the show consists of markedly inferior segments. John Hemphill is featured in three "Medical Minute" vignettes that blatantly copy show 68's funnier "Got a Minute?" Elsewhere, the oft-used and usually enjoyable "Melonville Calendar" series wears out its welcome with a weak installment concerning a new (and misspelled) city sign.

Show 134 *(SCTV Channel)*

1. SCTV promo: Edith Prickley
2. You're On part 1
3. Happy Hour (Six Gun Justice Final Episode: Toe to Toe with Tojo) part 1
4. SCTV promo: A Salute to the Oscars
5. Happy Hour (Six Gun Justice Final Episode: Toe to Toe with Tojo) part 2
6. You're On part 2
7. SCTV promo: We've Got it All (music)
8. You're On part 3
9. SCTV News: Earl's last show

What to watch for: SCTV News.
As newscasters Floyd Robertson and Earl Camembert, Joe Flaherty and Eugene Levy deliver one of the finest and most notable sketches of SCTV*'s final season. First appearing together on show 1, Floyd and Earl logged more appearances than any other characters in the history of* SCTV: *Out of 135 shows, a staggering 66 broadcasts featured original pieces with Levy's Earl Camembert; if episodes with Robertson's Count Floyd persona are included, Floyd Robertson's appearances are even more frequent. It's a testament to the strength and versatility of the characters that even with that many appearances, Floyd and Earl rarely grew tiresome.*

> *Floyd and Earl went through many changes throughout SCTV's run, from anchoring the "SCTV News" to "Nightline Melonville" to playing key roles in several of the wraparound elements in the NBC shows. One aspect of the characters remained solidly consistent, however: Floyd's utter contempt for Earl. Flaherty and Levy made sure this contempt was retained to the bitter end, as Floyd shows neither consideration nor respect for Earl even on Earl's last broadcast. To add insult to injury, Floyd shows up late and drunk for Earl's last show because he was at a party for the retiring soundman from "Monster Chiller Horror Theatre." And it is to the same soundman — and* not *to Earl — to whom Floyd delivers a touching tribute. At the end of the piece, Floyd staggers back to his other party, while Earl is left alone, hurt and embarrassed. A darkly hilarious sketch that closes the book on these characters exactly right.*

Besides the final "SCTV News" segment, there are only two other sketches on this episode, which is infuriatingly padded with three useless generic promos.

The second installment of the phone-in show "You're On," featuring Levy's snobbish Melonville councilman Max Lansky, is as solid as the first. This time Lansky is trying in vain to drum up support for an "exclusive" shopping district, while at the same time disregarding caller complaints about more pedestrian issues such as snow removal. And while he keeps his obvious anger a bit more in check this time around, he can't escape comments about his painfully obvious hairpiece.

Finally, the last episode of "Six Gun Justice" also airs here. The final installment is relatively plot-heavy and short on laughs (in contrast to the two better "Days of the Week" finales), and it also features an unsatisfying lengthy musical number. At least the sketch includes Happy Marsden's tearful confession that the "Six Gun Justice" actor playing Blackie was in real life his drug-addicted father, a revelation that helps to explain Marsden's own addictions. Sitting at his favorite bar stool at his favorite tavern, Marsden's goodbye coincides with "last call" for *SCTV*. Well, after just one more for the road.

Show 135 *(SCTV Channel)*

1. SCTV promo: Classics
2. Pledge Week: Edith Prickley, Guy Caballero
3. The Steve Bashekis Story part 1
4. Pledge Week: Bobby Bittman, Lola Heatherton, Jackie Rogers, Jr.
5. The Steve Bashekis Story part 2
6. Pledge Week: Troy Soren, Libby Wolfson
7. The Steve Bashekis Story part 3
8. SCTV promo: We've Got it All (generic)
9. Pledge Week: Ed Grimley, Count Floyd, Woody Tobias, Jr.
10. The Steve Bashekis Story part 4
11. Pledge Week: Edith Prickley, Guy Caballero

The final episode of *SCTV Network* on NBC featured one great sketch after another, suggesting that *SCTV* left network television in its prime. The final episode of *SCTV Channel*— the final episode of *SCTV*, period — unfortunately suggests that the end of *SCTV* was overdue.

While it will never be known if *SCTV* could have rebounded if given another chance, it's clear that by the eighteenth episode of its final year, the creative energy that had fueled the program for so long had been depleted. As writer Paul Flaherty said, "We were just tired. It was too hard."

So it is that this final episode of *SCTV* feels not like an episode at all, but rather like a long series of outtakes not intended for public consumption. One strike against this episodes is its redundancy, as Guy Caballero, Edith Prickley, and a host of the show's finest recurring characters once again — just as in shows 30, 98, and particularly 85 — shamelessly beg for viewer donations.

What pleasures there are in this episode come mostly from viewing the show with the benefit of hindsight. While it wasn't clear at the time of broadcast that this would be *SCTV*'s last episode (the ending of the program is purposefully vague), there is poignancy to it now that it stands as *SCTV*'s swansong. Not only are we seeing the final *SCTV* appearances of Count Floyd, Ed Grimley, Libby Wolfson, Bobby Bittman, and Lola Heatherton (an uncredited Catherine O'Hara), it's not hard to imagine that the kind words being said about *SCTV* by the characters are actually the cast members' feelings about the program.

Scattered between the SCTV staff's pleas for money is a movie entitled "The Steve Bashekis Story" (the movie's title refers to a friend of the late John Belushi, who, with Belushi and Tino Insana, formed the comedy group the West Compass Players prior to Belushi's admittance to Second City). The film is nothing more than segments of the 1934 movie *Of Human Bondage* with new dialogue dubbed over by the cast. The gimmick gets old quickly and the new dialogue is scarcely funny, although *SCTV* had the good sense to break up the movie into four short segments. (In contrast, show 77's single-segment "Cisco Kid" piece, which used the same device, was funnier but grew more tedious.)

At the end of the episode, having raised only $111, Prickley and Caballero sit defeated, fearing the end of SCTV. "Don't you care," Guy laments, "that we've worked and slaved to bring you the finest programming available?" The line is a thinly veiled plea at the North American TV audience: While the show received countless glowing notices from critics, the fact that *SCTV* never captured the public's attention like its counterpart *Saturday Night Live* meant that *SCTV*, in the words of Executive Producer Andrew Alexander, was "always shuffling toward the guillotine, the execution was always around the corner." That *SCTV* avoided the execution long enough to leave behind 135 episodes of mostly remarkable quality is a small miracle. Perhaps Andrea Martin's Edith Prickley states it best in the final seconds of the final episode: "Wherever there are people who cry out for superior television, there will be an SCTV." Although the masses did not cry out long or loud enough for the show, *SCTV* was indeed superior television.

APPENDIX A

The Compilations

Besides episodes that featured previously aired material (i.e., the first few NBC programs) and the 30-minute shows first syndicated in the mid-1980s that regularly complied sketches from disparate programs, there are five significant *SCTV* compilations: First, there were three "best of" 90-minute shows that aired on NBC in early 1982, with the initial installment being the first *SCTV* episode to be broadcast in *Saturday Night Live*'s time period.

The first NBC "best of" featured only material that had been part of the NBC broadcasts, including material that had originated in the show's first three seasons and then rerun during the initial *SCTV Network 90* shows. The other two "best of" compilations leaned heavily on material that had not been previously broadcast on NBC. Some of the sketches were edited for time.

The Best of SCTV Network 1

1. Dr. Shekter commercial (show 85)
2. Comment with David Brinkley: When will the street dealer be able to consistently provide quality smoke? (show 74)
3. Leave It To Beaver 25th Anniversary Party (show 15)
4. John McEnroe coffee commercial (show 86)
5. My First Time commercial (show 93)
6. The Merv Griffith Show promo (show 84)
7. National Midnight Star (show 84)
8. Indira commercial (show 80)
9. Great White North: Why are parking lots so small at donut places (show 73)
10. The Fishin' Musician: The Tubes (show 86)
11. The Brooke Shields Show promo (show 84)
12. Cooking with Edith Prickley (with Tex and Edna commercial) (show 43)
13. What's My Shoe Size? (show 37)
14. Sunrise Semester with Dr. Cheryl Kinsey: The Inability to Fake Orgasms (show 5)
15. Perry Como: Still Alive commercial (show 88)

16. SCTV Movie of the Week: Play It Again, Bob (show 59)
17. Mel Torme and Bob and Doug McKenzie anthems (show 64; the McKenzie anthem was deleted on a later rebroadcast)

The Best of SCTV Network 2

1. Guy Caballero: Welcome, Arabs (show 33)
2. Got a Minute? (show 68)
3. High Q (show 35)
4. The Johnny LaRue Show (show 1)
5. Point/Counterpoint: Alcohol (show 54)
6. My Fair Lady promo (show 53)
7. The Sammy Maudlin Show bumper (new)
8. Great White North: Back packing with beer on ski trips (show 60)
9. Long Distance commercial (show 40)
10. Danny Eubanks: Seminarian/Rookie Cop promo (show 57)
11. The Sammy Maudlin Show part 1: Edith Prickley (show 45)
12. Dr. Chet Vet the Dead Pet Remover commercial (show 45)
13. The Sammy Maudlin Show parts 2 and 3: Bobby Bittman, Lola Heatherton, Lin Ye Tang (show 45)
14. Graft recipes commercial (show 48)
15. Hats of the West (show 40)
16. Bad Acting in Hollywood (show 39)
17. Alpha Channel (show 70)
18. The Irwin Allen Show (show 67)

The Best of SCTV Network 3

1. Sunrise Semester: English for Beginners (show 2)
2. Harry Filth preview (show 25)
3. Taxi Driver with Gregory Peck promo (show 63)
4. Lola Heatherton in Concert promo (show 27)
5. Sid Dithers Private Eye (show 39)
6. Taxi Driver with Woody Allen promo (show 67)
7. SCTV Premiere: Return to the Planet of Empires (with VideoTech commercial) (show 65)
8. How the Middle East Was Won preview (show 33)
9. Taxi Driver with Sid Dithers promo (show 73)
10. Fillips Milk of Amnesia commercial (show 18)
11. Quincy: Cartoon Coroner (show 72)
12. The Dick Cavett Show: Dick Cavett (show 60)
13. Biller Hi-Lite commercial (show 39)
14. K-Tel's Fast Talking Playhouse: Who's Afraid of Virginia Woolf? (show 54)
15. Great White North: Star Wars (show 65)
16. The Young and the Wrestling promo (show 56)
17. SCTV Movie of the Week: Agatha Christie's Death Takes No Holiday (show 42)
18. Joni Mitchell "For Dogs Only" commercial (show 65)
19. Money Talks with Brian Johns: William E. Douglas (show 56)
20. Yellow Belly promo (show 37)
21. Monster Chiller Horror Theatre: Whispers of the Wolf (show 38)

After *SCTV*'s final cancellation, a two-hour "best of" aired on CBC in Canada and ABC in the United States in 1988, and, in 1992, an hour-long video called *The Best of John Candy on SCTV* was released.

The 1988 special featured new wraparound material with Flaherty's Guy Caballero and Martin's Edith Prickley testifying at an investigation into alleged misconduct by the SCTV network. Unlike previous compilations, sketches were often heavily edited into montages, a frustrating choice made ostensibly to spotlight the cast's range of impersonations and characters at the expense of presenting complete pieces. Some other sketches were obviously censored for content. (Apparently at least one of the censors had hearing difficulties, as the word "ship" was edited out of the phrase "ship building" in a "Great White North" segment.)

The most troubling aspect of the John Candy video is that the release pulls many clips out of wraparound stories, the plots of which therefore make no sense to new viewers. But as a collection of Candy's best moments (*not* best sketches) from *SCTV*, the video is passable entertainment. Note the video was never released on DVD.

The Best of SCTV Network

1. Investigation: Introduction (new)
2. Slinky ... Toy from Hell (show 91)
3. Martin Scorsese's Jerry Lewis Live on the Champs Elysees commercial (show 104)
4. High Q (show 35)
5. Sophia's Bath Oil commercial (show 127)
6. Yellow Belly promo (show 37)
7. Shower in a Briefcase commercial (show 114)
8. Perry Como: Still Alive commercial (show 88)
9. My First Time commercial (show 93)
10. Lola Heatherton's Way To Go, Woman! promo (show 88)
11. Investigation: Impersonations and pledge drives (new)
12. Guy Caballero Montage: Requests for cash (various)
13. Investigation: Pledge drives and movies (new)
14. SCTV Movies Montage 1: New York Rhapsody, The Godfather, My Fair Lady
15. SCTV promo: A Salute to the Oscars (show 134)
16. SCTV Movies Montage 2: Play It Again Bob, The Grapes of Mud
17. Investigation: Colorization and commercial interruptions (new)
18. Ben-Hur (heavily edited and interrupted by commercials including show 97's Al Peck's Used Cars, show 106's Moose Beer, show 101's Stairways to Heaven)
19. Investigation: Go Spuds, Go! (new)
20. Biller Hi-Lite commercial (show 39)
21. Hollywood Dirt Tonight (show 119)
22. Newsbreak with Rita Shubb (show 128)
23. SCTV Special Report: The Space Shuttle (show 83)
24. Investigation: Public affairs programming and favorite shows (new)
25. Gene Shalit's Critics' Special promo (show 86)
26. Sophia's Meatball Hut commercial (show 127)
27. The Ramblers Greatest Hits commercial (show 127)
28. Leave It To Beaver 25th Anniversary Party (show 15)

29. Mayberline commercial (show 88)
30. The Women Who Donahue Forgot promo (show 116)
31. Convert-A-Toup commercial (show 99)
32. Now "Nosy" the Short-Haired Terrier Dog Got His Name promo (show 105)
33. Harry Filth preview (show 25)
34. Great White North: How to stuff a mouse into a beer bottle (show 89)
35. Investigation: Pirini Sclereso (new)
36. SCTV Foreign Programming Montage: Oliver Grimley, Jane Eyrehead, Rome Italian Style, Whispers of the Wolf, Prickley Heat, Das Boobs
37. Bell Telephone commercial (show 103)
38. Investigation: Children's programming (new)
39. The Fella Who Couldn't Wait for Christmas promo (show 111)
40. Happy Hour Montage
41. Investigation: Recess (new)
42. Sophia's Muffler Shop commercial (show 127)
43. Investigation: Decision (new)
44. Mel Torme anthem (show 64)

The Best of John Candy on SCTV

1. Opening (includes clips of show 106's Garth and Gord and Fiona and Alice)
2. Street Beef wraparound part 1 (show 105)
3. Five Neat Guys Gold commercial (show 91)
4. The Battle of the PBS Stars part 1: Fred Rodgers and Julia Child box (show 103)
5. Half Wits (show 112)
6. The Millionaire (show 33)
7. Liberace's Musical Salute to the Holidays promo (show 94)
8. Monster Chiller Horror Theatre: Dr. Tongue's 3-D House of Stewardesses (show 84)
9. CCCP1: Hey Giorgy! promo (show 88)
10. Jake La Motta's Raging Bull-B-Que commercial (show 86)
11. Shmenge Travel commercial (show 101)
12. Farm Film Celebrity Blow-Up: Dustin Hoffman (show 112)
13. Harry's Sex Shop commercial (show 84)
14. Christmas wraparound part 1: Caballero kicks out LaRue (show 94)
15. Leave It To Beaver 25th Anniversary Party (show 15)
16. The Sammy Maudlin 23rd Anniversary Show: Lon Chaney, Jr. (show 106)
17. Stars In One promo: Steve Roman (show 112)
18. Fantasy Island (show 44)
19. Tommy Shanks commercial: Hospital (show 108)
20. Small Town Dick promo (show 91)
21. The Days of the Week montage (various)
22. What's My Shoe Size? (show 37)
23. K-I-L Target Leads commercial (show 96)
24. The Godfather wraparound part 1: Connie's Wedding (show 93)
25. Christmas wraparound part 4: Johnny LaRue's Street Beef part 1 (show 94)
26. The Dusty Towne Sexy Holiday Special (show 94)
27. Alfred Hitchcock Presents (show 40)
28. The Tim Ishimuni Show (show 80)
29. Christmas wraparound part 4: Johnny LaRue's Street Beef part 2 (show 94)
30. Credits (includes clips from show 13's Ben-Hur, show 88's Wet Nurse, show 116's South Sea Sinner, and show 115's Sweeps Week wraparound)

Appendix B

SCTV on DVD

After extended delays due to the complexities (and the costs) of securing home video rights to the music used in the original broadcasts, Shout! Factory released the 39 90-minute NBC programs (shows 79–117) in four separate DVD box sets from June of 2004 through September of 2005. The first volume features shows 79–87, the second volume includes shows 88–96, the third volume has shows 97–105, and the fourth volume completes the NBC run with shows 106–117. A three-disc set entitled *Best of the Early Years* that contains fifteen of the original half-hour shows — three shows from season two and twelve shows from season three — followed in October 2006.

The decision by Shout! Factory and the Second City to release the NBC shows first was a wise one; as Eugene Levy commented to *Video Store Magazine*, not only do many feel that they are "the best shows," but there were fears of releasing the first season due to the "chintzy" look of the episodes.

The DVD sets, while clearly the finest *SCTV* product ever made publicly available, are nonetheless frustrating. While the discs boast a fair amount of extras, they largely consist of dry interview clips and roundtable discussions that need editing. Also disappointing are the discs' limited commentary tracks: Joe Flaherty and Eugene Levy in particular seem to have little idea what they are watching and spend most of their commentaries trying to remember the sketches they worked on so long ago. Far better are tracks recorded by Andrea Martin and Catherine O'Hara, who seem to have lost none of their chemistry.

The biggest disappointment with the DVDs is the complete lack of deleted sketches, outtakes, alternate takes, or even NBC promos. The inclusion of this long sought-after material (Dave Thomas once claimed to have *boxes* of out-take tapes) would have made these DVD sets true gold mines for fans. Also, more should have been done to explain the sources for the show's parodies, most obviously via a subtitle trivia track like the one used to good effect on the superior *Seinfeld* DVD sets.

While Shout! Factory has done a fair job securing music rights, many changes had to be made that unfortunately greatly compromised some pieces. Among the most significant changes: The exclusion of Simon and Garfunkel's "Mrs. Robinson" from "The Days of the Week" (show 105), which dilutes the piece's effectiveness as a *Graduate* parody, and the alteration of all of the music in "The Happy Wanderers Salute John Williams" (show 108). The latter changes devastate the humor in the piece, since Yosh and Stan's ghastly polka versions of Williams's music are now just ghastly generic polka tracks. The most noteworthy edit in the DVDs is the complete removal of the "Stairways to Heaven" sketch from show 101 due to Led Zeppelin's notorious refusal to allow their music to be used in anything except lucrative advertising campaigns.

On the other hand, the near-complete form in which *SCTV*'s NBC episodes are presented on these DVDs is clearly preferable to how the same output had been seen for two decades in off-network syndication. Also of note are a couple of excellent extras: The *1999 U.S. Comedy Arts Festival SCTV Tribute* hosted by Conan O'Brien and a 1997 Museum of Television & Radio roundtable discussion notable for the participation of Rick Moranis, who is the only surviving member of the NBC cast to not otherwise contribute to the DVDs.

The release of the *Best of the Early Years* set in October 2006 appeared to signal an end to *SCTV* releases on DVD, as the cost of music clearances combined with what have been reportedly disappointing sales have apparently made releasing complete seasons of the first three years too cost-prohibitive for Shout! Factory. (Any future DVD release of *SCTV Channel* is also highly in doubt.) Given this latest development, as well as the music changes made to the shows that have been released, long-time fans looking for a complete representation of *SCTV* on DVD will need to rely on homemade dubs of their old VHS (or even BETA!) tapes.

Bibliography

Adams, Sam. "All Together Now." *The Philadelphia City Paper*, 12–19 October 2000. http://www.citypaper.net/articles/101200/mov.best.shtml.
"*Annie* History." *The Official Andrea McArdle Website*. http://andreamcardleasannie.homestead.com/anniehistory.html.
Basinger, Jeanine. *American Cinema: One Hundred Years of Filmmaking*. New York: Rizzoli, 1994.
Ben-Hur: The Making of an Epic. Warner Home Video and Turner Home Entertainment. 1993.
Boyles, Denis. "How Many Acrylics Had to Die to Make That Sweater?" *Penthouse*, June 1979: 134–139, 208–209.
Brennan, Sandra. "David Begelman." *MSN Entertainment*. http://entertainment.msn.com/celebs/celeb.aspx?mp=b&c=242337.
Brown, Ian. "The Comic Triumph of SCTV." *Macleans*, 27 December 1982: 28–32.
_____. "Two Hosers Take Off to the Movies." *Macleans*, 27 December 1982: 34.
Castleman, Harry, and Walter J. Podrazik. *Harry and Wally's Favorite TV Shows*. New York: Prentice Hall, 1989.
"A Chairy Tale." *National Film Board of Canada*. http://cmm.onf.ca/E/titleinfo/index.epl?id=11152.
Cocks, Jay. "Messages from Melonville." *Time*, 9 November 1981: 112.
David Letterman's Holiday Film Festival. NBC, 30 November 1985.
"Elizabeth I." *Britannia.com*. http://www.britannia.com/history/monarchs/mon45.html.
Erickson, Hal. "Eddie 'Rochester' Anderson." *MSN Entertainment*. http://entertainment.msn.com/celebs/celeb.aspx?mp=b&c=295100.
Errico, Marcus. "'Crying Indian' a Fake, Reports Say." *E! Online*, 7 January 1999. http://www.eonline.com/News/Items/0,1,4141,00.html.
Femyer, Mike. "Point/Counterpoint — Entertainment vs. News Division." *Farewell Analog*. http://www.farewellanalog.net/bothsides.html.
"The 50 Funniest TV Moments of All Time." *TV Guide*, 23–29 January 1999: 20–40.
Finan, Christopher M., and Anne F. Castro. *The Rev. Donald E. Wildmon's Crusade for Censorship, 1977–1992*. New York: The Media Coalition, 1994.

Finnan, Robert W. *The Bowery Boys Page.* http://users.arczip.com/fwdixon/BoweryBoys/.
Hartigan, Brian. "Silver City." *TV Guide Canada*, 30 June–6 July 2001: 10–13.
Hill, Doug, and Jeff Weingrad. *Saturday Night: A Backstage History of Saturday Night Live.* New York: Beech Tree, 1986.
Hobson, Louis B. "Redgrave Strikes Again." *Calgary Sun*, 19 August 1998. http://www.canoe.ca/JamMoviesArtistsR/redgrave_lynn.html.
Jacobsen, Karin, and Mary Ellen Snodgrass. *Jane Eyre (Cliffs Notes).* Indianapolis: John Wiley, 2000.
Jameson, Richard T. "Satire Comes to Video." *Film Comment*, May–June 1981: 76–77.
"Jerry Lewis Biography." The Jerry Lewis Website. http://members.aol.com/norky1995/bio.html.
"John Belushi: Made in America." *Rolling Stone*, 29 April 1982: 18–26, 57–61.
"Johnny Puleo." *The Space Age Pop Music Page.* http://www.spaceagepop.com/puleo.htm.
"Juvenile Delinquent, Bad Girl, & Hot Rod Movies." *The Video Beat!* http://www.thevideobeat.com/jd_biker_hotrod.htm.
Kenter, Peter, and Martin Levin. *TV North: Everything You Wanted to Know About Canadian Television.* Vancouver: Whitecap, 2001.
Late Night with David Letterman. NBC, 4 February 1982.
Late Night with David Letterman. NBC, 29 December 1982.
Late Night with David Letterman. NBC, 30 August 1983.
Late Night with David Letterman. NBC, 12 November 1987.
Late Night with David Letterman. NBC, 13 September 1989.
Later with Bob Costas. NBC, 21 June 1990.
Later with Bob Costas. NBC, 4 July 1990.
Macfarlane, David. "Taking Off with the McKenzie Brothers." *Macleans*, 11 January 1982: 16–17.
MacKay, Gillian. "SCTV's Revival Hopes." *Macleans*, 21 May 1984: 10–12.
MacKenzie, Robert. "SCTV Comedy Network." *TV Guide*, 31 October–6 November 1981: 1.
Mailer, Adele. *The Last Party.* Fort Lee, NJ: Barricade, 1997.
McCrohan, Donna. *The Second City: A Backstage History of Comedy's Hottest Troupe.* New York: Putnam, 1987.
Mikkelson, Barbara, and David P. Mikkelson. *Urban Legends Reference Page.* 20 March 2001 http://www.snopes.com/radiotv/tv/soupy1.htm.
Mills, Bob. "With Bob Hope on the Road to Peking." *Thinkers Network.* 1998. http://thinkers.net/expression/prosebase/0000000d.htm.
Mother's Day with Joan Lunden. Lifetime, 1984.
Moustaki, Nikki, and Gilbert Borman. *1984 (Cliffs Notes).* Indianapolis: John Wiley, 2000.
Nottingham, Stephen. "The French New Wave." *Steve's Cinema* Page. June 1998. http://ourworld.compuserve.com/homepages/Stephen_Nottingham/cintxt2.htm.
O'Toole, Lawrence. "A Southern Triumph for the Great White North." *Macleans*, 31 August 1981: 60.
"Pat Carroll." *Women's International Center.* http://www.wic.org/bio/pcarroll.htm.
Patinkin, Sheldon. *The Second City: Backstage at the World's Greatest Comedy Theater.* Naperville: Sourcebooks, 2000.
"Perry Como, Singer, Dies at 87." Associated Press. 13 May 2001.

"Rupert Holmes." *Rodney Walker's WENN Page.* http://rabat.liquidweb.com/grablab/ruperta/rupertvh1.html#hits.
"Salvador Dali's Biography." *Gala-Salvador Dali Foundation.* http://www.salvador-dali.org/eng/fdali/htm.
Second City Presents ... with Bill Zehme. Bravo,15 February 2002.
Shales, Tom. "SCTV Goes Cable." *The Washington Post,* 18 May 1983: B1.
Sloan, James Park. *Jerzy Kosinski: A Biography.* New York: Dutton, 1996.
Thomas, Dave, Robert Crane, and Susan Carney. *SCTV: Behind the Scenes.* Toronto: McClelland & Stewart, 1996.
"20 Questions: SCTV." *Playboy,* May 1982: 144–145, 238–243.
Vernon, Sharon, and Jaimie Vernon. "Rough Trade." *Jam! Music's Canadian Musi Encyclopedia.* http://www.canoe.ca/JamMusicPopEncycloPagesR/rough.html.
Waite, Ron. "The William Castle Story." *Horror-Wood Webzine.* http://www.horror-wood.com/castle.htm.
"Walter Ostanek." *CBC.ca.* http://artscanada.cbc.ca/artsNow/index.jsp?label=ostanek 230203&uid=.
Waters, Harry F. "Midnight Laughs in a New Key." *Newsweek,* 30 March 1981: 83–84.
Waters, Harry F., and Neal Karlen. "TV's Frozen Wasteland." *Newsweek,* 19 July 1982: 65.
Whitall, Susan. "SCTV Takes Off, Eh? (Thank You, Canada!)." *Creem,* March 1982: 26–31, 64–65.
Woodward, Bob. *Wired: The Short Life and Fast Times of John Belushi.* New York: Simon & Schuster, 1984.
"Yonge Street." *The City of Toronto.* http://www.city.toronto.on.ca/index.htm.

Index

Abbey Road 185
Abbott & Costello 93, 154, 219
The Admirable Crichton 61
Adultery, Italian Style 182
"The Adventures of Shake 'n' Bake" (sketch) 163, 165
Alda, Alan 92, 152, 249
Alexander, Andrew 68, 72, 103, 141, 227, 251
Alfred Hitchcock Presents 60
Alice 42, 219
"Alice the Wonder Dog" (sketch) 21
Alighieri, Dante 33
"Alistair Cook's Armenia" (sketch) 27
All Creatures Great and Small 40
"All-Girl Friday Night Pajama Party" (sketch) 156
"All the Long-Leggedy Beasties" (sketch) 40
All the President's Men 193
Allard, Dr. Charles 72, 83
Allen, Brad (character) 242–243
Allen, Irwin 88–89, 202
Allen, Woody 72, 79–80, 82, 137
"Alpha Channel" (sketch) 92
Altman, Robert 87
"A.M. Little America" (sketch) 41
Amedure, Scott 176
"American Orthodontal Group" (PSA parody) 138
American Pie 232
Ames, Ed 189
. . . And Justice for All 91, 147
Anderson, Eddie "Rochester" 200
Anderson, Loni 169
Andersson, Harriet 57

Andropov, Yuri 221
The Andy Griffith Show 118
"Angel Cortez: FBI Jockey" (sketch) 198–199
Angel Street 60
Angry Young Man (character) 109
Annie 174–175, 216
Annie Hall 82, 137
Antonioni, Michelangelo 182
Apocalypse Now 166
Arkin, Alan 5
"Artisans and Their Art" (sketch) 242
Astaire, Fred 64
Aykroyd, Dan 5, 58–59, 70, 142, 159, 163
Aykroyd, Peter 60

The B-52's 157
"The Babe Ruth Story" (parody) 42, 180
Bach, Catherine 179
"Backstage" (sketch) 13, 14, 18
Bacon, Francis 165
"Bad Acting in Hollywood" (sketch) 58–59
Bailey, F. Lee 230
Bain, Bonar 136–137
Baio, Scott 234
Baker, Senator Howard 110
Bakker, Jim, and Tammy Faye 90
Bakker, Tammy Faye 130
Ball, Lucille 207–208, 245
The Band 93, 105, 172
Band de Brava 205
Bannister, Roger 241
Barrett, Rona 31
"Barretta's Bird" (sketch) 38

"The Battle of the PBS Stars" (sketch) 179, 222
Beals, Jennifer 229, 247
The Beatles 185, 194
"Beauty and the Beets" (sketch) 21
Begelman, David 193
Belafonte, Harry 190
Belushi, John 5, 75, 142, 162, 163, 205, 251
Ben 184
"Ben-Hur" (parody) 3, 11, 27–28, 39, 48, 60, 200
Bennett, Tony 124–125, 159, 161, 194, 210
Benny, Jack 200
"Benny Hill Street Blues" (sketch) 130
Bergen, Candice 233
Bergman, Ingmar 57, 209–210
Bergman, Ingrid 64
Berle, Milton 125, 211, 241
Bernstein, Leonard 147–148
"Beside the Point" (sketch) 32
"The Best Is Yet to Come" 161
The Best of John Candy on SCTV (video release) 205-255–256
The Best of SCTV (1988 special) 28, 255–256
Betcha, Hugh (character) 85, 119–120
"Betty Bain: Professional Juror" (sketch) 46
The Bicycle Thief 182
"Big Brother" (episode) 89–90
"The Big Dude and the Kid"(sketch) 180
"Big Dude TV Dinners" (commercial parody) 180
"Big Giant Restaurant" (commercial parody) 69
Bildenhausen, Karl (character) 37, 213
"Bill Needle's Mailbag" (sketch) 86, 168, 187
The Birds 60
Bisset, Jacqueline 233
Bittman, Bobby (character) 11, 44, 105, 123, 169; "Bittman Does Dallas" and 74; Bob and Doug McKenzie and 160–161; "Christmas — That's All" and 207; "The Dick Cavett Show" and 99; final episode and 251; "Good-Bye America" and 31; "Maudlin's Eleven" and 164–165; "The Mirthmakers" and 53; "On the Waterfront Again" and 6, 65–66; retires 215–216; "The Sammy Maudlin Show" and 17, 37, 84, 107, 112, 135, 177, 190, 192; "SCTV Pledge Week" and 121; "SCTV Solid Gold Telethon" and 48; "SCTV Staff Christmas Party" and 150; Skip Bittman and 97, 143–144; "$211,000 Triangle" and 18

Bittman, Skip (character) 97, 143–144, 164–165, 168
"Bittman Does Dallas" (sketch) 74, 219
Black Like Me 240–241
"Black Perspective" (sketch) 20
Blackboard Jungle 180
Blanchard, John 72
Blasucci, Dick 12, 72, 83, 93, 107, 123, 131
Bleier, Rocky 180
"Blind Fists of the Furious Dragon" (sketch) 30
Blodgett, Esther (character) 210–211
"Blood Sucking Monkeys from West Mifflin, Pennsylvania" (sketch) 157–158
Blow-Up 182
"Blowin' in the Wind" 239
The Blues Brothers (film) 142, 168
The Blues Brothers (*SNL* characters) 120, 163
"Bob Hope Desert Classic" (sketch) 45–46, 50, 64, 71
"Bobby's Back" (sketch) 216
Body Heat 165–166
Bogart, Humphrey 64, 79
Boil, Edna (character) 172, 222, 229, 244
Boil, Tex and Edna (characters) 63, 68, 172
Bondanella, Peter 182
"Das Boobs" (sketch) 235
The Boomtown Rats 154–155
Das Boot 235
Bopper-Simpson, Sue (character) 132, 162
Borge, Victor 205
Borgnine, Ernest 245
Bosley, Tom 51, 58–59
"Botch & Lamb" (commercial parody) 54
"The Bowery Boys in the Band" (sketch) 199–200
Bowling for Columbine 138
Bowman, Dave 245
Boyd, Stephen 124–125
Boyle, Peter 5
The Boys from Brazil 94
The Boys in the Band 199–200
Bradley, Paul 188
Brando, Marlon 147
"Breaking Up Is Hard to Do" 225
Brinkley, David: "Buzz Aldrin's Mercury III Players" and 177; "Comment" and 61, 82, 91, 96, 111, 158, 180–181; "Point/Counterpoint" and 74; "SCTV Special Report: The Space Shuttle" and 114; "Walter Cronkite's Brain" and 139
"British Film Festival" (sketch) 109
"Broads Behind Bars" (sketch) 25–26

Brokaw, Tom 41
Bromfield, Valri 223, 234, 237
Bronson, E. Charles (character) 166
Brontë, Charlotte 200
Brooks, Albert 137
Brooks, Mel 237
Brown, Governor Jerry 58
Bruno (a.k.a. Woody Tobias, Jr.) (character) 11, 57, 210; "Death Motel" and 77, 80; "Dr. Tongue's Evil House of Wax" and 35; "Dr. Tongue's 3-D House of Slave Chicks" and 200–201; "The Making of 3-D Stake from the Heart" and 169–170; "The Russian Show" and 129; "Scary Previews" and 234; "Screen Acting" and 142; "SCTV Pledge Week" and 121; "3-D Firing Line" and 223; "3-D House of Beef" and 149; "The Towering Inferno" episode and 203–204; "2009: Jupiter and Beyond" and 245
Bruter, Dr. Ernest (character) 16
"Bubie's Chicken Medication" (commercial parody) 77
Buck Rogers in the 25th Century 237
Buckley, William F. 240
Buffett, Jimmy 183
"Building a Better House" (sketch) 37, 213
Bumme, Ben (character) 109
Burnett, Carol 224
Burton, Richard 2, 41, 52
Bush, George H.W. 221
Buttons, Red 89
"Buzz Aldrin's Mercury III Players" (sketch) 176–177

Caan, James 147
Caballero, Guy (character) 110, 144, 151, 174, 178, 210; *The Best of SCTV* and 255; Bob and Doug McKenzie and 159, 160–162; "Canadian Broadcasting Corporation" episode and 182, 188, 190; "Doorway to Hell" episode and 145; Edith Prickley and 32, 55; Ernest Kirsch and 44–45, 49; final episode and 251; first NBC show and 105; "Godfather" episode and 146–149, 214; "Indecent Exposure" episode and 193–194; Johnny LaRue and 14, 31, 113–114, 186, 206–207, 231; Lola Heatherton and 122–123; Moe Green and 23–24, 47, 89; "Moral Majority" episode and 116–117; "The People's Global Golden Choice Awards" and 167–168; pleas for money 48, 52, 78, 83, 121, 164; "The Russian Show" and 129;

SCTV Channel and 229, 238–239, 240, 245, 249; "Sweeps Week" episode and 218–219; third season and 72, 73, 74, 84, 86, 88, 90; "The Towering Inferno" episode and 203; "Zontar" episode and 136–137
Caddyshack 44, 186
Caged 25
Cagney & Lacey 9, 212
Caine, Michael 152, 234
California Fever 85
Camembert, Earl (character) 214, 231, 242, 247; "Election Central" and 196–197; "15 Minutes" and 21; "Indecent Exposure" episode and 193; Johnny LaRue and 50, 114; Lola Heatherton and 123; "Nightline Melonville" and 97, 162, 174; "One on the Town" and 97, 105, 158, 204; retires 97, 228, 249–250; "SCTV News" first season and 1, 11, 13, 15, 19, 20, 26, 29, 31, 34, 35, 37, 39, 40; "SCTV News" second season and 47, 49, 53, 55, 60, 62, 66, 67, 68–69, 70–71; "SCTV News" third season and 72, 73, 75, 80, 81–82, 85, 86, 91, 95, 96–97; "SCTV Staff Christmas Party" and 150–151; "SCTV 30th Anniversary Show" and 56–57; "60/20" and 77–78; "The Uncle Earl Show" and 41–42
Camembert, Merle (character) 56–57
"Canadian Broadcasting Corporation" (episode) 49, 104, 182, 188–192, 248
"Canadian Gaffes and Practical Amusements" (sketch) 248–249
"Can't Smile Without You" 194
Captain Combat (character) 1, 15, 23, 48, 90
Captain Kangaroo 15
Carlin, George 72, 75, 112, 137
"Carl's Cuts" (sketch) 141, 178, 187
The Carol Burnett Show 45
Carson, Johnny 45, 70, 78, 95, 135, 154, 189, 244
Carter, Jack 222
Casablanca 6, 64, 79
Cash, Johnny 178
Castle, William 62
Cat on a Hot Tin Roof 229
Cat Women of the Moon 245
Cavett, Dick 80, 99, 179
"Celebration" 128
Cerb [Cerf], Bennett 56
"The Chair" (sketch) 191
A Chairy Tale 191

Chamberlain, Richard 203
Chaplin, Charlie 245
Chapter Two 152
"Chariots of Eggs" (sketch) 177
Chariots of Fire 177
A Charlie Brown Christmas 208
Charlie's Angels 115
"Charlie's Kitchen" (sketch) 179, 181
Charo 55
Chase, Chevy 163, 239
Cheaters 176
"Check Please" (sketch) 42
Chekhov, Anton 2, 20
"Chest Fever" 172
Child, Julia 179
Chilliwack 164
The China Syndrome 76
Chinatown 107
"Chinese Fairy Tales" (sketch) 53
Christie, Agatha 62
A Christmas Carol 207, 231
"Christmas Day with the Shmenge Family" (sketch) 206, 231
The Cinema of Federico Fellini 182
"The Cisco Kid" (parody) 38, 100, 251
Clark, Bob (character) 63, 86
Clark, Bob (director) 235
Clark, Chuck (character) 58, 83
Clark, Dick 167
Clayburgh, Jill 76
Clift, Montgomery 241
A Clockwork Orange 109
Close, Del 6
Close Encounters of the Third Kind 166–167
The Coalition for Better Television 115, 117
Coco, James 152
Cohen, Irving (character) 236, 241, 245
Cole, Natalie 135
Collins, Clay (character) 171, 178, 185, 209
Coming Home 76
"Comment with David Brinkley" (sketch) 82, 91, 96, 156, 158, 180–181
Como, Perry 128–129
"Comrade Kangaroo" (sketch) 90
Conrad, William 97
"Consumer Action Line" (sketch) 68–69
Conte, Richard 164
Cooke, Alistair 40, 45, 61, 109, 180
"Cookery Crock" (sketch) 94–96, 170
"Cooking with Edith Prickley" (sketch) 63
"Cooking with LaRue" (sketch) 18, 31, 207
"Cooking with Marcello" (sketch) 82, 88, 93, 99
Cooper, Gordon 114

"Copacabana" 194
Copland, Aaron 169
Coppola, Francis Ford 146, 166, 170, 186, 202
Corman, Roger 171
Cosell, Howard 110, 179, 191
Cougar, John 194
Count Floyd (album) 239
Count Floyd (character) 8, 11, 26, 41, 123, 249; "Blood-Sucking Monkeys from West Mifflin, Pennsylvania" and 156–158; "Count Floyd's Have Yourself a Scary Little Christmas" and 208; "Death Motel" and 77; "The Dick Cavett Show" and 99; "Dr. Tongue's Evil House of Pancakes" and 153; "Dr. Tongue's Evil House of Wax" and 35; "Dr. Tongue's 3-D House of Slave Chicks" and 200–201; "Dr. Tongue's 3-D House of Stewardesses" and 117–118; final episode and 251; *Four for Texas* and 204; "Halloween Always Falls on Friday the 13th" and 246; "Madame Blitzman" and 3, 33–34; "The Making of 3-D Stake from the Heart" and 170; *Modern Problems* and 239; *The Odd Couple* and 82, 204; "Scary Previews" and 234; "SCTV Pledge Week" and 121; "3-D Firing Line" and 223; "3-D House of Beef" and 149; "Tip O'Neill's 3-D House of Representatives" and 210; "Whispers of the Wolf" and 57, 210
Cowper, Donald 20, 22, 31, 42
Crawford, Joan 144–145, 224
"Crazy Crafts with Molly Earl" (sketch) 75, 85, 93
"Crazy Hy's" (commercial parody) 108
Crenshaw, Marshall 114
"Cretin's Island" (sketch) 61
Cries and Whispers 57
"Critic's Corner" (sketch) 116, 187
Crock, Angus (character) 75, 81, 94–96, 158
Cronkite, Walter 91; "Buzz Aldrin's Mercury III Players" and 177; as "Dialing for Dollars" host 43, 76, 92; Edith Prickley and 98; "Point/Counterpoint" and 74; "SCTV News" and 95; "SCTV Special Report: The Space Shuttle" and 114; "Walter Cronkite's Brain" and 139
Crosby, Bing 6, 64, 79, 232
Cross, Christopher 119
"Crosswords" (sketch) 18
Crouch, Andrae 206–207
"Cruisin' Gourmet" (sketch) 91, 147

Cruising 91
Cujo 234
Currie, Dougall (character) 190, 248
The Czech Brothers (*SNL* characters) 159–160

"Da Doo Doo Da Da" 108
Dali, Salvador 184
Dallas 130
"Dallas Cowgirls Salute Copland" (sketch) 219
"Dan Money" (sketch) 40
Dance Fever 201
"Dance of the Goblins" 144
"Danny Eubanks" (sketch) 38, 77
"Dante's Inferno" (sketch) 33
"The Date Debate" (sketch) 228, 233
"The Dating Game" (parody) 95
Davis, Bette 224
Davis, Sammy, Jr. 17, 164
The Day the Clown Cried 99
"The Days of the Week" (sketch) 174, 178, 213; comparison to "Six Gun Justice" and 236–237, 248, 250; conclusion of 224–225; premiere of 171–172; second cycle premiere of 209; "Sweeps Week" episode and 220; wedding of Clay Collins and Sue Ellen and 185, 258
"Death Motel" (sketch) 77, 80, 142
"The Death of Emmett Till" 239
"Death Takes No Holiday" (sketch) 62
Deathtrap 234
DeCordova, Fred 78, 95
The Deer Hunter 199
Deliverance 187
Demme, Jonathan 110
Denver, John 93
De Sica, Vittorio 182
DeWitt, Joyce 159
"Dialing for Dollars" (sketch) 21, 23, 34, 37, 43, 63, 76, 92, 242
Diamond, Neil 130–131
"The Dick Cavett Show" (parody) 72, 80, 98–99
Dickens, Charles 244
Dickinson, Angie 61
"Did It in a Minute" 177
Diff'rent Strokes 136
Diller, Phyllis 237
"DiMaggio's on the Wharf" (sketch) 185–186
"Dining with LaRue" (sketch) 17, 23, 25, 26, 69, 70
Dirty Harry 41

Dithers, Sid (character) 19, 58, 131, 244
Divilbis, Yolanda (character) 205. 244
Divine 150, 202
The Divine Comedy 33
Divorce, Italian Style 182
"Do-It-Yourself Advertising" (sketch) 86–87
"Do-It-Yourself Dentistry" (sketch) 25
"Dr. Benson: The Credit Psychiatrist" (commercial parody) 34
Dr. Braino (character) 125
"The Dr. Braino Hour" (sketch) 67, 69
"Dr. Chet Vet: The Dead Pet Remover" (commercial parody) 66
Dr. Jekyll and Mr. Hyde 234
Dr. John 107, 211
Dr. Strangelove 129
Dr. Tongue (character) 11, 57, 210; absence from *SCTV Channel* and 234; absence from third season and 77, 81, 82, 99; "Dr. Tongue and His Animal Friends" and 30; "Dr. Tongue's Evil House of Pancakes" and 153; "Dr. Tongue's Evil House of Wax" and 35; "Dr. Tongue's 3-D House of Slave Chicks" and 200–201; "Dr. Tongue's 3-D House of Stewardesses" and 117–118; "The Making of 3-D Stake from the Heart" and 169–170; "The Russian Show" and 129; "Screen Acting" and 142; "SCTV Pledge Week" and 121; "SCTV Staff Christmas Party" and 150–151; "3-D Firing Line" and 223; "3-D House of Beef" and 149; "The Towering Inferno" episode and 203–204
"Dr. Tongue's Evil House of Pancakes" (sketch) 153
"Dr. Tongue's Evil House of Wax" (sketch) 35
"Dr. Tongue's 3-D House of Slave Chicks" (sketch) 200–201
"Dr. Tongue's 3-D House of Stewardesses" (sketch) 30, 35, 117–118, 200, 223
"Dr. X" (sketch) 169, 171, 183
The Doctors 49
Dolman, Bob 123
Dolman, Nancy 249
Donahue, Phil 78, 175, 222
Donny and Marie 108
Donohue, Brenda 19
"Don't Look Back in Anger" (*SNL* short film) 205
"The Doom Song" 133
"Doorway to Hell" (episode) 104, 143, 145–146

"Doublethink" (sketch) 89
Douglas, Kirk 56, 87
Doumanian, Jean 74
"Downtown" 118
Doyle-Murray, Brian 38
"Dream Interpretation" (sketch) 40
Dreyfuss, Richard 152
"The Driftwood Inn" (commercial parody) 208, 231
Dummar, Melvin 110
"The Dusty Towne Sexy Holiday Special" (sketch) 150, 231
Duvall, Robert 147
Dylan, Bob 239

Earthquake 89
Eastwood, Clint 41
Eastwood, Jayne 188–189
Easy Rider 139
Ebert, Roger 87
Ebony 160
The Ed Sullivan Show 164, 194
"Edith Prickley Live from the Melonville Baths" (sketch) 225, 244
Edmunds, Dave 180
Edwards, Geoff 55
"Eee-O-11" 164
8 1/2 182
Ekberg, Anita 79
"Election Central" (sketch) 50–51, 56, 196
The Elephant Man (character) 121
"The Elephant's Graveyard" 155
Eliot, T.S. 177
"Elvira Mad Again Part II" (sketch) 35
Embry, Joan 135
Emergency! 140
"Emergency Caterers" (sketch) 140–141
"Emergency Orderly and Court Clerk" (sketch) 29, 47
"English for Beginners" (sketch) 15, 105, 106, 110
The Enigma of Bobby Bittman 53, 99
"Enough About Me" (sketch) 42, 58
Entertainment Tonight 231
Entertainment Weekly 7
"Escape (The Pi_a Colada Song)" 153
E.T. 166
"Evelyn Wolf School of Speed Eating" (sketch) 66
"An Evening with Col. Sanders" (sketch) 26, 37
"Everybody's Talkin'" 223
Evita 108
"Exercise Is Easy" (sketch) 98

The Exorcist 140
"The Exorcist of Oz" (sketch) 18
"The Expert" (commercial parody) 120
"Extreme Close-Up" (sketch) 23

Face-Off 133–134
Faerie Tale Theatre 248
Fail-Safe 129
Fairchild, Morgan 159, 175
Falling from Grace 194
Falwell, Reverend Jerry 115–117
"Fame" 128
"Family Crisis" (sketch) 68
Fanny Hill 118
Fantasy Island 155, 167
"Fantasy Island" (parody) 6, 12, 61, 64–66, 75, 76, 126, 127, 245
"Farm Film Celebrity Blow-Up" (sketch) 63, 138, 153, 201, 209, 216
"Farm Film Report" (sketch) 52, 55, 121, 153, 155, 193, 209
"Farm Report" (sketch) 27
Farr, Jamie 219
Father Murphy 219
Father of the Bride 110
"Feedback" (sketch) 23–24
"The Fella Who Couldn't Wait for Christmas" (sketch) 208, 216
Fellini, Federico 182
Fender, Freddy 63
Ferrer, José 43
Ferrigno, Lou 83, 106
Field, Sally 76
Fife, Barney 118
"15 Minutes" (sketch) 21
"The 59th Street Bridge Song (Feelin' Groovy)" 214
"Fighting Air Dogs Over the Pacific" (sketch) 61
Filler, Reverend Gene (character) 199
Finkel, Mort (character) 25
"Finnian's Rainbow Meats" (commercial parody) 186
"Fireside Chat" (sketch) 58, 68
"The First Noel" 206
"Fish 'n Chips" (sketch) 99
"Fish Police" (sketch) 58–59
Fisher, Gil (character) 122, 133, 168, 173–174, 183, 223, 224
"The Fishin' Musician" (sketch) 122, 133, 168, 173–174, 183, 224
"A Fistful of Ugly" (sketch) 24
Fistinyerface, Paul (character) 37, 55, 213
Fitzgerald, Ella 88, 94

5 Neat Guys (characters) 108, 150, 167, 175
Flaherty, Paul 12, 72, 223, 228, 239, 246, 251
"The Flaming Turkey" (sketch) 70
Flashdance 229, 247
"Flashing Eyes" (sketch) 58, 83
Floyd the Barber 118, 146
Fodor, Eugene 143–145
"Folsom Prison Blues" 178
Fonda, Henry 129
Fonda, Jane 76, 179
Fonda, Peter 139
Four for Texas 204
"4th Degree" (sketch) 58, 83
"The Fracases" (sketch) 109–110
Franklin [Francis], Arlene 56, 248
Franklin, Bonnie 219
Franklin, Connie (character) 27
Freaks & Geeks 8
"The Fred Winston Show" (sketch) 238
The French Connection 140
"Frère Jacques" 214
Friday Night Videos 157
Fridays 7, 133
Friedan, Betty 169
Friends 166
"Friends of American Crooners and the Stop Julio Iglesias Committee" (PSA parody) 240
"From Small Things (Big Things One Day Come)" 180
"From Steve with Love" (sketch) 213
Front Page Challenge 190, 243
Frum, Barbara 191
"Funny Stuff" (sketch) 99

"Galaxy 66" (sketch) 32–33
Galbraith, John Kenneth 80
Gandhi, Indira 37, 108, 240
"Gangway for Miracles" (sketch) 140
Garfield, James 144–145
Garfunkel, Art 245
Garner, James 120
"Garth and Gord and Fiona and Alice" (sketch) 28, 188–189
"Gaslight" (parody) 60, 81
Gassman, Vittorio 182
Gayle, Crystal 210–211
"Gene Shalit's Critics Special" (sketch) 238
Gerard, Gil 237
Geeson, Judy 154
Geldof, Bob 154–155
"The Gerry Todd Show" (sketch) 108, 118–119, 134

"Get a Job" 110
Giacomelli, Marc 139
Gielgud, Sir John 18
Gifford, Frank 191
Gilligan's Island 61
"Gimme Jackie" (sketch) 228, 230
Gimme Shelter 228, 230
"The Girls of Vienna" (sketch) 13–14
"Give 'em Hell, Bess" (sketch) 154
Gleason, Jackie 41
Glick, Jiminy (character) 45, 197
"God Save the Queen" 223
Godard, Jean-Luc 24
Goddard, Bill 218
The Godfather 1, 23, 146–149, 170
"The Godfather" (episode) 7, 104, 146–149, 150, 194, 202, 214
The Godfather Part II 149
Goin' Down the Road 188–189
Going My Way 232
Goldfarb, Irv (character) 170–171
The Gong Show 22
"Good King Wenceslas" 92, 152
Good Will Hunting 199
"Good-Bye America" (sketch) 24, 31
The Goodbye Girl 152
Gordetsky, Eddy 176
Gordica, Terry 211
Gordon, Robert 114
Gordon, Ruth 233
"Gordon Lightfoot Sings Every Song Ever Written" (commercial parody) 92
Gorman, Norman (character) 78, 83, 150, 169
Gorme, Eydie 48
"Got a Minute?" (sketch) 249
Goulet, Robert 55
Goy, Luba 191
The Graduate 185, 223, 258
"Graft recipes" (commercial parody) 68
Graham, Virginia 139
Grant, Cary 80
"The Grapes of Mud" (sketch) 2, 28, 39
The Grapes of Wrath 39, 187
The Grateful Dead 67
"Grease" (commercial parody) 52
"The Great Debate" (sketch) 50
Great White North (album) 160
"Great White North" (sketch) 12, 74, 129, 157; *The Best of SCTV* and 255; final *SCTV* appearance of 183; first wraparound and 126–128; "How to Stuff a Mouse in a Beer Bottle" and 134; initial season of 84, 85, 86, 88, 90; NBC

episodes and 106, 108, 125, 138, 141, 158–159, 168; premiere of 73; "SCTV Staff Christmas Party" and 152
"Great White North Palace" (episode) 159–162, 168, 173, 178
The Greatest Story Ever Told 237
Green, Moe (character) 16, 19, 55; as accountant/first episode of 13; as "Dialing for Dollars" host 21, 28, 37, 42, 63, 76; Edith Prickley replaces and 72; "Extreme Close-Up" and 23; Guy Caballero and 24; kidnapping and 47, 89, 173; as "$129,000 Question" host 34; as SCTV station manager 40, 44
Greene, Lorne 219
Greene, Mean Joe 179–180
Greer, Dr. Hammond (character) 25
Griffin, Merv 83, 166–167
Grimley, Ed (character) 35; "The Fella Who Couldn't Wait for Christmas" and 207–208, 231; final episode and 251; "Grimley's Celebrity Fairie Tayles" and 249; "The Nutty Lab Assistant" and 194; "Oliver Grimley" and 244; *Stalag 17* episode and 238–239; "Sunrise Semester" and 198; "Sweeps Week" episode and 218; "The True Story of Billy the Kid" and 216; "What Ever Happened to Baby Ed?" and 224
"Grimley's Celebrity Fairie Tayles" (sketch) 249
"Grizzly Abrams" (sketch) 85
The Groove Tube 118
Guest, Christopher 129, 200, 242
Gumbel, Phyllis (character) 29
Gusstofferson, Gus (character) 1, 15, 113–114, 136, 207, 218
"Guy Friday" (sketch) 74, 78, 83

Haalmayer, Juul 123, 136, 207
Hackett, Buddy 213, 231
"Half Wits" (sketch) 54, 134, 208–209, 236, 246
Hall and Oates 176–177
Halsey, Janet (character) 209
Hamilton, Margaret 75
Hamlet 165
Hampshire, Keith (character) 29
"Happy Birthday to You" 92
Happy Days 51, 58
The Happy Hooker Goes to Hollywood 91
The Happy Hooker Goes to Washington 44
"Happy Hour" (sketch) 237, 238, 240, 241–242, 248

Happy Love 135
"The Happy Wanderers" (sketch) 173, 175
"The Happy Wanderers Salute Composer John Williams" (sketch) 195, 258
"The Happy Wanderers Salute New Wave Music" (sketch) 228–229
The Harlem Globetrotters on Gilligan's Island 103
"Harlett Romances" (commercial parody) 49
Harrington, Zach (character) 174
Harris, Richard 2, 41, 52, 97, 112, 167
Harry, Deborah 211
"Harry Filth" (sketch) 41, 128
"Harry's Sex Shop" (sketch) 116
Hartley, Mariette 120
"Harvey" (parody) 243
"Hats of the West" (sketch) 60
"Hawaii Five-Ho" (sketch) 87–88
Hayden, Sterling 1
"Headline Challenge" (sketch) 190–191, 243, 248
Heatherton, Joey 44
Heatherton, Lola (character) 105, 215; Bob and Doug McKenzie and 160–161; final episode and 251; "Lola! Bouncing Back to You" episode and 122–125, 151, 214; "Lola Heatherton in Concert" and 44; "The Love Spirit" and 207; "On the Waterfront Again" and 65; "The People's Global Golden Choice Awards" and 167; "The Sammy Maudlin Show" and 18, 99, 107, 135, 190; "SCTV Pledge Week" and 121; "SCTV Staff Christmas Party" and 151; "SCTV 30th Anniversary Show" and 56–57; "Way to Go, Woman!" and 130
Hedges, Vic (character) 107, 127, 196, 213, 241
Hefner, Hugh 31
"Hefty" (sketch) 29
Height, Dr. Cheryll (character) 24
"Hello Metric, Au Revoir Avoirdupois" (sketch) 191
Helm, Levon 105–106, 158
Hemingway, Mariel 169
Hemphill, John 178, 243; first appearance and 163; as Happy Marsden 237–238, 240, 248; "Headline Challenge" and 191; *SCTV Channel* and 228, 236, 245, 246, 249
"Henry" (sketch) 87
Hepburn, Katharine 2, 41
"Here Comes Santa Claus" 151–152
Heston, Charlton 28, 46, 89, 203

"The Heys of Our Lives" (sketch) 62
"High-Q" (sketch) 54, 106, 134
"High School Confidential" 141
Hill, Benny 130, 154
Hill Street Blues 221
"Him" 153
"Hinterland Who's Who" (parody) 189, 190, 191
"Hints for Homemakers" (sketch) 16
Hirsch, Judd 152
Hirschman, Crazy Legs (character) 193
Hitchcock, Alfred 60
Hitler, Adolf 26, 38
Ho, Don 87–88
Hoffman, Dustin 185, 209, 223
Holbrook, Hal 37, 193
"Hold On" 127
Holden, William 203
"Hollywood Dirt Tonight" (sketch) 201, 231
"Hollywood Salutes Its Extras" (sketch) 87
Holmes, Rupert 153
"Homelier You" (sketch) 21–22
The Honeymooners 218
Hope, Bob: "Bob Hope Desert Classic" and 45–46; "Fantasy Island" and 6, 64; "The People's Global Golden Choice Awards" and 168; "Pet Peeves of the Stars" and 175; "Play It Again, Bob" and 79–80; "The Sammy Maudlin Show" and 84; "Stars in One" and 237; "Taxi Driver" and 90
Hopkins, Linda 197
Hopper, Dennis 139
"A Horse Called Richard Harris" (bumper) 111
Hour of the Wolf 57
House Calls 130
"The House of Cats" (sketch) 46, 87
Houseman, John 199
"How Nosy the Short-Haired Terrier Dog Got His Name" (sketch) 186
"How the Middle East Was Won" (sketch) 41, 52, 74
Howard, Curly 3, 28, 110, 200
"Hugh Betcha's Short Story Playhouse" (sketch) 119–120
Hughes, Howard 110
"Human Sexual Response" (sketch) 197
Humoresque 143–145
Hurok, Billy Sol (character) 121, 151; absence from first "Farm Report" sketch and 27; blowing up of celebrities and 138, 154, 201, 209, 216, 225; first appearance and 52; "Rock Concert" and 63

Hutton, Timothy 120, 168

"I Cry Each Day I Die" (sketch) 36
"I Hate the Bloody Queen" 223
"I Owe Peking Two Thousand Dollars" (sketch) 84
I Love Lucy 79
"I Loves You, Porgy" 219
"I Was a Teenage Communist" (sketch) 179–180
I Was a Teenage Werewolf 180
"I Will Survive" 128
"I Wish I Were in Love Again" 159
"I Write the Songs" 194
"Identical Bellhops" (sketch) 183
"Identical Cheese Hostesses" (sketch) 183
"Identical OPEC Oil Ministers" (sketch) 183
"If You Could Read My Mind" 92
Iglesias, Julio 243
"Iko Iko" 107
"I'm Taking My Own Head, Screwing It On Right, and No Guy's Gonna Tell Me That It Ain't" (episode) 132–133
In Living Color 230
In Search Of... 121
"The Incredible Bulk" (sketch) 45
The Incredible Hulk 83, 106
Indecent Exposure 193
"Indira" (sketch) 37, 108, 162
Ingram, James 149
Insana, Tino 251
"International House of Panties" (commercial parody) 184
Invasion of the Body Snatchers 136–137
"The Irv Goldfarb Show" (sketch) 169, 170–171, 208
"The Irwin Allen Show" (sketch) 88–89
Ishimuni, Tim (character) 20, 109, 157, 180
"Island in the Sun" 190
It Conquered the World 136
Italian Cinema: From Neorealism to the Present 182
"It's a Wonderful Film" (sketch) 227, 231–233, 235
It's a Wonderful Life 232
"It's the Hard-Knock Life" 175
I've Got a Secret 241

"Jacques Costeau's Undersea World" (sketch) 54
Jaffe, Lou (character) 25, 29, 52, 61, 242
Jagger, Mick 230
"James Whitmore Tonight" (sketch) 37

"Jane Eyrehead" (sketch) 200, 213
Jarreau, Al 131
Jaws 195
"Jaws 23" (sketch) 55
"The Jazz Singer" (parody) 130–131
Jenny Jones 176
The Jerk 216
The Jerry Springer Show 176
Joel, Billy 169
John, Elton 152
"The Johnny LaRue Show" (sketch) 13–14, 128
Johnny Puleo and the Harmonica Gang 164
Johns, Brian (character) 76, 126–127, 183–184
"The Joint Is Jumping" 215
"The Journal" (parody) 191
Jules et Jim 24
"Jumping for Dollars" (sketch) 219
"Just for Fun" (sketch) 169, 240
"Just Once" 149
Juul Haalmayer Dancers 44, 123–124, 129, 150, 167, 207

Kael, Pauline 24, 223
Kanter, Stan (character) 169, 240
Kaplan, Gabe 27, 179
Karlov, Rabbi (character) 75, 95
Kaufman, Andy 215
Kazan, Elia 56
Keaton, Diane 79
Kelley, DeForest 75, 135–136
Kenter, Peter 190, 191, 197
Khaddafi, Muammar 191
"Kids Can Play on the Wagon" (PSA parody) 31
The Kids in the Hall 7
The King of Comedy 184
Kinsey, Dr. Cheryl (character) 18–19, 24, 56, 83, 156
Kirsch, Ernest (character) 45, 49, 55
Kirschner, Don 71
Kissinger, Henry 115, 229
Kitman, Marvin 107
"Klägg" (sketch) 38, 77
Klein, Calvin 229
Klein, Robert 5
Klugman, Jack 94, 167, 237
Koppel, Ted 191
Kosinski, Jerzy 204
Kraft, Christopher 177
Kramer vs. Kramer 76
"Krishna Sings Manilow" (commercial parody) 197–198, 244

Kristofferson, Kris 210
K-Tel, Harvey (character) 92, 169; comparisons to other pitchmen and 34, 61, 140, 216; first appearance and 24–25; "Harvey K-Tel's Fast-Talking Playhouse" and 74; "Speaking of Talk with Lou Jaffe" and 52; "Stairways to Heaven" and 175
Kubrick, Stanley 167
"Kwallada" (commercial parody) 108

Lafleur, Guy 20
Lake, Don 200
Lake, Veronica 84
Lansky, Max (character) 235, 250
LaRue, Johnny (character) 6, 11, 44, 105, 115, 123, 184, 210, 215; "All-Girl Friday Night Pajama Party" and 156; Bob and Doug McKenzie and 127, 160–161; Christmas episodes and 151, 206–207, 231; as city council candidate 50–51, 53, 196; as commercial pitchman 52, 54, 66; "Cooking with LaRue" and 18, 207; "Dining with LaRue" and 1, 17, 23, 26, 69, 70; "Family Crisis" and 68; final appearance and 219; first episode and 13–14; "A Fistful of Ugly" and 24; "Godfather" episode and 146; "Good-Bye America" and 31; "LaRue by Night" and 49; "Meet the Pawnbroker" and 70; "Mr. Science" and 20, 57, 112; "Polynesiantown" and 107–108, 112, 113, 144; "SCTV Solid Gold Telethon" and 48; "Street Beef" wraparounds and 113–114, 185–186
"LaRue by Night" (sketch) 49, 113
"LaRue Towers" (commercial parody) 54
"Lasermatic" (commercial parody) 1, 14
The Last of the Mohicans 61
The Last Party 186
The Last Polka 38, 173
"Last Train to Clarksville" 173
Late Night with David Letterman 134, 147, 247
Laugh-In 110
Laverne & Shirley 27
Lavin, Linda 219
Lawford, Peter 164, 204
Lawrence, Steve 48
Lean, David 244
Lear, Norman 116
Leave It to Beaver 91, 212
"Leave It to Beaver: 25th Anniversary Party" (sketch) 9, 30, 51

Index

Led Zeppelin 175, 258
"Lee A. Iococca's Rock Concert" (sketch) 71–72, 97, 101, 112
Lemmon, Jack 82
Lennon, John 185
Leone, Sergio 24
Lester, Buddy 164
"Let's Find Jerzy" (sketch) 204
Let's Make a Deal 22
Letterman, David 27, 189, 240
"The Leutonian Hour" (sketch) 16, 173
Leutonian Liberation Front 47, 89
Lewis, Jerry 48, 99, 184, 194, 209–210, 239
Liberace 67, 83, 152, 194, 231
"Liberace's Musical Salute to the Holidays" (sketch) 152
Liddy, G. Gordon 15, 108, 137–138
The Life and Times of Grizzly Adams 85
Lightfoot, Gordon 92
"The Lighting of the Melonville Christmas Tree" (sketch) 208
Linahan, Brock (character): Bob Hope and 237; "goes home" sketch and 225; Linda Hopkins and 197–198; "Oh! That Rusty!" and 212; Señor Wences's hand and 236; *Stalag 17* episode and 238; Steve Roman and 210
"The Lincoln-Douglas Debates" (parody) 61
Linehan, Brian 197
"The Little Skunk's Hole" 178
"Logos Galore" (commercial parody) 99
"Lola Heatherton in Concert" (sketch) 44
"The Lone Ranger Show" (sketch) 78, 88
The Loneliness of the Long Distance Runner 109
"The Long Hard War" (sketches) 220
"Longjeans G-11" (commercial parody) 24
Look Back in Anger 109
Loren, Sophia 66, 241
Losey, Joseph 182
The Love Boat 45, 219
"Love Craft" (sketch) 45
"Love Slaves of the Southwest" (sketch) 179, 181
"The Love Spirit" (sketch) 207
"Lowell Thompson Remembers" (sketch) 38
Lucas, George 166–167, 170
Lulu 154
Lust for Life 43
"Lust for Paint" (sketch) 2, 42–43
Lynn, Vera 129

"MacArthur Park" 98
"Macho Man" 63
Mackeral, Cassie (character) 97
MacLaine, Shirley 130
Macleans 5, 104
MacLeod, Gavin 219, 248
"Madame Blitzman" (sketch) 3, 33–34
Madame Curie 3, 33–34
"Magnum P.E.I." (sketch) 191, 198
Maharishi Mahesh Yogi 139
Mailer, Norman 186
"The Making of 3-D Stake from the Heart" (sketch) 142, 169–170
"The Making of 2009" (sketch) 245
"The Man Who Would Be King of the Popes" (sketch) 1, 41, 52, 75
Mandel, Howie 229
"Mandy" 194
Mane, John Norman (character) 210–211
Mangione, Chuck 153
Manilow, Barry 194
Marchand, Colette 43
Marks, Phillip (character) 248
Marley, John 147–148
"Marriage Counsellor" (sketch) 54
Married . . . with Children 117
Marsden, Happy (character) 237, 238, 240, 241–242, 248, 250
Martin, Dean 164
Martin, Remy (character) 231
Martin, Steve 73, 159
"Martin Scorsese's Jerry Lewis Live on the Champs Élysées" (sketch) 184
The Marx Brothers 245
M*A*S*H 219, 249
Mason, Marsha 92
"Master Ralph Roister Doister" (sketch) 49
"Master Sergeant Chef" (sketch) 47
Mastroianni, Marcello 182
"Match Unto My Feet" (sketch) 19
Matlock, May (character) 174, 209, 224
Matthau, Walter 82
Maudlin, Sammy (character) 6, 11, 105; anniversary show and 189–190, 192; with Betty Thomas 221; Bobby and Skip Bittman 143–144; with Bobby Bittman and Sir Kenneth Clark 36–37; with Christmas episode and 151–152; "drug abuse" sketch and 107; first appearance and 17; with Luciano Pavarotti and Sandler and Young 214; "Maudlin o' the Night" and 229; "Maudlin's Eleven" and 164–165; "On the Waterfront Again" and

65–66; "SCTV Solid Gold Telethon" and 48; "Zontar" episode and 135
"Maudlin o' the Night" (sketch) 229
"Maudlin's Eleven" (sketch) 163–165
Maui, Big Momma (character) 211
Maury 176
McAndrew, John 197, 204
McArdle, Andrea 175
McBob, Big Jim (character) 52, 121, 151; first "Farm Report" sketch and 27; blowing up of celebrities and 138, 154, 201, 209, 216, 225; "Rock Concert" and 63
McCarthy, Senator Joseph 56
McCartney, Linda 131
McCartney, Paul 185, 221
McClintick, David 193
McDonald, Michael 118
McElroy, Mel (character) 230, 236, 241
McGrath, Doug 188
McKay, Billy (character) 171–172
McKay, Violet (character) 171–172, 209, 224
McKean, Michael 242
McKenzie, Bob and Doug (characters) 12, 123, 215; Christmas episode and 151–152; comparison to Dr. Tongue and Bruno and 142; comparison to "Today Is Moscow" and 129; comparison to Yosh and Stan Shmenge and 173; final appearance of 183; first appearance of 73; first wraparound and 126–128; "Great White North" initial season and 84, 85, 86, 88, 90, 94, 96, 97; "Great White North" on NBC episodes and 106, 125, 138, 141, 168, 178; "Great White North Palace" and 159–161, 163; "How to Stuff a Mouse in a Beer Bottle" and 134; popularity of, 46, 104, 156, 158–159; *Strange Brew* and 7, 134, 161, 173
McMahon, Ed 78, 189
McNichol, Jimmy 85
McQueen, Steve 203
"Me and You and Yoga and Me" (sketch) 54
"Mean Joe Greene Playhouse" (sketch) 179–180
"A Medical Minute" (sketch) 249
Meehan, Margaret (character) 54, 134
"Meet the Pawnbroker" (character) 70
Meir, Golda 46
Melba the Disco Queen (character) 75
"Melba's Disco Jeans" (sketch) 75
"Melonville Calendar" (sketch) 205, 243–244, 247, 249
"A Melonville Moment" (sketch) 248

"Mel's Rock Pile" (sketch): premiere and 83; psychedelic music sketch and 243; punk music sketch and 223–224; Richard Harris/Slirrup brothers sketch and 97–98, 101, 111–112, 147, 167; "SCTV Boogie" and 36; "20th anniversary" sketch and 120
"Melvin and Howards" (sketch) 110
"The Memoirs of Anton Chekhov" (sketch) 2, 20
"Men on Women" (sketch) 40, 88
"Mental Illness" (PSA parody) 70
Meredith, Don 191
The Merv Griffin Show 118
"The Merv Griffin Show" (parody) 83, 106, 139
"The Merv Griffith Show" (sketch) 118, 130, 139
"The Merv Griffin Show: The Special Edition" (sketch) 166–167
Metal Priestess 133
Michaels, Lorne 6, 73, 103
"Mick Mason: Police Photographer" (sketch) 36, 38
The Mickey Mouse Club 218
Midler, Bette 225
"Midnight Cowboy II" (sketch) 35, 223, 234
Midnight Express 93
"Midnight Express Special" (sketch) 93, 97
The Midnight Special 71, 93, 103, 156
"Midnight Video Special" (sketch) 156–157
A Mighty Wind 242
"Milk of Amnesia" (commercial parody) 2, 34
"The Millionaire" (parody) 51, 110
The Mindbenders 155
Minnelli, Lorna 17, 18, 167, 189–190, 192, 221
Minyk, Linsk (character) 173, 175
The Miracle Worker 140
"The Mirthmakers" (sketch) 53
"Miss Leutonia Pageant" (sketch) 221–222
Mr. Blackwell 174
"Mr. Earl Doll" (sketch) 86
"Mr. Know-It-All" (sketch) 183
Mr. Mambo (character) 205
Mister Rogers's Neighborhood 41, 179
Mr. Sardonicus 62
"Mr. Science" (sketch) 20, 31, 57, 112
Mr. Show 7
Mr. Wizard 20
Modern Problems 239
Modern Romance 137

Modesty Blaise 182
"Mohicans Galore" (sketch) 61
Mojo (character) 172
Mommie Dearest 175
Monck, Chip 81
"Monday Night Curling" (sketch) 191
"Money Talks" (sketch) 76, 126, 183–184
Monk, Chick (character) 81, 92
The Monkees 173
Monroe, Tom (character) 108, 118
"Monster Chiller Horror Theatre" (sketch) 11, 30, 41, 250; "Blood-Sucking Monkeys from West Mifflin, Pennsylvania" and 156–158; "Death Motel" and 77; "The Dick Cavett Show" and 99; "Dr. Tongue's Evil House of Pancakes" and 153; "Dr. Tongue's Evil House of Wax" and 35; "Dr. Tongue's 3-D House of Slave Chicks" and 200–201; "Dr. Tongue's 3-D House of Stewardesses" and 117–118; *Four for Texas* and 204; "Halloween Always Falls on Friday the 13th" and 246; "The House of Cats" and 46; "Madame Blitzman" and 3, 33–34; "The Making of 3-D Stake from the Heart" and 170; *Modern Problems* and 239; *The Odd Couple* and 82, 204; "3-D Firing Line" and 223; "3-D House of Beef" and 149; "Tip O'Neill's 3-D House of Representatives" and 210; "Whispers of the Wolf" and 57, 210
Montalban, Ricardo 64, 75, 134, 154–155
Monterey International Pop Music Festival 81
Monty Python 1, 49, 79, 154, 233
Moore, Mary Tyler 120
Moore, Michael 138
The Moral Majority 115, 117
"Moral Majority" (episode) 6–7, 104, 114–119, 168
Mork and Mindy 199
"Morning Facial with Princess Carlotta" (sketch) 42
Morris, William (character) 37
Mother Teresa 64, 107, 130
Moulin Rouge 43
"Mouse House" (sketch) 184
Mouskouri, Nana 146
"Mrs. Falbo's Tiny Town" (sketch) 15, 118, 124, 137–138, 177–178, 194
"Mrs. Prickley's Jelly" (commercial parody) 32
"Mrs. Robinson" 185, 223, 258
Murder in the Cathedral 177

"Murder Is Bad for Your Health" (sketch) 60, 81
Murder on the Orient Express 38, 62
Murray, Anne 93
Murray, Bill 185–186, 192
"Murray's File" (sketch) 217, 242, 248
Musburger, Brent 148
"My Factory, My Self" (sketch) 76
"My Fair Lady" (parody) 15, 72
"My Girl" 164
"My Life One More Time" (sketch) 72
"Myra: Story of a Small Town Gypsy" (sketch) 247
Mystery Girl 120

"The Nana Mouskouri Story" (sketch) 146
"Nasex Nasal Deodorant" (commercial parody) 95, 216
"Natalie Ringneck" (sketch) 69
National Lampoon's Animal House 232, 235
"National Midnight Star" (sketch) 115, 166, 201, 231
"Naughty Chambermaids" (sketch) 45
Needle, Bill (character) 181, 202, 210, 235; "All-Girl Friday Night Pajama Party" and 156; "Big Brother" episode and 90; "Bill Needle's Mailbag" and 86; early versions of 25, 64; "Lola! Bouncing Back to You" episode and 122, 125; "Maudlin's Eleven" and 164; "Moral Majority" episode and 116–117; "The People's Global Golden Choice Awards" and 168; "SCTV Staff Christmas Party" and 151; "Shoot for the Stars" and 153; "Stand Up and Be Counted" and 174; "Starting Out" and 95; "Theatre Beat" and 132–133; "TV Talk" and 187
"The Needle and the Damage Done" 98
"Neil Jung: Psychiatrist" (sketch) 100
"Neil Simon's Nutcracker Suite" (sketch) 150–152
"Never in a Million Years" 154
"New York Rhapsody" (sketch) 28, 144–145
Newman, Paul 202
Newman, Randy 63
Newsday 107
The NFL Today 148
Night Flight 157
Night Gallery 85, 119–120
Night of 100 Stars 218–219
"Night of the Primetime Stars" (sketch) 218–219
"Night School High-Q" (sketch) 134

Night Tracks 157
Nightline 162
"Nightline Melonville" (sketch) 97, 162, 174, 250
Nilsson, Harry 223
Nimoy, Leonard 136
1984 89–90
Nixon, Richard 46
"The Nobel" (sketch) 124–125, 133, 194, 210
Norma Rae 76
"Northern Ireland Perspective '77" (sketch) 25
Nostradamus 183
"Nothin' But a Fool" 135
Nucleo, Johnny (character) 203–204
Nutley, Trish (character) 17–18, 21
"The Nutty Lab Assistant" (sketch) 194, 208
The Nutty Professor 194

O'Brien, Conan 7, 258
Ocean's Eleven 164–165
The Odd Couple 82, 204
Of Human Bondage 251
"Off and Running" 155
"Oh, Pretty Woman" 120
"Oh! That Rusty" (sketch) 212, 241
"Oil of Oil" (commercial parody) 66, 241
"Oliver Grimley" (sketch) 28, 228, 244
Oliver Twist 244
Olivier, Sir Laurence 80, 130–131
Olsen, Merlin 219
The Omen 57
"On the Waterfront Again" (sketch) 6, 12, 65–66
"Once in a Lifetime" 157
One Day at a Time 219
One from the Heart 170
"129,000 Question" (sketch) 34
"One Is Enough" (sketch) 51
"One on the Town" (sketch) 97, 105–106, 156, 158, 204
O'Neill, Tip 174, 210
"Only a Hobo" 239
"Only for Women" (sketch) 59
Only When I Laugh 152
Orbach, Lawrence (character) 209, 243
Orbison, Roy 120
Ordinary People 120, 121
Orlando, Tony 100, 112
Orwell, George 89–90
The Oscar 9, 124–125, 133, 161, 165, 194, 210
O'Toole, Peter 1–2, 41, 52

"Our Love Is on the Fault Line" 211
"Out-Patient" (sketch) 17
"Over the Rainbow" 18, 124

Pacino, Al 1, 23, 91, 147
Palmer, Charles 232
Parents Television Council 117
Paris Match 160
"Passport to Adventure" (sketch) 38, 67
Password 236
Patinkin, Sheldon 6, 8, 28, 34
The Patty Duke Show 183
"Paul's Workshop" (sketch) 37
Pavarotti, Luciano 175, 214; as "Johnny Pavarotti," 147
Peck, Al (character) 204, 239
Peck, Gregory 14, 85, 94, 170–171
Pennies from Heaven 216
"People and Things" (sketch) 53, 215–216
People for the American Way 116
People Magazine 166
"The People's Court" (parody) 201–202
"The People's Global Golden Choice Awards" (episode) 166, 167–168
"Pepi Longsocks" (sketch) 142–143, 235
Perkins, Carl 168, 173–174
Perlman, Itzhak 144
"Perry Como: Still Alive" (sketch) 128–129, 174
"Pet Peeves of the Stars" (sketch) 175
"Peter Pan" (parody) 202, 205
Peters, Bernadette 216
"Peter's Donuts" (*Great White North* album track) 96
Petersen, Wolfgang 235
Petri, Elio 182
"Petty Claims Court" (sketch) 47
"Philosophers at Work" (sketch) 248
"Philosophy Street" (sketch) 23
"Phil's Nails" (sketch) 61–62, 212
Pickens, Slim 129
"Pipeline" (sketch) 67
Pippi Longstockings 142
The Pittsburgh Midget (character) 223, 239, 246
"Plainclothes Mountie" (character) 16
The Plastics 157
"Play It Again, Bob" (sketch) 12, 79–80, 101, 106
Play It Again, Sam 79–80
"Pledge Week" (episode) 104, 119–121, 168
"The Point" (commercial parody) 35
"Point/Counterpoint" (sketch) 74
Poirot, Hercule 62

Poitier, Sidney 154–155
Polanski, Roman 107
Police Woman 61
"Polordak Camera" (commercial parody) 120
Poltergeist 218
"Polynesiantown" (sketch) 107–108, 112, 113–114, 127, 144, 151, 211
Pope, Carole 141
Popeye 87
Porgy & Bess 219
Porky's 235
"Power Play" (sketch) 133–134
"The Power to the Punk People Polka" 228–229
"The Praise Big Brother Show" (sketch) 90
Prentiss, Paula 169
"Pre-Teen World" (sketch) 141, 143, 163, 224
"Pre-Teen World Telethon for Pre-Teen World" (sketch) 163–164
Prickley, Edith (character) 42, 49, 78, 88, 105, 124, 242; *The Best of SCTV* and 255; Christmas episodes and 151, 207; "Cooking with Edith Prickley" and 63; "Edith Prickley Live from the Melonville Baths" and 225; final episode and 251–252; first appearance of 32; "Gangway for Miracles" and 140; "Give 'em Hell, Bess" and 154; Johnny LaRue and 107–108, 146; "The Mating Game" and 95; "Prickley Business" and 229; "Prickley Heat" and 165–166; replaces Moe Green 55, 72; "The Russian Show" episode and 129; "Sunrise Semester" and 93; "The Towering Inferno" episode and 203–204; "Tracking the Unknown" and 121; Walter Cronkite and 98
"Prickley Business" (sketch) 140, 229
"Prickley Heat" (sketch) 140, 165–166, 245
Primetime Glick 45, 197
Primetime News 191
The Prize 124
Prochnow, Jürgen 235
Psycho 60
The PTL Club 90, 130

Queen Elizabeth I 154
The Queen Haters (characters) 223, 233
Queen of Outer Space 245
Quicksilver Messenger Service 67
Quincy 167
"Quincy: Cartoon Coroner" (sketch) 94, 201

Radner, Gilda 5
Raiders of the Lost Ark 167, 187
Rain, Douglas 167
"The Ramblers Greatest Hits" (commercial parody) 242
Rasche, David 196
Rayburn, Norma (character) 203–204
"Real Live Girl" 243
Real People 193
The Recess Monkeys (characters) 163–164
The Red Skelton Show 165
Reddy, Helen 63
Redford, Robert 193
Redgrave, Lynn 130
Reed, Lou 150
"Relaxing with Raoul" (sketch) 69
Resnais, Alain 24
"Restless Doctors" (sketch) 49, 171
"Revenge" (sketch) 176, 178, 204
"Ricardo Montalban School of Fine Acting" (sketch) 134
Rich, Mort 123
Rich and Famous 233
"Rich and Jealous" (sketch) 233
Richardson, Sir Ralph 18
Rickles, Don 59, 137
"Ride Like the Wind" 119
Risky Business 229
Ritter, John 55
Rivera, Heraldo [Geraldo] 24, 31
Rivers, Joan 5
Road & Track 161
"Robco Up-Your-Nose Personal Pollution Filters" (commercial parody) 24–25
Roberts, Tony 79
Robertson, Cliff 193
Robertson, Floyd (character): as Count Floyd 3, 33, 41, 99, 249–250; drinking problem and 57, 67, 118, 174; "Election Central" and 196–197; "15 Minutes" and 21; "Lola! Bouncing Back to You" episode and 123; "Nightline Melonville" and 162, 174; *SCTV Channel* and 231, 242; "SCTV News" first season and 1, 11, 13, 19, 20, 26; "SCTV News" second season and 47, 53, 62, 66, 70–71; "SCTV News" third season and 72, 80, 81–82, 85, 86, 91, 95, 96–97; "Zontar" episode and 136
Robertson, Robbie 93
Rocco (character) 171–172, 209, 224
"Rock Concert" (sketch) 63, 71, 93, 121
Rocket, Charles 74
Rocky 29

"Rocky Mountain High" 93
Rodgers [Rogers], Fred 179
Rogers, Ginger 64
Rogers, Jackie, Jr. (character) 192, 207, 222, 230, 233, 247
Rogers, Jackie, Sr. (character) 192, 207, 222
Rolling Stone 160
The Rolling Stones 81, 230
Roman, Steve (character) 191, 198–199, 210, 213, 223
"Rome, Italian Style" (sketch) 182, 235
"Ronco Weiner Skinner" (commercial parody) 66
"Ronny Barrett's Sports" (sketch) 84
Rooster, Red (character) 129
Rough Trade 141
Route 66 32–33
"The Rowdyman" (sketch) 191
Rubinstein, Zelda 218
"The Russian Show" (episode) 7, 128–131
Ruth, Babe 43

"S & M Airlines" (commercial parody) 24
Sabian, Dr. Elliott (character) 171
Sagan, Carl 174, 179
Sahl, Mort 80
St. Marie, Buffy 175
Sales, Soupy 48
"Salt Buddy" (commercial parody) 244
Sammy & Company 6, 17, 164, 229
"The Sammy Maudlin Show" (sketch) 98, 153, 244; anniversary show and 189–190, 192; with Bobby and Skip Bittman 143–144, 147; with Bobby Bittman and Sir Kenneth Clark outtakes 36–37; with Bobby Bittman's Congressional drug abuse hearing outtakes 107; "Chariots of Eggs" and 177; Christmas episode and 151–152; first installment of 17–18; "I Owe Peking Two Thousand Dollars" and 45, 84, 112; with Luciano Pavarotti and Sandler and Young 212, 214; "On the Waterfront Again" and 65–66; "South Sea Sinner" and 221; "Zontar" episode and 135
Sand, Barry 132, 134
Sandler and Young 214, 221, 243–244
"Sandwich on the Orient Express" (sketch) 38
"Santa Bring My Baby Back to Me" 150
Santana 127
Saturday Night Live 5, 33, 60, 117, 141, 163, 199; comparisons to *SCTV* and 1, 6, 7, 20, 189, 251; The Czech Brothers and 159–160; "Don't Look Back in Anger" and 205; drug humor and 7, 60, 73–74; Ed Grimley and 194, 198, 208, 216; Lawrence Orbach and 209; Leonard Pinth-Garnell and 58–59, 70; Mr. Bill and, 86; Nick the Lounge Singer and 192; Robin Duke and Tony Rosato and 12, 93, 98, 103; *SCTV* airing in time period of 176–177, 253; *SCTV* parody ("Thursday Night") of 73–74; "Weekend Update" and 186
"Scary Previews" (sketch) 234, 245
Scenes from a Marriage 210
"Scenes from an Idiot's Marriage" (sketch) 209–210, 238
Scialfa, Patti 109
Schechtman, Beverly 46, 132
Schechtman, Lenny (character) 132–133
Schlesinger, John 223
Schmitz, Jonathan 176
Scleroso, Pirini (character) 15, 68, 72, 78, 110, 124, 141, 231
Scorsese, Martin 85, 184, 243
Scott, George C. 143
"Screen Acting" (sketch) 142
SCTV: Behind the Scenes 8–9
"SCTV Boogie" (sketch) 36, 37, 83, 120
"SCTV Disco" (sketch) 67, 75, 83, 120
"SCTV Live Theatre: Death of a Salesman" (sketch) 74–75
"SCTV News" (sketch) 118, 231; final appearance and 249–250; first season and 15, 19, 20, 26, 29, 31, 35, 37, 39, 40; "The Godfather" episode and 148; "Lola! Bouncing Back to You" episode and 123; premiere sketch and 13–14; replaced by "Nightline Melonville" and 162; second season and 47, 49, 53, 60, 62, 63, 66–67, 68–69, 70–71; "Sweeps Week" episode and 219–220; third season and 72, 75, 80, 81–82, 85, 86, 95, 96–97
"SCTV Solid Gold Telethon" (sketch) 12, 48, 56, 121
"SCTV Special Report: The Space Shuttle" (sketch) 114
"SCTV 30th Anniversary Show" (episode) 56–57, 110–111
Scutz, Carl and Fred (characters) 141, 160–161, 187
Sealy, Stephen (character) 141, 164, 224
Sebastiano, Marcello (character) 77, 82, 92–93, 95

Second City: Backstage at the World's Greatest Comedy Theater 8, 16
Second City Presents 192
Sedaka, Neil 225
Seigel, Larry (character) 108
Seinfeld 257
"Serfs" (commercial parody) 33
Serling, Rod 85
Sesame Street 23
Seth Dick III (character) 132–133, 172
"Seven Curses" 239
Severinsen, Doc 46
"Sex" (commercial parody) 32
The Sex Pistols 223
Shakespeare, William 165
"Shakespeare for College Credit" (sketch) 204
"Shakespeare in the Park" (sketch) 83
"Shakespeare's Greatest Jokes" (commercial parody) 18
Shalit, Gene 97
"Shangri-La Dance Studio" (commercial parody) 246
Shanks, Tommy (character) 58, 67, 68, 174, 196, 208
Shatner, William 136–137
Shearer, Harry 242
Shields, Brooke 154
"Shirt Glue" (commercial parody) 217, 244
Shmenge, Yosh and Stan (characters): "Christmas Day with the Shmenge Family" and 206; "The Happy Wanderers" premiere and 173; "Miss Leutonia Pageant" and 221–222; "Salute Composer John Williams" and 195, 258; "Salute New Wave Music" and 228–229
"Shock Theatre" (sketch) 22, 26
"Shoot at the Stars" (sketch) 55
"Shoot for the Stars" (sketch) 86, 95
"Shoplifting" (PSA parody) 29
Shore, Dinah 47, 71
Short, Mike 12, 72, 237
"Shower in a Briefcase" (commercial parody) 216
Shubb, Rita (character) 243
Shulman, Dr. Morton 217
Shulman, Murray (character) 217, 243
"Sid Dithers Private Eye" (sketch) 58
The Silhouettes 110
Sills, Beverly 179
"The Silly Bastard" (sketch) 51
Silver, Joel 108
Simmons, Matty 232
Simmons, Richard 194, 213

Simon, Neil 92, 151–152
Simon, Paul 74. 245
Simon and Garfunkel 185, 214, 223, 258
The Simpsons 8
Sinatra, Frank 88, 164–165
Siskel, Gene 87
Sittler, Darryl 20, 133
"Six Gun Justice" (sketch) 236–237, 240, 242, 248, 250
60 Minutes 21, 77
"60/20" (sketch) 77–78
Skelton, Red 165
"Slappy 2000 Home Comedy Center" (commercial parody) 140
Sledge Hammer! 196
Sleuth 234
"Slinky . . . Toy from Hell" (sketch) 245
Slirrup, "Rockin'" Mel (character): "Mel's Rock Pile" premiere and 83; "Mel's Rock Pile" tribute to psychedelic music and 243; "Mel's Rock Pile" tribute to punk music and 223; "Mel's Rock Pile" with Richard Harris and 97–98; "SCTV Boogie" and 36; "SCTV Disco" and 67; 20th anniversary of "Mel's Rock Pile" and 120
Smith, Gary L. 218
Smith, Maggie 152
Smith, Patti 63
Sneak Previews 87
"Snowbird" 92
Snyder, Jimmy "The Greek" 148
"So You're Dead, Now What?" (PSA parody) 19, 70
Solid Gold 135
Solzhenitsyn, Alexander 169
"Some Day, Some Way" 114
Somers, Suzanne 51
"Sometimes I Feel Like a Motherless Child" 168
Sommer, Elke 124
"Soon and Very Soon" 207
"Sophia's Bath Oil" (commercial parody) 241
Soren, Troy (character) 198, 229–230, 242, 246–247
"The Soren-Weiss Report" (sketch) 230
"South Sea Sinner" (parody) 220–221
Southside Johnny and the Asbury Jukes 109–110
"Speaking of Talk" (sketch) 52
Spence, Des 145
Spielberg, Steven 166–167, 170
"Spray-On Socks" (commercial parody) 18, 216, 244

Springsteen, Bruce 180
Squall, April (character) 36
"Stairway to Heaven" 173, 175
"Stairways to Heaven" (commercial parody) 175, 258
Stalag 17 238–239
"Stand Up and Be Counted" (sketch) 174, 235
"A Star Is Born" (parody) 125, 210–211
Star Trek 2, 20, 42, 75, 136–137
Star Wars 86, 87, 166, 195
"Stars in One" (sketch) 197, 210, 212, 225, 237
"Starting Out" (sketch) 95
The State 7
Steckler, Doug 123, 181
"The Steeler and the Pittsburgh Kid" (sketch) 179
"Steeplechase" (sketch) 141–142, 166, 209
Stefoff, Val 212
Stereopolis, Alki (character) 17, 18, 35, 45, 110, 146
"The Steve Bashekis Story" (final episode) 251
Stewart, Rod 154
"Stop" 72
Strange Brew 7, 134, 161, 173
Strassman, Marcia 27
Streep, Meryl 76, 138
"Street Beef" (sketch) 49, 113, 151, 185–186
Streisand, Barbra 47, 71, 72, 210, 233, 238
Strom, Don (character) 70
Stuart, Len 68, 72, 141
"Such a Night" 107
Sue Ellen (character) 178, 185, 209
Summer, Donna 98
"Summertime Blues" 106
"Sundown" 92
"Sunrise Semester" (sketch): Alki Stereopolis and 18, 98; Angus Crock and 81, 94, 96, 156, 158; April Squall and 36; "broadcast day" concept and 1, 6, 114; "Do-It-Yourself Advertising" and 86–87; "Do-It-Yourself Dentistry" and 25; Ed Grimley and 198, 208; Edith Prickley and 32, 93; final appearance and 216; "Gypsy Mythology" and 16; "The Inability to Fake Orgasms" and 18–19; "lost" episode of 44; Marcello Sebastiano and 77; "Melonville Calendar" and 205; Paul Fistinyerface and 55–56; premiere sketch and 13–14; Salvador Dali and 184; "Self-Defense for Women" and 24
Superman 195

Sutherland, Donald 120
Sutherland, Joan 179
Swanson, Gloria 84
"Sweeps Week" (episode) 7, 217–220
"Sweet Georgia Wine" 105–106
"Swinging with Mother Nature" (sketch) 192
"The Swish Buckler" (sketch) 33

"Talk to Ya Later" 123
"Talking Adventure Projector Serial" (sketch) 187, 213
Talking Heads 157
Tang, Lin Ye (character): "Blind Fists of the Furious Dragon" and 30–31; "Chinese Fairy Tales" and 53; "Dining with LaRue" and 25; "Doorway to Hell" episode and 145–146; "Fighting Air Dogs Over the Pacific" and 61; first appearance of 17; "On the Waterfront Again" and 65; potential offensiveness of 20, 61, 74, 109, 180; "SCTV Staff Christmas Party" and 150; "Sunrise Semester" and 44
"Tax Advice" (sketch) 67
"Taxi Driver" (parody) 84, 90
"The Taxidermist" (sketch) 8, 22, 26
Taylor, Elizabeth 167, 175
Taylor, Rip 194
"Teacher's Pet" (sketch) 154–155
"Ted Gordon: Malpractice Lawyer" (sketch) 14
"Ted Gordon: Overbooked Attorney" (sketch) 14, 138
The Temptations of Dr. Antonio 182
Tenth Victim 182
Terrio, Denny 201
"Theatre Beat" (sketch) 86, 132–133
"Theatre North America" (sketch) 16–17
"Thérèse et Joe" (sketch) 24
Thicke, Alan 229
Thicke of the Night 6, 229
Third World 168
Thomas, Betty 220–222
Thomas, Danny 112, 165
Thomas, Ian 126–127
Thorson, Scott 194, 231
"Those Funny Guys" (sketch) 29
"Those Two Zany Ambulance Drivers" (sketch) 67
"Three Blind Mice" 214
"3-D Firing Line" (sketch) 142, 223
"3-D House of Beef" (sketch) 149, 150
The Three Stooges 3, 28, 30, 39, 154, 200
Three's Company 51, 115, 148, 200, 231

Index

"Thursday Night" (sketch) 73–74
"Tie a Yellow Ribbon 'Round the Ole Oak Tree" 100
Tilton, Charlene 130
Time magazine 104, 229
"Tiny Bubbles" 211
"Tip O'Neill's 3-D House of Representatives" (sketch) 210
To Sir, with Love 154–155
"Today Is Moscow" (sketch) 129
The Today Show 41
Todd, Gerry (character) 108, 134, 150, 151, 157
"Tom Thumb" (parody) 249
The Tonight Show: adjacency to *SCTV* on NBC schedule and 6, 103; Bob Hope and 45; Brooke Shields and 154; "The Lone Ranger Show" and 78; "The Sammy Maudlin Show" and 135, 189; "SCTV News" and 70
Tootsie 209
"Top Secret Man" 157
Torme, Mel 85
The Total Film-Maker 99
Total Request Live 157
Toulouse-Lautrec, Henri de 43
"The Towering Inferno" (episode) 202–205
Towne, Dusty (character) 131, 150
"Tracking the Unknown" (sketch) 120, 121
The Traveling Wilburys 120
Trebel [Trebek], Alex 54, 134, 236, 246
"Triple Feature Movie" (sketch) 53
Trudeau, Pierre 190, 240
True Love 211
"The True Story of Billy the Kid" (sketch) 216
Truffaut, François 24
Truman, Bess 154
Truth or Consequences 39
The Tubes 122, 123, 173
"Turk Gruman: Police Dispatcher" (sketch) 163
"Turning Japanese" 108
TV Guide 79
TV North 190
"TV Talk" (sketch) 187
TV's Bloopers and Practical Jokes 248
"12 Angry Men" (parody) 194
"20 Depressing Hits" (commercial parody) 27
20/20 77
The $25,000 Pyramid 18
"The $211,000 Triangle" (sketch) 18

2001: A Space Odyssey 166–167, 245
"2009: Jupiter and Beyond" (sketch) 228, 245
"Two-Way TV" (sketch) 91
"The Typewriter Song" 210, 238

"UFO Sharkey" (sketch) 59
Ugazzo, Turk (character) 147–149, 211
Ullmann, Liv 57
"The Uncle Earl Show" (sketch) 41–42
Undeclared 8
"Undercover Policewoman" (sketch) 61
An Unmarried Woman 76
"Unnecessary Surgeon" (sketch) 14, 29
Upright Citizens Brigade 7

Vaccaro, Brenda 108
Van Reddick, Rusty (character) 212, 241
Vannelli, Gino 72
Vereen, Ben 215
"Vic Arpeggio: Private Investigator" (sketch) 213, 240–241
Vidal, Gore 186
Video Store Magazine 257
"Videotech Video Dinners" (commercial parody) 134
"The Vikings and the Beekeepers" (sketch) 149
The Viletones 82
Village People 63
Villechaize, Hervé 64, 167
Vinton, Bobby 46
Voudry, Idella (character) 245, 247

"The Wacky World of Poverty" (sketch) 22
Wainwright, Dr. William (character) 171, 209, 224
Waiting for Guffman 129
"Wake Up" (sketch) 35
The Wall Street Journal 186, 193
Wallace, General Lew 28
Wallace, Mike 78
Waller, Fats 215
Walsh, Joe 224
"Walter Cronkite's Brain" (sketch) 139–140, 145, 158
Walter Cronkite's Universe 139
"Wara! Wara! Wara!" (sketch) 15, 68
Warhol, Andy 202
Warmel, Claire (character) 216
Warren, Rusty 131, 150
Waters, John 202
Watson, Patrick 19
Waxberg, Hal (character) 105

"Way to Go, Woman!" (sketch) 107
"We Got a Maid" (sketch) 231
We Got It Made 231
"We May Never Love Like This Again" 203
"Weekend Update" (*SNL* sketch) 186
Weese, Duard (character) 247–248
Weiss, Joel (character) 229–230, 242, 246–247
"Welcome Back, President Kotter" (sketch) 27
"We'll Meet Again" 129
Wells, Orson 53, 90, 97, 152
Wellsley, Robert (character) 196
We_ces, Senor 236
Wendy O'Williams and the Plasmatics 133
"We're in This Love Together" 131
"Western Redundancy Playhouse Theater" (commercial parody) 220
"Wet Nurse" (sketch) 130
"What Ever Happened to Baby Ed?" (sketch) 224
What Ever Happened to Baby Jane? 224
"What Fits Into Russia" (sketch) 129–130
"What I Did for Love" 128
What's My Line? 56, 190, 218
"What's My Shoe Size?" (sketch) 56
"Which Way You Running, Johnny?" (sketch) 245
"Whispers of the Wolf" (sketch) 57, 210
White, Barry 131, 175
"White Christmas" 151
"Whiter Shade of Pale" 172
Whitman, Slim 72, 108, 115, 173, 175
Whitmore, James 37
The Who 93
Who's Afraid of Virginia Woolf? 74
Who's Minding the Store? 210
"Who's on First?" 93
Wicks, Sondra (character) 248
"Wide World of High Voices" (sketch) 98
Wilcox, Mary Charlotte: as Deborah Harry 211; first appearance and 186; as Idella Voudry 245, 247; as Janet Halsey 209; "Koffier & Meltzer" and 212; as Pauline Kael 24, 223; "People and Things" and 215–216; SCTV Channel and 228; "The Towering Inferno" episode and 203
Wild Kingdom 121
Wilder, Billy 238
Wildmon, Reverend Donald 115–117
Will & Grace 74, 166
"Will: The Movie" (sketch) 108

Willard 184
Willard, Fred 5, 193, 238–239
"The William B. Show" (sketch) 214–215
Williams, John 195, 258
Williams, Paul 210
Williams, Robin 199–200, 213
Williams, William B. (character): absence from third season and 84, 98–99; "Maudlin's Eleven" and 164–165; "On the Waterfront Again" and 65–66; quits "The Sammy Maudlin Show" and 189–190, 192; returns to "The Sammy Maudlin Show" and 221; "The Sammy Maudlin Show" and 17, 37, 107, 143–144; "The William B. Show" and 214–215; "Zontar" episode and 135
Wilson, Bob and Betty (characters) 38, 67
Wilson, Dr. Raoul (character): Dr. Rawl Withers and 115; "Dream Interpretation" and 40; "Men on Women" and 88; offensiveness of 150, 156; "Relaxing with Raoul" and 69; "Sermonette" and 81
The Winds of War 218, 220
"Winning Chess" (sketch) 31
Winston, Fred (character) 238–239
Winters, Shelley 97, 134, 221
Withers, Dr. Rawl (character) 40, 115, 166, 167–168, 231
"Witness to Yesterday" (sketch) 19
The Wizard of Oz 6, 64–65, 75, 122, 124, 213, 245
"Wok on the Wild Side" (sketch) 179–180
Wolfman Jack 93
Wolfson, Libby (character): city council election and 196; "exercise" sketch and 162; final episode and 251; first appearance of 122, 124; as playwright 131–133, 137, 172; "Stars in One" and 239–240
"Women Say the Darndest Things" (sketch) 67
"The Women Who Donahue Forgot" (sketch) 222
Women's Prison 25
Wonder Woman 41
"Words to Live By" (sketch): Angus Crock and Rabbi Karlov and 75; "broadcast day" concept and 1, 6, 13, 114; Dr. Ernest Bruter and 16; Ernest Kirsch and 45; Mr. Mambo and 205
"Working for the Man" 120
"The World at War" (sketch) 38
"The Wrong Side of the Bed" (sketch) 122
Wyler, William 28

X: The Man with the X-Ray Eyes 171

"Yellow Belly" (sketch) 110–111
"You Don't Bring Me Flowers" 72
"You! with Libby Wolfson" (sketch) 124, 131–133, 162, 196
Young, Neil 98
The Young and the Restless 49, 174
"Young Turks" 154
"The Young Weasels" (sketch) 68
"You're On with Max Lansky" (sketch) 235, 250

Zanuck, Darryl F. 90
Zmed, Adrian 201
"Zontar" (episode) 135–138, 167, 218, 235
The Zontar Thing from Venus 136–137
Zoom! 141

www.ingramcontent.com/pod-product-compliance
Ingram Content Group UK Ltd.
Pitfield, Milton Keynes, MK11 3LW, UK
UKHW041916140426
5217IPUK00013B/181